The World Trade Organization and Human Rights

The World Trade Organization and Human Rights

Interdisciplinary Perspectives

Edited by

Sarah Joseph

Professor of Human Rights Law and Director, Castan Centre for Human Rights Law, Monash University, Australia

David Kinley

Professor of Human Rights Law, University of Sydney, Australia

Jeff Waincymer

Professor of Law, Monash University, Australia

Edward Elgar

Cheltenham, UK • Northampton, MA, USA

Published by
Edward Elgar Publishing Limited
The Lypiatts
15 Lansdown Road
Cheltenham
Glos GL50 2JA
UK

Edward Elgar Publishing, Inc.
William Pratt House
9 Dewey Court
Northampton
Massachusetts 01060
USA

A catalogue record for this book is available from the British Library

Library of Congress Control Number: 2009933365

FSC
Mixed Sources
Product group from well-managed forests and other controlled sources
www.fsc.org Cert no. SA-COC-1565
© 1996 Forest Stewardship Council

ISBN 978 1 84720 661 9

Typeset by Cambrian Typesetters, Camberley, Surrey
Printed and bound by MPG Books Group, UK

Contents

Contributors

Professor Pranab Bardhan is Professor of Economics at University of California at Berkeley. He was educated at Presidency College, Calcutta and Cambridge University, UK, and has been the author of twelve books, twelve co-edited books, and more than 100 journal articles, primarily in the areas of economic development, international trade, political economy, and institutional economics. He was the Chief Editor of the *Journal of Development Economics* from 1985–2003. More details are available at http://emlab.berkeley.edu/users/webfac/bardhan/bardhan.htm.

Graciela Chichilnisky has worked extensively in the Kyoto Protocol process, creating and designing the carbon market concept that became international law in 2005. She also acted as a lead author of the Intergovernmental Panel on Climate Change, which received the 2007 Nobel Prize. A frequent keynote speaker, special adviser to several UN organizations and heads of state, her pioneering work uses innovative market mechanisms to reduce carbon emissions, conserve biodiversity and ecosystem services and improve the lot of the poor. Dr Chichilnisky is a Professor of Economics and Mathematical Statistics at Columbia University and the Sir Louis Matheson Distinguished Professor at Monash University. More details are available at www.chichilnisky.com.

Dr Patrick Emerton is a Lecturer in the Faculty of Law, Monash University. His areas of research include philosophy of language, political philosophy, and legal responses to political violence. His doctoral thesis, 'Moral Relativism and Political Legitimacy: An argument for a global social contract', argues that international political arrangements can be legitimate only if they respect and conform to the deep commitments of all who participate in them.

Dr Caroline E. Foster is a former adviser with the New Zealand Ministry of Foreign Affairs and Trade. Her interests lie in the fields of dispute settlement, trade, human rights, international environmental law, and the law of the sea, as well as Antarctica. She has published widely in international legal journals and her monograph on science, the precautionary principle, and the rules of evidence in international courts and tribunals will be published next year by Cambridge University Press.

Professor Robert Howse is the Lloyd C. Nelson Professor of International Law at New York University. He has also taught at the University of Michigan, Harvard, Tel Aviv, Toronto, Tsing Hua, and Paris (Sorbonne-Pantheon) Universities and is a regular instructor at the World Trade Institute, Berne. He is the author of, among other works, *The Regulation of International Trade* (with Michael Trebilcock), a contributor to the American Law Institute project on WTO Law, and series editor for Oxford University Press's Commentaries on the WTO Treaties.

Professor Sarah Joseph is a Professor of Law at Monash University and the Director of the Castan Centre for Human Rights Law. She is the main author of the leading text, *The International Covenant on Civil and Political Rights: Cases, Materials and Commentary* (OUP, 2004). She has published on numerous topics, including corporations and human rights, freedom from torture, and Australian constitutional law. She is a lead investigator on two major grants funded by the Australian Research Council, on the WTO and Human Rights, and Multinational Corporations and Human Rights.

Professor David Kinley holds the Chair in Human Rights Law at the University of Sydney. He has previously held positions at universities in Australia, the UK and the US, and has lectured on human rights matters in many other countries. He is the author of many books and articles, the most recent of which is *Civilising Globalisation: Human Rights and the Global Economy* (CUP, 2009). He has worked for more than 15 years as a consultant and adviser on international and domestic human rights law, especially in Asia, with a variety of governments, corporations, NGOs and international bodies including the World Bank and the UN.

Dr Andrew T.F. Lang is a Senior Lecturer in the Law Department of the London School of Economics. He previously studied at the University of Sydney, and the University of Cambridge, where he received his PhD, and was then a Junior Research Fellow at Trinity Hall, Cambridge.

Dr Shervin Majlessi is a programme management officer at the United Nations Office on Drugs and Crime (UNODC – New York). Prior to joining UNODC he was an advisor on trade/globalization and good governance/corruption issues at the Office of the UN High Commissioner for Human Rights (OHCHR – Geneva). He has also worked as a consultant for the World Bank and as a deputy counsel for the Independent Inquiry Committee into the UN Oil-for-Food Programme (Volcker Committee).

Odette Murray is an LLM candidate at the University of Cambridge, specialising in international law. She holds a BA and LLB from the University of Sydney, graduating with first class honours. She was a member of the University of Sydney team which won the 2007 Phillip C. Jessup International Law Moot Court Competition in Washington, DC. She is a solicitor of the Supreme Court of NSW practicing in class action litigation at Maurice Blackburn Lawyers, and is an Affiliate of the Sydney Centre for International Law.

Hai Nguyen is a researcher at the Vietnamese Institute for Human Rights. Currently, she is a PHD student at the Law Faculty, The University of Sydney. She has published a number of articles on human rights issues in Vietnam.

Professor Ernst-Ulrich Petersmann is Professor of International and European Law and Head of the Law Department at the European University Institute (EUI) in Florence, Italy. He was previously Professor of International and European law at the University of Geneva, Switzerland, and its Graduate Institute of International Studies. During his 30 years of legal practice, Professor Petersmann represented Germany in various international organisations (EC, OECD, UN), acted as legal advisor to the GATT as well as legal consultant for the WTO, and participated in numerous GATT and WTO dispute settlement proceedings as legal advisor, member or chairman of dispute settlement panels.

Professor Hélène Ruiz Fabri has degrees in law and political science, a Doctorate in Law and is Agrégée des Facultés de droit (1990). She is currently Professor at the University of Paris I – Panthéon Sorbonne, Director of the Institute of Comparative Studies of Paris (UMR de droit comparé Paris I/CNRS), Director of the Master 2 Degree Program in International Economic Law and President of the European Society of International Law. She teaches and researches International Law and she also got expertise notably at the French administration and at the Agence internationale de la Francophonie as a legal consultant on the cultural diversity.

Dr Kenneth C. Shadlen is a political scientist in the Development Studies Institute (DESTIN) at the London School of Economics and Political Science. His current research addresses the politics of intellectual property (IP), and the politics of North-South economic integration. He is the co-editor of *The Politics of Intellectual Property: Contestation over the Ownership, Use, and Control of Knowledge and Information* (Edward Elgar, 2009), and *The Political Economy of Hemispheric Integration: Responding to Globalization in the Americas* (Palgrave Macmillan, 2008). He is writing a book on the politics of IP, technology and innovation in Latin America.

Professor Ruti G. Teitel is the Ernst C. Stiefel Professor of Comparative Law at New York Law School. She has also taught in the School of International and Public Affairs at Columbia University and at Yale Law School, as a Senior Fellow at the Orville H. Schell Jr Center for International Human Rights. Her book, *Transitional Justice* (Oxford University Press, 2000), examines the 20th century transitions to democracy in many countries. She is a member of the Council on Foreign Relations, and is also on the Steering Committee of Human rights Watch Europe/Central Asia, as well as HRW's Terrorism and Counter-Terrorism Steering committee.

Professor Chantal Thomas joined Cornell University in 2007 as Professor of Law, and has also taught at law faculties in Beijing, Cairo, London, Minneapolis, New York City, Paris and Suzhou. Professor Thomas focuses her scholarship on international trade and development, with emphasis on the relationships between international law, political economy, and global social justice. She is co-editor (with Joel Trachtman) of *Developing Countries in the WTO Legal System* (Oxford University Press, 2009).

Professor Jeff Waincymer is a Professor at the Faculty of Law, Monash University. He is the author of *WTO Litigation: Procedural Aspects of Formal Dispute Settlement*, and *Australian Income Tax: Principles and Policy* (2nd edn) and is a joint author of *A Practical Guide to International Commercial Arbitration* and also *International Trade Law: Commentary and Materials* (2nd edn). He is an Australian Government Nominee as a non-governmental panellist for the WTO and has acted as a panellist. He is also a nominated ICSID panellist.

Preface

This book is the culmination of a four-year project examining the relationship between the World Trade Organization and human rights. A key moment in the relationship between these regimes occurred in Seattle in December 1999. Internally, key WTO Members sought to use that meeting as the launching pad for a new Round of multilateral trade negotiations. Externally, a range of critics, including influential non-governmental organizations, engaged in public demonstrations that criticized the processes and goals of the WTO. From that time, challenges as to the consistency or otherwise of the international trade law and human rights law regimes have been debated in both public fora and scholarly circles.

The politicized nature of the debate meant that much of the dialogue was polarized and rarely displayed a genuine attempt to analyze and synthesize competing arguments. Even in scholarly circles many of the criticisms directed from the trade camp towards the human rights camp and vice versa, were based on misunderstandings or at least questionable generalizations as to the norms, processes and goals of the other field. One reason for this is the historical lack of dialogue between scholars from each camp. A number of earlier worthy projects had begun to redress this. This project also aimed to do so and, to that end, a range of multidisciplinary scholars were invited to a conference in Prato, Italy, to present and debate their views, organized by the Castan Centre for Human Rights Law. This volume contains revised versions of those papers.

Mindful of the fact that we, the editors, are all legal scholars, an important aspect of the project was to attempt a more comprehensive interdisciplinary analysis of the central questions posed, namely, whether the WTO unduly interferes with the promotion of international human rights and/or fails to do enough in a positive sense to promote such rights? Questions of this nature inevitably require a deeper understanding of the philosophical and economic rationales underpinning each of the regimes and of the political and sociological insights that might be brought to bear on the way they currently operate and on the means by which the relationship between them can be optimized. The chapters in this volume range from general analyses of the way certain disciplines impact upon the debate, to case study analysis concentrating on particular arenas where the trade and human rights interface is most problematic. Because of the breadth of the topic and the legitimate differences in view within and between each interdisciplinary field touched upon, this project can only seek to advance the debate in a meaningful way, not resolve it once and for all.

Both the conference and this volume have been supported with funds from the Australian Research Council. We are grateful to the Council for its significant support. We also wish to thank the following research assistants who have supported us in our work: Cameron Miles and Rachel Ball.

Sarah Joseph
David Kinley
Jeff Waincymer

1. The trade and human rights debate: Introduction to an interdisciplinary analysis

Jeff Waincymer

1. INTRODUCTION AND METHODOLOGY

There has been a growing debate about the compatibility between the international trade regime and the promotion of universal human rights. In this volume we seek to analyse this relationship.[1] There are two related aspects of

[1] This volume builds upon earlier work in the field including F M Abbott et al. (eds) *International Trade and Human Rights: Foundations and Conceptual Issues* (University of Michigan Press, Michigan, 2006); Padideh Ala'i, 'Global Trade Issues in the New Millennium: A Human Rights Critique of the WTO: Some Preliminary Observations' (2001) 33 *George Washington International Law Review* 537; Philip Alston, 'Linking Trade and Human Rights' (1980) 23 *German Yearbook of International Law* 126; Thomas Cottier, 'Trade and Human Rights, a Relationship to Discover' (2002) 5 *Journal of International Economic Law* 111; Thomas Cottier et al. (eds) *Human Rights and International Trade* (Oxford University Press, Oxford, 2005); Frank J Garcia, 'The Global Market and Human Rights: Trading Away the Human Rights Principle' (1999) 25 *Brooklyn Journal of International Law* 51; Frank J Garcia, *Trade, Inequality and Justice: Toward a Liberal Theory of Just Trade* (Transnational Publishers, New York, 2003); S Leader, 'Human Rights and International Trade' in P F J Macrory et al. (eds) *The World Trade Organisation: Legal, Economic and Political Analysis* (Springer, New York, 2005) 664; H Lim, 'Trade and Human Rights: What's At Issue?' (2001) 35 *Journal of World Trade* 275; Ernst-Ulrich Petersmann, 'From Negative to Positive Integration in the WTO: Time for Mainstreaming Human Rights into WTO Law?' (2000) 37 *Common Market Law Review* 1363; Stephen J Powell, 'The Place of Human Rights Law in World Trade Organization Rules' (2004) 16 *Florida Journal of International Law* 219; Friedl Weiss et al. (eds) *International Economic Law with a Human Face* (Kluwer Law International, The Hague, 1998); Lorand Bartels, 'Trade and Human Rights' in D Bethlehem et al. (eds) *Oxford Handbook of International Trade* (Oxford University Press, Oxford, 2008) Ch 21; Wolfgang Benedek, 'The World Trade Organisation and Human Rights' in W Benedek et al. (eds) *Economic Globalisation and Human Rights* (Cambridge University Press, Cambridge, 2007) 143; Andrew Lang, 'Rethinking Trade and Human Rights' (2007) 15 *Tulane Journal of International and Comparative Law* 335.

this endeavour. The first is to consider whether the World Trade Organisation ('WTO') unduly interferes with the promotion of human rights as a result of the promises governments make to each other through WTO treaty provisions. Some of these provisions are seen to directly or indirectly limit governmental ability to regulate for the benefit of human rights. Key areas where this debate arises involve government measures in relation to health and the environment and the potential use of trade sanctions as a counter to human rights abuses. These measures are sometimes threatened with challenge through the WTO dispute settlement system on the basis that they might impact negatively upon the rights of international traders. The second is to consider whether the WTO ought to do more in order to promote the attainment of universal human rights. If it can legitimately be argued that the ultimate goal of all governance systems is to promote human rights, then any institution is failing in its obligations if it does not prioritize that goal.

At the extreme, some critics argue that globalization in general and the WTO in particular allow for markets to improperly take primacy over international human rights law;[2] that the WTO is unfair, opaque and undemocratic and that certain of the WTO's specific norms undermine the rights to sustainable development, health, education, knowledge, culture and labour rights.[3]

The purpose of this chapter is to set the scene for this debate and situate the specific chapters that follow. It seeks to outline some of the key methodological issues that face anyone attempting to answer these questions. How should we approach the analysis of the topic? What intellectual disciplines and data sets are relevant? What are the proper parameters for any useful study? Can we keep our study within manageable limits or will that detract from the validity of any postulated conclusions? What are the difficulties in establishing causal links between actions and outcomes and what other problems of proof arise when we seek to provide persuasive conclusions? After outlining the challenges facing any attempt at a comprehensive analysis, this volume then deals with a selection of the more significant topics.

These questions show how wide-ranging the debate could prove to be and why it would be impossible to resolve all relevant questions through any one intellectual discipline alone.[4] For example, as to the possible interference with

---

[2] Marjorie Cohn, 'The World Trade Organisation: Elevating Property Interests Above Human Rights' (2001) 29 *Georgia Journal of International and Comparative Law* 427.

[3] See, for example, Anne-Christine Habbard and Marie Guiraud, 'The World Trade Organisation and Human Rights' (FIDH Position Paper, 1999) FIDH, www.fidh.org/IMG/pdf/omc320A.pdf at 14 December 2008.

[4] A similar interdisciplinary approach has been adopted with respect to human rights analysis per se: see Michael Freeman, *Human Rights: An Interdisciplinary*

human rights by the WTO, this will overlap with challenges as to the role of globalization per se and the suggested value of market-based mechanisms. Such a challenge can be divided into two further sub-questions. The first is whether trade liberalization as encouraged by the WTO is inherently antithetical to the development goals of human rights. Conversely, can it be argued that the promotion of economic efficiency is a useful precondition to the ultimate advancement of human rights via increased world welfare? From an economics perspective, we might wish to consider the extent to which the WTO does in fact promote efficiency and the extent of any positive correlation between increased efficiency and world welfare. Alternatively, what merit is there in modern critiques of neo-classical economic postulates?[5]

Secondly, even if it is hypothesized that efficiency can have a useful instrumental value for human rights, are there other conflicts between the two regimes? For example, even if trade liberalization is desirable from an efficiency perspective at least, does it nonetheless interfere with some human rights by shifting resources from less efficient, but still deserving people, to more efficient traders who accumulate wealth but do not show any responsibility for the welfare of those who may have lost out in the process? Such economic questions then naturally segue into philosophical ones. If some groups in society are winners and others losers as a result of trade liberalization, we might ask by what philosophical construct will we determine whether such an outcome is fair or not? To the extent that it is not, what redistribution obligations arise as a result? Can we ameliorate the problem by adopting redistribution processes that remove any a priori unfairness flowing from a liberal trading regime? What do different philosophical schools of thought say about short- and long-term compensatory obligations or about hierarchies of norms?

A consideration of distributional processes as well as outcomes also asks us to consider the functions and limits of political and legal institutions and hence the fields of political science and political economy. For example, what does

---

Approach (Policy Press, Cambridge, 2002). While the WTO has been the focus of a number of studies from other disciplines (for example Bernard M Hockman and Michel M Kostecki, *The Political Economy of the World Trading System from GATT to WTO* (Oxford University Press, Oxford, 1995); K Bagwell and R W Staiger, *The Economics of the World Trading System* (MIT Press, Cambridge, 2002); Jeffrey L Dunoff and Joel P Trachtman, 'Economic Analysis of International Law' (1999) 24 *Yale Journal of International Law* 1; P F J Macrory et al. (eds) *The World Trade Organisation: Legal, Economic and Political Analysis* (Springer, New York, 2005), and while the leading WTO scholars draw on a range of disciplines (see generally the works of Robert Howse and Ernst-Ulrich Petersmann, contributors to this volume) there have been few significant interdisciplinary studies of the WTO.

[5] For a critical legal studies perspective see Roberto Unger, *Free Trade Reimagined: The World Division of Labour and the Method of Economics* (Princeton University Press, Princeton, 2007).

political science have to say about the ability of legal mechanisms to prevent vested interests capturing international institutions and interfere unduly with the hoped for fair and efficient outcomes from the activities of the institutions concerned? Is there merit in the neo-realist critique of international law? At the extreme this would place serious doubts on the ability of international trade and human rights lawyers to create legal mechanisms that could meaningfully enhance outcomes within each field or enhance the relationship between the two fields. Alternatively, if some organizational structures are more likely to be successful than others, how do the international trade and human rights regimes measure up? Would significant structural changes in either enhance their individual utility and their compatibility?

These examples show how many of the sub-themes involve complex interdisciplinary questions about which there can be legitimate debate. Because of the central place of these interdisciplinary questions in the overall theme of this volume, a number of the chapters seek to provide insights from the key fields of philosophy, economics, political science and sociology. In this way we hope to advance the growing debate about the optimal relationship between trade and human rights, defuse the overly polarized nature of that debate and in turn, avoid what a former director general of the WTO, Renato Ruggiero, described as a 'dialogue of the deaf'.[6]

We have separated the key interdisciplinary areas, but inevitably there is overlap and interdependence as is shown in most of the contributions. For example, a utilitarian philosophical perspective would more naturally be accepting of liberal trade policies and would be less inclined to accept the notion of universal and equal human rights than would be the case with a social contractarian perspective.

It should also be understood that other intellectual disciplines not directly covered in this volume can be brought into the analysis. Both philosophy and economics bring us to issues of cognitive psychology. Psychological perspectives are one element of the critique of the assumptions of rationality underpinning welfare economics. Psychological perspectives can also be drawn into philosophical discourse. For example, Patrick Emerton's chapter looks at the degree to which more fortunate countries owe duties to those less fortunate.[7] He considers the work of the philosopher John Rawls, who used a thought experiment to argue for a particular model of a liberal social contract. Rawls suggested that imaginary risk-averse subjects operating behind a veil of ignorance would support a political system which evaluates the justice in their

[6] Renato Ruggiero, 'A Shared Responsibility: Global Policy Coherence for Our Global Age' (Address to the Conference on 'Globalization as a Challenge for German Business', Bonn, 9 December 1997).

[7] See Chapter 6.

society through a consideration of how the worst off in that society are treated.[8] Cognitive psychologists would see their field having much to say about such risk-averse proclivities. Psychological perspectives might also help us to better understand why there are demands for cultural diversity even in instances where this comes at the expense of economic efficiency. This is dealt with in the chapter by Hélène Ruiz Fabri on trade and culture.[9] Anthropologists have indirectly considered related issues by analysing the phenomenon of globalization.[10]

While we have adopted a strong interdisciplinary focus and have sought contributions from a range of scholars, our dominant focus is to consider the role of law and legal institutions in providing an optimized relationship between the WTO and human rights. In one sense, that debate is simply a subset of broader governance issues. What are the rights of each individual in a just society, howsoever that is to be defined? How are these rights agreed upon? How should decisions be made, particularly where some trade-off is required between different legitimate aspirations? What regulatory mechanisms will optimize the attainment of those rights? This aspect of the debate is obviously not unique to the question of the WTO and human rights. It occurs at national and regional levels. As to the latter, the debate has been conducted at a particularly sophisticated level in the context of the European Union. The EU is always a useful model for scholarly analysis in relation to our theme as the *Treaty of Rome* contains key GATT-type norms and there has been a rich jurisprudence and literature on the integration of trade and social welfare goals.[11]

Where the WTO is concerned, it is an aspect of the *global* governance problem. Global governance is inevitably more challenging and more naturally a

---

8 John Rawls, *A Theory of Justice* (Harvard University Press, Cambridge, 1971).

9 See Chapter 8.

10 See for example L Sklair, 'Competing Conceptions of Globalization' in C Chase-Dunn and S J Babones (eds) *Global Social Change: Historical and Comparative Perspectives* (Johns Hopkins University Press, Baltimore, 2006) 59; D Held and A McGrew, *Globalization/Anti-Globalization* (2002); Immanuel Wallerstein, *The Modern World System* (Academic Press, New York, 1974–1989) .

11 *Treaty establishing the European Economic Community*, opened for signature 25 March 1957, 298 UNTS 11 (entered into force 1 January 1958) ('*Treaty of Rome*'). See Joseph Weiler, *The EU, the WTO, and the NAFTA: Towards a Common Law of International Trade?* (Oxford University Press/Academy of European Law, Florence, 2000); Joseph Weiler and Marlene Wind, *European Constitutionalism Beyond the State* (Cambridge University Press, Cambridge, 2003); Ernst-Ulrich Petersmann, 'Time for a United Nations "Global Compact" for Integrating Human Rights into the Law of Worldwide Organisations: Lessons from European Integration' (2002) 13 *European Journal of International Law* 621.

field for second-best analysis and solutions than is the still-complex governance debate at any national level. We can never expect the same level of efficiency and coordination between international political systems as we could expect within any individual domestic government system. Yet many of the most pressing problems can only be dealt with at the international level. In this sense, our concern with the WTO and human rights might indeed be seen as just one part of the 'linkage' or 'trade and . . .' debate as described in much recent WTO related literature.[12] This debate looks at the way the trade regime can be properly integrated with other policy fields such as health, environment and technology, the latter including knowledge and technology transfer. It will also cover questions as to the optimal international regulatory structure to deal with linkage questions. This issue has been raised in the influential study by Martti Koskenniemi as to the fragmentation of international law and legal institutions.[13]

The next key methodological concern is to determine what combination of inductive, deductive and empirical analysis is most appropriate to the question we have posed. There is also the question of the breadth of the field of analysis and the appropriate data to be considered. While our central question relates to issues of governance, there is a need to separate the WTO debate from other fields of analysis. The WTO debate should not be confused with such broader questions as the role of globalization per se although there may be a significant overlap.[14] Furthermore, while the WTO is a central element of international economic law, its role and responsibilities should not be confused with other aspects of the system, as for example the International Monetary Fund and the adverse impact its lending practices have been argued to have on human rights in least developed countries.[15]

The debate can remain at the general level or might look at particular features of the system, both substantive and procedural. As to substantive

[12] Symposium, 'The Boundaries of the WTO' (2002) 96 *American Journal of International Law* 1.

[13] Martti Koskenniemi, *Fragmentation of International Law: Difficulties Arising from the Diversification and Expansion of International Law: Report of the Study Group of the International Law Commission*, UN Doc A/CN.4/L.682 (13 April 2006).

[14] See for example Eleanor M Fox, 'Globalisation and Human Rights: Looking out for the Welfare of the Worst Off' (2002) 35 *New York University Journal of International Law and Politics* 201; Mary Robinson, 'Shaping Globalisation: The Role of Human Rights' (2003) 19 *American University International Law Review* 1.

[15] See for example A Brysk (ed.) *Globalisation and Human Rights* (University of California Press, Berkeley, 2002); S Skolgy, *Human Rights Obligations of the World Bank and the International Monetary Fund* (Cavendish Publishing Limited, London, 2001).

norms, we would naturally look at those rules which are most affected by the WTO and human rights interface, rules such as those pertaining to health, in particular the *Agreement on Sanitary and Phytosanitary Measures* ('SPS'),[16] the *Agreement on Trade Related Intellectual Property Rights* ('TRIPS')[17] and similar agreements as to their human rights implications. This includes examination of both the express and implied linkage of trade liberalization and human rights and the hierarchy of express norms. The SPS Agreement is touched upon in a range of chapters in this volume.[18]

There might even be a preliminary question as to whether we can meaningfully debate the topic at the general level without looking at specific instances, for example, which human right is arguably being affected; is it accepted as such a right; what trade liberalization norm impacts upon it; how should any conflict between those two specific norms be resolved and why? Such an approach would be unlikely to lead to uniform conclusions about the relationship between the regimes. For example, most commentators have found a justifiable basis for criticizing the very inclusion of the TRIPS regime within the WTO and its impact upon human rights concerns such as the AIDS crisis in Africa.[19] Other sectoral issues might conversely raise broader policy debates. A key question in the field of permitted health regulation is the degree of scientific certainty that is required. This involves principles of risk management theory and the relevance or otherwise of precautionary principles under international law. Here there can at least be legitimate debate about optimal models and trade-offs.[20]

---

16 *Marrakesh Agreement Establishing the WTO*, opened for signature 15 April 1994, 1867 UNTS 3 (entered into force 1 January 1995) Annex 1A (*Agreement on Sanitary and Phytosanitary Measures*).

17 *Marrakesh Agreement Establishing the WTO*, opened for signature 15 April 1994, 1867 UNTS 3 (entered into force 1 January 1995) Annex 1C (*Agreement on Trade-Related Aspects of Intellectual Property Rights*).

18 See, respectively, Chapters 2, 10, 11, and 12.

19 Sarah Joseph, 'Pharmaceutical Corporations and Access to Drugs: The "Fourth Wave" of Corporate Human Rights Scrutiny' (2003) 25 *Human Rights Quarterly* 425.

20 See, for example, Vern R Walker, 'Keeping the WTO from Becoming the "World Trans-Science Organization": Scientific Uncertainty, Science Policy and Fact Finding in the Growth Hormones Dispute' (1998) 31 *Cornell International Law Journal* 251; Jeffrey Atik and David A Wirth, 'Science and International Trade – Third Generation Scholarship' (2003) 26 *Boston College International and Comparative Law Review* 171; Alan O Sykes, 'Exploring the Need for International Harmonisation: Domestic Regulation, Sovereignty and Scientific Evidence Requirements: A Pessimistic View' (2002) 3 *Chicago Journal of International Law* 353.

Alternatively, one might ask, as Thomas Cottier has, whether a comprehensive view and theory is needed, rather than a sector-by-sector analysis of conflicting norms.[21]

A consideration of governance from a lawyer's perspective could segment the analysis in other ways, in particular by looking at the WTO and human rights systems from a legislative, executive[22] and adjudicative perspective[23] as well as through analysing the value of the core substantive norms themselves.

After a both top-down conceptual analysis and an inductive analysis of past experiences we might then ask whether there are legitimacy challenges to the WTO regime in the absence of an express link and priority ordering with human rights norms and if so why?

2. WHAT IS THE WTO, WHAT ARE HUMAN RIGHTS AND WHAT DO EACH AIM TO DO?

In order to properly understand the relationship between the regimes of international trade and human rights we need to understand what each aims to do and why its goals are independently worthy. What can and should the two regimes do for each other? Do they conflict in any way and if so, how should this be avoided or resolved?

Where the WTO is concerned, it is best understood as a legal response to protectionist behaviour by domestic governments.[24] History shows that protectionism is likely to reduce world welfare and constitute a barrier to harmonious and cooperative intergovernmental relationships. Political economy shows why even governments that believe in the value of free trade are likely to follow their own self-interest and pander to protectionist interests,

---

21 Thomas Cottier, 'A Theory of Direct Effect in Global Law' in A von Bogdany et al. (eds) *European Integration and International Coordination: Studies in Transnational Economic Law in Honour of Claus-Dieter Ehlermann* (Kluwer Law International, The Hague, 2002) 99, 113.

22 For example see Daniel Esty, 'Good Governance at the World Trade Organisation: Building a Foundation of Administrative Law' (2007) 10 *Journal of International Economic Law* 509.

23 Gabrielle Marceau, 'WTO Dispute Settlement and Human Rights' (2002) 13 *European Journal of International Law* 753. Chantal Thomas, in Chapter 10, compares legislative and adjudicative responses and they might apply in the trade and labour interface.

24 For an analysis of the development of the World Trade Regime see Joost Pauwelyn, 'The Transformation of World Trade' (2005–2006) 104 *Michigan Law Review* 1.

absent any regulatory or other mechanisms that discourage them from doing so.[25]

In responding to the problem of protectionism via intergovernmental legal constraints, the core feature of the WTO is the requirement of non-discrimination by governments through their international trade rules. This entails both non-discrimination as to the treatment of goods and services emanating from different foreign supplier countries[26] and also between local and foreign producers,[27] save in the latter case for the permitted form of protection, namely, a tariff on imported goods.[28] Thus the aim of the WTO is to limit protection to transparent and non-discriminatory taxes. It supports this goal through the proscription of bans on international trade and through norms that limit other non-tariff barriers to trade.[29]

Those who are less familiar with the international trade regime need to understand that the WTO rules do not require free trade or even demand trade liberalization, although the organization supports the latter by providing a negotiating forum in which countries may lower and then bind their tariff levels on a non-discriminatory basis.[30] Importantly, however, there is no legal obligation to reduce these permitted tariffs. Nevertheless, the system encourages such reductions and in that sense is based on the economic theory of *comparative advantage*, which suggests that nations should concentrate their productive endeavors in those fields where they have a comparative advantage as against other supplier countries. They should then trade the surpluses from such specialization to obtain the goods and services where they do not have sufficient comparative advantage. Even if one country is more efficient in all sectors than another, if the first concentrates on what it does best and lets the

---

25 Arye L Hillman, *The Political Economy of Protection* (Harwood Academic Publishers, Switzerland, 1989) 2.

26 *Marrakesh Agreement Establishing the WTO*, opened for signature 15 April 1994, 1867 UNTS 3 (entered into force 1 January 1995) Annex 1A (*General Agreement on Tariffs and Trade 1994*) ('GATT 1994') Article I; *Marrakesh Agreement Establishing the WTO*, opened for signature 15 April 1994, 1867 UNTS 3 (entered into force 1 January 1995) Annex 1B (*General Agreement on Trade in Services*) ('GATS') Article II.

27 Article III GATT 1994; Article XVII GATS.

28 The GATS Agreement allows countries to designate which service sectors they wish to bring under non-discriminatory norms. These commitments are found within each country's Schedules to the Agreement.

29 Where goods are concerned, this occurs through Article XI GATT 1994. Again, services are somewhat different as WTO members only promise to open services markets where they expressly include those markets in positive schedules to the GATS Agreement.

30 Commitments as to bound tariffs are contained in Article II GATT 1994 and the individual Member's tariff schedules.

other concentrate on the things it is closer to in efficiency, then both will be better off through trade. This is crucial from a development perspective as the theory postulates that even the poorest and least efficient country will have some *comparative* advantage. Thus the very existence of the WTO is justified by the argued benefits of trade liberalization, but has no direct liberalization obligations.

From its inception, the GATT system contained exceptions to the above obligations, which in part covered human rights concerns, although the exceptions do not utilize that concept expressly. The best example is Article XX GATT 1994 which among other things, allows for exceptions in fields such as health and the environment. These are not blanket exceptions and depend upon certain factors being established. The best-known examples are exceptions for measures 'necessary to protect human, animal or plant life or health';[31] and measures 'relating to the conservation of exhaustible natural resources'.[32] Much of WTO legal analysis looks at adjudication of disputes in this arena.

Some well-publicized disputes in the health and environment arena tend to hold centre stage in the WTO and human rights scholarship to date.[33] In terms of our project, the first methodological concern with these disputes is that the sample for analysis is particularly small. Here it is necessary to not only consider the outcomes in individual cases but also the nature of international adjudication and its strengths and weaknesses. If the outcomes are thought to be problematic, is it the fault of the rules or the adjudicatory processes or both?

One recurring problem in any field of international legal regulation is that the rules are often last-minute compromises made between countries with very divergent interests. Hence they are often poorly drafted and pose greater strain on adjudicatory processes. Nevertheless, a key aim of WTO regulation must be to ensure a proper distinction on a case-by-case basis between acceptable and unacceptable behaviour, with enough bright line certainty in the rules and their interpretation to decrease transaction costs and decrease incentives to protectionism, while still supporting desirable social policies.

---

31 Article XX(b) GATT 1994.

32 Article XX(g) GATT 1994.

33 See for example *United States – Import Prohibition of Certain Shrimp and Shrimp Products*, WTO Doc WT/DS58/AB/R (12 October 1998) (Report of the Appellate Body) ('*Shrimp/Turtle*'); *European Communities – Measures Concerning Meat and Meat Products (Hormones)*, WTO Doc WT/DS26/AB/R; WT/DS48/AB/R (13 February 1998) (Report of the Appellate Body); *European Communities – Measures Affecting Asbestos and Products Containing Asbestos*, WTO Doc WT/DS135/R (18 September 2000) (Report of the Panel); *European Communities – Measures Affecting the Approval and Marketing of Biotech Products*, WTO Docs WT/DS291/R, WT/DS292/R, WT/DS293/R (29 September 2006) (Panel Report).

Cases at the interface of the trade and human rights debate pose particular problems for adjudicators. Even if one started with the hypothesis that human rights are more important than trade liberalization benefits, (to the extent that they might be incompatible), the WTO system still has a real need to prevent protectionism. This is accepted as a legitimate concern by many of our commentators, including those arguing for a strong human rights focus.[34] A particular problem would be where protectionist measures are inappropriately labelled as human rights measures simply to protect them from successful challenge. There are real examples of protectionist measures whose construction is based on a strict literal interpretation of WTO rules. Examples beyond the human rights arena include the variable levy of the European Union's Common Agricultural Policy and Australia's tariff quota system used in the past in the fields of textiles, clothing and footwear. Neither formally imposes bans, but impose tariffs in some circumstances at such high levels as to be tantamount to the same thing from a commercial perspective. This kind of governmental behaviour in the face of international legal commitments has to be a legitimate concern even for those who wish to increase the opportunity of States to regulate for human rights purposes. The need to prevent abusive protectionist practices does not trump that right or mean that human rights proponents need to guarantee that their policy prescriptions can block any potential protectionist misuse of human rights provisions, but the issue is a key part of the regulatory challenge. On the other hand, there is a need to consider whether protectionism itself can ever be a means by which to promote human rights.

From a legal perspective, we might at some stage ask if there are any tensions to be found within the rules or their application and interpretation. This is a theme taken up in the chapter by Robert Howse and Ruti Teitel.[35] While this chapter covers a broad range of topics, the authors look at the possible conflicts between the WTO's norms and the rights to work, health and food emanating from the *International Covenant on Economic, Social and Cultural Rights* ('ICESCR')[36] to determine whether there is a conflict in the rules or in the jurisprudence pertaining to them. The authors conclude that there is no inherent conflict in this aspect of the rules and that sensible WTO jurisprudence can avoid any potential conflict.[37] The authors also conclude that any

34 See, for example, Chapters 2, 10, 11, and 12.

35 See Chapter 2.

36 Opened for signature 16 December 1966, 999 UNTS 3 (entered into force 3 January 1976).

37 This is to be contrasted with Frank J Garcia who argues that there are fundamental incompatibilities between the two regimes as currently constituted: Frank J Garcia, 'The Universal Declaration of Human Rights and the Challenge of Global Markets: Trading Away the Human Rights Principle' (1999) 25 *Brooklyn Journal of*

potential problems arise primarily from the traditional isolation of the trade regime's culture from human rights perspectives. They suggest that WTO adjudication that gives sufficient attention to human rights norms should not lead to conflict, although they do identify instances where adjudicatory behaviour did not meet their recommended approach. This question is also taken up in the chapter by Caroline Foster with respect to the relationship between trade rules and governmental entitlements to provide optimal health and safety policies. The chapter is less sanguine on this issue of potential conflict and the sensibilities of the jurisprudence, although its critical conclusions are a result of the distinct thesis that in the context of scientific uncertainty, a WTO Member should be able to defend health and safety measures on the basis that the population does not want to adopt the particular risk. Such a call to consider subjective preferences in the context of this interdisciplinary volume raises questions as to the relevance of such preferences for the identification of human rights norms, in particular in helping to set proper parameters for civil and political rights as well as the right to health.[38] That in turn raises important questions as to the foundations of a liberal democracy, an issue taken up in Patrick Emerton's chapter in relation to the political theories of John Rawls.[39] Sarah Joseph and Chantal Thomas, in their respective contributions, include an analysis of the jurisprudence in this arena as part of an examination of the legislative processes. Sarah Joseph looks at it in the context of analysing alleged democratic deficit, and Chantal Thomas looks at it in the context of alternative reform models in the trade and labour arena.[40] Our ultimate conclusions about the relationship between the two legal regimes may depend on an inductive analysis of a range of such sector specific papers,[41] coupled with a concern for such interdisciplinary challenges.

International Law 51. For a broader analysis of the compatibility of WTO norms with other international law norms, see Joost Pauwelyn, *Conflict of Norms in Public International Law: How WTO Law Relates to Other Rules of International Law* (Cambridge University Press, London, 2003).

[38] See Robert Howse, 'Democracy, Science and Free Trade: Risk Regulation on Trial at the World Trade Organisation' (2000) 98 *Michigan Law Review* 2329, who points to the view that deliberative democracy is not only about representation of the will of the people but also moral justification for the policies selected. Moral perspectives also entail the possibility of giving concern to the interests of foreign citizens although this again calls into question the Pogge/Rawls debate discussed in Chapter 6.

[39] Chapter 6.

[40] See, respectively, Chapters 12 and 10.

[41] Examples include Lorand Bartels, 'Article XX of GATT and the Problem of Extraterritorial Jurisdiction: The Case of Trade Measures for the Protection of Human Rights' (2002) 36 *Journal of World Trade* 353; Robert Howse and E Tuerk, 'The WTO Impact on International Regulations: A Case Study of the Canada–EC Asbestos Dispute' in G De Burca and J Scott (eds) *The EU and the WTO: Legal and Constitutional Issues* (Hart Publishing, Oxford, 2001).

These papers at least show that there are differing views as to how much reliance can be placed on adjudicators to get the balance right. Some of our contributors advocate strengthening the legal relationship between trade and human rights norms. For example, Ernst-Ulrich Petersmann[42] concludes with a declaration that he successfully proposed for adoption by the International Law Association as to the need for WTO adjudication to give sufficient deference to international human rights law. Shervin Majlessi,[43] in his contribution, supports a broad adoption of the WTO Director-General's Geneva Consensus, which calls for concern for the negative impacts of trade liberalization being taken into account at the same time as trade opening is advocated.

3. THE NATURE OF HUMAN RIGHTS

The previous section sought to identify a relatively narrow aim of the WTO system. In turn, one cannot say whether the WTO unduly interferes with human rights without knowing what is comprised in that concept. There is a need to accept that the ambit, nature and level of legal obligations with regard to many human rights are contentious, particularly where economic rights are concerned. In part, this is caused by a lack of consensus as to the sources of human rights.

One can take a positivist approach and look to the treaty documents that establish such rights, plus customary law norms of the same nature, or instead approach the question from a broader philosophical perspective. Where the first approach is concerned, key human rights sources are the references to human rights in the Preamble and Articles 1, 55 and 56 of the *Charter of the United Nations*, the *Universal Declaration of Human Rights* ('UDHR');[44] the *International Covenant on Civil and Political Rights* ('ICCPR');[45] and the ICESCR.

A positivist approach is more conservative in nature, as the developments via international agreement on core norms are slow. Some look at a whole range of statements, declarations and practices, seeking to argue human rights have entered the realms of customary law.[46] As Philip Alston notes

42 See Chapter 3.

43 See Chapter 14.

44 GA Res 217A (III), UN Doc A/810, 71 (1948).

45 Opened for signature 16 December 1966, 999 UNTS 171 (entered into force 23 March 1976).

46 For example, Theodor Meron, *Human Rights and Humanitarian Norms as Customary Law* (Oxford University Press, Oxford, 1989).

however, few would include economic and social rights through this form of analysis.[47]

Even a purely treaty-based approach has interpretational uncertainties. Integrating WTO and human rights under a positivist framework requires consideration of the legal implications of differing but overlapping membership of the two international legal regimes, positivist approaches to identifying any hierarchy or other means of resolving conflict, such as through the use of the norms contained in the *Vienna Convention on the Law of Treaties* ('VCLT'),[48] and many difficult dispute settlement issues such as interpretation of rules, approaches to evidence, standing and jurisdiction and sources of law. For example, the WTO is criticized for not allowing civil society or individuals to have standing. Jurisdictional questions can also be raised as to whether a panellist who is empowered solely through the WTO Dispute Settlement Understanding can nevertheless consider other international law norms.

There is also a question of interpretation of meaning of any express norms. For example, what do we mean by the 'highest attainable standard' for health?[49] The more there are difficulties in interpreting individual norms, the more difficulties there might be for any adjudicator seeking to resolve linkage and trade-off issues between trade and human rights. In addition there are important reservations and exceptions within the human rights treaty provisions that require similar balancing as occurs under Article XX GATT 1994. Examples include 'emergencies' as expressed in Article 4 ICESCR and 'public policy' requirements per Article 8(2) ICESCR.

There may also be conflicts between different human rights norms. On one level, all are equal in importance and are interdependent[50] but some are written in softer language which would be relevant from a positivist perspective. In addition, they often impose differing constraints on how governments should act and how rights should be enforced. Thomas Cottier has pointed out that some human rights are suitable for articulating immediate individual legal rights, while others are of a programmatic nature, needing elaboration and guidance legislatively.[51] Yet not all would agree on which fall into either cate-

---

47 Philip Alston, 'Ships Passing in the Night: The Current State of the Human Rights Development Debates Seen Through the Lens of the Millennium Development Goals' (2005) 27 *Human Rights Quarterly* 755, 773.

48 Opened for signature 23 May 1969, 1155 UNTS 331 (entered into force 27 January 1980).

49 Article 12 ICESCR; Paul Hunt, *The Right of Everyone to the Enjoyment of the Highest Attainable Standard of Physical and Mental Health, Report of the Special Rapporteur, Addendum, Mission to the World Trade Organisation*, UN Doc E/CN.4/2004/49/Add.1 (1 March 2004).

50 Article 2 UDHR.

51 Cottier, above n 21, 112.

gory. Sarah Joseph's contribution on democratic deficit also analyses which specific human rights might arguably be breached as a result of WTO norms and practices.[52] Philip Alston deals with the question whether poverty itself involves a breach of human rights.[53]

One difficulty is seeking to integrate various potentially conflicting norms that arise through different legal sources. Here, as in any legal system, there needs to be a balancing device, whether this is some form of *proportionality* test as applied in EU and Canadian constitutional law or the *reasonableness* test of the WTO Appellate Body per Article XX GATT 1994 jurisprudence.[54] There are also risk management issues and the degree of scientific certainty alluded to above in relation to the SPS Agreement.

A further issue in a positivist debate as to the ambit of human rights is whether the rights are limited to negative rights against undue interference or entail positive rights that impose obligations on others to help their attainment. While ICESCR clearly includes positive rights, the interpretation challenge still exists, particularly in the face of the softer language of some norms. A right might be stated more positively, but could still be expressed more in aspirational language as well. Furthermore, if a positive right requires considerable expenditures to be fulfilled, to what extent is it an inherent right where a government has limited resources? The debate would also lead to some positivist philosophers concluding that ICESCR is generally aspirational and not about existing human rights. Paul Hunt believes that this argument is misleading because State intervention is also required for the protection of civil and political rights as well as economic rights. Both sets of rights may require State intervention and a substantial amount of expenditure and should not be distinguished on this basis.[55]

---

52 See Chapter 12.

53 Philip Alston, above n 47, 785ff.

54 Donald Regan, 'The meaning of "Necessary" in GATT Article XX: The Myth of Cost-Benefit Balancing' (2007) 6 *World Trade Review* 347; Federico Ortina, *From 'Non-Discrimination' to 'Reasonableness': A Paradigm Shift in International Economic Law?* (2002) Jean Monnet Program, www.jeanmonnetprogram.org/papers/05/050101.html at 12 December 2008; OHCHR, *Human Rights and World Trade Agreements: Using General Exception Clauses to Protect Human Rights* (2005) UNHCHR, http://www.ohchr.org/Documents/Publications/WTOen.pdf at 12 December 2008.

55 Paul Hunt, 'Reclaiming Economic, Social and Cultural Rights' (1993) *Waikato Law Review* 141, 153. For arguments that the rights carry concomitant obligations see Office of the High Commissioner for Human Rights ('OHCHR'), *Draft Guidelines: Human Rights Approach to Poverty Reduction Strategies* (2002) OHCHR, [13], www.unhchr.ch/development/povertyfinal.html at 14 December 2008; United Nations Development Program, *Human Development Report 2003* (United Nations, Geneva, 2003) 28.

Even a narrow positivist approach could also lead to questions as to the role of some alleged rights not expressly covered. An example might include rights not seen themselves as established human rights, but which might nevertheless be argued to be *inherent* elements of such rights by reason of being necessary *preconditions* for the attainment of express human rights. For example, Amartya Sen saw freedom to exchange goods as a human right given the relationship to the right to work and the right to food.[56]

James Harrison has addressed our central question as to the compatibility of the two regimes from a perspective that concentrates on a positivist conception of human rights even though he himself does not presume that such rights should be so limited.[57] Nevertheless, within that framework, he concluded that there were still particular problems although he suggested that there were 'few inherent actual conflicts'.[58] He noted the trend towards WTO rules aiming at more internal regulation of Members in fields that cannot all be justified under neo-classical economic postulates of trade liberalization. While economists could debate the characterization, political science perspectives suggest no surprise when powerful Members use the WTO to impose such things as intellectual property protections that are far removed from the trade barrier concerns that faced the GATT from its inception. Harrison also raises concerns as to conditionality-based trade restrictions that aim to promote human rights. He concludes that fear of scrutiny under the WTO acts as a disincentive to such action against extreme human rights abuses. He also notes that use of such mechanisms under regional or preference regimes comes with insufficient scrutiny mechanisms to counter imbalances in power between donor and donee.[59] This dual concern suggests how delicate the balancing needs to be if both too much and too little scrutiny can be legitimate problems as circumstances change. The regulatory chill factor is in part proportional to the uncertainty in the rules and Harrison calls for more precision in articulation of key concepts.[60]

The challenges grow exponentially when we move beyond a purely positivist approach to the identification of human rights norms.[61] If the basis of human rights is philosophical and not purely within positivist notions of legal philosophy, what are its sources? Is it religious as per natural law, can it be devised from moral philosophy, or from the specific field of ethics as Peter

56 Amartya Sen, *Development as Freedom* (Knopf, New York 1999) 26.

57 James Harrison, *The Human Rights Impact of the World Trade Organisation* (Hart Publishing, Oregon, 2007).

58 Ibid 249.

59 Above, n 57, 121.

60 Above, n 57, 250.

61 Burns Weston, 'Human Rights' (1984) 3 *Human Rights Quarterly* 257, 259.

Singer asserts,[62] can it be even justified economically or under game theory as the basis of a stable and sustainable society? While some human rights advocates eschew an attempt to articulate philosophical foundations,[63] Jerome Shestak has observed that there are a range of practical reasons to consider the philosophic foundations of human rights. Understanding the foundations may promote the authority of the international law of human rights:

> [h]ow one understands the meaning of human rights will influence one's judgment on such issues as which rights are regarded as universal, which should be given priority, which can be overruled by other interests, which call for international pressures, which can demand programs for implementation, and for which one will fight.[64]

Michael Freeman argues that the positivist approach misrepresents human rights and can have dangerous implications. In his view, '[o]ne appeals to human rights precisely when legal institutions fail to recognize and enforce them. If legal positivism were true, an important basis for criticizing unjust legal systems would be eliminated'.[65]

A converse argument is that we should simply concern ourselves with the actual problems in the world and not get bogged down in the competing theories. Thus even if we have differing views as to global justice, we can still readily say that we wish to do something about extreme poverty as is evidenced by the Millennium Development Goals as adopted.[66] Nevertheless, a concern for the philosophical questions will help us understand whether we have gone far enough. To the extent that equality is an element of justice, concerns for the world's poor need to arise far earlier than when they are found to be starving.

---

62 Peter Singer, *One World: The Ethics of Globalization* (Yale University Press, New Haven, 2002).

63 In fact it was the very lack of a consistent view about the nature of human rights that led James Harrison to limit his analysis of the WTO and human rights to a positivist one: Harrison, above n 57. Philip Alston has also cautioned against an unprincipled proliferation of alleged human rights: Philip Alston, 'Conjuring Up New Human Rights: A Proposal for Quality Control' (1984) 78 *American Journal of International Law* 607.

64 Jerome J Shestak, 'The Philosophic Foundations of Human Rights' (1998) 20 *Human Rights Quarterly* 201, 201–2.

65 Michael Freeman, *Human Rights: An Interdisciplinary Approach* (Policy Press, Cambridge, 2002) 12.

66 Thomas Nagel, 'The Problem of Global Justice' (2005) 23 *Philosophy and Public Affairs* 113, 118; UN, *Millennium Development Goals* (2000) UN, www.un.org/millenniumgoals/ at 14 December 2008; UN, *United Nations Millennium Declaration*, GA Res 55/2 , UN GAOR, 55th sess, 8th plen mtg, UN Doc A/Res/55/2 (8 September 2000).

Philosophical views about human rights have varied significantly as different philosophical theories as to law, politics and liberty have emerged. Legal positivism, which dominated much of jurisprudential thought in the nineteenth and twentieth centuries, is the natural justification for the positivist view of the international law of human rights. At the extreme, a positivist perspective did not treat international law as a proper legal system because the absence of a sovereign authority with enforcement powers was antithetical to its notion of law as such.[67] The more expansive view stems from the natural law tradition, beginning with religion-based notions of fundamental rights and values. Secular developments in natural law theory also provided a justification for international law as law. The natural law theories of scholars such as Grotius were particularly relevant in justifying international law per se as a mechanism to promote the moral imperative of peaceful and harmonious cooperation between people and nations.[68] In considering the rights of individuals and the role of government, John Locke argued that the fundamental right of individuals was for life, liberty and property, with governments being a result of a social contract to avoid the worst aspects of interpersonal behaviour under an unconstrained state of nature.[69] The French Philosophers, particularly Rousseau and Voltaire, built upon these ideas, in turn inspiring developments in America and its domestic Bill of Rights.[70]

Some philosophical perspectives were closely aligned with certain economic perspectives. For example, the utilitarianism of Jeremy Bentham calls for governmental policies that promote the greatest benefit for the greatest number. That is less concerned with the individual and certainly the least fortunate individual. As a result, Bentham was sceptical of the notion of human rights.[71]

---

[67] John Austin, *The Province of Jurisprudence Determined* (Weidenfeld and Nicholson, London, 3rd edn, 1954).

[68] Shestak, above n 64, 206.

[69] John Locke, *Two Treatises of Government* (Cambridge University Press, New York, Peter Laslett ed., 1963).

[70] See, for example, Jean-Jacques Rousseau, *The Social Contract* (Penguin, London, Maurice Cranston ed., 1968).

[71] Modern scholars have also questioned the determinacy of human rights: for example, Chris Brown, 'Universal Human Rights? An Analysis of "Human-Rights Culture" and its Critics' in R G Patman (ed.) *Universal Human Rights?* (Palgrave Macmillan, London, 2000) 31, or have argued that they need to be understood in their historical context, for example, Norberto Bobbio, *The Age of Rights* (Policy Press, Cambridge, 2nd ed., 1996); Jack Donnelly, *Universal Human Rights in Theory and Practice* (Cornell University Press, Ithaca, 2003); Eugene Kamenka, 'Human Rights: Peoples' Rights' in James Crawford (ed.) *The Rights of Peoples* (Oxford University Press, New York, 1988) 127. Critical legal studies indeterminacy challenges have also been directed to human rights themselves. See for example Duncan Kennedy, *A Critique of Adjudication* (Cambridge University Press, Cambridge, 1997).

From a human rights perspective, it is not only the nature of these philosophical schools of thought, but also their focus that is important. Locke's views begin with individual rights and postulate a minimal role for government, purely in order to effectively support those rights. On the other hand, the utilitarian perspective looks at the collective good rather than the individual's rights.[72] Some of the excesses of the twentieth century show how problematic notions of the collective good may prove to be. The post-World War II international legal framework, including the United Nations and the Bretton Woods system, including the related GATT as the precursor to the WTO, were in part inspired by greater thought about the value of individual liberty and mechanisms which might protect it. The Kantian perspective has been particularly influential in developing a moral philosophy that supports cooperation and values and behaviour that ought to be applicable to all.[73] Kant argued that humans and humanity should be seen as ends and not means, a view which resonates strongly with the core values espoused in the UDHR. He also argued that a cosmopolitan view of such rights would support our aspiration to perpetual peace.[74]

While there is certainly no consensus on the basis of a non-positivist theory, certain recent scholars have been particularly influential in advancing the debate. Ronald Dworkin sought to reconcile natural rights and utilitarian perspectives in his seminal work, *Taking Rights Seriously*.[75] Probably the most influential modern philosophical perspective is that of John Rawls, who sought to identify rights and duties within a society based on a coherent theory of justice. Using a thought experiment of a negotiated social contract between persons conducting the exercise behind a 'veil of ignorance', he argued that two principles of justice would be selected. The first is that 'each person is to have an equal right to the most extensive total system of equal basic liberties compatible with a similar system of liberty for all'.[76] The second principle asserts that 'social and economic inequalities are to be arranged so that they are both: (a) to the greatest benefit of the least advantaged, consistent with the just savings principle, and (b) attached to offices and positions open to all under conditions of fair equality of opportunity'.[77]

At first, it might have been thought that the second principle was a justification for redistributional rules at the international level in favour of the least

---

72 Shestak, above n 64, 212.

73 Fernando Teson, 'The Kantian Theory of International Law' (1992) 92 *Columbia Law Review* 53.

74 Immanuel Kant, 'Perpetual Peace: A Philosophical Sketch' in H Reiss (ed.) *Kant – Political Writings* (Cambridge University Press, Cambridge, 2nd edn, 1991) 107.

75 Ronald Dworkin, *Taking Rights Seriously* (Duckworth, London, 1977).

76 John Rawls, *A Theory of Justice* (Harvard University Press, Cambridge, 1971) 302.

77 Ibid.

advantaged countries, although Rawls did not assert this in that book. Indeed in due course, he argued to the contrary in a separate book, *The Law of Peoples*.[78] One difficulty is that for obvious reasons, human rights scholars never sought to incorporate trade law norms into a comprehensive philosophical theory of human rights until such time as the WTO and international economic law were seen as problematic. Human rights law was first concerned with the most egregious crimes against humanity and individuals. More recently it is dealing with the more intellectually challenging concern with the notion of socio-economic justice. It has only been relatively recently that the relationship between these two fields has begun to be examined. These themes are explored in Patrick Emerton's chapter which deals with the Rawls/Pogge debate about the duty of industrialized countries towards developing countries. Thomas Pogge has taken issue with Rawls' argument as to why his justice principles do not operate internationally.[79] Rawls applied his theory of justice on a two-step basis. Once persons had collected into a people based on a social contract they would owe different duties to other peoples. Decent societies would not only wish to help others but it would be strategically sensible to stabilize the world. Rawls argued that the main reason for poverty is the lack of institutional infrastructure. If the cause of poverty is institutional defects, then in his view, the limits of the moral obligation are to assist in developing these. Pogge challenges this view on a range of levels, both factual and moral. Patrick Emerton explores that debate and also seeks to identify the core content of human rights that might flow from the basic theory of justice.[80]

Modern proponents of a non-positivist theory of human rights have based their arguments on dignity,[81] justice[82] and liberalism.[83] Philip Alston has made

---

78 Rawls, *The Law of Peoples, with the Idea of Public Reason Revisited* (Harvard University Press, Cambridge, 1999).

79 Thomas W Pogge, *Kant, Rawls and Social Justice* (PhD Thesis, Harvard University, 1983); Thomas W Pogge, 'An Egalitarian Law of Peoples' (1994) 23 *Philosophy and Public Affairs* 195; Thomas W Pogge, *World Poverty and Human Rights* (Polity Press, Cambridge, 2002).

80 Chapter 6.

81 For example, Oscar Schachter, 'Human Dignity as a Normative Concept' (1983) 77 *American Journal of International Law* 848; Jack Donnelly, *Universal Human Rights in Theory and Practice* (Cornell University Press, New York, 2003); Michael J Perry, *Towards a Theory of Human Rights* (Cambridge University Press, Cambridge, 2007); Raymond J Vincent, *Human Rights and International Relations* (Cambridge University Press, Cambridge, 1986); Louis Hencken (ed.), *Human Dignity: The Internationalisation of Human Rights* (Aspen Institute for Humanistic Studies, New York, 1979).

82 Rawls, above n 76; Ronald Dworkin, above n 75.

83 David P Forsythe, *Human Rights in International Relations* (Cambridge University Press, Cambridge, 2006).

the point that general terms such as equity, dignity and governance need to be rooted in identified standards.[84] Christian Tomuschat has argued for certain human rights deductively as an essential element of a viable legal order.[85] Alston postulated a revision of Tomuschat's thesis namely:

> [N]o right should be excluded when the following two conditions are present: (i) the right is indispensable to a meaningful notion of human dignity (upon which human rights are based) and (ii) the satisfaction of that right is demonstrably within the reach of the government in question assuming reasonable support from the international community.[86]

Sociological and anthropological perspectives may also be relevant in the identification of the ambit of human rights. Given that human rights law has emanated from the international legal system which has been dominated by Western thought and power, some have questioned whether its values, including human rights norms, can be challenged from the perspective of cultural relativism. John Finnis contends that a comprehensive survey of different anthropological literature shows that there are universal basic values shared by all cultures, albeit that these values may be realized in different ways. He argues that such universal values include, inter alia, concern for human life, concern for truth and for education.[87] Michael Trebilcock notes the policy advocacy of many globalization critics 'who on the one hand ostensibly oppose the imperialistic expansion of Western cultural influences, while at the same time selectively promoting distinctly homogeneous concepts of universal human rights, labour standards and environmental protection'.[88]

---

84 Philip Alston, above n 47, 760.

85 Christian Tomuschat, *Human Rights: Between Idealism and Realism* (Oxford University Press, Oxford, 2004) 35.

86 Philip Alston, above n 47, 774.

87 John Finnis, *Natural Law and Natural Rights* (Clarendon Press, Oxford, 1980) 83. See also Arvind Sharma, *Are Human Rights Western?* (Oxford University Press, New York, 2006); Richard A Wilson (ed) *Human Rights, Culture and Context: Anthropological Perspectives* (Pluto Press, London, 1997); A Pollis and P Schwab (eds) *Human Rights: Cultural and Ideological Perspectives* (Praeger, New York, 1979); Fernando Teson, 'International Human Rights and Cultural Relativism' (1985) 25 *Virginia Journal of International Law* 869.

88 Michael J Trebilcock, 'Critiquing the Critics of Economic Globalization' (2005) 1 *Journal of International Law and International Relations* 213, 217.

4. PHILOSOPHICAL PERSPECTIVES ON THE BROADER DEBATE

The previous section looked at philosophy in the context of defining the ambit of human rights, but there are a range of other philosophical questions that present themselves when we look at the compatibility between the regimes. The question to ask in tandem is what is the philosophical justification for trade liberalization. As noted above, efficient solutions by definition increase total welfare. They do not guarantee allocation in ways that all would see as just, but at least a larger total allocatable amount provides greater opportunities for just distributions, however they are to be defined. The economic premise is therefore the first issue. The WTO is bound up in the economics of efficiency, so if it does not even promote efficiency or raise total welfare it would not be a just outcome for that reason alone. Even where it raises welfare, because it has no distributional norms, the justice of its immediate outcomes depends on one's views as to distributive justice ranging from the classical utilitarian perspective to Rawlsian perspectives. To the latter school of thought, at the national level, even an optimal outcome from an efficiency perspective would not be fair without any adjustment mechanisms along the way. A philosophical argument in favour of a libertarian free market was provided by Robert Nozick.[89] Because Nozick's libertarian perspective includes arguing that a person has the right to the fruits of their labour, he argues against redistributive taxation policies as being tantamount to forced labour.

A key issue is how to respond to data that shows increased wealth of the very poor in most societies, but also even more rapidly increasing disparities between rich and poor individuals and generally between North and South. Again a Rawlsian perspective has concerns with this, although his own work showed that there are complex questions of liberal political philosophy when one moves from national to international perspectives.

There are a number of other specific philosophical questions posed by aspects of WTO activities. These might include: the notion of sovereignty and the propriety of extra-territorial norms in cases such as *Shrimp/Turtle* where US laws sought to ban shrimp imports from foreign suppliers who did not do enough to protect endangered sea turtles; the more general relationship between sovereignty and justice;[90] unequal and unconscionable bargaining

---

[89] Robert Nozick, *Anarchy, State and Utopia* (Basic Books, New York, 1974).

[90] Thomas Nagel has pointed out the need to consider justice alongside concepts of sovereignty. This forces us to choose between cosmopolitan and political constructs of justice as epitomized in the Pogge/Rawls debate. Nagel, above n 66, p 120; Peter Singer, *One World* (Yale University Press, New Haven, 2002). A cosmopolitan view

within negotiating Rounds;[91] de facto discrimination through such phenomena as tariff escalation, where the WTO's reciprocal and unconstrained negotiating forum tends to lead to negotiated outcomes where there are higher tariffs on products that are of most interest for developing country exports and generally weaker norms in fields such as agriculture.

There are also philosophical questions as to adjudicatory methodology such as in relation to approaches to interpretation. Once again the chapter by Howse and Teitel argues strongly for an approach which pays sufficient deference to human rights. This methodology is strongly reinforced in the chapter by Ernst-Ulrich Petersmann.

Justice issues also have temporal dimensions. This is because economics argues that trade liberalization that can be expected to cause short-term harm to inefficient traders and consequential problems for employees in that sector will lead to increased welfare in the long term. There is then a philosophical question as to the degree to which economic harm can be allowed to occur to current citizens, with a view to providing greater benefits for future citizens. Again the question only becomes relevant if the economic arguments are hypothesized to be true. This again reminds us that the different interdisciplinary perspectives must be integrated. Another example of the intersection between philosophy and economics is the Pogge/Rawls debate alluded to above. Pogge based his views, in part at least, on a belief that international economic law causes harm to the extreme poor, while Rawls took issue with that assertion. Philosophers must then turn for assistance to economists. Economics may also help to resolve other tensions such as the morality underpinning utilitarianism.

5. ECONOMIC PERSPECTIVES

While few if any would support the idea of efficiency as an ultimate goal, economists argue that it is an extremely desirable means to the attainment of more meritorious goals. As noted above, neo-classical economics argues that many utilitarian policies would provide sufficient welfare gains to allow the winners to fully compensate the losers and still be better off. As also noted, the WTO is premised on the economic theory of *comparative advantage* as a means to maximize wealth through specialization and trade. Neo-classical economics also points out that trade barriers on imports adversely affect the import country's export sector as well as imposing excessive costs on

was presented by Charles Beitz, *Political Theory and International Relations* (Princeton University Press, Princeton, 1999).

[91] This issue is discussed in Chapter 12 in the context of democratic deficit.

consumers, and that growth is generally better than redistribution alone as a mechanism to increase welfare. Neo-classical economics also points to the regulatory importance of price signals as incentives towards efficient allocation of resources. The Coase theorem also points to the regulatory benefits in adopting the most efficient response to the regulation of social issues such as environmental protection.[92]

An efficient solution is one where total value is maximized and hence at least increases the potential distributable benefits to the individuals within a society. While there may be winners and losers from any market-based endeavour, neo-classical economic theory asserts that a domestic political system can redistribute the efficiency gains from trade liberalization to those who suffer in the short term, either through immediate income transfers or through retraining schemes and the like. Economists describe this as a Kaldor/Hicks transfer payment at the domestic level, where winners from efficiency gains are able to fully compensate losers and still be better off. Neo-classical economic theory also postulates that even though there will commonly be short-term losers, the efficiency gains in the short term will provide greater opportunities for short-term losers in the long term beyond the option of immediate compensatory transfers. Economists describe this as a Kuznets curve analysis which predicts short-term losses before long-term gains.

Such a market-based system contemplates transfers but does not mandate them, leaving this as economic theory does, to domestic political systems. In this sense, the WTO is not inherently utilitarian, simply because it leaves the distributional justice questions to domestic politics.

Those in the early 'pro-WTO' camp in the human rights debate tended to rely on the above postulates of liberal trade theory and tended to ignore the problem of the observable disparity of benefits from trade and the challenge as to whether there is any systemic bias against the extreme poor. Many supporters tended to rely on the neo-classical economic views above, that disparities will be alleviated over time and/or are domestic redistribution issues outside the purview of economic prescription. Yet the utility of liberal trade policies as a means to promote human development is not without its critics and the degree of poverty and disparities in wealth cannot be ignored, whatever their true cause.[93] As the current problems in the world economy

---

92 Ronald H Coase, 'The Problem of Social Cost' (1960) 3 *Journal of Law and Economics* 1.

93 For an analysis of some of the key challenges see Trebilcock, above n 88. For survey analyses of the challenges from development theory see Kevin E Davis and Michael J Trebilcock, 'The Relationship Between Law and Development: Optimists versus Skeptics' (Working Paper No 08-14, NYU School of Law, Public Law and Legal

show, markets will inevitably fail without appropriate regulatory mechanisms. It is extremely difficult to find the right balance between regulation and liberalization and to have that adopted and nurtured by a democratic constituency subject to pressures from vested interests. This issue will be discussed further below in relation to the political dimension.

Returning to economic concerns, debates about the incontrovertible data as to an unconscionable amount of truly poor people in the world,[94] bring us to complex causation questions and in turn, philosophical debates dependent upon the conclusions on those causation questions. Sceptical economists and some philosophers have relied heavily on the data as to extreme poverty as part of a critique of liberalization. For example, Pogge noted that a quarter of the world's population lives below the international poverty line.[95] Complex causation questions have been noted. For example, is the disparity in gains from trade in favour of industrialized countries proof of exploitation or is it the natural corollary of higher labour productivity in the richer countries? Is the latter shown by China taking over textiles market share from countries such as the Philippines and Bangladesh? Economics has tried harder in recent times to explain such outcomes. More recently, much has been done in modelling growth and analysing developing country economic performance.[96] At times the results will be mixed in terms of benefits and detriments. For example, Winters et al.[97] survey the empirical literature and note increased income from trade liberalization but also note higher volatility through variances in prices and income sources.

Many human rights critics of the trade regime have looked to the work of economists such as Dani Rodrik that seeks to draw sceptical causal conclusions from statistical data and econometric modelling. For example, Rodrik compared Mexico, a participant in the WTO and NAFTA, unfavourably with

Theory Research Paper Series, 2008); John K M Ohnesorge, 'Development Theory: Law and Development Orthodoxies and the North East Asian Experience' (2008) 28 *University of Pennsylvania Journal of Economic Law* 219; Francisco Rodriguez and Dani Rodrik, 'Trade Policy and Economic Growth: A Skeptic's Guide to the Cross-National Evidence' (Working Paper No W7081, National Bureau of Economic Research, Harvard University, 1999).

94 Detailed data is provided in Chapter 4. See also Daron Acemoglu and Ventura Jaume, 'The World Income Distribution' (2002) 117 *Quarterly Journal of Economics* 659.

95 Pogge, above n 79 (2002), 7–9.

96 For example, John M Antle and Gregg Heidebrink, 'Environment and Development: Theory and International Evidence' (1995) 43 *Economic Development and Cultural Change* 603.

97 Alan L Winters et al. (2004) 'Trade Liberalization and Poverty: The Evidence So Far' (2004) 42 *Journal of Economic Literature* 72.

Vietnam, then outside the WTO system.[98] The contribution in this volume from David Kinley, Hai Nguyen and Odette Murray[99] adds a more recent analysis of Vietnam through the time frame when it acceded to the WTO Agreement. Their chapter looks critically at some of the pressures imposed on developing countries through their relationship with more powerful trading partners under this system, which again brings the political science perspective into our analysis. Even if Rodrik's comparative cautions are appropriate, however, one needs to be careful as to what conclusions one would draw. If Vietnam has advanced more favourably outside of the WTO system than Mexico has done within it, do we now expect a downturn in Vietnam's economic welfare and human rights as a result of joining the system? If so, for what reasons? If this does not eventuate, what implications would this have for our theoretical perspectives?

A number of leading economists have questioned aspects of free market equilibrium analysis. Alan Blinder has cautioned as to the implications of off-shoring of impersonal jobs, although he did so from the perspective of the impact upon a developed country, the USA. He points to the fact that significant transitional shocks creating millions of losers lead to political problems from shifts in trading patterns.[100] Some economists seek to analyse markets from the perspective that they are significantly more complex systems than is theoretically postulated.[101] Nobel Prize winner George Akerlof has presented a detailed study of the role of psychological norms as they affect neo-classical postulates.[102] Psychological insights into mass commercial behaviour underlie the behavioural finance school of economics.[103] Psychologists have also argued that as nations become wealthier, such wealth ceases to be a good indicator of general well-being.[104]

Pranab Bardhan in his chapter[105] reminds us of the perennial research prob-

---

98 Dani Rodrik, *The Global Governance of Trade as if Development Really Mattered* (United Nations Development Program, New York, 2001) 21ff.

99 See Chapter 9.

100 Alan S Blinder, 'Offshoring: Big Deal, or Business as Usual?' (CEPS Working Paper No 149, June 2000), www.princeton.edu/~ceps/workingpapers/149blinder.pdf at 15 December 2008.

101 See for example W Brian Arthur et al. (eds), *The Economy as an Evolving Complex System II* (Addison-Wesley, Reading, 1997).

102 George A Akerlof, 'The Missing Motivation in Macro Economics' (2007) 97 *American Economic Review* 5.

103 See for example Robert Shiller, 'Behavioural Economics and Institutional Innovation' (2005) 72:2 *Southern Economic Journal* 269.

104 Ed Diener and Martin E P Seligman, 'Beyond Money: Toward an Economic of Well-Being' (2004) 5:1 *Psychological Science in the Public Interest* 1.

105 Chapter 4.

lem of correlation versus causation. He points out that past economic regression studies are all flawed. These can only look at correlations and also have analytical problems. For example, why have China and India grown; is it trade, or internal infrastructure, land reform, internal migration, anti-poverty programs internally or the like? Why has sub-Saharan Africa fallen behind? Is it instability, war, civil conflict, and corruption, which frighten off foreign investors and traders? Pranab Bardhan's chapter seeks to drill down to a more analytical perspective on the various ways that trade liberalization may impact upon the poor as a discrete group. He finds a complex picture where benefits are largely dependent on the domestic political and economic institutions of the countries concerned.

Some analysts take an economic history perspective and present a pessimistic picture as to the extent of time that developing countries need to suffer social and political injustice while pursuing growth.[106] Joseph Stiglitz has presented an insider's critique and in part has highlighted the natural economic observation that asymmetrical information and market power and inadequate institutions will not lead to efficient outcomes. Furthermore, he sees some of these problems as ethical issues. Rodrik and Stiglitz have not abandoned economic theory, however. Stiglitz notes that developing countries cannot afford the inefficiency losses from poor resource allocation and policies that are a disincentive to foreign investment and which promote an exodus of their best and brightest.[107] Indeed in another publication, Rodrik accepts that all countries have been shown to succeed in growth if they integrate with the global economy, install adequate institutional environments to protect property rights and enforce contracts and adopt sound government financial practices.[108]

Another aspect of economic analysis would look at the interrelationship between trade regulation and human rights. We can consider the positive and negative correlations between the regimes that economic theory might predict. An example of a negative impact is the effect of TRIPS norms on the generic pharmaceutical industry. On the other hand, many trade law reforms would be expected to have positive effects on some human rights at least. An example

---

[106] Sylvia Ann Hewlett, 'Human Rights and Economic Realities: Tradeoffs in Historical Perspective' (1979) 94 *Political Science Quarterly* 453.

[107] Joseph E Stiglitz, 'Two Principles for the Next Round, or How to Bring Developing Countries in from the Cold' (2000) 23 *World Economy* 438. See also Joseph Stiglitz and Andrew Charlton, *Fair Trade for All: How Trade Can Promote Development* (Oxford University Press, Oxford, 2007); Joseph Stiglitz, *Making Globalisation Work* (Allen Lane, New York, 2006).

[108] Dani Rodrik, *One Economics, Many Recipes: Globalisation, Institutions and Economic Growth* (Princeton University Press, Princeton, 2008).

would be the positive environmental impact of reducing agricultural subsidies.[109] There is also the correlation between higher stages of development and demand for higher levels of human rights, with environment again being the key example, although we might need to factor in the negative impact on the environment of commercial activity.[110]

Another NGO challenge that economists have sought to examine is whether trade competition leads to a race to the bottom in terms of the human rights infrastructure that might impose costs on traders. Examples would include direct environment, labour and social welfare standards or the indirect impact of reduced government revenue through tax competition aimed at attracting foreign investment.[111] The scholarship to date suggests that there is little evidence of such a race.[112]

Economics also provides insights as to the relative efficiency of direct versus indirect policy instruments. For example, direct allowance of labour migration would do much more for labour standards than trying to force foreign policy changes through a social clause. Trade in goods is simply a substitute for trade in other factors. Another direct labour approach would be to provide income transfers to stop child labour.

Another specific challenge is whether sanctions should be permitted in aid of human rights goals and whether the WTO norms unduly interfere with this.[113] To date, many economic and political commentators challenge the

---

109 Daniel C Esty, 'Greening World Trade' in J J Schott (ed.) *The World Trading System: Challenges Ahead* (Peterson Institute for International Economics, Washington DC, 1996).

110 Antle and Heidebrink, above n 96.

111 It is worth noting that any problems with investment as opposed to trade policy fall outside the range of legitimate criticisms of the WTO given its limited brief.

112 For example, Robert C Feenstra and Gordon H Hanson, 'Global Production and Inequality: A Survey of Trade and Wages' in E Kwan Choi and James Harrigan (eds) *Handbook of International Trade* (Blackwell, Oxford, 2002) Ch 6. Eskeland and Harrison found no evidence of correlation between foreign investment and home country pollution abatement costs and also found that foreign companies in developing countries are cleaner and more energy efficient than locals: see generally Gunnar A Eskeland and Ann Harrison 'Moving to Greener Pastures? Multinationals and the Pollution Haven Hypothesis' (2003) 70 *Journal of Development Economics* 1. This is not to say there are not significant instances of inappropriate multinational behaviour or the need for developments in corporate social responsibility. This literature simply relates to the challenge as to whether there is a systemic race to the bottom implied by the notion of competition per se.

113 See for example Patricia Stirling, 'The Use of Trade Sanctions as an Enforcement Mechanism for Basic Human Rights: A Proposal for Addition to the World Trade Organisation' (1996) 11 *American University Journal of International Law and Policy* 1.

benefits of such strategies.[114] Most commentators argue that they hurt innocent parties. Thus they take away some human rights to promote others, raising 'ends justifying means' philosophical questions. It is also difficult to apply sanctions in a non-discriminatory way, that is target everyone who needs change, or decide where the cut-off line is. They often involve double standards. They generally have no review mechanism. Sanctions will not work when the target prefers to forgo the gains from trade, although this might mean that trade sanctions work best on those who believe in trade the most and who benefit the most from it. Even when changes are made, they are often poorly administered.[115] Political science would suggest that for sanctions to be approved there will usually need to be an alliance between altruists and protectionists, hence encouraging protectionism.

Economics could also look at the efficiencies or otherwise of trade and human rights regimes and the cost/benefit of linkage.[116] Failing to link has extra transaction costs, fragmentation and non-coherence issues. There are differing approaches; one would be to prioritize. Another is to have a streaming mechanism such as Article XX GATT 1994; a third approach is to simply relax the standards in the substantive norms and provide for greater deference. Caroline Foster's chapter calling for deference to domestic public opinion is an example of the latter, as are the chapters of Howse and Teitel and Petersmann demanding interpretation consistent with human rights norms.[117]

There has also been some analysis of the WTO from a new institutional economics perspective.[118] An important question is to consider what we should be properly comparing with what. To simply analyse a particular system without considering its alternatives makes it too easy to criticize and

---

[114] See, for example, Gary C Hufbauer et al., *Economic Sanctions Reconsidered* (Peterson Institute for International Economics, Washington DC, 3rd edn 1990).

[115] See generally Jim Rollo and Alan L Winters, 'Subsidiarity and Governance Challenges for the WTO: The Examples of Environmental and Labour Standards' (2000) 23 *The World Economy* 561.

[116] Jack L Goldsmith and Eric A Posner, 'The Theory of Customary International Law' (1999) 66 *University of Chicago Law Review* 1113; Jeffrey L Dunoff and Joel P Trachtman, 'Economic Analysis of International Law' (1999) 24 *Yale Journal of International Law* 1; Alan Sykes, 'International Trade and Human Rights: An Economic Perspective' in F M Abbott et al. (eds) *International Trade and Human Rights: Foundations and Conceptual Issues* (University of Michigan Press, Detroit, 2006) 69.

[117] See, respectively, Chapters 11, 2, and 3; see also Chapter 12.

[118] Based on the earlier works of economists such as: Coase, above n 92; Oliver E Williamson, *The Economic Institutions of Capitalism* (Free Press, New York, 1985); Beth V Yarbrough and Robert M Yarbrough, *Cooperation and Governance in International Trade: The Strategic Organizational Approach* (Princeton University Press, Princeton, 1992).

misunderstand the problems of second-best analysis. Economics might thus look at the cost/benefit of the system as opposed to unconstrained protectionism, uncertainty, and the impact of a shift to bilateralism. Thus a key question is whether major economic powers would be more or less able to exploit the poor absent a regulatory mechanism such as the WTO? This again leads on to political science questions, to be discussed below.

Methodologically, we might also need to consider second-best analysis where we consider trade and human rights regimes as they are, not as they ought to be. For example, where the WTO is concerned, there is an anti-developing country bias through tariff escalation, managed protection through anti-dumping, countervailing and safeguards regimes and continued protection in sensitive fields such as agriculture. At times, the major critique of the WTO is that it is failing in its mandate to prevent protectionism, particularly where that protectionism is applied against those industries where the least developed countries have a comparative advantage. This naturally integrates with political science analysis, which asks why the institution is captured in this way and how, if at all, this might be overcome.

We also need to be careful of using inappropriate generalizations in our analysis. For example, a useful study might look to the gains and losses from removing agricultural export subsidies as both WTO advocates and pro human rights NGOs decry agricultural protectionism. Yet while most presume that opening agricultural markets is of immediate benefit to developing countries, it is a fact that net food importing developing countries currently benefit from rich country export subsidies.

Economics might also query what are the implications of imposing human rights standards that cannot be met efficiently at current levels of development and which might have major opportunity costs vis à vis development itself. Thomas Cottier described this as 'the deepest conceptual flaw and irony of the international human rights system'.[119] The converse argument, which is not mutually exclusive, is that imposing trade liberalization norms without the domestic infrastructure to allow just distributions, or even distributions that promote further efficiencies, could equally be flawed.

We might look at the missing infrastructure that arguably keeps too many in abject poverty. A related question is to ask what do both economics and philosophy say about efficiency reforms that are unlikely to be successful until such domestic infrastructure problems are fixed? Pranab Bardhan suggests that there may be disastrous results, as countries with better safety nets and means of responding domestically do better out of trade liberalization.[120] We

---

[119] Cottier, above n 21.

[120] See Chapter 4

have the work of scholars such as Amartya Sen[121] arguing for certain minimum standards to allow for adequate development. In his seminal work, he argued for critical freedoms as a means to that end, namely freedom of political association and criticism; freedom to engage in market transactions; freedom from disease; freedom from disabling effects of inadequate education and literacy; freedom from extreme poverty. In his view these have both intrinsic and instrumental values.

This is just one example of how economics regularly considers the problems of short-term goals and long-term objectives, as Graciela Chichilnisky has dubbed them in her chapter.[122] Her analysis of carbon markets raises a major example of a global risk management problem. While environmental NGOs sometimes say one cannot put a price on the environment, economists such as Chichilnisky have long pointed out that there are insufficient prices flowing from lack of property rights that cause overuse and degradation. Lack of well-defined property rights or enforcement leads to negative social cost externalities. Trade liberalization can exacerbate this but the first best solution is to address the property rights. Sometimes this is easy, for example, ensuring proper pricing of domestic inputs such as energy and water. The chapter by Chichilnisky explains the importance of property rights for environmental protection in the crucial field of climate control. Few would expect the WTO to directly seek to allocate property rights on a worldwide basis. Nevertheless, the lack of appropriate infrastructure in the poorest countries and the second-best problems that this poses at least calls on analysts to re-evaluate the timing and importance of WTO reforms.

We should be concerned with these issues even if they are not the fault of the WTO, in circumstances where their absence would make WTO prescriptions sub-optimal, for example how important are property rights, or assistance programs to enhance capacity to utilize increased market access openings. If the first-best policy is not yet feasible, for example property rights, then some staged trade restriction might be a second-best interim solution otherwise the harm may be too costly.

6. POLITICAL SCIENCE PERSPECTIVES

A discussion of infrastructure and domestic mechanisms invites us to return our attention to the field of political science, although again the fields overlap and the views from one field are commonly dependent on conclusions from

---

121 Sen, above n 56.

122 See Chapter 13.

the others. A range of scholars from other disciplines note the importance of infrastructure. The philosopher Thomas Nagel goes so far as to argue that there is inevitably a need to allow important structures to be developed illegitimately by unjust entities and then take them over for more justifiable purposes.[123] As another example, if a major cause of poverty is the lack of institutional infrastructure as Rawls argues and Sen supports in part, then we might be looking to limit reforms to indirect mechanisms, such as promotion of the rule of law, democracy and efficient market infrastructure on the understanding that voters will call for redistribution in due course.

In addition to considering what the WTO and human rights regimes actually do, it is also desirable to consider their role and utility as international legal systems and remember that there are different theories of international law that would impact upon our analysis.

Because the greatest challenge facing international law is the problem of promoting compliance within a system without an effective enforcement process, a key aspect of any theory of international law is to consider why nations do or do not comply and how compliance can best be promoted.[124] Such views vary from consent-based theories, which suggest that States face binding commitments in international law because of that consent,[125] cooperative models as for example suggested by Chayes and Chayes,[126] the legitimacy theory of Thomas Franck[127] and a focus on the transnational legal process as suggested by Harold Koh.[128] While these questions are aimed at the utility of international legal systems, the various theories are impacted upon by differing perspectives of political science.[129] Any governance system,

---

[123] Nagel, above n 66, 146.

[124] Benedict Kingsbury, 'The Concept of Compliance as a Function of Competing Conceptions of International Law' (1998) 19 *Michigan Journal of International Law* 345.

[125] Louis Henkin, *How Nations Behave* (Columbia University Press, New York, 1979).

[126] A Chayes and A H Chayes, *The New Sovereignty: Compliance with International Regulatory Agreements* (Harvard University Press, Cambridge, 1995).

[127] Thomas M Franck, *Fairness in International Law and Institutions* (Clarendon Press, Oxford, 1995); Thomas M Franck, 'Legitimacy in the International System' (1998) 83 *American Journal of International Law* 705; Andrew T Guzman, 'International Law: A Compliance Based Theory' (Public Law and Legal Theory Working Paper No 47, University of California at Berkeley, 2001); Martti Koskenniemi, 'Legal Cosmopolitanism: Tom Franck's Messianic World' (2003) *New York University Journal of International Law and Policy* 471.

[128] Harold H Koh, 'Transnational Legal Process' (1994) 75 *Nebraska Law Review* 181; Harold H Koh, 'Why Do Nations Obey International Law?' (1997) 106 *Yale Law Journal* 2599.

[129] See for example Kenneth W Abbott, 'International Relations Theory,

whether the WTO or a national government, is merely a means to an end. At one extreme, a neo-realist perspective sees the application and pursuit of power as the essence of international relations, with legal institutions and rules having little impact on the behaviour of states.[130] The contribution by Ken Shadlen looks at various theories of international relations and concludes that the neo-realist perspective does not explain some of the actual outcomes in the WTO system.[131] Such a conclusion holds out hope for meaningful outcomes as a result of greater attention to the development of international legal rules and institutions. On the other hand this does not guarantee that the outcomes will be fair. Here, there are a range of critical legal perspectives that point to a range of fairness problems in current international law practice.[132]

The contribution by Andrew Lang brings a sociological element to the political science debate.[133] Lang's contribution brings a constructivist perspective, looking at the role of the key players in defining the nature of the debate. Political theories that look at the role of individuals and complex organizations will consider the range of networks that apply.[134] The contribution by Shervin Majlessi analyses the history of international trade law scholarship and situates it within the perspective of different international relations theories. In particular, he seeks to look at the implications of different theories, drawing on the works of other contributors to this volume.[135]

There are a number of other political perspectives with both theoretical and practical dimensions. A key aspect of politics is the lessons from political science as to the way organizations and vested interests work or don't work for optimal outcomes. Political science explains why we might seek institutions to promote certain outcomes in the face of inherent barriers. It helps us determine

International Law, and the Regime Governing Atrocities in International Conflicts' (1999) 93 *American Journal of International Law* 361; Anne-Marie Slaughter et al., 'International Law and International Relations Theory: A New Generation of Interdisciplinary Scholarship' (1998) 93 *American Journal of International Law* 367.

130 Hans J Morgenthau, *Politics Among Nations: The Struggle for Power and Peace* (Knopf, New York, 3rd edn, 1960); Stephen D Krasner, *Sovereignty: Organised Hypocrisy* (Princeton University Press, Princeton, 1999); Jack Goldsmith and Eric A Posner, *The Limits of International Law* (Oxford University Press, Oxford, 2005).

131 See Chapter 5.

132 David Kennedy, *International Legal Structure* (Nomos, Krakow, 1987); Martti Koskenniemi, *From Apology to Utopia: the Structure of International Legal Argument* (Cambridge University Press, Cambridge, 2005); H Charlesworth et al., 'Feminist Approaches to International Law' (1991) 85 *American Journal of International Law* 613.

133 See Chapter 7.

134 Examples include Anne-Marie Slaughter, *A New World Order* (Princeton University Press, Princeton, 2004); John Braithwaite and Peter Drahos, *Global Business Regulation* (Cambridge University Press, Cambridge, 2000).

135 See Chapter 14.

when and why legal institutions may support these ends and how to optimize this. If every government was fully supportive of the economic theory of comparative advantage and supportive of the widest range of human rights, there would be little need for the institutions. While economists argue that unilateral trade liberalization is in a country's best interests, local vested interests opposed to efficient reforms mean that reciprocity is generally needed to sell the reforms politically.[136] WTO obligations allow sensible governments to resist domestic protectionist pressures and still say they would have liked to help.

This does not mean that the mechanism selected by the WTO will be optimal. The WTO operates via a consensus mechanism. In theory even the smallest country can block any initiative by withholding its support. On the other hand, we would expect countries with significant economic power to use their influence to encourage uptake of such developments. Consensus has a range of costs and benefits as a decision-making mechanism. It seems fair to think that there was unanimous support for any key developments. On the other hand, requirements of unanimity lead us to expect that the system will be very slow to complete needed reforms. There is the overall question whether Rounds and reciprocity are a good way to improve rules requiring careful drafting as opposed to tariff reductions.

We might then ask whether reciprocity is sensible from a political science perspective even though it is poor from an economic perspective? On the one hand it allows the free trade lobby to counter protectionists, but it may do the opposite as well by ensuring we must 'get' something in return for adopting beneficial economic policies. Sauvé and Subramanian thus called it a peace treaty among mercantilists.[137]

Some analyse the debate from a sovereignty perspective. At the broadest level, what level of domestic political autonomy should be tolerated under an international trade treaty?[138] This is a part of the challenge of global governance and determining the appropriate regulatory levels and the way they interact. A number of questions present themselves. Is there a crisis of legitimacy as some postulate?[139] Can participatory rights flow from ICCPR? What

---

136 Nigel Grimwade, *International Trade Policy: A Contemporary Analysis* (Routledge, London 1996) 39.

137 Pierre Sauvé and Arvind Subramanian, 'Dark Clouds over Geneva? The Troubled Prospects of the Multilateral Trading System' in Pierre Sauvé et al. (eds) *Efficiency, Equity, Legitimacy: The Multilateral Trading System at the Millennium* (Brookings Institution Press, Washington DC, 2001) 19.

138 Michael H Trebilcock and Robert Howse, *The Regulation of International Trade* (Routledge, London, 3rd edn, 2005) 84.

139 Daniel Esty, 'The World Trade Organization's Legitimacy Crisis' (2002) 1 *World Trade Review* 7; Robert O Keohane and Joseph S Nye, *Power and Interdependence* (Addison Wesley Longman, New York, 3rd edn, 2001).

is their actual content and how do we combine rights with effective governance, for example confidentiality and need to keep bargaining parameters from other countries? Is the WTO an unreasonable constraint on a sovereign's right to promote health, environment and labour rights? The traditional pro-WTO response is to say that Article XX and SPS constraints are examples of the *exercise* of sovereign power for mutual best interest. A sub-set of the sovereign rights issue is the entitlement to extra-territorial demands or at least impact as arose in *Shrimp/Turtle*.

Sarah Joseph in her chapter looks, inter alia, at the question of democratic deficit and its human rights implications.[140] She notes concerns with entry into the WTO and performance under it. After noting various problems, including lack of public input and imbalance in bargaining power, she identifies various strategies for alleviating some of the problems, including technical support and transparency mechanisms. The role of transparency and monitoring systems to minimize the power of vested interests has been an issue upon which there has been some analysis of the WTO in the past.[141] The Trade Policy Review Mechanism of the WTO and UNHR Committees are examples of transparency mechanisms that provide some promise. Trade negotiating committees at domestic levels, if appropriately established, might also help in part to overcome democratic deficit concerns. Another transparency device is an obligation to undertake human rights impact statements when key reforms are proposed. This is akin to the idea of a tax expenditure budget in tax policy.

Another governance issue is the question of linkage between the regimes and problems of fragmentation. Koskeniemmi notes the biases that are generated in a fragmented but interrelated set of international institutions.[142] Linkage through the UN could overcome such biases, although that might be unworkable.

Political science can also give insights on specific sectoral issues and the way by which they may best be regulated. Bureaucrats, for example, who

---

140 See also Rahul Singh, 'The World Trade Organisation and Legitimacy: Evolving a Framework for Bridging the Democratic Deficit' (2008) 42:2 *Journal of World Trade* 347; Robert Dahl, 'Can International Organisations be Democratic? A Sceptic's View' in Ian Shapiro and Casiano Hacker-Cordon (eds) *Democracies Edges* (Cambridge University Press, Cambridge, 1999) 23; Albert O Hirschman, *Exit, Voice and Loyalty: Responses to Decline in Firms, Organisations and States* (Harvard University Press, Cambridge, 1970); Alois Stutzer and Bruno S Frey, 'Making International Organisations More Democratic' (2005) 1:3 *Review of Law and Economics* 305.

141 See for example Gabrielle Marceau and Peter N Pedersen, 'Is the WTO Open and Transparent?' (1999) 33 *Journal of World Trade* 5, discussing NGO criticisms and providing a partial defence.

142 Koskenniemi, above n 13.

establish technical standards will naturally do so in conjunction with local industry, but such industry-vested interests might include protectionist criteria.

While changes could be made to the WTO's political processes, its current limitations need to be understood at the same time as consideration is given to the feasibility of any significant changes. This flows into the second key question we have posed, namely whether the WTO should do more to promote human rights. On this issue, many commentators from both sides of the spectrum have cautioned against such initiatives. Frieder Roessler argues that most linkage attempts are inefficient responses to policy differences.[143] Better options are harmonization where possible and tariffs and subsidies otherwise. Linkage should be used to support domestic political coalitions among interest groups. Jose Alvarez argues against trade and human rights linkage because the latter is more in the nature of soft law, and incomplete and without universal consensus as to its key obligations.[144] In a similar vein Dunoff argues that increasing legalization of other areas through WTO linkage may not be proper.[145] Alston argued that the WTO is not set up to do justice to human rights concerns.[146] In terms of the WTO and human rights interface, the WTO also does not have an optimal mechanism for debating non-trade norms. At best it carves out ambiguous exceptions.

The political perspective could also look at specific challenges in individual sectors. An example of the regulatory problems in the linkage field is the interface between trade and labour discussed in the chapter by Chantal Thomas.[147] This field could cover working conditions, both in terms of hours and physical environment; exploitation of children; wage rates and acceptance of unionism. There are many difficulties in addressing these through the WTO or anywhere for that matter. Labour and environmental standards are not absolutes. There is no consensus as to the content of the right to unionize and collectively bargain. Many labour standards are of little relevance to the extreme poor, such as the rural self-employed. Economics suggests that diversity of labour standards is also a source of comparative advantage. Trade liberalization ought to be particularly beneficial to labour in developing countries because labour is the key factor of production. The interdisciplinary perspectives thus raise a range of challenging questions. If we were to ban child labour,

---

143 Frieder Roessler, 'Diverging Domestic Policies and Multilateral Trade Integration' in J Bhagwati and R E Hudec (eds) *Fair Trade and Harmonization Vol 2: Legal Analysis* (MIT Press, Cambridge, 1996) 21, 36–7.

144 Jose Alvarez, 'The WTO as Linkage Machine' (2002) 96 *AJIL* 146.

145 Jeffrey Dunoff, 'The WTO in Transition: of Constituents, Competence and Coherence' (2001) 33 *George Washington International Law Review* 979, 1012.

146 Philip Alston, 'International Trade as an Instrument for Positive Human Rights Policy' (1982) 4 *Human Rights Quarterly* 155.

147 Chapter 10.

by what criteria would we draw the line? How would we police the rule? What tolerance if any would there be for breaches? Will it hurt comparative advantage? Will it hurt the children and their families? Is this unimportant compared to the moral issue or the long-term economic positive externalities from education rather than work? Chantal Thomas's chapter analyses a range of legislative responses in the context of this field. She canvasses the possibility of providing broadly for positive obligations, the inclusion of general soft law principles, amendments or relying on existing style exceptions. She contrasts the lack of political will to deal with labour with the decision to include the TRIPS Agreement, of obvious benefit to leading developed economies. Overall she finds enough problems with the legislative option to seriously consider reliance on the judiciary as a preferred alternative.

There can be legitimate debate as to whether there are actual biases in negotiations, rule articulation, and adjudication. The latter might cover issues of who are to be panellists, what is their jurisdictional coverage and sources of law and how they should approach interpretation. The data is perhaps equivocal. Supporters of the status quo would point to the express precedence for Article XX options and the direct rights in SPS. The jurisprudence is more equivocal. An expansive interpretation of 'necessary' in Article XX GATT allowed wider scope for the exception as has the concern for the procedural manner of promulgation and execution rather than the substantive content, while a superimposed 'reasonable and least trade restrictive' chapeau interpretation goes the other way, albeit to a point where supporters might suggest there is a reasonable policy balance. That debate might depend on further dispute settlement issues such as burden and standard of proof and deference. An entitlement that looks balanced but which cannot be applied in that way is obviously problematic. Trade and labour is a key area where it would be questionable as to how to differentiate between protectionist and legitimate measures, particularly as political support would bring together both groups of supporters. Chantal Thomas has provided an analysis of the strengths and weaknesses of the adjudicatory record in aid of her moderate support for this tactical response to the problem.[148]

The chapter on culture by Hélène Ruiz-Fabri points to other regulatory issues including the question of culture as an economic value; the challenges as to soft law; short-term gains versus long-term costs; fragmentation concerns and the historical failure in having culture dealt with within the WTO.[149]

---

148 Chapter 10

149 See Chapter 8. See also Cécile Fabre and David Miller, 'Justice and Culture: Rawls, Sen, Nussbaum and O'Neill' (2003) 1:1 *Political Studies Review* 4.

7. CONCLUSION

This chapter has sought to argue that the allied questions as to whether the WTO interferes with human rights and/or ought to do more to promote their attainment, requires complex interdisciplinary analysis. Too much of the debate to date has been polarized. Extreme positions can often be shown to be dependent on presumptions from other disciplines that are rarely supported within those fields. As has sought to be shown, economic theories depend in part on psychological predictions and philosophical perspectives as to resource distribution. Philosophical perspectives depend in part on attitudes to social interaction, appropriate political institutions and the relationship between sovereign states. Political perspectives in turn depend in part upon economic analyses as to the likely distributional outcomes in different political models and the philosophical perspectives alluded to above. Any attempt to properly answer the question as to whether the WTO unduly interferes with human rights and/or fails to do enough to promote them, must therefore involve a more nuanced and integrated approach to the analysis of past experiences in the context of these interdisciplinary insights. It is hoped that the interdisciplinary perspectives contained in this volume constitute a significant advance in that line of analysis.

2. Beyond the divide: the International Covenant on Economic, Social and Political Rights and the World Trade Organization

Robert Howse and Ruti G. Teitel

1. INTRODUCTION[1]

Since the end of the Cold War, two main visions have guided the evolution of international law and institutions – the vision of human rights and humanity and that of economic globalisation. Both visions have offered challenges to traditional understandings of sovereignty: both have given a new significance to non-state actors in the evolution and implementation of international law. Both have often given rise to demands and aspirations to global politics and/or constitutionalism as well as new relationships between local, national, regional and global levels of governance.

However the legal, institutional and policy cultures of international human rights law and of international trade, financial and investment law have developed largely in isolation from one another.

As a matter of international law, both the *International Covenant on Economic, Social and Economic Rights* ('ICESCR')[2] and the World Trade Organization ('WTO') are, in the first instance, treaty regimes. A fundamental structural characteristic of the international legal system is that of decentralization without hierarchy.[3] Treaty norms in the ICESCR have an equal legal

---

[1] This chapter is derived from a previous paper written by the authors: see R Howse and R G Teitel, 'Beyond the Divide: The Covenant on Economic, Social and Cultural Rights and the World Trade Organization (Occasional Paper No 30, Freidrich Ebert Stiftung, 2007) http://library.fes.de/pdf-files/iez/global/04572.pdf at 11 November 2008.

[2] Opened for signature 16 December 1966, 999 UNTS 3 (entered into force 3 January 1976).

[3] See generally, International Law Commission, *Fragmentation of international law: Difficulties arising from the diversification and expansion of international law*, Report of the Study Group of the International Law Commission, finalised by Martti Koskenniemi, UN Doc. A/CN.4/L/682 (13 April, 2006).

status to those in the WTO. A majority of states are parties to both the WTO Single Undertaking (the core WTO treaties) and the ICESCR. The principle of decentralization without hierarchy, along with that of giving full effect to international obligations, implies the need to interpret and to develop these regimes in a complementary and consistent fashion to the extent possible. As the report of the International Law Commission ('ILC') on fragmentation of international law notes: 'In international law, there is a strong presumption against normative conflict'.[4]

Since the WTO Seattle Ministerial, now almost a decade ago, there has been a concerted effort in the international human rights community, by activists, academics, and the Office of the High Commissioner to overcome this isolationism, attempting to understand how trade affects the realisation of human rights and what implications human rights obligations have for the interpretation and negotiation of trade agreements.[5] It is fair to say that these efforts have not been matched by a comparable openness on the part of the international trade law and policy community: the WTO negotiations in the Doha Round are occurring without any explicit reference to human rights.

The Cold War legacy of economic and social rights brought with it an association with discredited collectivist approaches to economic and social organisation. The concept was often viewed as polarizing along East/West, North/South fault lines; this is a heritage that must be overcome if economic and social rights are to gain purchase in the international economic regimes. The conventional economic policy ideology prevalent in the international trade law and policy knowledge communities views the issues surrounding access to essential services, food, housing, and healthcare as a matter of trade-offs under scarcity. From that perspective, there may be a tension between the role of the market in generating the wealth necessary to obtain these goods and the capacity to guarantee wider access to them through redistribution; thus, speaking of rights in these contexts is often viewed as incoherent, mere posturing or wishful thinking. The problem here is a lack of awareness in the international trade policy community about how economic and social rights have been interpreted and elaborated in the policy and practice of the international human rights institutions.

---

4 Ibid [37].

5 See for example, UN High Commissioner for Human Rights ('UNHCHR'), *Liberalization of trade in services and human rights*, UN Doc E/CN.4/Sub.2/2002/9 (25 June 2002); UNHCHR, *Globalization and its impact on the full enjoyment of human rights*, UN Doc E/CN.4/2002/54 (22 April 2003); UNHCHR, *Human rights, trade and investment*, UN Doc E/CN.4/Sub.2/2003/9 (2 July 2003); UNHCHR, *Impact of the TRIPS Agreement on the Enjoyment of all Human Rights*, UN Doc E/CN.4/Sub.2/2001/13 (28 June 2001).

At the same time, the collapse of the Washington Consensus, the mixed track record of 'liberal' economic reform in contributing to improvement in living standards in developing countries, and the new economics of globalisation reflect a fundamental crisis of confidence in the capacity of economics oriented towards liberalisation of global markets to provide a universal 'formula' for the attainment of human well-being.[6] There is an absence today of a plausible, agreed normative economic framework that can inform debates about globalisation as well as related domestic reforms. This provides a window of opportunity for international human rights law to supply an alternative normative structure for such a debate. To realise this possibility, rights must be capable of being linked to specific policy options and choices and must be capable of translation into a framework for analysing the effects of alternative trade and related domestic policies, including alternative possible new rules in trade agreements. The promising work of Armartya Sen on development as freedom may be highly relevant in this regard.[7]

The *Declaration on Trade Related Intellectual Property Rights and the Public Health*[8] and the *Kimberley (Conflict Diamonds) Waiver*[9] reflect an unacknowledged debt to human rights consciousness in the WTO. The current Director-General of the WTO, Pascal Lamy, has written about globalisation with a human face and his conception of the economic sphere, including the international economic sphere, is deeply rooted in the notion of humanity.[10] More recently, a joint study by the ILO and the WTO Secretariat explicitly refers to freedom of association and the right to collective bargaining as 'universally recognized human rights', urges their respect as such (and not just for instrumental reasons of social peace), and refutes with empirical evidence the notion that respect for such rights harms competitiveness.[11]

---

[6] See, for example, D Rodrik, *The Global Governance of Trade: as if Development Really Mattered* (United Nations Development Programme, Geneva, 2001).

[7] See, for example, Amartya Sen, *Development as Freedom* (Anchor Books, New York, 2000).

[8] WTO Doc WT/MIN(01)/DEC/2 (20 November 2001) http://www.wto.org/english/thewto_e/minist_e/min01_e/mindecl_trips_e.htm at 11 November 2008.

[9] WTO Doc WT/L/676 (19 December 2006) http://www.kimberleyprocess.com/download/getfile/359 at 11 November 2008.

[10] See, most notably, Pascal Lamy, 'Humanizing Globalisation' (Speech delivered in Santiago de Chile, 30 January 2006) http://www.wto.org/english/news_e/sppl_e/sppl16_e.htm at 11 November 2008.

[11] International Labor Office and the Secretariat of the World Trade Organization, *Trade and Employment: Challenges for Policy Research* (ILO and WTO, Geneva, 2007) 66, http://www.ilo.org/wcmsp5/groups/public/---dgreports/---dcomm/---webdev/documents/publication/wcms_081742.pdf at 8 August 2008.

Reconstructing globalisation on the basis of a human rights consciousness, and in particular with a view to fully realising the vision of the ICESCR, is a daunting task which would need to engage many policy disciplines and many institutions. Apparent lack of consensus concerning the legal status and precise meaning of some social and economic rights is an obstacle to their influence in the international trade regime.

In our view, a short- to medium-term strategy is needed to identify some fairly *precise and specific* interconnections between the legal concepts and doctrines in the treaty texts of both regimes. As international lawyers whose collective expertise extends across both regimes, we seek in this chapter to conceive the challenge as a legal question of the interaction and interpretation of treaty norms.[12] But how does one achieve that deeper level of cooperation and cross-communication, given the different languages or idioms in which the human rights community and the trade policy community understand the challenges of globalisation?

When we examine the features of the WTO treaties as legal instruments – as opposed to the way that the trade policy community has often viewed the WTO regime – it quickly becomes evident that the treaties themselves have been structured in many ways so as to ensure that the means adopted in the WTO to achieve economic goals are not inconsistent with the human purposes and values intrinsic to the norms in the ICESCR.

The preamble to the WTO Agreement states the purposes of the WTO system in terms that are broadly consistent with the human ends that underlie the rights in the ICESCR:

> . . . raising standards of living, ensuring full employment and a large and steadily growing volume of real income and effective demand, and expanding the production of and trade in goods and services, while allowing for the optimal use of the world's resources in accordance with the objective of sustainable development, seeking both to protect and preserve the environment and to enhance the means for doing so in a manner consistent with their respective needs and concerns at different levels of economic development, *Recognizing* further that there is need for positive efforts designed to ensure that developing countries, and especially the least developed among them, secure a share in the growth in international trade commensurate with the needs of their economic development.

The values that permeate the WTO preamble gel with the obligation provision in Article 2(1) ICESCR, which reads:

> Each State Party to the present Covenant undertakes to take steps, individually and through international assistance and co-operation, especially economic and techni-

---

12 See generally International Law Commission, above n 3.

> cal, to the maximum of its available resources, with a view to achieving progressively the full realization of the rights recognized in the present Covenant by all appropriate means, including particularly the adoption of legislative measures.

It is difficult to imagine how the progressive fulfilment of economic and social rights could be achieved, particularly in developing countries, without the advancement of the goals stated in the WTO Preamble. Furthermore, it should be noted that Article 2 ICESCR clearly indicates that the responsibility of states is engaged not just individually with respect to the rights of persons on their territory but also with respect to international assistance and co-operation, especially economic and technical.

In most cases, the WTO treaties contain exceptions or limitations clauses that allow deviation from trade liberalisation rules where the realisation of fundamental human values, such as health, is at stake. This approach has not been fully honoured or achieved in all respects in existing WTO law, especially in the case of intellectual property rights. Even in these cases, much of the problem, however, is arguably a question of the interpretation of the existing treaty rules in the WTO. In some other instances, on which we shall elaborate, commitments within these rules to address economic and social rights-related concerns have not been properly implemented.

The exercise of interpretation and implementation provides an international law-based means of advancing the consistency of the WTO treaty regime with the ICESCR, that is a means that does not depend on the broader transformation of international economic policy or a political rebalancing of globalisation.

With respect to interpretation, the Appellate Body of the WTO has suggested that non-WTO legal norms have several uses in WTO dispute settlement, such as, for example, the interpretation of exceptions to WTO obligations (for example, the interpretation of 'exhaustible natural resources' in Article XX GATT[13] in the *Shrimp/Turtle*[14] case); the articulation of legal benchmarks related to the situation in developing countries (for example, the interpretation of the meaning of 'development needs' in the *EC – Tariffs*[15] case); the establishment of an international recognition of

[13] *Marrakesh Agreement Establishing the World Trade Organization*, opened for signature 15 April 1994, 1867 UNTS 3 (entered into force 1 January 1995), annex 1A (*General Agreement on Tariffs and Trade*) 1867 UNTS 190 ('GATT').

[14] *United States – Import Prohibition of Certain Shrimp and Shrimp Products*, WTO Doc WT/DS58/AB/R (12 October 1998) (Report of the Appellate Body) ('*Shrimp/Turtle*').

[15] *European Communities – Conditions for the Granting of Tariff Preferences to Developing Countries*, WTO Doc WT/DS246/AB/R (20 April 2004) (Report of the Appellate Body) ('*EC – Tariffs*').

a relevant state of affairs (for example, that certain species were endangered in the *Shrimp/Turtle* case); and the indication of an appropriate standard of deference or sensitivity to domestic regulatory action (for example, the precautionary principle by the Appellate Body in the *EC – Hormones* case).[16]

Article 31(3)(c) of the *Vienna Convention on the Law of Treaties* ('VCLT') provides that among the mandatory sources of treaty interpretation is 'any relevant rules of international law applicable to the parties'.[17] A recent WTO panel, in the *EC – GMOs* case, declined to consider an international convention, the *Biosafety Protocol*,[18] in its interpretation of relevant WTO treaty provisions because it read this provision as requiring that all the parties of the WTO be also parties to the Protocol, for it to be considered as an interpretative aid.[19] This narrow approach to Article 31(3)(c) has been rejected both by the Study Group on Fragmentation of the International Law Commission[20] and by the International Court of Justice in the recent *Oil Platforms*[21] decision. In any case, the Appellate Body of the WTO has used international law as reflective of broad agreement in the international community even where not all of the parties to dispute were bound by the instrument in question (the *Rio Convention*[22] in *Shrimp/Turtle*).

One limit on the use of non-WTO law reflected in the recent *Mexico – Soft Drinks*[23] case is that the Appellate Body will not on its own make a determination as to whether a particular WTO Member has violated its obligations under a non-WTO legal instrument. This does not significantly narrow the role for non-WTO law in interpretation. Regarding economic social and cultural rights, the issue will not normally be whether a WTO Member has violated a

---

16 *European Communities – Measures Concerning Meat and Meat Products*, WTO Doc WT/DS26/AB/R, AB-1997-4 (13 February 1998) (Report of the Appellate Body) ('*EC – Hormones*') 46ff.

17 Opened for signature 23 May 1969, 1155 UNTS 331 (entered into force 27 January 1980).

18 *Cartagena Protocol on Biosafety to the Convention on Biodiversity*, opened for signature 29 January 2000, 39 ILM 1027 (entered into force 11 September 2003).

19 *European Communities – Measures Affecting the Approval and Marketing of Biotech Products*, WTO Docs WT/DS291/R, WT/DS292/R, WT/DS293/R (29 September 2006) [7.58ff] (Panel Report) ('*EC – GMOs*').

20 International Law Commission, above n 3, [448], [450], [471].

21 *Oil Platforms (Islamic Republic of Iran v United States of America)* [2003] ICJ Reports 161, http://www.icj-cij.org/docket/files/90/9715.pdf at 8 August 2008.

22 *Rio Declaration on Environment and Development*, UN Doc A/CONF.151/5/Rev.1 (14 June 1992).

23 *Mexico – Tax Measures on Soft Drinks and Other Beverages*, WTO Doc WT/DS308/AB/R, AB-2005-10 (6 March 2006) (Appellate Body Report) ('*Mexico – Soft Drinks*').

provision of the ICESCR, but rather, what is necessary in terms of relaxation of WTO disciplines for the Member to fulfil its duties under the ICESCR.

There are narrower or more expansive ways of reading the idea of consistency between treaty norms in the ICESCR and those in the WTO. In this commentary, we have chosen to focus on a relatively narrow conception: namely the notion that one treaty regime should not undermine the existing effectiveness of the other. This does not mean that in the longer run it would not be desirable to explore the possibility of restructuring the WTO system to enhance the capacity of states to respect, protect and fulfil the rights in the ICESCR. Our estimate is, however, that the current level of dissent about the relationship of trade liberalisation to economic development, and the divergent views of different states on notions of equity in the WTO system, make this a difficult agenda to pursue for the moment, from the perspective of the UN human rights institutions and the WTO itself.

Instead, we have decided to concentrate on a set of situations where the concern is that the WTO treaty regime could operate to undermine ICESCR norms such that the effects would almost universally be viewed as unacceptable by states and peoples with different positions and perspectives on many of the fundamental debates about economic globalisation, development and global justice.

Here we avert to the concept of human security, as articulated in the 2003 Report of the UN Commission on Human Security:

> [h]uman security complements human development by deliberately focusing on downside risks. It recognizes the conditions that menace survival, the continuation of daily life and the dignity of human beings . . . Human security helps identify the rights at stake in a particular situation. And human rights help answer the question: How should human security be promoted?[24]

A focus on human security so articulated is broadly consistent with the idea of 'minimum core obligation' and 'minimum essential levels' of economic, social and economic rights, which has been articulated by the Committee on Economic, Social and Cultural Rights ('CESCR').[25]

Making economic, social and cultural rights as they relate to basic human security a priority, and addressing the risk of human security being undermined by the WTO treaty regime, is justified not only because of the broad consensus around human security-related norms, but also due to the fact that

---

[24] *Human Security Now: Final Report of the Commission on Human Security* (United Nations Publications, New York, 2003) 10, http://www.humansecurity-chs.org/finalreport/index.html at 15 November 2008.

[25] CESCR, *General Comment No 3: The Nature of State Parties' Obligations*, UN Doc E/1991/23 (14 December 1990).

the progressive fulfillment of all the rights in the ICESCR clearly depends on social and political conditions that are fundamentally compromised when human security itself is threatened. A minimum of human security is in many ways a prerequisite for the social cooperation, citizen and worker participation, and good governance that are needed if the full vision of the Covenant is to be achieved in each country. Conversely, when human security is menaced, whether by economic crisis, natural disaster or war, the *acquis* of social, economic and cultural rights can be rapidly undermined. Moreover, where human security itself is threatened by the denial of economic, social and cultural rights, the rights in the *International Covenant on Civil and Political Rights* ('ICCPR')[26] are likely to be menaced or unachievable, as well.

Not all Members of the WTO are parties to the ICESCR, but in the case of the human-security dimensions of rights such as the right to health, to food, and to work, even non-parties of the Covenant have participated in various legal and policy instruments and initiatives that affirm these dimensions, whether the declaration on core labor rights of the International Labor Organization ('ILO')[27] or the Food and Agriculture Organization's ('FAO') initiatives on food security,[28] or the World Health Organization's constitution, which affirms the right to health as fundamental.[29] Moreover, the human security dimensions of economic and social rights are arguably already implicit in the notion of the right to life in the ICCPR.[30]

In our view, the connection of the rights in the ICESCR to human security makes these rights something more than provisions of a specialised treaty regime. They form part of what the Report of the Study Group of the International Law Commission refers to as the 'normative environment' of the international legal order, which must be taken into account in interpreting and applying particular treaties.[31] This presupposes that there is a minimum substantive normativity inherent in the international legal order, a kind of foundation or floor, grounding the aspirations and efforts of the international legal system. It is our view that the notion of human security captures this

---

26 Opened for signature 16 December 1966, 999 UNTS 14668 (entered into force 23 March 1976).

27 See *Declaration on Fundamental Principles and Rights at Work* (1998) ILO http://www.ilo.org/dyn/declaris/DECLARATIONWEB.static_jump?var_language=EN&var_pagename=DECLARATIONTEXT at 8 August 2008.

28 See http://www.fao.org/ at 15 November 2008.

29 *Constitution of the World Health Organization*, opened for signature 22 July 1946, 2 *Official Records of the World Health Organization* 100 (entered into force 7 April 1948), http://www.who.int/governance/eb/who_constitution_en.pdf at 8 August 2008.

30 See Art 6(1) ICCPR.

31 International Law Commission, above n 3, [415ff.].

minimum substantive universal normativity. The idea of human security as such a normative floor for the interpretation and application of the WTO treaties is acknowledged in the WTO Appellate Body's suggestion that WTO law must be interpreted and applied in light of the notion that the 'preservation of human life and health' is a value that 'is vital and important in the highest degree'.[32]

The access to medicines and conflict diamonds examples suggest that the international trade regime would be open to human rights culture as a culture of human security. In the case of access to medicines, the WTO Members were prepared to modify the rights and obligations in TRIPS in order to facilitate affordable access to medications necessary to deal with devastating life-threatening illness.[33] In the case of conflict diamonds, the WTO Members created a waiver that affirmed as a matter of legal certainty that Members could restrict trade in diamonds to conflict areas in a manner consistent with their WTO obligations (this is especially notable, because such restrictions could anyhow have been justifiable as an exception under the relevant WTO treaty).[34] These examples show that the WTO as a treaty community is susceptible to concerns of human security.

In our view, there are several dimensions to the downside risk that WTO norms may undermine or be inconsistent with the human security dimensions of social, economic and cultural rights; appreciation of these concrete dimensions allows us to make very concrete suggestions as to how such tensions between treaty regimes can be addressed within the idiom and structures of international law.

2. DOMESTIC POLICY SPACE

Various WTO treaties contain constraints on the ability of WTO Members to use domestic policy instruments, whether compulsory licensing in the case of TRIPS, subsidies including food subsidies in the case of the *Subsidies and Countervailing Measures Agreement* ('SCM')[35] and the *Agreement on*

---

[32] *European Communities – Measures Affecting Asbestos and Asbestos-Containing Products*, WTO Doc WT/DS135/AB/R (00-1157) AB-2000-11 (5 April 2001) [174] (Report of the Appellate Body) ('*EC – Asbestos ABR*'). This case is discussed below in connection with the right to health.

[33] See the *Doha Declaration on the TRIPS Agreement and Public Health*, WTO Doc WT/MIN(01)/DEC/2 (20 November 2001).

[34] See above n 9.

[35] *Marrakesh Agreement Establishing the World Trade Organization*, opened for signature 15 April 1994, 1867 UNTS 3 (entered into force 1 January 1995), annex 1A (*Subsidies and Countervailing Measures Agreement*).

Agriculture,[36] or industrial policy measures such as local content requirements.[37] In addition, WTO Members could bind themselves under the *General Agreement on Trade in Services* ('GATS')[38] to liberalise market access in sectors related to essential services, such as health care and water, limiting in important ways their ability to impose public goals related to the human security dimensions of economic and social rights (such as universal affordable access to clean water) on private economic operators who have a right to participate in the market under the GATS commitments. So far, there have been few commitments negotiated that directly affect such public services; in the current round of negotiations, NGO activists have effectively raised awareness of the risks to policy space, and to human rights, of acceding to demands of some WTO Members for guaranteed market access in these areas.[39]

With respect to policy space, there are several very specific legal challenges posed by these aspects of the WTO regime. First, it must be ensured that existing flexibilities in the treaties, including exception and limitation clauses (such as those in Article XX GATT) are interpreted so as to allow WTO Members to meet their obligations with respect to human-security dimensions of economic and social rights. In addition, the full implementation of flexibilities that have already been added by agreement of WTO Members, for instance those based on the *Doha Declaration on TRIPS and Public Health*,[40] must be guaranteed. Third, areas where enhanced or new flexibilities are required in order to ensure that WTO Members can meet their obligations with respect to human security dimensions of economic and social rights must be identified (for instance, the inclusion of emergency safeguards in the GATS and the creation of a 'safe

---

36 *Marrakesh Agreement Establishing the World Trade Organization*, opened for signature 15 April 1994, 1867 UNTS 3 (entered into force 1 January 1995), annex 1A (*Agreement on Agriculture*).

37 Such measures are generally prohibited under the *Marrakesh Agreement Establishing the World Trade Organization*, opened for signature 15 April 1994, 1867 UNTS 3 (entered into force 1 January 1995), annex 1A (*Agreement on Trade Related Investment Measures*) ('TRIMS').

38 *Marrakesh Agreement Establishing the World Trade Organization*, opened for signature 15 April 1994, 1867 UNTS 3 (entered into force 1 January 1995), annex 1B (*General Agreement on Trade in Services*).

39 See, for example, Oxfam, *EU Hypocrisy Unmasked: Why EU Trade Policy Hurts Development* (Oxfam, London, 2003) Oxfam, http://www.oxfam.org.uk/resources/policy/trade/downloads/eu_hypocrisy.pdf at 15 November 2008; The Alliance for Democracy, *Stop the GATS Attack Now!* (2001), http://www.thealliancefordemocracy.org/html/eng/1331-AA.shtml at 15 November 2008; 3D, 'Practical Guide to the WTO', Chapter 5, at http://www.3dthree.org/en/complement.php?IDcomplement=36 (15 November 2008).

40 *Declaration on the TRIPS Agreement and Public Health*, WTO Doc WT/MIN(01)/DEC/2 (14 November 2001).

haven' for subsidies necessary for the realisation of human security-related human rights). Finally, instances where proposed new WTO disciplines, including additional commitments in services sector liberalisation, may risk constraining policies necessary to realise the human security dimensions of economic, social and cultural rights must be identified with as much precision as possible (for example, water privatisation and GATS).

As a general matter, it is important that policy space be understood as a permissive concept: allowing flexibility to a WTO Member to use a particular policy instrument need not imply that this will be the optimal or desirable instrument for realising a given economic or social right in all contexts. For example, in some national contexts, monopolisation and privatisation of essential services may lead to greater access and lower prices, thus helping to fulfil the economic and social rights in question; in others, the effects may be higher prices and universal access may be compromised.

A. The Direct Effects on Social, Economic and Cultural Rights of Reduction in Trade

While the trade policy community has generally assumed that reduction in explicit trade barriers such as tariffs leads to increased overall domestic welfare in WTO Members, more recent economic research has shown that opening up domestic markets to foreign competition leads to social and economic dislocation in many countries; this social and economic dislocation affects the enjoyment of human security dimensions of social and economic rights such as the right to work.

The challenges we see here are firstly, to facilitate the best possible *ex ante* analysis of what the likely effects will be in a given country of increased competition from imports due to negotiated reduction of trade barriers, including on particularly vulnerable groups. Additionally, where the overall balance of effects is positive, but there are negative impacts on the enjoyment by some individuals and groups of human security-related dimensions of economic, social and cultural rights, specific policy strategies must be formulated to address these possible negative impacts (adjustment policies, for example) and to ensure that such policy responses are permissible under WTO rules (which relates to policy space, as discussed above). Some of the strategies in question may imply agreement on technical assistance or development aid, in the case of developing countries. Third, in cases where the negative effects have not been anticipated, steps must be taken to ensure that there is sufficient possibility within the WTO treaty regime for temporary reversal of market opening commitments to deal with effects on human security dimensions of economic, social and cultural rights ('safeguards'), or through actual rebalancing of commitments of the particular WTO Member. Finally, the actual effects of trade liberalisation commitments on the enjoyment of human security-related dimensions of economic, social and cultural rights must be analysed *ex post*, so as to provide a basis where necessary for adjustment of commitments through further multilateral negotiations, where challenges appear to be common to a range of WTO Members.

In the next part of this chapter, we proceed to examine aspects of rights in the Covenant that are directly and obviously connected to the concept of human security, and elements of which have been affirmed in terms of legal obligation in a variety of other instruments and institutions. We have chosen the right to work, the right to health and the right to food, although there are others as well, no doubt. Given our international law-based approach, we focus on those aspects of the interaction of the WTO system with these rights that are most closely grounded in existing treaty norms and their interpretation, related commitments and instruments, and matters that are the subject of existing treaty-rule negotiations in the present Doha Round.

3. THE RIGHTS TO WORK, HEALTH AND FOOD IN INTERACTION WITH THE WTO REGIME

A. The Right to Work

Article 6 of the Covenant provides:

> (1) The States Parties to the present Covenant recognize the right to work, which includes the right of everyone to the opportunity to gain his living by work which he freely chooses or accepts, and will take appropriate steps to safeguard this right.
>
> (2) The steps to be taken by a State Party to the present Covenant to achieve the full realisation of this right shall include technical and vocational guidance and training programs, policies and techniques to achieve steady economic, social and cultural development and full and productive employment under conditions safeguarding fundamental political and economic freedoms to the individual.

(i) Human security, international trade, and worker dislocation

The human security dimension of the right to work has been identified by the Committee on Economic Social and Cultural Rights (CESCR), the body which monitors implementation and compliance with ICESCR, in its General Comment 18: 'The right to work contributes . . . to the survival of the individual and to that of his or her family . . .'.[41] Loss of employment from trade

41 CESCR, *General Comment No 18: The Right to Work*, UN Doc E/C.12/GC/18 (6 February 2006) [1].

liberalisation and foreign competition may threaten survival so understood unless appropriate adjustment policies are undertaken. It should be recalled that the Preamble of the WTO Agreement affirms the commitment of WTO Members that 'their relations in the field of trade and economic endeavour should be conducted with a view to raising standards of living, ensuring full employment and a large and steadily growing volume of real income and effective demand'. Both the negotiation and application of WTO rules must be guided by this commitment, *inter alia*, to full employment and raising standards of living, which may be regarded as having largely incorporated the right to work into the WTO regime.[42]

While the optimal policies for moving toward full employment and higher standards of living may be a matter of controversy in the WTO, from a human security perspective on the right to work, there is an obligation to ensure that survival-threatening job losses due to trade liberalisation are predicted and avoided as much as possible through the crafting of trade rules and concessions, and that WTO rules permit to member states the policy space to address the impact on the right to work through appropriate adjustment policies, such as retraining, education, and income support. This includes the kinds of policies explicitly indicated in Article 6(2) ICESCR. In this respect we note that the Secretariats of both the ILO and the WTO have emphasised the importance of active labour market policies in their recent report on employment and trade:

> Active labour market policies may also be a useful tool to facilitate adjustment to changes in the structure of production brought about by trade liberalization. Measures to provide retraining for displaced workers and job search assistance to facilitate labour mobility will be important in this connection.[43]

It should be acknowledged that many adjustment policies such as funding for generally available vocational training are entirely consistent with WTO rules. However, as explained below, if policies are targeted at specific sectors or firms with adjustment needs, there is a risk of the policies being viewed as impermissible subsidies.

What is firstly required is a serious effort to assess and estimate *ex ante* the possible negative employment impacts of alternative positions in WTO negotiations, with special attention to the duty of non-discrimination in Article 2(2)

---

42 Along such lines, in the *Shrimp/Turtle* case, the Appellate Body found that the reference to 'sustainable development' in the Preamble made the international law of biodiversity relevant as a standard for interpreting and applying relevant WTO norms: see *Shrimp/Turtle* [17], [67], [129], [131], [153].

43 ILO and WTO, above n 11, 64.

ICESCR and therefore the distribution of potential employment effects along gender lines as well as the other statuses enumerated therein. Complementing this would be the provision of technical assistance to States that are unable otherwise to make such estimates, along with a structure and timetable to negotiations that permit such assessments to influence the negotiation of concessions and treaty rules in a timely and effective fashion. Moreover, effective 'safeguard' provisions in WTO Agreements, which allow WTO Members adequate policy space to deal with negative effects of trade concessions on the right to work, must be introduced, especially where the effects have not been predicted or predictable through *ex ante* assessment.

A fourth relevant measure would be a plan by each Member as to how it will safeguard the right to work given anticipated negative employment affects on some sectors due to trade concessions. Finally, the program would be completed via interpretation and perhaps modification of WTO rules on subsidies and safeguards, and perhaps other rules as well, in order to allow WTO Members to address the threat to human security from trade liberalisation-induced job losses (or indeed dislocation for other reasons that threatens human security).

(ii) Subsidies

Policies that provide a financial contribution to a recipient and a benefit (that is, a competitive advantage) and that are specific to particular industries or sectors, may be actionable 'subsidies' under the SCM, depending on their effects on international trade. Article 8 SCM originally entailed a defined list of subsidies to be deemed 'non-actionable', those subsidies were immunised from challenge in WTO dispute settlement as well as countervailing duty action, even if they were to be found to meet the criteria discussed above. This list included certain subsidies for research and development, environmental protection, and to disadvantaged regions. However, this provision for deemed non-actionability applied provisionally, for only the first five years that the SCM was in force. Since its effective expiration, WTO Members have been unable to agree to either continue with the list as it now stands or to create a different list. Therefore, today there are no subsidy programs that are explicitly protected as non-actionable. During the Doha Round negotiations, proposals from developing countries (most notably Venezuela and Cuba) have emerged for the reinstatement of a category of non-actionable subsidies.[44]

44 See, e.g. WTO doc. TN/RL/W/41/Rev.1, 10 March, 2003.

Based upon the joint work of the ILO and the WTO, and in collaboration with the Committee on Economic, Social and Cultural Rights, it should be possible to draw up a list of policy instruments, including those already mentioned in Article 6 ICESCR, that may be necessary for WTO Members to enact, in order to address the human security dimensions of the right to work, and particularly to prevent the threat to human security through loss of employment from trade-liberalisation induced industrial dislocation. These policy instruments could form part of a new 'non-actionable' category in an amended SCM in the Doha Round.

Moreover, in the case of those instruments explicitly indicated in Art 6 SCM, any interpretation of the agreement should be based on a presumption that, since most WTO Members were bound by the ICESCR when they negotiated the SCM, Members deemed the instruments in question consistent with SCM. This derives from the basic international law principle that, to the extent possible, the interpretation of one treaty should not render obligations under other treaties ineffective. This may have significance in the interpretation of specificity, which is a complex judgment not determined by bright line rules. In particular, Article 2.1(b) SCM appears to be aimed at guaranteeing some policy space for subsidies that are provided on the basis of 'objective criteria':

> Where the granting authority, or the legislation pursuant to which the granting authority operates, establishes objective criteria or conditions governing the eligibility for, and the amount of, a subsidy, specificity shall not exist, provided that the eligibility is automatic and that such criteria and conditions are strictly adhered to. The criteria or conditions must be clearly spelled out in law, regulation, or other official document, so as to be capable of verification.

Arguably, subsidy measures aimed at realising the right to work should be deemed to have been understood to fall within the notion of measures based on 'objective criteria or conditions', where the features of these programs are reasonably related to the right to work as articulated in Article 6 of the Covenant.

TRIMS identifies some investment-related measures that are deemed to be impermissible under the WTO. These include measures that require an enterprise to use local content or sourcing in its production activities; such measures are deemed to be inconsistent with Article III:4 GATT, the national treatment obligation. However, TRIMS also provides that the exceptions otherwise applicable to the GATT apply as well in the case of TRIMS that are deemed to violate specific provisions of the GATT. Thus, where a Member needed to impose such requirements in the context of a national economic crisis, for instance, to prevent the enjoyment of the right to work being undermined, the measures might be justifiable under Article XX(a) GATT, as necessary for the protection of public morals. In the *US – Gambling*[45] decision, the Appellate Body referred to public morals in Article XIV GATS as concerning 'the preservation of the fundamental interests of a society, as reflected in public policy and law'.[46] Almost by definition, rights recognised internationally can be considered 'fundamental interests . . . as reflected in . . . law'.

With respect to the right to work as it is relevant to employment in service industries, the GATS does not contain any explicit disciplines on subsidies in the context of services. The future negotiation of such provisions is anticipated by Article XV GATS, which recognises the role of subsidies in the development programs of developing countries.

It has been argued that the national treatment obligation in the GATS, which prohibits discrimination against like services and service providers of other WTO Members, would make subsidies targeted at local workers questionable.[47] However, a WTO Member might be able to offer subsidies to any service provider with a commercial presence and the capacity to create employment or train workers in the Member concerned.

Article XIX GATT provides that a WTO Member may impose 'safeguards' on a temporary basis, increasing tariffs above the ceilings it has committed in WTO negotiations, under certain circumstances where a domestic industry is suffering injury due to surges in imports. The definition of injury includes *inter alia* a situation of declining employment. In light of the right to work the narrow interpretation of safeguards that is prevalent in WTO jurisprudence may need to be re-examined. A strict demonstration that the events leading to the surge of imports could not reasonably have been foreseen has been required by the Appellate Body in order for a member to invoke safeguards, and also a strict demonstration of a casual relation between the surge of imports and the injury.[48] Since it is hard through economic methodology to identify a surge in imports as a factor separate from others affecting the fate of an industry,[49] the consequence is that safeguard relief is very difficult to come

---

45 *United States – Measures Affecting the Cross Border Supply of Betting and Gambling Services*, WTO Doc WT/DS285/AB/R, AB-2005-1 (7 April 2005) (Report of the Appellate Body) ('*US – Gambling*').

46 *US – Gambling* [296].

47 See, for example, Report of the United Nations High Commissioner for Human Rights, *Liberalization of Trade in Services and Human Rights*, UN Doc E/CN.4/Sub.2/2002/9 (25 June 2002) [60].

48 *United States – Safeguard Measures on Imports of Fresh, Chilled or Frozen Lamb from New Zealand and Australia*, WTO Doc WT/DS177/AB/R, WT/DS178/AB/R, AB-2001-1 (1 May 2001) (Report of the Appellate Body) [166], [172] ('*US – Lamb*').

49 See Gene Grossman and Petros Mavroidis, 'United States – Definitive Safeguard Measures for Imports of Circular Welded Carbon Quality Line Pipe from Korea' in H Horn and P Mavroidis (eds) *The WTO Case Law of 2002* (Cambridge University Press, New York, 2005) 122.

by in the WTO. Horn and Mavroidis have argued that the rationale for safeguards should be seen in significant measure as to address social adjustment costs from trade liberalisation.[50]

In light of that consideration, are such readings of the treaty texts in question really required, especially given the right to work is reflected in the 'full employment' objective stated in the WTO Agreement Preamble? Of course, safeguards may have negative impacts on the right to work in the countries of export that are consequently faced with higher tariffs. However, there are other facets that balance this concern of the exporting country with the concern for adjustment of the importing country and its workers. These include the requirement that safeguard relief be temporary and that compensation be offered to affected exporting states. Also, there is an obligation on the state taking safeguards to take other adjustment measures to ensure that the underlying problem is addressed. A proper understanding of the right to work could be relevant to defining appropriate compensation, determining whether there is an ongoing justification for safeguards, and what alternative adjustment policies a Member can be expected to take to address the underlying situation.

In this context, it should be noted that the WTO contains a mechanism for examining the trade-related policies of WTO Members and their effects, the *Trade Policy Review Mechanism* ('TPRM').[51] The function of the TPRM is stated as the 'impact of a Member's trade policies and practices on the multilateral trading system'. As already noted, the WTO Agreement (to which the TPRM treaty is annexed) states as an objective of the WTO, *inter alia*, that 'relations in the field of trade and economic endeavour should be conducted with a view to raising standards of living, ensuring full employment and a large and steadily growing volume of real income and effective demand'. The references to 'raising standards of living' and 'full employment' suggest that the mandate of the TPRM should include a consideration of the effects of trade and related policies, including those implementing WTO rules, on the realisation of the right to work. But this turns out not to be the case. Take for example, the policy review of Senegal earlier in this decade. The Secretariat report does note policies of Senegal that have impacts on the realisation of the objectives in the WTO Preamble, including positive initiatives to enhance

---

50 Henrik Horn and Petros Mavroidis, 'What Should be Required of a Safeguard Investigation. A Discussion of the Appellate Body Report on *United States – Safeguard Measures on Imports of Fresh, Chilled or Frozen Lamb Meat from New Zealand and Australia*' in H Horn and P Mavroidis (eds) *The WTO Case Law of 2001* (Cambridge University Press, Cambridge, 2004) 72.

51 *Marrakesh Agreement Establishing the World Trade Organization*, opened for signature 15 April 1994, 1867 UNTS 3 (entered into force 1 January 1995), annex 3 (*Trade Policy Review Mechanism*) Art A(i).

educational and workforce opportunities for women.[52] On the other hand, the report does not consider how Senegal's trade and related policies, such as privatization, may either enhance or threaten such initiatives, which have obvious relevance to the right to work.

(iii) Human security, trade in people, and the General Agreement on Trade in Services

While the above discussion has focused, in relation to the right to work, on the risk to human security from loss of employment opportunities, human security can also be threatened by certain conditions of work. The right to work has important implications for the situation of migrant and trafficked workers,[53] for example, whose treatment often raises issues of human security. Under the WTO, GATS liberalisation of trade in services includes so called Mode 4 trade, the temporary physical presence of the service provider in the host country. The characterisation of persons who temporarily go to another WTO Member country for purposes of employment as transboundary 'service providers' rather than workers, raises the issue of whether it is an assumption of GATS that such persons are to be exempt from the protections of labor or human rights regulation, either in the host or the home country or both.

Under the GATS so far there have been only limited commitments by individual WTO Members to liberalise Mode 4 services trade. There is thus the opportunity for human rights institutions to focus on the relationship of such commitments to the right to work, providing guidelines on how WTO Members should define such commitments in light of their obligation with respect to the right to work – at a minimum, in such a way as to not further undermine the human security of migrant and trafficked workers. For example with respect to the existing commitments under GATS, Caroline Dommen notes:

> Most countries that have made GATS Mode 4 commitments also provide for wage and labor standard parity [with indigenous workers]. Over 50 WTO members have included the wage-parity stipulation in their Mode 4 commitments. In addition, to prevent foreign 'strike breakers' 22 members have reserved the right to suspend Mode 4 commitments in the event of labor-management disputes.[54]

---

52 See *Trade Policy Review Body – Trade Policy Review – Senegal – Report by the Secretariat*, WTO Doc WT/TPR/S/119 (30 June 2003).

53 The concept of trafficking includes not only obviously non-consensual movement of workers (with coercion or threat of force) but also movement that constitutes exploitation, which would include subjection to employment conditions threatening to human security, that is denial of the minimum human conditions of work as required by the core content of Art 6 ICESCR. See Jacqueline Bhabha, *Trafficking, Smuggling and Human Rights* (March 2005) Migration Policy Institute, http://www.migrationinformation.org/feature/display.cfm?ID=294 at 8 August 2008.

54 Caroline Dommen, *Migrants' Human Rights: Could GATS Help?* (March

Building upon these individual country experiences with scheduling commitments, it would be useful for the ILO, the WTO and UN bodies concerned with migration and trafficking to collaborate on a set of guidelines for scheduling future commitments under GATS Mode 4 in order to protect the human security of migrant or trafficked workers. This might include the possibility of excluding from commitments altogether sectors or sub-sectors where trafficking is rampant.

At the same time, even apart from the specific commitments that WTO Members make with respect to Mode 4 under GATS, the Most-Favoured-Nation clause applies generally to all services trade. This means that, whether or not it has made specific commitments, a WTO Member cannot discriminate between different countries in its approach to regulating services. This raises the issue of whether, even if it had not made any specific commitments, a WTO Member could restrict or prohibit trade in workers from a country that is not taking effective measures to deal with trafficking problems. Presumably here the public morals exception to GATS obligations could be invoked (Article XIV(a) GATS). The right to work might be used as part of the normative context for interpreting this exception. Again, since there is little awareness or attention in the WTO to the situation of migrant and trafficked workers, it is important that the relevant agencies provide guidance as to appropriate measures for addressing the human security of such persons, to ensure that the GATS is interpreted in a manner that allows such measures to be taken and to be effective.

B. The Right to Health

Article 12 ICESCR provides:

1. The States Parties to the present Covenant recognize the right of everyone to the enjoyment of the highest attainable standard of physical and mental health.

2. The steps to be taken by the States Parties to the present Covenant to achieve the full realisation of this right shall include those necessary for:

    (a) The provision for the reduction of the stillbirth-rate and of infant mortality and for the healthy development of the child;
    (b) The improvement of all aspects of environmental and industrial hygiene;

2005) Migration Policy Institute, http://www.migrationinformation.org/Feature/display.cfm?id=290 at 8 August 2008.

(c) The prevention, treatment and control of epidemic, endemic, occupational and other diseases;
(d) The creation of conditions which would assure to all medical service and medical attention in the event of sickness.

(i) Trade in goods

A fundamental aspect of the right to health is the duty of the state to protect against disease and related health risks – especially, from a human security perspective those that are life-threatening or can result in a fundamentally reduced capacity to live with dignity. As the dramatic examples of avian influenza and mad cow disease illustrate, in an era of globalisation threats to health security can spread across national boundaries at breakneck pace, through the movement of goods and natural persons.

Several WTO treaties have provisions that could limit the ability of WTO Members to control the entry and conditions of sale of imported products in order to discharge their duty under Article 12(2)(c) of the Covenant.

In the *EC – Asbestos* case, Canada challenged a health-based ban by France on all asbestos and asbestos-containing products, whether domestic or imported. The panel held that asbestos and asbestos-containing products were 'like' substitute products on the domestic market in France, and therefore that France had violated Article III:4, the National Treatment provision, which requires that 'like' domestic and imported products be treated even-handedly.[55] In effect, the panel was saying that a product that has a long history of causing loss of human life has to be treated under WTO law the same as a non-lethal substitute, for the sake of free trade. The Appellate Body reversed this ruling, finding that the panel erred in law in deciding that health effects could not be taken into account in the determination of likeness, and went on to find that, on account of the different health effects that stemmed from the different physical characteristics of, respectively, asbestos and substitute products that were permitted in France, these two groups of products were 'unlike': there was thus no violation of National Treatment.[56] From the perspective of the right to health, this is a landmark ruling, because it indicates that considerations of health as a human value must be considered not only in interpreting and applying exceptions to WTO disciplines, but in understanding the very scope of those disciplines themselves. Even where an exception exists – as it does for measures necessary to protect, *inter alia*, human health – at the same time WTO Members should not be lightly assumed to have undertaken

[55] *European Communities – Measures Affecting Asbestos and Products Containing Asbestos*, WTO Doc WT/DS135/R (18 September 2000) 419ff. (Report of the Panel) ('*EC – Asbestos PR*').

[56] *EC – Asbestos* ABR, [116], [117].

in the first place substantive obligations that are inconsistent with the right to health, when those obligations can be read and applied otherwise, consistent with the rules of interpretation in the VCLT.

In this respect, it is significant that the Appellate Body went on, even though it had already reversed the panel's finding of a violation of III:4, to make a point of indicating that France's measure would in any case have been justified under the health exception in Article XX. In so doing, the Appellate Body noted that: 'it is undisputed that WTO Members have the right to determine the level of protection of health that they consider appropriate in a given situation'. Further the Appellate Body held:

> The more vital or important [the] common interests or values pursued, the easier it would be to accept 'necessary' measures designed to achieve those ends. In this case, the objective pursued by the measure is the preservation of human life and health through the elimination, or reduction, of the well-known, and life-threatening, health risks posed by asbestos fibres. The value pursued is both vital and important in the highest degree.[57]

It is clear that where the WTO adjudicator concludes that 'the value pursued is both vital and important in the highest degree', an additional degree of deference will be afforded to domestic regulatory action aimed at vindicating the value in question: this in itself suggests a particular role for the rights in the Covenant. By binding themselves to respect, protect and fulfil economic, social and cultural rights, the parties to the Covenant evidence the acceptance of the human values underlying the rights as fundamental – having priority over less fundamental, or secondary, human interests.

(ii) Domestically prohibited products

The issue of domestically prohibited products illustrates the complexity of the Right to Health in relation to WTO disciplines. Article XI GATT bans restrictions and prohibitions on exports. Where a WTO Member prohibits the sale of a product on grounds of health risks, the member may enact such a ban without regard to whether the sale is domestic or for export. In such a situation, where the measure is not targeted at exports in particular, would that aspect nevertheless violate Article XI GATT? From a right to health perspective, such a prohibition as applied to exports could be seen as a fulfilment of the duty to engage in international cooperation to fulfil the right to health. There are concerns that developed countries could 'dump' products which are viewed as dangerous to health in their domestic spheres on developing countries, which may have limited resources and capacities to detect health risks when products

57 *EC – Asbestos* ABR [172].

cross the border. According to the UN Special Rapporteur on the Right to Health:

> Sometimes drugs, rejected in the North because they have passed their expiry date, are sold in the South. Thus, States need to have in place a basic system for monitoring essential drug quality . . . The duty to respect requires States to refrain from interfering, directly or indirectly, with the enjoyment of the right to health. Thus, a State should not market unsafe drugs.[58]

However, on some scenarios the imposition of export controls based on domestic regulatory approaches could undermine the country of importation's ability to decide on what is required to protect the right to health of its own citizens. Take the example of new experimental medications to treat HIV/AIDS. In countries such as the US, such medications may be only available legally on the market after years of clinical trials to ensure their relatively benign effect on human health. Another country's government may determine however that the right to health requires allowing patients access to such novel treatments more rapidly – especially if their health condition is grave in the short term. The logic of a humanity-based conception of international law is that the obligations of human rights are not limited to a state's own citizens. However, the ICESCR affirms a norm of self-determination in Article 1, suggesting that each society is entitled to a large degree of autonomy in realising its course of social and economic development.

The issues raised by export of domestically prohibited products have not received any definitive treatment in the WTO itself.[59] There is a gap here, as the treaty texts do not seem to explicitly address this dilemma, and thus an opportunity to frame this issue, inasmuch as it relates to human health, in terms of the right to health.

(iii) The right to health, the TRIPS Agreement, and access to essential medicines

Article 31 TRIPS provides the flexibility for WTO Members to compulsory-license patented goods, where certain conditions are met, including reasonable compensation to the rights-holder, and provided the license only applies to the

---

[58] Paul Hunt, *Report of the Special Rapporteur on the Right of Everyone to the Enjoyment of the Highest Available Standard of Physical and Mental Health*, UN Doc E/CN.4/2004/49/Add.1 (1 March 2004) [38]–[40].

[59] The issue is largely unaddressed in the scholarly literature, with the rare exception of Tobias Bender, 'Unilaterale Exportverbote von Domestically prohibited goods zum Umwelt: der Gesundheitsschutz im Ausland und ihre Rechtmäßigkeit nach dem GATT ein Betrag zur Dogmatik der Artikel 11 und XX GATT' (2003) 4 *Zeitschrift für ausländisches öffentliches Recht und Völkerrecht* 1007.

market of the WTO Member in question. Despite this flexibility, which is even greater where an emergency situation exists (some of the conditions are lifted), drug industry interests and some developed governments tried to discourage developing countries who sought to use this flexibility to address the health crisis of HIV/AIDS, by taking an extremely narrow view of the flexibilities in question. The TRIPS division of the WTO Secretariat appears to have largely collaborated in this undertaking, sending a message as to the strictness of TRIPS disciplines, and underemphasising the flexibilities.

In response, the WTO *Doha Declaration on the TRIPS Agreement and Public Health* made clear that the TRIPS Agreement should not provide obstacles to the availability of essential medicines at affordable prices, at least in relation to certain critical diseases. Article 4 reads:

> We agree that the TRIPS Agreement does not and should not prevent Members from taking measures to protect public health. Accordingly, while reiterating our commitment to the TRIPS Agreement, we affirm that the Agreement can and should be interpreted and implemented in a manner supportive of WTO Members' right to protect public health, and in particular, to promote access to medicines for all.

Article 5 specifies some of the implications of this affirmation:

> [I]ncluding the right to grant compulsory licenses and the freedom to determine what constitutes a national emergency or other circumstances of extreme urgency, it being understood that public health crises, including those relating to HIV/AIDS, tuberculosis, malaria and other epidemics, can represent a national emergency or other circumstances of extreme urgency.

In the debate over the usefulness of compulsory licensing as an instrument to ensure affordable access to essential medicines, it was widely put about that Article 31 TRIPS did not cover a situation where a developing country wanted to grant a compulsory license in respect of a drug it was importing, that is manufactured in another country. Thus, if an African country with no indigenous capacity to manufacture compulsorily licensed products wanted to import for its domestic market a generic from India, it could not, it was believed, use Article 31 TRIPS. India could only grant a compulsory license for the Indian domestic market, according to the terms of the same. This argument ignores the exception of Article 30 TRIPS.[60] There are good reasons to

---

60 Article 30 TRIPS reads as follows:

> Members may provide limited exceptions to the exclusive rights conferred by a patent, provided that such exceptions do not unreasonably conflict with a normal exploitation of the patent and do not unreasonably prejudice the legitimate interests of the patent owner, taking account of the legitimate interests of third parties.

think that the granting of a compulsory license could be extended to the market in another WTO Member country as an Article 30 TRIPS exception, where that other WTO Member indicates that were it to possess its own manufacturing capacity, it would itself have granted such a license for production of generics domestically. Such an exception does not conflict with the normal exploitation of the patent, in the sense that the government of the importing state would be entitled to limit anyhow the patent-holder's right through compulsory licensing, and the only thing that prevents it from doing so is a current lack of manufacturing capacity domestically. It would not fundamentally undermine the patent holder's legitimate interests because, in the case of a poor country, the amount of revenue forgone would not be substantial, and in any case the country granting the license (India) would still have to comply with various conditions (albeit mitigated by the emergency nature of the situation in the case of HIV/AIDS drugs). For these reasons, in our view, the problem of a poor country not having domestic manufacturing capacity could be solved within the four corners of TRIPS.

However, especially in light of various interpretations issued by the industry and to some extent from within the WTO Secretariat, many developing countries wanted additional legal security on this point. Thus, Article 6 of the Declaration provides:

> We recognize that WTO Members with insufficient or no manufacturing capacities in the pharmaceutical sector could face difficulties in making effective use of compulsory licensing under the TRIPS Agreement. We instruct the Council for TRIPS to find an expeditious solution to this problem and to report to the General Council before the end of 2002.

The resulting agreement, as Correa explains:

> [T]akes the form of an interim waiver, which allows countries producing patented products under compulsory license to export the products to eligible importing countries, provided that a compulsory license has also been granted in the importing country.[61]

According to Correa, however, this solution is not very practicable, given all the onerous conditions that must be fulfilled to take advantage of the waiver, including the requirement that the product for export be clearly distinguishable from the patented version in appearance ('shape, coloring, labeling and packaging'), and the provision of exact information about the quantities being produced and shipped, as well as imposing responsibility on

---

[61] Carlos Correa, 'Access to drugs under TRIPS: A not so expeditious solution' (2004) 8 *Bridges* 21.

the generic producer for proving the 'bio-equivalence' of the generic product and the possibility, if data are not disclosed by the patent-holder, that it would have to conduct its own toxicity and efficacy studies. In Correa's view, these various conditions entail such costs for generic manufacturers that the solution will be of no practical benefit to poor countries who lack their own manufacturing capacity. Moreover, whether a developing country does or does not have such capacity is not a matter of self-declaration, but is subject to challenge, for instance, if a developed WTO Member questions the actual existence of incapacity.

Correa's skepticism seems vindicated by virtue of the fact that only one importing country has thus far declared its intention to use the mechanism.[62] A recent Oxfam briefing paper notes:

> Rich countries, for their part, seem to be in no hurry to make it work. Many have been slow to implement the deal, and no country has successfully used the mechanism to export medicines to countries with insufficient manufacturing capacity. The USA has not enacted legislation to implement the solution, while the European Union only approved regulations implementing the public health solution in mid-2006.[63]

Rich countries that did implement the law made it more complicated. Despite the efforts of civil-society groups and generic manufacturers, Canada enacted legislation that has proved 'unworkable' according to Médecins Sans Frontières ('MSF'), which spent two years trying to export generic ARVs under Canada's legislation.[64] The inability of the Paragraph 6 solution to deliver medicines is a serious threat to the legitimacy of the WTO. The current WTO Director-General has just started to acknowledge the solution's present weakness. Civil-society skepticism towards Paragraph 6 is shared by most countries. By October 2006, only three countries, the USA, Switzerland and

---

62 See WTO Doc IP/N/9/RWA/1 (notification by Rwanda to import from Canada: 17 July, 2003); see also WTO Doc IP/N/10/CAN/1 (notification by Canada to export to Rwanda: 8 October, 2007).

63 Oxfam Canada, *Oxfam Canada's Submission to Consultation on Canada's Access to Medicines Regime* (Oxfam, Ontario, 2007) http://www.camr-rcam.gc.ca/review-reviser/camr_rcam_oxfam_22-eng.pdf at 15 November 2008.

64 MSF Canada, *Neither Expeditious, Nor a Solution: The WTO August 30th Decision is Unworkable*, (Paper prepared for the XVI International AIDS Conference, Toronto, August 2006) http://www.msf.ca/features/aids2006/files/REP_JCPA_en.pdf at 15 November 2008; MSF Canada, *Too Little for Too Few: Challenges for Effective and Accessible Antiretroviral Therapy* (Briefing document prepared for the XVI International AIDS Conference, Toronto, August 2006) http://www.msf.ca/features/aids2006/files/REP_IACbriefingdoc_en.pdf at 15 November 2008.

El Salvador, had formally accepted the solution.[65] That said, by the end of 2008, numerous other parties had come to the table, including the Republic of Korea, Norway, India, the Philippines, Israel, Japan, Australia, Singapore, China and Hong Kong, the European Communities, Mauritius, Egypt, Mexico, Jordan and Brazil.[66]

The Special Rapporteur on the Right to Health noted in 2004: 'the effectiveness of the Decision [on Implementation of Paragraph 6] will depend on the extent to which it actually does lead to increased access to medicines for the poor'.[67] The failure to implement adequately the decision, and the nature of the measures taken by WTO Members pursuant to the Decision should arguably be examined in depth from the perspective of the right to health. Here we are dealing with the frustration of rights under WTO law acquired after protracted negotiations, which has clearly negative consequences for human-security related dimensions of the right to health.

C. The Right to Food

Article 11 of the Covenant provides:

1. The States Parties to the present Covenant recognize the right of everyone to an adequate standard of living for himself and his family, including adequate food, clothing and housing, and to the continuous improvement of living conditions. The States Parties will take appropriate steps to ensure the realization of this right, recognizing to this effect the essential importance of international co-operation based on free consent.

2. The States Parties to the present Covenant, recognizing the fundamental right of everyone to be free from hunger, shall take, individually and through international co-operation, the measures, including specific programmes, which are needed:

   (a) To improve methods of production, conservation and distribution of food by making full use of technical and scientific knowledge, by

---

[65] Oxfam International, 'Patents versus Patients: Five Years after the Doha Declaration' (Oxfam Briefing Paper 95, Oxfam International, 2006) Section 5, http://www.oxfam.org.uk/what_we_do/issues/health/downloads/bp95_patents.pdf

[66] For a complete list of parties to the 30 August 2003 waiver and the 6 December 2005 motion that amended TRIPS, see http://www.wto.org/english/tratop_e/trips_e/amendment_e.htm at 15 November 2008.

[67] Above n 58, [43].

disseminating knowledge of the principles of nutrition and by developing or reforming agrarian systems in such a way as to achieve the most efficient development and utilization of natural resources;

(b) Taking into account the problems of both food-importing and food-exporting countries, to ensure an equitable distribution of world food supplies in relation to need.

General Comment 12 on the right to food defines the responsibilities of states at the international level among others: (a) to respect the right to food in other countries; (b) to facilitate access to food and to provide the necessary food aid when required, but in a manner that does not adversely affect local producers and markets; and (c) to ensure that in international agreements the right to food is given adequate consideration.[68]

A 2002 report of the Office of the UN High Commissioner for Human Rights ('OHCHR') considered in depth the implications of agricultural trade rules and negotiations in the WTO for, *inter alia*, the right to food.[69] Determining an optimal set of international trade rules from the perspective of fully realising the right to food is a daunting task; the accessibility of food at affordable prices and adequate nutritional quality may depend on a careful balance of elements of local capacity and self-sufficiency and open and competitive world markets. The current rules in the WTO *Agreement on Agriculture* may not strike such a balance, requiring too much liberalisation of developing countries' agricultural markets that threatens local capacity and self-sufficiency, on the one hand, and not requiring sufficient liberalisation of developed country agricultural markets, on the other.[70] But the negotiations on agriculture in the Doha Round reflect considerable controversy and uncertainty as to the best mix of liberalisation commitments and safeguards of some aspects of local production.

Even apart from the challenge of devising an optimal set of rules to promote food security through agricultural trade liberalisation, however, there is, from a human security perspective, the more basic, and arguably less controversial challenge of ensuring that whatever set of rules is in place does not have negative effects, including short-term effects, on the realisation of the right to food, and that governments remain able to discharge their responsibilities with respect to the right to food through direct policies such as consumer

[68] CESCR, *General Comment No 12: The Right to Food*, UN Doc E/C.12/1999/5 (12 May 1999) [36].

[69] See UNHCHR, above n 5 (22 April 2003).

[70] See for example, Jean Ziegler, *Report of the Special Rapporteur on the Right to Food*, UN Doc E/CN.4/2006/44 (16 March 2006) [40].

subsidies that ensure that food is affordable to their citizens despite price fluctuations on world markets. Along similar lines, the WTO rules concerning export subsidies on agricultural products must be compatible with the proper role of food aid in assuring the right to food. In other words, whatever the overall design of agricultural trade liberalisation in the WTO may be, there need to be certain specific legal safeguards or mechanisms to protect the right to food in its most basic human-security related dimensions.

Although not articulated in terms of the right to food, the Marrakesh Decision that accompanied the Uruguay Round *Agreement on Agriculture* reflects a recognition of this need for specific safeguards and mechanisms. Because Net Food-Importing Developing Countries ('NFIDCs') may experience higher food prices due to the reduction of export subsidies as required in the *Agreement on Agriculture*, special mechanisms are to be made available under the Marrakesh decision to counter such negative effects, including the establishment of financing mechanisms to ensure affordable accessibility of imported food.[71] As well, a new *Food Aid Convention* was to be established, to lay down appropriate criteria for the granting of food aid consistent with WTO rules. The Convention came into force in 1999.[72]

It is widely acknowledged that a number of the specific mechanisms envisaged by the Marrakesh Decision have never been implemented, in particular those requiring compensation or financial assistance to NFIDCs. Despite concerns expressed by the FAO and the United Nations Conference on Trade and Development ('UNCTAD'), both the International Monetary Fund ('IMF') and the WTO have apparently decided not to move forward on such assistance.[73] The effects of the failure to implement the Marrakesh Decision on the right to food deserve urgent attention: the undertakings in the Decision were integral to the bargain on agricultural trade liberalisation negotiated in the Uruguay Round.

Moreover, in 2007 the *Food Aid Convention* was up for renegotiation; the deadline for the necessary conversation has since lapsed and the Convention has expired.[74] It may yet be resurrected, but it is important that proposals for

---

71 See *Decision on Measures Concerning the Possible Negative Effects of the Reform Programme on Least-Developed and Net Food-Importing Developing Countries*, WTO Doc G/AG/2 33–4 (15 December 1993 and 14 April 1994) http://www.wto.org/english/docs_e/legal_e/35-dag.pdf at 15 November 2008.

72 Opened for signature 13 April 1999, done at London (entered into force 1 July 1999).

73 Kevin Gray, *Right to Food Principles vis à vis Rules Governing International Trade* (British Institute of International and Comparative Law, London, 2003) 27, http://www.cid.harvard.edu/cidtrade/Papers/gray.pdf at 8 August 2008.

74 Sophia Murphy, *Food Aid Emergency* (2008) Institute for Agriculture and Trade Policy, http://www.iatp.org/iatp/commentaries.cfm?refID=103587 at 15 November 2008.

modification of the Convention, concerning issues such as the degree of concessionality of food aid and targeting of food aid, be examined carefully from the perspective of the right to food.

Thinking in the WTO on the question of food aid is apparently moving in the direction of an approach that would only permit an exception or carve-out for food aid in situations of emergency.[75] The question is whether such an approach would be consistent with the responsibilities of states in respect of food aid under the right to food. Would such a constraint impede the delivery of food aid to prevent or forestall an emergency occurring, requiring that human disasters have already taken place in order for aid to be permissible? From a human-security perspective, can emergencies be distinguished from situations in a number of developing countries where the human security of people is threatened on a daily basis by lack of access to adequate food? In any case, attention to the impact on the right to food of evolution of rules on food aid in the *Food Aid Convention* and the WTO is clearly warranted from a human-security perspective.

4. CONCLUSION

It is often suggested that there is a profound normative tension between the regime of human rights on the one hand and that of the WTO on the other. The authors of this chapter, both international lawyers, each with a specialisation in one of the two regimes, do not believe that the issue should be conceived as one of conflicting legal rights and obligations. The problem stems largely from the historical isolation of the institutional culture of the trade regime from that of the human rights regime. The challenge, both intellectual and practical, is to end this isolation, such that the interpretation and evolution of the norms of the one regime are conducted in a manner that is consistent with the norms of the other.

With this challenge also comes an extraordinary opportunity to provide, in a post-Cold War context, an orientation for the international trade system that is based on widely agreed norms of human rights and humanity. In the absence of such an orientation, the future evolution of the trading system is likely to be hostage to conflicting national and regional interests and perspectives, especially after the collapse of the Washington consensus, and the accompanying scepticism – including among leading economists themselves – about the ability of economics to provide a general formula for development.

75 WTO Committee on Agriculture, *Chair's Reference Paper: Food Aid* (WTO, Geneva, 10–11 April 2006), http://www.wto.org/english/tratop_e/agric_e/refpapers_apr06_e.htm at 8 August 2008.

In this chapter, the authors have chosen to focus on aspects of the ICESCR that clearly bear on human security and their interrelationship with WTO treaty norms, both in respect to the interpretation of existing rules and in the context of the continuing evolution of those rules. We believe that human security (here understood in terms of the protection of human life and health) as a fundamental value has already been recognized in various provisions of the WTO Agreements and in their interpretation by the Appellate Body.

As international lawyers, we have sought to focus in particular on the compatibility of different treaty norms and regimes, based on the notion that the avoidance of conflict of norms and the imperative to give effectiveness to all international obligations are fundamental principles of the international legal system. This approach leads to the identification of a select number of very concrete issues that may be pursued by the UN human rights institutions with respect to the WTO system, going beyond open-ended debate and speculation about the overall relationship between human rights and globalisation.

We believe that it is through consideration of specific relationships between treaty norms and their interpretation that concern for economic, social and cultural rights can most effectively penetrate the rather isolated institutional culture of the WTO.

3. International trade law, human rights and the customary international law rules on treaty interpretation

Ernst-Ulrich Petersmann

1. 'PRINCIPLES OF JUSTICE' IN INTERNATIONAL TRADE LAW?

Similar to Article 1 of the *Charter of the United Nations* ('UN'), the Preamble to the *Vienna Convention on the Law of Treaties* ('VCLT')[1] prescribes that 'disputes concerning treaties, like other international disputes, should be settled by peaceful means and in conformity with the principles of justice and international law.' The Agreement establishing the World Trade Organization ('WTO')[2] recognizes 'basic principles and objectives [. . .] underlying this multilateral trading system'. Some of these principles are specified in WTO provisions, for instance in the *General Agreement on Tariffs and Trade* ('GATT')[3] and other WTO agreements on trade in goods, services and trade-related intellectual property rights. Other principles are incorporated into WTO law by reference to other international law rules, for example in the WTO *Dispute Settlement Understanding* ('DSU')[4] which requires interpreting WTO law 'in accordance with customary rules of interpretation of public international law'. These customary rules, as codified in Articles 31 to 33 VCLT, include rules and principles for textual, contextual and teleological interpretation of treaties (such as *lex specialis*, *lex posterior*, *lex superior*)

[1] *Vienna Convention on the Law of Treaties*, opened for signature 23 May 1969, 1155 UNTS 331 (entered into force 27 January 1980).

[2] *Marrakesh Agreement Establishing the WTO*, opened for signature 15 April 1994, 1867 UNTS 3 (entered into force 1 January 1995) ('*Marrakesh Agreement*').

[3] *Marrakesh Agreement Establishing the WTO*, opened for signature 15 April 1994, 1867 UNTS 3 (entered into force 1 January 1995) Annex 1A (*General Agreement on Tariffs and Trade 1994*).

[4] *Marrakesh Agreement Establishing the WTO*, opened for signature 15 April 1994, 1867 UNTS 3 (entered into force 1 January 1995) Annex 2 (*Dispute Settlement Understanding*).

aimed at mutually coherent interpretations on the basis of legal presumptions of lawful conduct of states, of the systemic character of international law, and the mutual coherence of international rules and principles. The customary law requirement of interpreting treaties 'in conformity with principles of justice', including 'universal respect for, and observance of, human rights and fundamental freedoms for all' (Preamble VCLT), also calls for clarifying the *substantive principles of justice* underlying WTO law, like freedom, non-discrimination, rule of law, independent third-party adjudication and preferential treatment of less-developed countries ('LDCs'). For, rules that are not perceived as just by governments, citizens and courts, are unlikely to be effective over time.

The worldwide recognition of inalienable human rights and of corresponding obligations of all 192 UN member states entails that citizens increasingly challenge the democratic legitimacy of power-oriented structures of international law, such as the lack of effective, individual legal and judicial remedies in UN human rights law. In the field of economic relations, citizens increasingly claim that freedom from poverty is a human right, and that the unnecessary poverty of some two billion people requires far-reaching changes of international economic law. Yet, the basic WTO principle of progressive liberalization and legal protection of liberal trade can be justified by all liberal theories of justice, such as:

- utilitarian theories defining justice in terms of maximum satisfaction of individual preferences and consumer welfare through consumer-driven competition and division of labor in global markets;
- libertarian theories focusing on constitutional protection of individual liberty and property rights for empowering individuals to enhance their welfare through mutually beneficial cooperation;
- egalitarian concepts defining justice not only in terms of equal freedoms and rule of law, but also in terms of social human rights and democratically agreed redistribution and 'difference principles' benefiting poor people; and
- international theories of justice based on sovereign equality and effective empowerment of states to increase their national welfare through liberal trade subject to 'public interest exceptions' that give priority to sovereign rights to protect non-economic citizen interests.

Hence, the diversity of utilitarian, libertarian, egalitarian and constitutional value preferences should not affect recognition that the WTO guarantees of liberalization of discriminatory trade barriers, non-discriminatory treatment and rule of law – by enhancing individual liberty, non-discrimination and opportunities for mutually beneficial trade and poverty reduction across frontiers – reflect, albeit imperfectly, basic principles of justice. In terms of the Aristotelian distinction between 'general principles of justice' (like liberty, equality, fair procedures, promotion of general consumer welfare) and particular principles of justice requiring adjustments depending on particular circumstances, WTO rule-making and WTO dispute settlement procedures can also contribute to 'corrective justice' and 'reciprocal justice', just as the special, differential and non-reciprocal treatment of less-developed WTO Members in numerous WTO provisions may contribute to 'distributive justice'.

2. CONSTITUTIONAL JUSTICE IN WTO LAW?

The prohibition of denial of justice is one of the oldest principles of state responsibility in international law. Under the customary international law rules for the protection of aliens, the international minimum standard with respect to the duties of states to provide decent justice to foreigners focused on procedural due process of law and the duty of states 'to create and maintain a system of justice which ensures that unfairness to foreigners either does not happen, or is corrected';[5] state responsibility for denial of justice depended on proof of a systemic failure in the national administration of justice, either by a miscarriage of justice by the judiciary or by non-judicial authorities (for example, if they prevented the judiciary from administering justice in a fair manner). The universal recognition – in regional and worldwide human rights conventions as well as in national laws – of human rights of access 'to a fair and public hearing within a reasonable time by an independent and impartial tribunal established by law' for the 'determination of civil rights and obligations or of any criminal charge' has reinforced the intergovernmental prohibition of a denial of justice by individual rights of access to justice.[6] The progressive

---

[5] See Jan Paulsson, *Denial of Justice in International Law* (Cambridge University Press, Cambridge, 1995) 7, 36.

[6] The quoted text is from Article 6 of *Convention for the Protection of Human Rights and Fundamental Freedoms*, opened for signature 4 November 1950, 213 UNTS 222 (entered into force 3 September 1953) ('ECHR') and similar guarantees in other regional human rights conventions, for example, Article 8 of the *American Convention on Human Rights*, opened for signature 1969, 1144 UNTS 123 (entered into force 18 July 1978); UN human rights conventions (for example Article 14 of the *International Covenant on Civil and Political Rights*, opened for signature 16 December 1966, 999 UNTS 171 (entered into force 23 March 1976); and other UN human rights instruments (for example, Article 10 of the *Universal Declaration of Human Rights*, UN Res 217A (III) UN Doc A/810, 71 (1948) ('UDHR'), which have given rise to a comprehensive case-law clarifying the rights of access to courts and

extension – by an ever-increasing number of international treaties, notably in the field of international economic and environmental law – of individual rights of access to courts and to effective legal remedies increasingly confronts judges with a 'constitutional problem': do the human rights obligations of all government bodies require judges to interpret intergovernmental rules as protecting and empowering not only states, but also their citizens, as has been increasingly recognized by national and international courts in European law as well as in other areas of international law (such as investment law, intellectual property law, social and labor law, and human rights law)?

The functional interrelationships between law, judges and justice are reflected in legal language from antiquity (for example, in the common core of the Latin terms *jus, judex, justitia*) up to the modern Anglo-American legal traditions of speaking of courts of justice, and giving judges the title of Justice, Lord Justice or Chief Justice. The independence and impartiality of judges, and their application of rules of law and evidence as determined in fair procedures protected by guarantees of due process of law, are defining elements of courts. Like the Roman god Janus, justice and judges face two different perspectives; their 'conservative function' is to apply the existing law and protect the existing system of rights so as to render to each person what is his right. Yet, laws tend to be incomplete and subject to change. Impartial justice and judicial 'balancing' of conflicting legal claims may require 'reformative interpretations' of legal rules in response to changing social conceptions of justice. For example, former UN Secretary-General Kofi Annan warned – in his final address as UN Secretary-General to world leaders assembled in the UN General Assembly on 19 September 2006 – that the 'unjust world economy, world disorder and widespread contempt for human rights and the rule of law' entailed divisions that 'threaten the very notion of an international community, upon which the UN stands'.[7] Should national and international judges interpret and apply WTO law as empowering and protecting only the rulers, but not their citizens? Can the explicit task of 'the dispute settlement system of the WTO [. . .] in providing security and predictability to the multilateral trading system'[8] be realized if producers, investors, traders and consumers are treated as mere objects of an 'international law among states' rather than as legal and economic subjects of the international division of labor and 'democratic principals' of the government agents that claim to represent citizen interests in the intergovernmental WTO negotiations?

---

related guarantees of due process of law. Cf Francesco Franconi (ed.), *Access to Justice as a Human Right* (Oxford University Press, Oxford, 2007).

[7] The speech of Kofi Annan is reproduced in UN Doc GA/105000 (19 September 2006).

[8] Article 3 DSU.

The WTO rules and procedures for the settlement of disputes require all members of WTO dispute settlement panels, the WTO Appellate Body and WTO arbitrators to settle disputes independently and impartially on the basis of the agreed WTO rules. Even though WTO dispute settlement reports become legally binding only upon adoption by the WTO's Dispute Settlement Body composed of WTO government representatives, the DSU provisions ensuring quasi-automatic adoption of WTO panel reports, Appellate Body reports and arbitral awards – subject to the, so far, never applied possibility of 'negative consensus' on rejection of a WTO dispute settlement report – justify qualifying WTO dispute settlement procedures as quasi-judicial. Does the adoption of all of the more than 220 WTO dispute settlement reports since 1996 mean that WTO dispute settlement bodies have succeeded in administering justice?

From a 'realist', state-centered approach to international relations, the adoption and, in more than 80 per cent of all disputes, regular implementation of WTO dispute settlement findings within 'a reasonable period of time' (Article 21 DSU) are widely celebrated as evidence of a successfully operating dispute settlement system. From a 'liberal approach' evaluating law in terms of its contribution to the protection and promotion of human rights and general citizen-interests, however, consent by governments offers insufficient proof of 'constitutional justice'. As international trade is governed primarily by private decisions of investors, producers, traders and consumer-driven competition, as well as by democratic governance inside countries rather than in the WTO, realist analyses of multilevel trade governance must go beyond the level of intergovernmental trade diplomacy and examine also why business support, civil society support and parliamentary support for the ongoing Doha Development Round negotiations in the WTO have so much declined (for example, compared with the previous Uruguay Round negotiations).[9]

3. ABSENCE OF HUMAN RIGHTS ARGUMENTS IN GATT/WTO DISPUTE SETTLEMENT PROCEEDINGS

According to John Rawls, 'justice is the first virtue of social institutions, as truth is of systems of thought';[10] rules that are not perceived as just by those affected by the rules risk being disregarded by domestic courts, national

---

[9] See Christian Joerges and Ernst-Ulrich Petersmann (eds), *Constitutionalism, Multilevel Trade Governance and Social Regulation* (Hart Publishers, Oxford, 2006).

[10] John Rawls, *A Theory of Justice* (Harvard University Press, Cambridge, 1973) 3.

parliaments and citizens. In his *Theory of Justice*, Rawls used the idea of reasonableness for justifying fair procedures that would prompt reasonable citizens (as autonomous moral agents) to agree on basic equal freedoms and other principles of justice that must legally limit the rational pursuit of self-interests so as to enable and induce citizens to cooperate in peaceful and mutually beneficial ways. In his later book on political liberalism,[11] Rawls reframed his theory of justice as fairness by emphasizing the importance of the public use of reason for maintaining a stable, liberal society confronted with the problem of reasonable disagreement about individual conceptions for a good life and a just society. Reasonableness requires legal guarantees of basic equal rights (for example freedoms to participate as equals in public discourse) and a democratic constitution (for example independent judicial protection of basic rights) as legal and institutional preconditions for public debate defining the conditions for a stable consensus on the principles of justice.[12] The universal recognition of human rights and the international legal requirement to settle disputes 'in conformity with principles of justice' and human rights entail that citizens increasingly challenge the power-oriented logic of intergovernmental trade negotiations on the ground that consumer welfare, human rights and the general citizen interests in democratic self-government are nowhere mentioned in WTO law. The admission, by WTO dispute settlement panels as well as by the WTO Appellate Body, of amicus curiae submissions from non-governmental organizations also reflects judicial concerns that WTO dispute settlement procedures might benefit from more inclusive decision-making procedures.

The intergovernmental structures and narrow mandates of WTO institutions entail that WTO decision-making processes hardly ever refer to human rights. WTO law prescribes independent dispute settlement procedures at national, intergovernmental and also at private levels (for example, in Article 4 of the WTO *Agreement on Preshipment Inspection*),[13] including regional (for example, in the EC) and sub-national legal and judicial remedies (for example, in Hong Kong, Macau and Taiwan as parts of China). The purpose of this multilevel 'dispute settlement system' is not only 'to preserve the rights and obligations of Members under the covered agreements, and to clarify the

---

11 John Rawls, *Political Liberalism* (Columbia University Press, New York, 1993).

12 On these dual functions of reasonableness in Rawls's theory of justice, see Jürgen Habermas, 'Reconciliation through the Public Use of Reason: Remarks on John Rawls' Political Liberalism' (1995) 92 *Journal of Philosophy* 109.

13 *Marrakesh Agreement Establishing the WTO*, opened for signature 15 April 1994, 1867 UNTS 3 (entered into force 1 January 1995) Annex 1A (*Preshipment Inspection*).

existing provisions of those agreements in accordance with customary rules of interpretation of public international law'; the DSU also aims at providing 'security and predictability to the multilateral trading system' (Article 3 DSU) at all levels of international trade. Yet, in hardly any of the more than 370 WTO dispute settlement proceedings since 1995 have plaintiffs, respondents or third-party interveners referred to the human rights obligations of all 153 WTO Members (for example, under the *UN Charter*, under more than 100 UN and regional human rights instruments, under customary law and 'general principles of law recognized by civilized nations'). The limited jurisdiction of WTO dispute settlement bodies, the intergovernmental structures of WTO dispute settlement proceedings, the national sovereignty and vast policy discretion of each WTO Member to regulate and restrict international trade entail that neither complainants and respondents nor WTO dispute settlement bodies have considered it necessary to base legal claims and arguments on human rights.

Yet, there is no evidence (for example, in the various reports by the UN High Commissioner for Human Rights on the human rights dimensions of WTO law) that the legal findings in the almost 400 GATT and WTO dispute settlement reports since 1948 have contributed to violations of human rights.[14] Nor is there evidence that WTO rules are not flexible enough to permit each WTO Member to conduct its trade policy in accordance with its human rights obligations. As WTO law is based on principles of freedom, non-discrimination, rule of law, transparent policy-making and national sovereignty to protect non-economic public interests, it appears also unlikely that any basic conflicts between WTO rules and the human rights obligations will arise in the future. This optimistic assessment seems warranted also in view of the case-law of the European Court of Justice ('ECJ'), the European Free Trade Area ('EFTA') Court and the European Court of Human Rights; notwithstanding the recognition, by these European courts as well as by national courts inside the EC and EFTA countries, of the human rights obligations of EC and EFTA member states as 'general principles' of European law and their examination of alleged conflicts between EC trade rules and human rights, none of the thousands of judgments by these European courts and national courts appear to have established conflicts between the EC's trade rules and human rights that could not be reconciled by interpreting European economic law in conformity with the human rights obligations of European states.[15] The few ECJ findings that

14 See Ernst-Ulrich Petersmann, 'The "Human Rights Approach" Advocated by the UN High Commissioner for Human Rights and by the ILO: Is It Relevant for WTO Law and Policy?' (2005) 7 *Journal of International Economic Law* 605.

15 For a discussion of relevant case-law see: Ernst-UlrichPetersmann, 'The WTO and Regional Trade Agreements as Competing Fora for Constitutional Reforms:

human rights arguments can be relevant for interpreting trade rules, as well as for justifying trade restrictions, related to specific transactions (for example, the sale of imported laser games simulating killing of human beings), specific restrictions (for example, of freedom of transit in order to respect freedom of association and public demonstrations on motorways) and specific economic regulations (such as EC rules on the patenting of isolated body parts and biotechnological inventions), without revealing systemic inconsistencies between trade law and human rights.

4. NEED FOR INTERPRETING WTO RULES IN CONFORMITY WITH HUMAN RIGHTS AND OTHER 'PRINCIPLES OF JUSTICE'

The absence of systemic conflicts between WTO rules and human rights law in the past, and the pragmatic responses of WTO bodies to such alleged conflicts (for example, in case of the WTO waivers for the rights of WTO Members to protect access to medicines and to control trade in 'conflict diamonds'), does not mean that trade rules and human rights may not conflict in the future. Indeed, many of the legal complaints over alleged conflicts between trade rules and human rights in the ECJ could be similarly brought to the WTO dispute settlement system, for example:

- if national governments restrict imports, transit trade or freedom of commercial speech in order to protect the human rights of domestic citizens (for example, as in the *Omega*[16] and *Schmidberger*[17] cases in the ECJ, the *Hertel*[18] case in the European Court of Human Rights), or in

Trade and Human Rights' in L Bartels and F Ortino (eds) *Regional Trade Agreements and the WTO Legal System* (Oxford University Press, Oxford, 2006) 281.

16 *Omega Spielhallen-und Automatenaufstellungs – GmbH v Oberbürgermeisterin der Bundesstadt Bonn* [2004] ECR I-9609. The case concerned the prohibition by the Bonn police of a commercialized laser game that simulated armed combat. The argument was that this game constituted an affront to human dignity as guaranteed in Article 1 (1) of the *German Constitution*. Despite the fact that the prohibition inhibited the freedom of the applicant to import and sell laser games, the ECJ upheld the government's decision as necessary to preserve respect for human rights.

17 *Case C-112 Eugen Schmidberger* [2003] ECR I-5659. The case concerned the closure of the Brenner motorway by the Austrian government to allow for a protest. A German lorry company argued that this measure impeded its ability to conduct trade over the Alps with Italy. The ECJ held that this restriction was justified and that the government had been entitled to authorize the demonstration.

18 *Hertel v Switzerland*, Application No 25181/94 (Unreported, European Court of Human Rights, Trial Chamber, 25 August 1998). In this case, the applicant carried

case of trade restrictions responding to human rights violations abroad;
- if intergovernmental measures (for example, by the EC) restrict trade-related, individual freedoms (as in the *Stauder*[19] case in the ECJ) or property rights (as in the *Hauer*[20] case in the ECJ); or
- in case of conflicts between 'market freedoms' (for example, GATS market access commitments) and core labor rights (as in the *Viking*[21] and *Laval*[22] cases in the ECJ).[23]

As it may only be a matter of time until respondents, third parties or *amici curiae* may confront WTO dispute settlement bodies with human rights arguments, it is important to contribute to the clarification of how WTO bodies should respond to human rights arguments in order to promote the mutual coherence of human rights and trade law. Just as the EC Court has succeeded in preventing conflicts between trade rules and human rights by interpreting EC law in conformity with the human rights obligations of EC member states,

---

out a study of the effects on human beings of the consumption of food prepared in microwave ovens, drawing some alarming conclusions. Following an application by the Swiss Association of Manufacturers and Suppliers of Household Electrical Appliances, the study was censored by the Swiss Federal Court on the basis that publication of the study would unfairly impact on their business. The European Court of Human Rights overturned this measure.

19 [1969] ECR 419. In this case, a German citizen challenged a German decision to allow the sale of surplus butter at a reduced price. The contention was that the German requirements under the Decision violated his right of privacy. Although the ECJ determined that the Decision did not violate the applicant's rights, the ECJ did state that it would protect fundamental human rights enshrined in the general principles of EU law.

20 [1979] ECR 3727. In this case, a viticulturalist was refused permission to plant vines on the basis that this was contrary to an EC regulation designed to adjust wine-growing potential to market requirements. The ECJ acknowledged the legal requirement to protect freedom of profession and property rights of the applicant, but upheld the regulation.

21 *Viking Line v International Transport Workers' Federation* [2008] ECR 741. The case centred on cross-border collective action by unions. The unions were protesting at the reflagging of one of Viking Line's ferries, so that a cheaper Estonian crew could be employed. The Court found that the unions' action amounted to a restriction on the company's right to establish wherever it wished in the EU, but such a restriction was still capable of justification.

22 *Laval v Svenska Byggnadsarbetareförbundet* , Case C-341/05 (ECJ judgment of 18 December 2007, nyr). The case concerned collective action by Swedish trade unions against construction services provided by Latvian construction firms, whose freedom of providing services inside the EC was – according to the ECJ – disproportionately restricted by the exercise of the fundamental rights of trade unions to take collective actions.

23 For discussion of these cases see Petersmann, above n 15 and T Cottier et al. (eds) *Human Rights and International Trade* (Oxford University Press, Oxford, 2005).

so is it important for the future legitimacy and democratic support of the WTO legal and dispute settlement system that WTO dispute settlement bodies and domestic courts respond to human rights arguments by WTO complainants, defendants, third-party interveners or *amici curiae* in conformity with the customary rules of international treaty interpretation and avoid unnecessary conflicts between trade and human rights obligations of WTO Members.

The customary rules of international treaty interpretation not only require interpreting WTO law in its context, including any relevant rules of international law applicable in the relations between the parties' (Article 31.3(c) VCLT), as well as 'in the light of its object and purpose', including 'sustainable development' (which is mentioned in the WTO Preamble as one of the objectives of the *Marrakesh Agreement*).[24] They also require the settlement of 'disputes concerning treaties [. . .] in conformity with the principles of justice and international law', including 'universal respect for, and observance of, human rights and fundamental freedoms for all' (Preamble VCLT). Human rights constitute not only individual rights, but also corresponding obligations of governments and 'general principles of law recognized by civilized nations' (Article 38 of the *Statute of the International Court of Justice*) that may be important for interpreting international treaties, for example for clarifying the interpretation of the 'general exceptions' and 'public interest provisions' in WTO law and 'the basic principles [. . .] underlying this multilateral trading system' (Preamble to the *Marrakesh Agreement*).

WTO law provides for compulsory jurisdiction of national and WTO dispute settlement bodies for the settlement of transnational trade disputes so as to make the 'dispute settlement system of the WTO [. . .] a central element in providing security and predictability to the multilateral trading system' (Article 3(2) DSU). The phrase 'multilateral trading system' confirms the need for protecting legal security not only in intergovernmental relations among WTO Members but also in international trade relations among private economic actors.[25] Yet, the diverse conceptions of rule of law and of justice at national and intergovernmental levels impede cooperation among national and international judges and undermine the effectiveness of the multilevel WTO dispute settlement system – to the detriment of traders, investors, producers and consumers involved in international trade. For example:

---

[24] On the evolving methods of interpreting WTO law see: Ernst-Ulrich Petersmann, 'WTO Dispute Settlement Practice 1995–2005: Lessons from the Past and Future Challenges' in Y Taniguchi et al. (eds) *The WTO in the Twenty-first Century* (Cambridge University Press, Cambridge, 2007) 38.

[25] See Ernst-Ulrich Petersmann, 'Multilevel Judicial Governance of International Trade Requires a Common Conception of Rule of Law and Justice' (2007) 10 *Journal of International Economic Law* 529.

- just as the absence of references to human rights in the more than 100 investor–state arbitration awards during the past years has led to democratic distrust (for example, in the Americas) regarding the appropriate balancing of investor rights with public interests, so has the absence of references to human rights and to general consumer welfare in WTO dispute settlement case-law prompted human rights bodies and civil society to claim that WTO negotiations and WTO dispute settlement proceedings one-sidedly favor producer interests and may 'trade away human rights'.
- Most parliaments do not effectively control WTO decision-making processes[26] and – due to parliamentary distrust of intergovernmental rule-making in the WTO – are not fully committed to domestic implementation of WTO dispute settlement rulings.
- As long as WTO rules treat citizens as mere objects of intergovernmental trade governance, domestic courts are also likely to continue their frequent disregard for WTO rules and WTO dispute settlement rulings.

From the independent and impartial perspective of judges mandated to settle disputes 'in conformity with principles of justice' and human rights, respect for human rights and for the legal autonomy of citizens as producers, traders, consumers and 'democratic principals' of government agents may require interpreting WTO rules not only as reciprocal rights and obligations among governments, but also as protecting consumer welfare and rule of law in international trade among citizens.

5. MULTILEVEL JUDICIAL GOVERNANCE OF INTERNATIONAL TRADE MUST AIM AT CITIZEN-ORIENTED CONCEPTIONS OF RULE OF LAW AND JUSTICE

WTO law and the DSU aim at protecting legal security for all public and

---

26 See the comparative study of national parliaments in *The Role of Parliaments in Scrutinising and Influencing Trade Policy – A Comparative Analysis*, European Parliament Study (PE 370-166v01-00, 2005). On the inadequate 'input legitimacy' (for example, in terms of explicit respect for human rights and democratic procedures) as well as 'output legitimacy' (for example, in terms of consumer welfare, public understanding and democratic support by citizens and parliaments) of the WTO see, for example, Ernst-Ulrich Petersmann, 'Citizens, Parliaments, Democracy and the WTO: Need for Strengthening the Democratic Dimensions of the WTO' in *The Parliamentary Dimension of the WTO* (European Parliament, Strasbourg, 2006) 24.

private actors involved in international trade. Also, civil society support for reciprocal trade negotiations in GATT and the WTO, as well as for GATT and WTO dispute settlement proceedings and domestic trade policy-making (which are often initiated and influenced by private complaints), has proven to be of crucial political importance for the successful conclusion of multilateral trade negotiations, for the progressive development of GATT/WTO law and for its dispute settlement system. Citizen-oriented conceptions of international law are today widely shared in European economic integration law governing trade among more than 480 million EC citizens, as well as in the protection of human rights by regional human rights courts and UN human rights bodies. As explained by Lon Fuller, law must order social life not only by 'subjecting human conduct to the governance of rules';[27] law must also aim at establishing a *just* order and procedures for the *fair* resolution of disputes.[28] Since the American and French democratic revolutions in the eighteenth century, fairness and justice are increasingly defined not only in terms of rule-following and procedural justice (such as rights to a fair hearing and due process of law, democratic participation, access to courts) but also in terms of substantive justice and human rights. The present-day universal recognition of human rights entails that claims to 'legal authority' by national and international legal systems must also be evaluated in terms of their contribution to the protection and fulfillment of human rights and to the empowerment of citizens. As long as WTO Members interpret WTO rules one-sidedly as reciprocal rights and obligations among governments, without regard to the citizen-oriented functions of WTO rules to promote consumer welfare and rule of law in international trade among citizens, domestic courts and citizens will continue to challenge power-oriented conceptions of 'international law among states' for their failure to respond to 'citizen-oriented conceptions' of rule of law and justice in international trade among citizens.

The increasing judicial recourse – in the case-law not only of WTO dispute settlement bodies but also of domestic trade courts – to 'principles' and 'balancing' for justifying interpretive choices is in line with modern constitutional theories of adjudication, such as Dworkin's 'adjudicative principle of integrity' which requires judges to regard law as expressing 'a coherent conception of justice and fairness'.[29] The WTO requirement of making the

---

[27] Lon Fuller, *The Morality of Law* (Yale University Press, New Haven, 1969) 96.

[28] For Fuller's criticism of positivist conceptions of law see Lon Fuller, 'Positivism and Fidelity to Law – A Reply to Professor Hart' (1958) 71 *Harvard Law Review* 630.

[29] See Ronald Dworkin, *Law's Empire* (Harvard University Press, Cambridge, 1986) 225, 243.

'dispute settlement system of the WTO [. . .] a central element in providing security and predictability to the multilateral trading system' (Article 3(2) DSU) should be construed in conformity with the 'consistent interpretation principle' recognized in most national legal systems, that is, the requirement of interpreting domestic laws in conformity with international legal obligations of the country concerned so as to also promote rule of law in transnational relations among citizens and in the judicial protection of rule of law by domestic courts (as required, for example, by Article X GATT and the corresponding provisions in other WTO agreements).

Yet, national and international judges often fail to cooperate in their interpretation and judicial protection of trade law because they perceive international and domestic trade law as being based on mutually conflicting conceptions of justice. For instance, just as US courts claim that WTO dispute settlement rulings 'are not binding on the US, much less this court',[30] so has the EC Court refrained long since – at the request of the political EC institutions who have repeatedly misled the ECJ about the interpretation of WTO obligations in order to limit their own judicial accountability[31] – from reviewing the legality of EC measures in the light of the EC's GATT and WTO obligations. Even though national and international judges are usually required to interpret domestic trade laws in conformity with WTO obligations (for example,

---

[30] US Court of Appeals for the Federal Circuit, judgment of 21 January in *Corus Staal BV v Department of Commerce*, 395 F.3d 1343 CA Fed 2005. In the *Corus Staal* dispute, the US Supreme Court denied petition for certiorari on 9 January 2006 (*Corus Staal BV v Department of Commerce*, 546 US 1089, 126 S Ct 1023 (Mem) US 2006) notwithstanding an *amicus curiae* brief filed by the EC Commission supporting this petition:

> We argue that the Federal Circuit went too far by construing the Uruguay Round Agreements Act to make considerations of compliance with international obligations completely irrelevant in construing a Department of Commerce anti-dumping determination, and further argue that the Department's 'zeroing' methodology held invalid by both a WTO Appellate Body and a NAFTA Binational Panel – is not entitled to Chevron deference because it would bring the United States into noncompliance with treaty obligations.

Available at http://www.robbinsrussell.com/pdf/265.pdf at 4 January 2009.

[31] Cf P J Kuijper, 'WTO Law in the European Court of Justice' (2005) 42 *Common Market Law Review* 1313, who claims (at 1334) that 'it is difficult to point out one specific moment at which it can be established beyond doubt that WTO rules have been breached, even after a decision of a panel or report of the Appellate Body', and 'that it is rarely or never possible to speak of a sufficiently serious breach of WTO law' by the political EC institutions justifying the EC's non-contractual liability for damages pursuant to Article 288 EC Treaty.

pursuant to the 'consistent interpretation principle' recognized in most domestic legal systems), domestic judges – like international judges – often refrain from applying international rules unless they are explicitly required to do so. Similar to the *dictum* by US Supreme Court justice Oliver Wendell Holmes that his judicial task was not to administer justice, but to apply the positive rules of law,[32] so does multilevel judicial governance in international trade often neglect the legal requirement and judicial task of interpreting international treaties 'in conformity with principles of justice', including 'universal respect for, and observance of, human rights and fundamental freedoms for all' (Preamble VCLT) as required by the universal human rights obligations of all WTO Members under international law. If law is perceived – from a democratic citizen perspective – as a struggle for ever more precise legal protection of constitutional rights of citizens, it is up to civil society to challenge the one-sidedly intergovernmental structures of WTO law as well as the frequent legal and judicial incoherencies in multilevel trade governance, for instance by using the admissibility of *amicus curiae* submissions in WTO and ICSID dispute settlement proceedings.

6. PROPOSAL FOR AN ILA DECLARATION ON 'INTERNATIONAL TRADE LAW AND HUMAN RIGHTS'

Respect for the human rights of citizens requires constitutional safeguards of democratic self-governance not only inside constitutional democracies, but also in international rule-making and in the intergovernmental supply of 'international public goods' (including a mutually beneficial world trading system protecting rule of law and human rights) necessary for enabling individual and democratic self-development in a globally interdependent world. Regrettably, only very few national parliaments (like the US Congress and the Swiss Parliament) appear to effectively control intergovernmental rule-making in the WTO; all governments pursue national self-interests in the WTO (such as protection of 'rent-seeking' domestic industries in exchange for domestic political support, limitation of judicial accountability of governments in domestic courts for violations of WTO obligations) rather than maximization of the general consumer welfare of their citizens. Civil society and non-governmental organizations have, therefore, good reasons to insist that the ever more complex 'multilevel governance' in worldwide organizations

---

[32] For a discussion of this *dictum* see: Ronald Dworkin, *Justice in Robes* (Oxford University Press, Oxford, 2006) Ch 1.

must not undermine human rights. The more UN human rights bodies continue to assess the impact of trade agreements on human rights and criticize the neglect of human rights in international trade negotiations,[33] the more trade diplomats and WTO bodies should acknowledge the legitimacy of such concerns and take into account the human rights dimensions of international trade rules.

The International Law Association ('ILA'), since its foundation in 1873, has regularly contributed – through its more than 65 national branches as well as through its international conferences, legal committees, ILA reports and ILA resolutions – to the progressive development of international law by elaborating draft conventions and clarifying legal problems in all fields of international law. The ILA Resolution on 'The Rule of Law in International Trade', adopted at the 69th ILA conference at London in 2000,[34] emphasized the legal as well as economic and political benefits of the rule of law in international trade. Since then, all reports of the ILA's International Trade Law Committee ('ITLC') have discussed, inter alia, the complex interrelationships between human rights and international trade law. The 7th ITLC Report adopted at the 72nd ILA conference at Toronto included text proposals for a future ILA Declaration on 'International Trade Law and Human Rights' in order to promote a global discussion on the relevance of human rights for the future interpretation and progressive development of international trade law and its multilevel dispute settlement system.[35] The following draft proposal, discussed by the ITLC at its meeting in June 2007, deliberately avoided certain controversies over the interpretation of human rights law (for example, the current state of customary human rights law), international trade law (for example, the limited jurisdiction of WTO dispute settlement bodies), and of the customary international law rules on treaty interpretation (for example, concerning the interpretation of Article 31.3(c) VCLT). Its primary aim was limited to helping clarify how trade dispute settlement bodies should respond to human rights arguments with due respect for the diversity of national and regional human rights traditions, the limited mandate of trade institutions, due process of law requirements and the customary methods of international treaty interpretation. As noted below, it was discussed at the 73rd ILA Conference in August 2008.

---

[33] See the critical remarks by the UN Committee on Economic, Social and Cultural Rights on the *Report submitted by Costa Rica pursuant to Articles 16 and 17 of the UN Covenant on Economic, Social and Cultural Rights*, UN Doc E/C.12/CRI/CO/4 (23 November 2007), regarding the human rights impact assessment of the Central American Free Trade Area Agreement.

[34] ILA, *Report of the 69th Conference* (ILA, London, 2000) 23–25.

[35] ILA, *Report of the 72nd Conference* (London 2006), 279ff.

Draft Proposal for a 2008 ILA Resolution

– *Recalling* that the practice of the UN and of UN Specialized Agencies confirms that all UN member states have human rights obligations under the UN Charter, and that the recognition of human rights in the primary law (for example, the 'fundamental right to the enjoyment of the highest attainable standard of health' recognized in the Constitution of the World Health Organization by 193 member states) and in the secondary law of UN Agencies (for example, in the 1998 ILO Declaration on Core Labor Standards) has contributed to the progressive development, protection and universal recognition of human rights in the practice of states.

– *Recalling* also that all 151 WTO Members have human rights obligations (for example, under the UN Charter, under UN human rights conventions, under customary international law and under 'general principles of law recognized by civilized nations') not only in intergovernmental relations among states, but also vis-à-vis domestic and foreign citizens. Even though the precise scope and content of such human rights obligations often remains contested, international courts have determined that some human rights obligations have evolved into international *ius cogens*;

– *Recalling* further that WTO dispute settlement bodies – in their task to interpret and 'clarify the existing provisions of those agreements in accordance with customary rules of interpretation of public international law' (Article 3(2) DSU) – may have to examine claims by WTO Members to interpret WTO rules (for example, on protection of 'public morals', human health and other public interests) in conformity with human rights obligations of WTO Members, taking into account 'any relevant rules of international law applicable in the relations between the parties' (Article 31.3(c) VCLT);

– *Recalling* the 'Declaration on the Rule of Law in International Trade' adopted by the 69th Conference of the ILA in 2000 at London, as well as numerous other ILA Resolutions aimed at promoting mutually coherent interpretations and synergies of multilateral international treaties, and noting the extensive discussions on legal interrelationships between international trade law and human rights in the bi-annual reports of the ILA's International Trade Law Committee since 2000 as well as in numerous books and other publications by ILA members;

– *Welcoming* the WTO Declaration on Trade Related Intellectual Property Rights and Health, the WTO Waivers for the 'Kimberley Rules for conflict diamonds' and for 'access to medicines', and the 2007 Joint Study by the ILO and the WTO on 'Trade and Employment' (for example, its explicit reference to freedom of association and the right to collective bargaining as 'universally recognized human rights'), all of which acknowledge the need for interpreting WTO rules with due regard to human rights concerns;

The 73rd Conference of the ILA at Rio de Janeiro declares:

(1) It may only be a matter of time until WTO dispute settlement bodies may be confronted – as it has happened in regional economic courts and arbitral tribunals – with human rights arguments in support of interpreting trade and economic rules in conformity with human rights obligations of the countries concerned, or with related requests for 'judicial comity' or 'judicial deference'. Notwithstanding their limited jurisdiction and their right to exercise 'judicial economy', WTO dispute settlement bodies may be required by the customary methods of international treaty interpretation to examine whether human rights arguments invoked by WTO Members may be relevant for justifying, for example, restrictions of imports of goods and services in conformity with WTO rules if such restrictions are 'necessary to protect public morals' (Articles XX(a) GATT, XIV(a) GATS), 'to maintain public order' (Article XIV(a) GATS), to protect security (Articles XXI GATT, XIV*bis* GATS), human health (Articles XX(b) GATT, XIV(b) GATS) and other basic human needs. Judicial deference towards legal protection of human rights inside the importing country, without prejudice to the judicial review of the WTO obligations of the countries concerned, may be in conformity not only with the human rights obligations of WTO Members, but also with the legal findings of WTO dispute settlement bodies,[36] especially if the non-discriminatory application of restrictions to like goods and services regardless of their origin demonstrates their non-economic objectives.

(2) WTO Members have not expressed any intention to deviate from their human rights obligations when they negotiated and ratified the WTO Agreements. They have recognized in numerous WTO provisions the rights and obligations of all WTO Members to protect human life, human health,

[36] See, for example, the Appellate Body's reference to public morals in Article XIV GATS as concerning 'fundamental interests [. . .] as reflected in law', and the Appellate Body's acknowledgment that the more vital the value pursued by import restrictions, the higher may be the degree of judicial deference towards the protective measure: see *United States – Measures Affecting the Cross-Border Supply of Gambling and Betting Services*, WTO Doc WT/DS298/AB/R (20 April 2005) (Report of the Appellate Body) and *European Communities – Measures Affecting Asbestos and Products Containing Asbestos*, WTO Doc WT/DS135/AB/R (5 April 2001) (Report of the Appellate Body) respectively.

human security and other human needs and public interests. Hence, in their examination of legal claims to interpret WTO rules in conformity with human rights, trade dispute settlement bodies should proceed from the legal presumption that WTO provisions can and should be interpreted consistent with the human rights obligations of WTO Members under international law.

(3) In examining legal claims concerning an alleged impact of human rights on the interpretation of WTO rules, WTO dispute settlement bodies must respect their limited jurisdiction and the legitimate diversity of national and regional human rights traditions provided such diverse traditions remain consistent with universal human rights obligations.

(4) In conformity with the worldwide recognition – for example, in the 1993 Vienna Declaration of the UN World Conference on Human Rights – that 'democracy, development and respect for human rights and fundamental freedoms are interdependent and mutually reinforcing' (at [8]), the ILA endorses the calls by the UN High Commissioner for Human Rights (for example, in its reports on the human rights dimensions of WTO rules that directly affect citizen interests) to interpret and apply WTO rules in conformity with the respective human rights obligations of WTO Members. Just as human rights and public discourse on the human rights dimensions of economic law have played an important role in promoting civil society support for European law and the legal consistency of European integration law with human rights, so can respect for universal human rights and public discourse on the human rights dimensions of WTO law promote civil society support for the WTO and help to ensure that WTO rights and obligations contribute to the protection of general citizen interests as defined by universal human rights.

(5) Respect for the universal human rights obligations of WTO Members is warranted also by the legal requirement (as stated in the Preamble to the VCLT as well as in Article 1 of the *Charter of the United Nations*) to settle disputes concerning treaties, like other international disputes, 'in conformity with the principles of justice and international law', including 'respect for, and observance of, human rights and fundamental freedoms for all'. National and international tribunals should cooperate in promoting the rule of law not only in intergovernmental relations among states but also in international trade transactions among citizens, including the just settlement of international trade disputes for the benefit of citizens whose life and welfare are ever more influenced by international trade.

7. THE FINAL TEXT OF THE 2008 ILA RESOLUTION: ANOTHER STEP ON THE ENDLESS ROAD TOWARD 'CONSTITUTIONAL JUSTICE'

There is a diplomatic adage that likens a camel to a horse drafted by a committee. Fortunately, draft proposals from the more than twenty ILA Committees are double-checked in a review process under the guidance of the ILA's Executive Council and the ILA Director of Studies before being submitted to the ILA Plenary Assembly for approval. Thanks to the legal wisdom and drafting skills of the ILA's President, the Rt Hon Lord Slynn of Hadley, the compromise text resulting from years of discussions in the ITLC Committee was further reduced to its legal essentials. The final text approved by the 73rd ILA Plenary Assembly reads as follows:

RESOLUTION No. 5/2008
INTERNATIONAL TRADE LAW

The 73rd Conference of the International Law Association, held in Rio de Janeiro, Brazil, 17–21 August 2008:

HAVING CONSIDERED the report of the International Trade Law Committee, especially the reasoning in Chapter VIII on International Trade Law and Human Rights;

RECALLING that by virtue of the UN Charter and human rights conventions and under customary international law and general principles of international law, states have human rights obligations;

CONSIDERING that it is likely that WTO dispute settlement bodies will be confronted – as has happened in national and regional economic courts and arbitral tribunals – with human rights arguments in support of interpreting trade and economic rules in conformity with the human rights obligations of the countries concerned, or with related requests for 'judicial comity' or 'judicial deference';

DECLARES WTO members and bodies are legally required to interpret and apply WTO rules in conformity with the human rights obligations of WTO members under international law.

From the point of view of customary law, this text does not go beyond what WTO Members have recognized in numerous legal instruments. The text avoids clarifying the contested status, precise legal meaning and scope of specific human rights obligations (for example, of international organizations and other non-state actors) in transnational economic relations in order to respect the reality of 'reasonable pluralism' among governments and citizens about how UN human rights standards should be legally implemented in domestic legal and economic systems with diverse democratic traditions and conceptions for a good life and for just societies.[37] UN human rights law, like WTO law, often prescribes only minimum standards that may be implemented in domestic legal systems in legitimately diverse ways, depending on the respective democratic preferences and available resources of the societies concerned.

According to Rawls, it is 'the fact that in a democratic regime political power is regarded as the power of free and equal citizens as a collective body' which requires that the democratic exercise of coercive power over one another can be recognized as being democratically legitimate only when 'political power [. . .] is exercised in accordance with a constitution (written or unwritten) the essentials of which all citizens, as reasonable and rational, can endorse in the light of their common human reason'.[38] The today almost universal commitment by nearly all of the 192 UN member states to national constitutions and human rights also limits and 'constitutionalizes' the transnational legal regulation of economic cooperation among citizens, for example by prompting states to constitute ever more international courts for judicial protection of rule of law in transnational economic relations. According to Rawls, 'in a constitutional regime with judicial review, public reason is the reason of its supreme court'; transparent, rules-based and impartial judicial reasoning, subject to procedural guarantees of due process of law, makes independent courts less politicized 'fora of principle' that are of constitutional importance for an 'overlapping, constitutional consensus' necessary for legally stable and just relations among free, equal and rational citizens who tend to remain deeply divided by conflicting moral, religious and philosophical doctrines.[39] Also in international law, Article 1 of the *Charter of the United Nations* and the VCLT recall the general international law obligation 'that disputes concerning treaties, like other international disputes, should be settled by peaceful means and in conformity with the principles of justice and international law', including 'universal respect for, and observance of, human rights and fundamental freedoms for all' (Preamble VCLT). The ECJ, the European Court of Human Rights and the EFTA Court have successfully trans-

---

37 On the 'idea of a well-ordered society' respecting the 'fact of reasonable pluralism' and pursuing only a limited conception of 'political justice' see Rawls, above n 11, 35ff.

38 John Rawls, *Justice as Fairness: A Restatement* (Harvard University Press, Cambridge, 2001) 41.

39 Rawls, above n 11, 231ff.

formed the intergovernmental EC treaties and the ECHR into constitutional orders founded on respect for human rights. Their incremental 'judicial constitutionalization' of intergovernmental treaty regimes was accepted by citizens, national courts, parliaments and governments because their judicial 'European public reason' protected more effectively individual rights and European 'public goods' (like the EC's common market). The '*solange* method' of cooperation among European courts 'as long as' constitutional rights are adequately protected, reflects an 'overlapping constitutional consensus' on the need for 'constitutional justice' in European integration law among the 30 member countries of the 'European Economic Area' ('EEA') and, increasingly, also among the 47 member states of the ECHR.[40]

The increasing calls from civil society, their NGOs (like the ILA) and democratic governments for stronger legal and judicial protection of rule of law in international trade continue to promote ever stronger legal and judicial remedies in transnational trade and investment relations. The ILA's 2008 Resolution may assist WTO dispute settlement bodies and regional and national courts of justice in meeting their existing legal duties, under national and international laws, of 'providing security and predictability to the multilateral trading system' (Article 3 DSU) by settling international disputes 'in conformity with principles of justice' and human rights (VCLT). True, just as only a dozen among the thousands of ECJ judgments over the past 50 years have explicitly reviewed the EC's economic regulations in the light of the human rights obligations of the EC and its 27 member states, so are human rights challenges to WTO rules and to national trade regulations of WTO Member States likely to remain rare exceptions (for example in view of the numerous WTO 'exceptions' protecting the sovereign rights and obligations of WTO members to protect non-economic 'public interests'). Yet, democratic and parliamentary support for the world trading system risks being undermined if trade courts interpret and apply trade rules without 'administering justice'. According to Dworkin's 'adjudicative principle of integrity', judges should interpret law – in conformity with its objectives of legality, rule-of-law and its underlying constitutional principles of justice – as expressing 'a coherent conception of justice and fairness':

> Law as integrity asks judges to assume, so far as this is possible, that the law is structured by a coherent set of principles about justice and fairness and procedural due process, and it asks them to enforce these in the fresh cases that come before them, so that each person's situation is fair and just according to the same standards.[41]

---

[40] See Ernst-Ulrich Petersmann, 'Human Rights, International Economic Law and "Constitutional Justice"' (2008) 19 *European Journal of International Law* 769.

[41] Dworkin above n 29, 225, 243.

Reducing the unnecessary poverty of some two billion people living on 2 dollars or less per day is not only a 'moral imperative', but also a legal requirement of modern human rights law. As stated already in the Preamble to the UDHR, 'it is essential if man is not to be compelled to have recourse, as a last resort, to rebellion against tyranny and oppression, that human rights be protected by the rule of law.' The ILA's 2008 Resolution on international trade law and human rights reminds lawyers and judges all over the world of their customary law obligation of interpreting and applying trade rules with due regard to 'principles of justice' and human rights.

4. Globalisation and human rights: an economist's perspective

Pranab Bardhan

1. INTRODUCTION

As is common in most contentious public debates, different people mean different things by globalisation. Some interpret it to mean the global reach of new technology (particularly in information and communications) and capital movements, some refer to outsourcing by domestic companies of rich countries, others protest against the tentacles of corporate capitalism or US hegemony in cultural and economic matters. In this chapter I shall mainly confine myself to globalisation in its economic aspects, and that too primarily in the sense of openness to foreign trade and *long-term* capital flows (ignoring other aspects of economic globalisation like speculative short-term capital movements or immigration).[1] Of course, the trade aspects of globalisation are very much linked to the World Trade Organisation ('WTO').[2] I shall discuss:

a) How globalisation in this sense may have affected extreme poverty in the world which is a violation of human rights; and
b) Its impact on labour rights.

Even without insisting on a full-scale normative framework for shaping trade and investment laws, many will agree that extreme poverty is a degradation of human dignity and that there is a basic human right to minimum subsistence (part of the 'right to life').[3] UNESCO and several human rights

[1] Parts of the material in this chapter may be found in Pranab Bardhan, 'The Global Economy and the Poor', in Abhijit Vinayak Banerjee et al. (eds), *Understanding Poverty* (Oxford University Press, New York, 2006), 98–109.

[2] The *raison d'etre* of the WTO is to supervise rules regarding liberalisation of trade, which indirectly has an impact on long-term capital flows, and to serve as a negotiating forum for further commitments to open trade.

[3] The right to life is protected in a variety of human rights treaties, such as article 6 of the International Covenant on Civil and Political Rights (16 December 1966) 999 UNTS 171, entered into force 23 March 1976 ('ICCPR').

activists have claimed that poverty is a violation of human rights.[4] A discussion of the impact of economic globalisation on poverty is thus relevant.

A common cliché in the media as well as in street protests is that globalisation is making the rich richer and the poor poorer. But the data on inequality[5] suggest that over the last two decades or so:

- Inter-country disparity in per capita incomes is increasing.
- But population-weighted disparity (for example, giving larger countries more weight than smaller countries) is decreasing.
- Intra-country inequality is increasing in some countries but is decreasing or ambiguous in other countries (for example, it has increased over the last two decades in China, but it went up, then down, in Brazil).
- If one combines population-weighted inter-country inequality and intra-country inequality, the *World Development Report 2006*[6] reports a small decline in this combined inequality between 1988 and 2000.

Again contrary to the cliché, the summary picture on poverty for developing countries as a whole (see Figure 4.1 and Table 4.1) suggests a poverty *decline* between 1981 and 2004 (with or without China), with the largest declines in East and South Asia, in terms of the proportion of people below a common international poverty line (the admittedly crude one of the World Bank at $1 per day at 1993 purchasing power parity).

We do not know how much of these results on inequality or poverty are driven by globalisation. Pro-globalisers, for example, point to the large decline in poverty in China and India in the recent decades of international economic integration. But no one has yet convincingly demonstrated that this decline is mainly due to globalisation. It could instead be, to a large extent, due to internal factors like expansion of infrastructure or the massive 1978 land reforms or the relaxation of restrictions on rural-to-urban migration in China, or the spread of green revolution in agriculture, large anti-poverty programs or social movements in India. Those who are more dubious of global processes point out that in the same decades poverty has remained stubbornly high in sub-Saharan Africa. But this may have little to do with globalisation, and more to

---

4 UNESCO, 'The fight against extreme poverty: an intersectoral challenge' (2006) 14 *SHS Views* 8; UNESCO, 'Interview with Sylvie Kayatesi Zaïnabo: "poverty is a denial of human rights"' (2008) 20 *SHS Views* 6.

5 See, for example, B Milanovic, *Worlds Apart: Measuring International and Global Inequality* (Princeton University Press, Princeton, 2005).

6 World Bank, *World Development Report 2006* (World Bank, Washington DC, 2005).

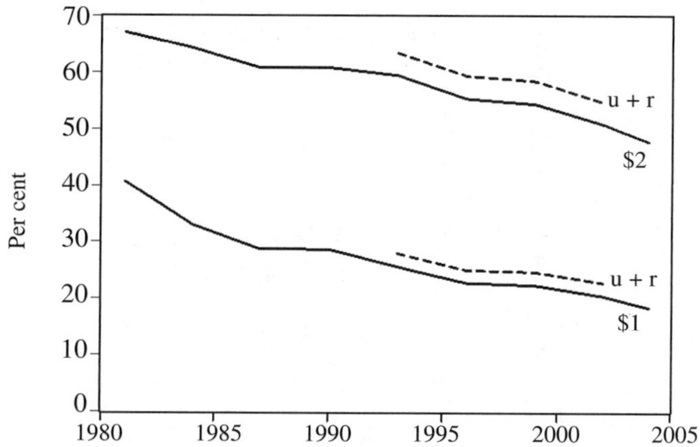

Note: The poverty measures are the proportions of people below the alternative poverty lines of \$1 a day and \$2 a day at 1993 purchasing power parity, estimated on the basis of household survey data in different developing countries. The series labeled 'u + r' incorporates the urban-rural poverty line differential.

Figure 4.1 Poverty measures over time, 1981–2004[7]

do with unstable or failed political regimes, wars and civil conflicts which afflicted several countries in Africa; if anything, such instability only reduced their extent of globalisation, as it scared off many foreign investors and traders.

In general it is empirically difficult to disentangle the effects of trade or foreign investment liberalisation from those of ongoing technological changes (skill-biased, for example, as in the case of information or telecommunication technology) or reform in macro-economic stabilisation policies, deregulation, privatisation, removal of capital controls, and so on.

2. THE POOR AS SELF-EMPLOYED

If one goes beyond simple correlations, the causal processes through which international economic integration can affect poverty primarily involve the poor in their capacity *as workers*, *as consumers*, and *as recipients of public services*, or *users of common property resources*.

7 M Ravillion and S Chen, 'Absolute Poverty Measures for the Developing World: 1981–2004' (Working Paper No 4211, World Bank Policy Research, Washington DC, 2007) 25.

Table 4.1 Poverty measures for $1 a day[8]

(a) Percentage of population

Region	1981	1984	1987	1990	1993	1996	1999	2002	2004
East-Asia and Pacific (EAP)	57.73	39.02	28.23	29.84	25.23	16.14	15.46	12.33	9.05
China	63.76	41.02	28.64	32.98	28.36	17.37	17.77	13.79	9.90
Eastern-Europe and Central Asia (ECA)	0.70	0.51	0.35	0.46	3.60	4.42	3.78	1.27	0.94
Latin America and Caribbean (LAC)	10.77	13.07	12.09	10.19	8.42	8.87	9.66	9.09	8.64
Middle East and North Africa (MNA)	5.08	3.82	3.09	2.33	1.87	1.69	2.08	1.69	1.47
South Asia (SAS)	51.55	46.64	44.90	43.02	37.11	36.57	35.76	34.68	31.95
India	54.31	49.50	45.88	44.29	42.13	40.61	38.76	37.49	35.78
Sub-Saharan Africa (SSA)	42.26	46.20	47.22	46.73	45.47	47.72	45.77	42.63	41.10
Total	**40.64**	**33.03**	**28.67**	**28.66**	**25.60**	**22.76**	**22.32**	**20.43**	**18.39**
Total excl. China	32.03	30.11	28.68	27.14	24.65	24.60	23.84	22.59	21.10

(b) Number of people (in millions)

Region	1981	1984	1987	1990	1993	1996	1999	2002	2004
EAP	796.40	564.30	428.76	476.22	420.22	279.09	276.54	226.77	169.13
China	633.66	425.27	310.43	374.33	334.21	211.44	222.78	176.61	128.36
ECA	3.00	2.27	1.61	2.16	16.94	20.87	17.90	6.01	4.42
LAC	39.35	50.90	50.00	44.60	38.83	42.96	49.03	48.13	47.02
MNA	8.81	7.26	6.41	5.26	4.53	4.38	5.67	4.88	4.40
SAS	473.44	456.90	468.96	478.87	439.58	459.41	474.63	485.17	462.22
India	381.67	371.08	366.45	376.21	378.93	385.30	387.27	393.16	386.37
SSA	167.53	199.78	222.80	240.34	252.26	286.21	296.07	296.11	298.30
Total	**1488.54**	**1281.41**	**1178.55**	**1247.45**	**1172.36**	**1092.92**	**1119.84**	**1067.08**	**985.50**
Total excl. China	854.88	856.14	868.12	873.12	838.15	881.49	897.06	890.47	857.14

8 Ibid 28.

Let us first take the case of *poor workers*. They are mainly either self-employed or wage earners. The self-employed work on their own tiny farms or as artisans and petty entrepreneurs in small shops and firms. The major constraints they usually face are in credit, storage, marketing and insurance, access to new technology, extension services, and to infrastructure (like roads, power, ports, telecommunication, and irrigation), and government regulations (involving venal inspectors or policemen, insecure land rights and so forth). To relieve these constraints often requires substantive domestic policy changes, and foreign traders and investors are not directly to blame. In fact they may sometimes help in relieving some of the bottlenecks in infrastructure and services and in essential parts, components, technology, and equipment. If these changes are not made and the self-employed poor remain constrained, then, of course, it is difficult for them to withstand competition from large agri-business or firms (foreign or domestic).

When small producers are heavily involved in exports (for example, coffee producers of Uganda, rice growers in Vietnam, garment producers in Bangladesh or Cambodia) the major hurdle they face is often due to not more globalisation but *less*. As is by now well known, developed country protectionism and subsidisation of farm and food products and simple manufactures (like textiles and clothing) severely restrict their export prospects for poor countries. This is a matter on which the Doha negotiations of the WTO are currently foundering.[9]

Another increasingly important barrier to trade many small farmers of developing countries face in world markets is that rich countries now shut out many of these imports under a whole host of safety and sanitary regulations (sometimes imposed under pressure from lobbyists of import-competing farms in those countries).[10] There are also the barriers to entry raised by the cartels of global retail chains. In agri-business, for example, in recent years through mergers, acquisitions and business alliances the agri-food corporations have concentrated enormous market power: companies like Monsanto, Cargill, Nestlé and Wal-Mart have come to dominate supply chains for food and agricultural goods, from seeds and pesticides all

---

[9] See generally the WTO website, in particular the gateway for the Doha Development Agenda: http://www.wto.org/english/tratop_e/dda_e/dda_e.htm at 1 July 2008.

[10] See generally, A O Sykes, *The WTO Agreement on Safeguards: A Commentary* (Oxford University Press, Oxford, 2006); K Anderson, 'The Future Agenda of the WTO' in WTO Secretariat (ed.) *From GATT to the WTO: The Multilateral Trading System in the New Millennium* (Kluwer, The Hague, 2000) 7. See also the WTO website, particularly the comments on the Sanitary and Phytosanitary Measures Agreement and the Technical Barriers to Trade Agreement: http://www.wto.org/english/thewto_e/whatis_e/tif_e/agrm4_e.htm at 1 July 2008.

the way to produce on the supermarket shelf.[11] In food retail sales the largest supermarkets like Wal-Mart, Carrefour, Ahold, Tesco and Kroger are dominant.[12]

Similarly, it may be very difficult, costly, and time-consuming for small producers of manufactures or services in developing countries to establish brand name and reputation in quality and timely delivery, which are absolutely crucial in marketing, particularly in international markets. This is where multinational marketing chains with global brand names, mediating between domestic suppliers and foreign buyers, play their role. Coordinated attempts on the part of developing countries, with technical assistance from international organisations, to build international quality certification institutions for their products should be a high priority in providing an alternative. Those who are justifiably outraged by the extremely high marketing margins the monopoly multinational companies currently charge the poor producers should agitate more for anti-trust action, not anti-trade action. There should also be more energetic international attempts to certify codes against international restrictive business practices and to establish an international anti-trust investigation agency, possibly under WTO auspices. Even if such an agency may not have much enforcement powers, internationally publicised reports of anti-trust investigations by a recognised international body will have some impact on rapacious monopolies, and strengthen the hands of domestic competition commissions in developing countries, and also partially relieve the current lack of information on price-setting and business practices of global companies.

It is also important to keep in mind that trade liberalisation, even when increasing the mean incomes of the poor producers, may heighten their vulnerability, particularly by increasing the variance of prices or income sources. The evidence on this is mixed, but it is clear that the capacity of the poor to cope with negative shocks is usually much weaker than the rest of the population.[13]

3. THE POOR AS WAGE EARNERS

Turning to *poor wage earners*, the traditional international trade theory suggests that the workers in a poor country (presumably having abundant

---

[11] See D Eagleton, *Power Hungry: Six Reasons to Regulate Global Food Companies* (Actionaid International, London, 2005) http://www.actionaid.org.uk/_content/documents/power_hungry.pdf at 1 July 2008.

[12] Ibid.

[13] For a brief summary of the empirical literature on this question, see L A Winters et al., 'Trade Liberalisation and Poverty: The Evidence So Far' (2004) 42 *Journal of Economic Literature* 72.

supplies of unskilled labour) having a comparative advantage in products intensive in unskilled labour should benefit from trade liberalisation. The improvement in wages and employment of garment workers in Bangladesh or Vietnam with expanding exports is an obvious example. The matter is, of course, complicated by the fact that developing countries (say, Brazil or Mexico or Turkey) may import labour-intensive products from even poorer countries (say, China or Indonesia or Bangladesh), so that trade, consistent with the traditional theory, may lead to lower wages in the former set of developing countries, for which there seems to be some evidence.[14] Similarly, if a poor country has large supplies of other factors of production (like land or mineral resources), trade liberalisation may not benefit the labour-intensive sectors, as the mineral sector may expand at the expense, say, of farmers or artisans.

What about the presence of large and powerful multinational companies hiring people with low bargaining power in poor countries? There is little evidence that poor unskilled workers get lower wages (or fewer jobs) in the presence of those companies, compared to what they will get in their absence, other things remaining the same.[15] Contrary to the impression created by the campaign in affluent countries against 'sweatshops' run by multinational companies in poor countries, it can be pointed out that the poor are often banging at the gates of these sweatshops for a chance of entry, since their current alternative is much worse, in inferior occupations or work conditions or in unemployment. We shall come back to this issue in section 5. Of course, sometimes the large companies, instead of hiring labour themselves, outsource their activities to smaller firms and household enterprises, where the wages and overhead costs are lower, to the detriment of the formal sector employees, but the net effect on the workers of the country should take into account the resultant improvement in wages and employment among the usually much poorer informal sector workers.

There are, however, two important reasons why opening the economy may worsen the conditions of workers: one relates to the nature of technical change, and the other to that of collective bargaining. As much of technical change in rich countries is biased against the services of unskilled labour, and if multinational companies transplant those new techniques in poor countries, employment and wage of unskilled labour will go down, as has been report-

14 For detailed evidence from Colombia, see P Goldberg and N Pavcnik 'Trade Protection and Wages: Evidence from the Columbian Trade Reforms' 66 *Journal of International Economics* 75.

15 See, for example, B Aitken et al., 'Wages and Foreign Ownership: A Comparative Study of Mexico, Venezuela and the United States' (1996) 40 *Journal of International Economics* 345.

edly the case, for example, with global tenders to construction companies like Bechtel or Mitsui using labour-saving technology rendering many construction workers unemployed in India.[16]

Globalisation often leads to a weakening of unions. As foreign competition (or even the threat of it) lowers profit margins, the old rent-sharing arrangements between employers and unionised workers come under pressure. Rents decline both for capital and labour, but labour may have to take a larger cut as internationally less mobile labour faces more mobile capital, or as companies can more credibly threaten substitution of foreign factors of production, including intermediate inputs, for domestic factors. This may lead to lower wages, and, sometimes more important, increased risk of unemployment.

Even when poor unskilled workers lose from international liberalisation, it may be possible to combine a policy of liberalisation with a domestic policy of compensating the losers at low cost. The main problem, of course, is that of credible commitment on the part of the ruling politicians that losers will be compensated. Recent history in many countries is full of reneged promises on the part of governments to displaced workers. Obviously, this is a particularly important matter in poor countries where there is very little effective social protection available from the state. Rich countries have better social safety nets and have some programs in place helping, however imperfectly, displaced workers to adjust. International organisations that preach the benefits of free trade should take the responsibility of funding and facilitating such adjustment assistance programs in poor countries that can help workers in coping with job losses and getting retrained and redeployed. There should be more of the income support programs like the Trabajar program in Argentina or programs to train and help the unemployed in finding new jobs like the Probecat in Mexico.[17]

Until issues of general economic security for poor workers in developing countries are satisfactorily resolved, globalisation is bound to raise anxiety and hostility among workers worried about their job security. If mass politics in a country is organised, as it usually is, in such a way that the nation-state is the primary political forum for demanding and getting the necessary redistributive and insurance functions of a society (rendered more important by the economics of international specialisation), to the extent that the nation state is weakened by forces of international economic integration, it is a matter of serious concern. Much depends, of course, on a society's institutions of conflict

16 See, for example, R Jhabvala and R Kanbur, 'Globalisation and Economic Reform as Seen from the Ground' in Contract Basu (ed.) *India's Emerging Economy* (MIT Press, Cambridge, 2004) 293.

17 See M Rama and W Maloney, *Income Support Programs for the Unemployed in Latin America* (World Bank, Washington DC, 2000).

management and coordination. It is not a coincidence that countries that have a better record in building these institutions have coped better with the dislocations brought about by international trade: the major example is the case of Scandinavian countries where in spite of a strong tradition of organised labour movement and worker solidarity over many decades of the last century, the unions there in general have been in favour of an open economy and the worker dislocations have been better managed, in contrast to the case in the US, where a weaker social safety net and the lack of portable health insurance make globalisation more unpopular with workers.[18]

The general issue of the weakening of the nation state is rather complex. There is a possible loss of national policy options brought about by a poor country's participation in international trade and investment and in the framework of global institutions and rules that govern them. I agree with the anti-global protesters that many of the international organisations that define the rules of this order are accountable more to the corporate and financial community of rich countries than to the poor, and that the decision-making processes in these organisations need to be much more transparent and responsive to the lives of the people their decisions crucially affect.[19] But the protesters' demand for the abolition of international organisations like the WTO is, however, misplaced. If the alternative to a multilateral organisation like the WTO is for a developing country to face the US in bilateral trade negotiations, the US is likely to be much more dominant and arbitrary in such negotiations than in the dispensations of the WTO (which in its arbitration decisions has sometimes ruled against the US position). Of course, serious efforts are needed to strengthen the technical negotiation capacity of poor countries in international trade forums where they face the well-equipped and well-funded teams of lawyers and negotiators representing rich countries.[20]

Coming to the issue of a government's fiscal options in a global economy, many people are of the opinion that the scope for taxing capital to raise revenue is severely limited by the threat of capital flight in the long run, even

---

18 See, for example, K Scheve and M Slaughter, 'A New Deal for Globalisation' (2007) 86 *Foreign Affairs* 34.

19 It is also to be noted that in the WTO each member country has one vote (the convention is to reach decisions by 'consensus'), whereas in the Bretton Woods institutions (IMF and the World Bank) voting is dollar-weighted. But there is no denying the fact that the rich countries (and their large corporate lobbies) exercise a dominant effect on the agenda-setting and decision-making of the WTO, as with the Bretton Woods institutions. See also Chapter 12, pp. 316–22.

20 E-U Petersmann, 'WTO Dispute Settlement Practice 1995–2005: Lessons from the Past and Future Challenges' in Y Taniguchi et al. (eds), *The WTO in the Twenty-First Century: Dispute Settlement, Negotiations and Regionalism in Asia* (Cambridge University Press, Cambridge, 2005) 38, 43.

if we ignore the problem of short-term speculative capital flows. While this limitation can be serious, one should not exaggerate its effects. Most countries collect only a small part of their revenues from capital taxation, even in relatively closed economies. In any case there are strong arguments for funding redistributive policies through progressive consumption taxes (say, VAT) rather than taxes on capital or labour.[21] There is, however, a short-run problem in some developing countries whose public budgets are heavily dependent on customs duties which decline with trade liberalisation.[22]

4. THE ACCESS OF THE POOR TO PUBLIC AND ENVIRONMENTAL RESOURCES

This brings us to the issue of the poor *as recipients of public services*. If cuts in public budgets on health, education and public works programs are necessitated by the decline in customs revenue as a result of trade reform, the poor may suffer. Much depends on the nature of customs administration, the degree of complexity of the tariff structure, and the scope for expansion of the revenue base following trade reform. The low quality and quantity of public services like education and health in poor countries is, of course, not just due to their relatively low share in the public budget. To a large extent even the limited money allocated in the budget does not reach the poor because of all kinds of top-heavy administrative obstacles and bureaucratic and political corruption. Again this is a domestic institutional failure, not largely an external problem related to globalisation. The major effort required here is to strengthen the domestic institutions of accountability.

The poor are also *users of common property resources*. This brings us to the complex issues of trade and environment, the decline in which is not usually taken into account in the standard estimates of poverty, based as they are on either household surveys of private consumer expenditure or national income

[21] Studies in Turkey have shown, through a computable general equilibrium model, that a direct income subsidy to the losers of trade reform, financed by a VAT, is quite cost-effective when compared to a flat tax on capital and labour: G W Harrison, 'Trade Liberalization, Poverty and Efficient Equity' (2003) 71 *Journal of Development Economics* 97. The main problem, of course, is that of credible commitment on the part of the ruling politicians that losers will be compensated: P Bardhan, 'Globalization, Inequality, and Poverty: An Overview' (Paper presented at the Trade and Poverty in Latin America and the Caribbean Workshop, Washington DC, 19 June 2006) 16, http://idbdocs.iadb.org/wsdocs/getdocument.aspx?docnum=751258 at 1 July 2008.

[22] For an argument that tariff revenues fall much slower than tariff rates, see L Pritchett and G Sethi, 'Tariff Rates, Tariff Revenue and Tariff Reform' (1994) 8 *World Bank Economic Review* 1.

accounts. Environmentalists argue that trade liberalisation damages the poor by encouraging overexploitation of the fragile environmental resources (forestry, fishery, surface and groundwater irrigation, grazing lands, etc.) on which the daily livelihoods of particularly the rural poor crucially depend. Here also the answers are actually complex and mere trade restriction is not the solution.

The environmental effects of trade liberalisation on the rural economy depend on the crop pattern and the methods of production. Take, for example, an African rural economy where the exportable product is a capital-intensive tree crop (like coffee or cocoa), the import-substitute is a land-intensive crop (like maize), and there is a labour-intensive subsistence (non-traded) crop (like roots and tubers). The economy may have a comparative advantage in tree crops. In this case an increase in import substitution leads to an expansion of cultivated land under the land-intensive crop as well as a shortening of the fallow period, leading to depletion of natural vegetation and biomass. Trade liberalisation in this context, through encouraging the production of the less land-intensive tree crop, can significantly improve the natural biomass, as has been shown by Lopez in a study published in 2000 for Côte d'Ivoire in the latter part of the 1980s, using the data from the Living Standards Survey and some remote sensing data from satellite images.[23] There are, of course, some cases where international trade may push a country into a narrow range of cropping specialisation, and the resulting loss of diversity may make the local eco-system less resilient and more vulnerable to shocks.[24]

One reason why land-intensive crops may lead to overuse of land and depletion of natural vegetation (or that expansion of the agricultural frontier in general leads to deforestation) is the lack of well-defined property rights or lack of their enforcement in public or communal land. In such cases the private cost of expanding production is less than the social cost and there is overuse and degradation of environmental resources. If the country exports such resource-intensive products, foreign trade may make this misallocation worse. International trade theorists point out that trade restriction is not the first-best policy in this situation, correcting the property rights (or the regulation) regime is.[25] But the latter involves large changes in the legal-regulatory or community institutional framework which take a long time to implement, and

---

23 R Lopez, 'Trade Reform and Environmental Externalities in General Equilibrium: Analysis for an Archetype Poor Tropical Country' (2000) 5 *Environment and Development Economics* 377.

24 See, for example, R Aggarwal, 'Globalisation, Local Ecosystems and the Rural Poor' (2006) 34 *World Development* 1405.

25 See, for example, P Bardhan and C Udry, *Development Microeconomics* (Oxford University Press, Oxford, 1999) Ch 13.

given the threshold effects and irreversibilities in environmental degradation (forest regeneration requires a minimum stock, for example), one may not afford to wait. In that case some program of (time-bound) trade restriction coupled with serious attempts at the overhaul of the domestic institutional framework may be necessary. In other cases domestic policy changes can be implemented much more quickly, and restricting trade is unnecessary and undesirable. For example, administered under-pricing of precious environmental resources (irrigation water in India, energy in Russia, timber concessions in Indonesia)[26] is a major cause of resource depletion and correcting it should not take much time. Domestic vested interests, not globalisation, are responsible for the prolongation of such socially damaging policies.

In the case of some resource-intensive exports it is difficult for a country by itself to adopt environmental regulations if its international competitors do not adopt them at the same time and have the ability to undercut the former in international markets. Here there is an obvious need for coordination, in the environmental regulation policies of the countries concerned. Given the low elasticity of demand for many resource-intensive primary export commodities from developing countries in the world market, such coordinated policies, while raising prices and the terms of trade need not lead to a decline in export revenue.[27]

A common charge against multinational companies is that they flock to developing country 'pollution havens' to take advantage of lax environmental standards. In one of the very few careful empirical studies on the question, Eskeland and Harrison examine the pattern of foreign investment in Mexico, Venezuela, Morocco and Côte d'Ivoire. They find no evidence that foreign investment in these countries is related to pollution abatement costs in rich countries. They also find that within a given industry foreign plants are significantly more energy-efficient and use cleaner types of energy compared to their local peers.[28]

5. THE POOR AS CONSUMERS

Finally, let us briefly discuss the case of the poor *as consumers*. Whether they gain as consumers from trade depends on:

---

[26] Ibid.

[27] For examples of such commodities, see R Repetto, 'Trade and Sustainable Development' in M G Quibria (ed), *Critical Issues in Asian Development: Theories, Experiences and Policies* (Oxford University Press and Asian Development Bank, Hong Kong, 1995) 186.

[28] See G Eskeland and A Harrison, 'Moving to Greener Pastures? Multi-nationals and the Pollution Haven Hypothesis' (2003) 70 *Journal of Development Economics* 1.

a) Whether they are net buyers of tradable goods – for example, the landless labourers in Bangladesh who are net buyers of rice may gain from imports of cheaper rice from Thailand, but the landed peasants will lose; or
b) How monopolistic is the retail market structure which often blocks the pass-through from border prices to domestic prices – for example, in Mexico after NAFTA the cartelised tortilla sector largely maintained prices even with the availability of cheaper North American corn.[29]

We should also discuss here the likely impact on prices of some technology-intensive products (like life-saving drugs) which the poor buy that follows the patent regime of the TRIPS under WTO global rules. Exorbitant prices for life-saving drugs under the monopoly power for global drug companies granted with TRIPS can be a crushing burden on poor people and public health programs in poor countries. A detailed counterfactual study by Chaudhuri et al. in 2006[30] of four products in the fluoroquinolone segment of antibiotics in the Indian pharmaceuticals market shows that in 1999–2000 (when TRIPS did not yet apply in India) product patents in this segment of the market would have raised the prices from between 100 and 400 per cent in the absence of any price control. Of course, the main rationale of patents is in terms of the necessary inducement for research and innovations. But even with TRIPS, there is much more research on diet pills and anti-wrinkle creams and very little on tropical diseases that kill the poor of the world by the millions.[31] There are also other ways of encouraging research on drugs and vaccines for these diseases (for example, upfront research subsidy, purchase commitment by a Global Fund, public buyouts of patents), different from ensuring temporary monopoly through patents. Finally, to the extent existing knowledge is an ingredient or stepping stone for future research, TRIPS provide major disincentives for the latter.[32]

---

29 See Winters et al., above n 13.

30 S Chaudhuri et al., 'Estimating the Effects of Global Patent Protection in Pharmaceuticals: A Case Study of Quinolones in India' (2006) 96 *American Economic Review* 1477.

31 M K Kyle and A M McGahan, *Investments in Pharmaceuticals Before and After TRIPS* (2008) 18–20, http://emertech.wharton.upenn.edu/ConfReports_TechConfApr08/Kyle_McGahan.pdf at 1 July 2008.

32 For a discussion of the major issues around intellectual property rights, see P Bardhan, *Scarcity, Conflicts and Cooperation* (MIT Press, Cambridge, 2005) Ch 12.

6. GLOBALISATION AND WORKER RIGHTS

Many advocates of human rights worry about the implications of globalisation on worker rights. There are several distinct issues involved here:

(a) If the sweatshops producing goods for the global economy use forced labour, it is a clear violation of basic human rights and should not be permitted under any circumstances.[33] The same applies to unsafe or hazardous work conditions.[34] There is, however, not much evidence that global production particularly encourages forced labour. What is common is that the wages paid for work in the global companies are often 'paltry' particularly compared to those paid in rich countries. But more often than not these wages are higher than what domestic companies pay for comparable work. In any case one should distinguish between unsafe or hazardous work conditions and forced labour on the one hand and low-wage jobs on the other. Under capitalism just as workers willing to sell themselves as serfs are not permitted, unsafe work conditions that can cause bodily injury are to be strictly regulated. But the case for stopping workers from accepting low-wage jobs is much weaker, particularly if high minimum wages keep some poorer workers unemployed. We should look at the reality of the severely limited opportunities faced by the poor workers and the unintended consequences of trying to restrict rich-country imports of 'sweatshop' products in terms of the harm it may cause to these workers.

(b) What about child labour?[35] The issue of child labour has attracted a great deal of international attention in connection with the globalisation debate. Contrary to popular impression in the West, most working children in poor countries work for their family enterprises. According

---

[33] Forced labour is prohibited under a number of human rights treaties and also a number of International Labour Organization [ILO] Conventions. See, for example, article 8 of the ICCPR.

[34] See, in this respect, article 7 of the International Covenant on Economic, Social and Cultural Rights [ICESCR] (16 December 1966) 993 UNTS 3, entered into force 3 January 1976. Rights to just and favourable working conditions are also found in ILO Conventions. Unsafe working conditions can also threaten one's right to an adequate standard of physical and mental health (article 12 ICESCR) and, at worst, one's right to life (for example, article 6 ICCPR).

[35] Child labour (with some carefully defined exceptions) constitutes a breach of a number of ILO Conventions, as well as Articles 31 and 32 of the Convention on the Rights of the Child (20 November 1989) 1577 UNTS 3, entered into force 2 September 1990, and article 24 of the ICCPR.

to UNICEF-coordinated detailed household surveys in 36 low-income countries for 124 million children in the 5–14 age group, and tabulated by Edmonds and Pavcnik in 2005, 25 per cent of these children work in gainful employment but less than 3 per cent work outside their family enterprises for pay. About 70 per cent of the children attend school, and of those who do not, only about a quarter work in what can at least partly be described as gainful work (including in family enterprises), the rest of the non-attendees either do not work or only do domestic chores.[36]

Theoretically, trade-induced expansion of an industry that employs children may increase the demand for child (and adult) labour but the resultant income effect will reduce the supply of child labour from poor (or credit-constrained) households. Edmonds and Pavcnik, in a 2005 study,[37] analysed the effect of national and international rice market liberalisation in rural Vietnam in the 1990s on the basis of household survey data, and found that the income effect dominated: an increase of 30 per cent in the real price of rice in this period was associated with a 9.2 per cent decline in the probability that a child works. The result could have been, of course, different in a country where the majority of the poor are net rice consumers. But the point remains that a policy that increases earning opportunities for poor households (rather than good-intentioned but simplistic punitive policies like boycotting products of child labour) are much more effective in reducing the incidence of child labour. Policy interventions like contingent transfer programs (payments to mothers contingent on the child's school attendance) like the *Oportunidades* in Mexico or the Food for Education Program in Bangladesh have been particularly effective.[38]

(c) To create favourable conditions for multinational companies in Export Processing Zones (EPZs) the governments of poor countries often waive some labour rights, for example, those relating to freedom of association and collective bargaining (a 'core' labour standard of the ILO)[39] or those relating to unsafe and hazardous work conditions (not

---

36 E V Edmonds and N Pavcnik, 'Child Labour in the Global Economy' (2005) 18 *Journal of Economic Perspectives* 199.

37 Ibid.

38 See Bardhan, above n 32, Ch 12.

39 See ILO Convention 87 on Freedom of Association and Protection of the Right to Organise (1948) 68 U.N.T.S. 17, and ILO Convention 98 on the Right to Organise and Collective Bargaining (1949) 96 U.N.T.S. 257.

a part of the 'core' labour standards).[40] Many poor workers are quite willing to give up those rights for the benefits of working in the EPZs. Are there grounds for legal interventions in such free market contracts?

Most Chicago School law and economics people who go by the principle of voluntary contracts are opposed to such legal interventions in voluntary contracts.[41] But I agree with Basu[42] that there can be three types of situations where such interventions may be justified:

(i) We all know that individuals do not always act in their best interests, or properly estimate long-run costs of their action, or there is 'cognitive dissonance'. There are many examples of society restricting individual action on such grounds (for example, in the case of addictive behaviour like smoking). Similar arguments can be made for restraining people from working in unsafe working conditions.

(ii) There may be multiple equilibria, one where everybody works under hazardous conditions, and another where everybody works under safe conditions. A law banning unsafe work conditions may help in moving from a bad equilibrium to a good equilibrium

(iii) There are cases where some workers, who want to work under hazardous conditions or without freedom of association, may bring down the available wage rates for those workers who do not want to work under such conditions. This is a case of what economists call 'pecuniary externalities'. If society decides that no one should have to pay a penalty for a preference that he or she wants to follow some work norms (like safety of working conditions or freedom to join unions), there is a case for legal intervention.

(d) We have mentioned before that the churning caused by globalisation causes job anxiety, and some people may actually lose their jobs. What does it imply for the right to work? I do not think there is much moral

---

40 However, unsafe working conditions do breach a number of human rights, as well as non-core ILO Conventions. See above, n 34.

41 See, for example, J Bhagwati, 'Trade Liberalisation and "Fair Trade" Demands: Addressing the Environmental and Labour Standards Issues' 18 *World Economy* 745; K Basu, 'Global Labour Standards and Local Freedoms' in UNU-WIDER (ed.), *WIDER Perspectives on Global Development* (Palgrave Macmillan, New York, 2005) 175, 178.

42 Basu, above n 41.

> or economic basis for the right to work per se. If, for example, I am a horrible worker, and nobody wants to hire me, I should be entitled to some basic economic security (part of the right to life or subsistence), maybe even to facilities and opportunities for job training and information, but not guaranteed job security. There is a lot of confusion on this issue among well-meaning activists.[43]

In conclusion, let us say that in this paper we have pointed to the complexities and ambiguities in the impact of economic globalisation on human rights, both in the matter of extreme poverty as a violation of human rights and of some basic rights of workers. In general, globalisation can cause many hardships for the poor but it also opens up opportunities which some countries can utilise and others do not, largely depending on their domestic political and economic institutions, and the net outcome is often quite complex and almost always context-dependent, belying the glib pronouncements for or against globalisation made in the opposing camps.

---

[43] The General Comment on the Right to Work, issued by the Committee on Economic Social and Cultural Rights in late 2005, confirmed that while States should adopt, as quickly as possible, measures aimed at achieving full employment, article 6 of the International Covenant on Economic Social and Cultural Rights does not recognise an unconditional right to be employed. See General Comment 18: 'Article 6 of the ICESCR', E/C.12/GC/18, paras 6, 19. See also para 27 on the duty of States to provide appropriate technical and vocational education, and para 28 on the provision of informational programmes.

5. Resources, rules and international political economy: the politics of development in the WTO

Kenneth C. Shadlen

1. INTRODUCTION

The Uruguay Round of multilateral trade negotiations, which began in 1986 and concluded with the signing of the 'Final Act' in 1994, marked a watershed in the making of the international political economy. In addition to giving birth to a new international organization,[1] the World Trade Organization ('WTO'), the Uruguay Round introduced binding agreements in new areas that had previously been left out of the international trading regime. While the WTO's predecessor organization, the General Agreement on Tariffs and Trade ('GATT'), addressed national policies in tariffs and non-tariff trade measures, the Uruguay Round addresses policies in a variety of 'trade-related' activities, such as intellectual property ('IP') and investment.

The broadening of the international trade regime to include binding constraints in these new issue areas was fiercely resisted by many developing countries. Yet, despite their resistance to negotiating IP and investment, and the unfavourable nature of the subsequent agreements, developing countries accepted the final outcome. Developed countries' insistence that the Uruguay Round be an all or nothing affair – a 'single undertaking' – meant that developing countries could not approve the Final Act, with its promises of increased access to North American and European markets, the final elimination of the onerous *Multi-Fibre Arrangement*,[2] and the establishment of a more useful system for dispute resolution, without also accepting agreements that imposed new multilateral disciplines on IP and investment (along with other areas, such as services and subsidies and so on).

[1] *Marrakesh Agreement Establishing the WTO*, opened for signature 15 April 1994, 1867 UNTS 3 (entered into force 1 January 1995).

[2] *Arrangement Regarding International Trade in Textiles*, opened for signature 1 January 1974, 930 UNTS 166 (entered into force 1 January 1974).

In the period after the Uruguay Round, the 'North–South' conflicts over IP and investment remain politically charged. Developed countries have sought to secure commitments beyond that stipulated by the WTO. In both policy areas, developed countries were unsatisfied with the settlements reached in the Uruguay Round and sought to impose additional limitations on developing countries' policy options. And in both policy areas developing countries adamantly resisted and successfully turned back these efforts.

How have weak countries managed to prevail in an important international setting like the WTO? To address this question I draw on the insights from two approaches to the study of international political economy ('IPE'), structuralism and institutionalism. The structuralist approach focuses on the distribution of *resources* as the key determinant for explaining international outcomes, while the institutionalist approach focuses on the effects of *rules*. What we see is that, within a broad set of constraints that is determined by the distribution of resources, the rules of the WTO drive the outcomes. In particular, the WTO's rules of unweighted voting and consensus decision-making have inflated developing countries' influence in the post-Uruguay Round setting and allowed them to block the efforts of wealthier countries to impose new constraints on national policy in the areas of IP and investment.

In the second part of the chapter I present these two analytic approaches to the study of IPE, deriving a set of expectations about North–South relations. In Parts 3 and 4 I consider the North–South politics of IP and investment, respectively, both in the Uruguay Round and the post-Uruguay Round period. These issue areas are marked by endemic and underlying sources of conflict, which I highlight in each instance. In both cases we see developing countries blocking developed countries' efforts to impose new international regulations, and in both instances the power that allows developing countries' to 'prevail'[3] is derived from rules and not resources. In the fifth and concluding section, I summarize the findings and I address a subsequent question that logically follows from the analysis: why, if developing countries can block developed countries' initiatives now, were they unable to do so during the Uruguay Round?

Before proceeding, a caveat is in order. Throughout the chapter I refer to 'developed' and 'developing' countries, and I treat them as homogenous

[3] As we shall see, in both instances developing countries blocked outcomes that they regarded as worse than the status quo, so they 'prevailed' by securing the better (less worse) of two outcomes. Yet most developing countries also oppose the status quo, and they have not been able to replace it by achieving agreements on international rules that are more aligned with their preferences. Hence the need to qualify the verb 'prevail'. I address these issues throughout the chapter.

blocks. Doing so is problematic, to say the least, and invites criticisms from all corners. To be sure, not all wealthy countries share the same interests on all issues and nor do all poorer countries; plenty of issues in the international political economy – and even the WTO – are marked by cross-cutting alliances where some coalitions of developed and developing countries are pitted against other coalitions of developed and developing countries. Notwithstanding these observations, it is also true that there exist certain underlying cleavages in the international political economy that are based on income – that countries of different levels of economic development are likely to have different interests in the regulation of the international political economy, and that these differences are the source of persistent and endemic conflict. Indeed, an examination of the politics of the post-World War II international trading system leaves the undeniable sense that the 'North–South' cleavage has been – and continues to be – a prevailing axis of conflict.[4]

2. RESOURCES, RULES, AND NORTH–SOUTH CONFLICT

Traditionally the field of IPE has been organized around the topic of international cooperation and coordination.[5] Scholars have concerned themselves

---

4 See, for example, Jock A Finlayson and Mark W Zacher, 'International Trade Institutions and the North South Dialogue' (1981) 36 *International Journal* 732; Stephen D Krasner, *Structural Conflict: The Third World Against Global Liberalism* (University of California Press, Berkeley, 1985); David A Lake, 'Power and the Third World: Toward a Realist Political Economy of North–South Relations' (1987) 31 *International Studies Quarterly* 217; John Gerard Ruggie, 'Political Structure and Change in the International Economic Order: The North–South Dimension' in J G Ruggie (ed.) *The Antinomies of Interdependence: National Welfare and the International Division of Labor* (Columbia University Press, New York, 1983) 423; Kenneth C Shadlen, 'Patents and Pills, Power and Procedure: The North–South Politics of Public Health in the WTO' (2004) 39 *Studies in Comparative International Development* 76. Diana Tussie, *The Less Developed Countries and the World Trading System: A Challenge to the GATT* (St Martin's Press, New York, 1987); Robert H Wade, 'The Ringmaster of Doha' (2004) *New Left Review* 146.

5 Stephen D Krasner (ed.) *International Regimes* (Cornell University Press, Ithaca, 1983); Kenneth A Oye (ed.) *Cooperation under Anarchy* (Princeton University Press, Princeton, 1986); Arthur A Stein, *Why Nations Cooperate: Circumstance and Choice in International Relations* (Cornell University Press, Ithaca, 1993). For a more recent review of this body of literature, see Vinod K Aggarwal and Cédric Dupont, 'Collaboration and Co-ordination in the Global Political Economy' in John Ravenhill

with how countries with overlapping but non-identical interests and preferences can act collectively. With the basic metaphor being the prisoners' dilemma, where the result of each country striving for its most-preferred choice is an outcome that is worse for all actors than had they cooperated and settled mutually on second-best choices, much of the field of IPE has been constructed around the problem of collective action and the challenges to achieving international cooperation. Thus, a major strand of IPE scholarship was over the dynamics of 'international regimes', the formal and informal arrangements established by countries to establish order and achieve international cooperation.[6]

Scholars of IPE working from varying analytic perspectives offer different solutions to the problem of cooperation. Structuralists (also called 'realists') emphasize the role of dominant countries to either supply public goods and essentially permit others to free-ride on their efforts or to impose order by punishing free-riders.[7] Institutionalists (also called 'liberals') emphasize the cooperation-enhancing effect of information provided by procedures and rules and context.[8] Constructivists focus on the importance of ideas, the emergence of norms, and the role of experts in generating common causal visions of the world.[9] In this chapter I extend the first of these two perspectives, structuralism and institutionalism, to the topic of international cooperation in North–South economic relations.

(ed.) *Global Political Economy* (Oxford University Press, Oxford, 2nd edn, 2007) 67; Lloyd Gruber, *Ruling the World: Power Politics and the Rise of Supranational Institutions* (Princeton University Press, Princeton, 2000); Lisa L Martin and Beth A Simmons, 'Theories and Empirical Studies of International Institutions' (1998) 52 *International Organization* 729.

6 Krasner, above n 5. See also, Aggarwal and DuPont, above n 5; Beth Simmons and Stephan Haggard, 'Theories of International Regimes' (1987) 41 *International Organization* 491; Robert Keohane, *After Hegemony* (Princeton University Press, Princeton, 1984).

7 Stephen Krasner, 'State Power and the Structure of International Trade' (1976) 28 *World Politics* 317; Charles Kindelberger, *The World in Depression 1929–1939* (University of California Press, Berkeley, 1973).

8 Keohane, above n 6; Robert Axelrod and Robert Keohane, 'Achieving Cooperation Under Anarchy: Strategies and Institutions' in Oye, above n 5, 226; Lisa L Martin, 'The Political Economy of International Cooperation' in I Kaul et al. (eds) *Global Public Goods: International Cooperation in the 21st Century* (Oxford University Press, Oxford, 1999) 51.

9 Ernst B Haas, 'Why Collaborate? Issue-linkage and International Regimes' (1980) 32 *World Politics* 357; Ernst B Haas, *When Knowledge Is Power: Three Models of Change in International Organizations* (University of California Press, Berkeley, 1990). See also (1992) 46 *International Organization*, the special issue dedicated to the theme 'Knowledge, Power, and International Policy Coordination'.

In applying regime analysis to North–South relations, the first thing to emphasize is that the metaphor of the prisoners' dilemma – and the underlying assumption of common interests – may not be appropriate for the task at hand. With many of the issues of salience in a North–South context, actors' interests and the larger context of strategic interaction are different from in the traditional IPE approaches noted above. Different types of economic issues have different political characteristics, and the 'deep integration' issues introduced in the UR have different implications for economic development and thus inter-state politics than standard issues of trade.[10] The sorts of rules on IP and investment, for example, that developed countries promote on behalf of their firms are unlikely to be embraced by developing countries, and the sorts of policy approaches that many developing countries would prefer are likely to be resisted by their counterparts in the 'north'. In the subsequent sections I shall explain the underlying cleavages on IP and investment; for now the key point is simply that the distributional conflicts in these issue-areas are more accentuated and intense than in standard IPE frameworks. Indeed, the political challenges are not so much how to achieve collective action but how to reconcile conflicting and often incompatible interests. As many scholars have noted, placing too much attention on how countries achieve international cooperation risks masking the distributive implications of cooperative outcomes.[11] The substantive issue-areas analysed in this chapter call for a focus on the more starkly distributive dimensions of international cooperation.

Structuralists and institutionalists bring different tools and emphases to bear in analysing conflict resolution. The former focus on the distribution of resources as the determinant of countries' strategies and the underlying power differentials among countries, while the latter focus on the constraining effects that rules and context have on countries' strategies and forms of behaviour. Actors have conflicting interests, and those with the most 'power' prevail, of course – but what determines which actors have more or less 'power'? To answer that question, structuralists look at the material resources that actors have at their disposal, and institutionalists emphasize rules and procedures.

---

[10] Nancy Birdsall and Robert Z Lawrence, 'Deep Integration and Trade Agreements: Good for Developing Countries?' in I Kaul et al., above n 8, 128; Stephan Haggard, *Developing Nations and the Politics of Global Integration* (Brookings Institution, Washington DC, 1995); Kenneth C Shadlen, 'Exchanging Development for Market Access? Deep Integration and Industrial Policy under Multilateral and Regional-Bilateral Trade Agreements' (2005) 12 *Review of International Political Economy* 750.

[11] Stephen D Krasner, 'Global Communications and National Power: Life on the Pareto Frontier' (1991) 43 *World Politics* 336; Martin and Simmons, above n 5; Gruber, above n 5.

When applied to conflict between developed and developing countries, the expectations derived from a structuralist approach are rather simple and straightforward. If rich and poor countries have conflicting interests, to the extent that rich countries have more resources (which by definition they do) and thus power, we should expect rich countries' interests to prevail. Thus structuralists expect the international political economy to reflect the interests of the more developed countries.[12]

While the distribution of resources may be a useful predictor of how conflicts will be resolved, it is not without its shortcomings. Actors with more resources obviously do not always impose their will; actors often consent to institutional arrangements (or rules) that mitigate resource differentials and produce outcomes that would be reflective of alternative distributions of power. The question, then, is why actors with more resources would accept institutions that constrain the exercise of their own resources? After all, from a structuralist perspective, such rules distort the 'natural' order of things.

Institutionalists provide an answer to this question by concerning themselves with the reasons why actors want rules in the first place. Actors demand institutions because of the invaluable functions that they perform: institutions reduce transaction costs involved in securing information, monitoring activities, and enforcing compliance. Furthermore, by providing standards of behaviour that demarcate likely patterns of conduct, institutions increase predictability and reduce uncertainty.[13] Actors cannot know what the precise outcome of any given interaction will be, but the array and probability of different scenarios can be anticipated, and this certainty and predictability are cherished.

Integrating these simple observations derived from the structuralist and institutionalist approaches leads to the following implications regarding North–South politics in the international economy. First, and most fundamentally, developed countries write the rules. To paraphrase Krasner, there are 'makers, breakers, and takers'[14] of international institutions: developed

---

[12] Examples of such analyses include Krasner, above n 4; Lake, above n 4; Susan Strange, '*Cave! Hic Dragones*: A Critique of Regime Analysis' in Krasner, above n 5, 337; Robert Tucker, *The Inequality of Nations* (Basic Books, New York, 1987). What drives countries' interests, however, is a further question. Some scholars regard interests as a function of actors' position in the international system, while others focus on how domestic policymaking processes shape national interests and goals.

[13] Examples of prominent institutionalist approaches to IPE that emphasize the uncertainty-reducing role of rules include Keohane, above n 6; Martin, above n 8; Kenneth Abbott and Duncan Snidal, 'Why States Act through Formal International Organizations' (1998) 42 *Journal of Conflict Resolution* 3.

[14] Stephen D Krasner, 'US Commercial and Monetary Policy: Unraveling the Paradox of External Strength and Internal Weakness' (1977) 31 *International Organization* 636.

countries are makers, developing countries are takers (and, at times, breakers).

Yet notwithstanding their prevailing rule-making capacities, developed countries may create and abide by rules that fail to reflect underlying distributions of power in order to secure compliance on the part of developing countries and thereby reduce the costs of monitoring and enforcement. Indeed, the prevalence of information asymmetries, which raise the costs of monitoring and enforcement, gives developed countries incentives to establish rules that encourage self-enforcement. That is, more powerful actors' demand for international rules may lead them to accept, as a side effect, the distorting effects that rules can have on the 'natural' order of things.

Developing countries are likely to accept, and perhaps appear to embrace, even unfavourable agreements because of the stability and predictability that institutions promise to deliver. For developing countries, the principal advantages of – and thus source of demand for – institutions are the provision of predictability and reduction of uncertainty. The stability that comes from knowing what is and what is not acceptable behaviour can help ameliorate some of the vulnerability that marks developing countries' position in the international system. Subjecting interaction to institutions gives actors greater confidence that conflicts will be resolved, if not entirely to their liking at least according to known and recognized procedures. Stability and predictability come at a high price, however. To secure developed countries' formal commitment to mutually-recognized rules, and thus the bounding of the uncertainty that is endemic to weakness, developing countries must accept and adapt to rules and regulations that are generally not of their making. The upshot, then, is that developing countries may demand and seek to strengthen institutions, even institutions with unfavourable distributional effects, to secure stability and predictability. The key point here is that for weak actors, bad rules that are universally acknowledged are better than no rules, for under conditions marked by power asymmetries no rules *are* bad rules – they are simply less predictable, changing with the whims of the more powerful actors, and they do not promise reciprocal constraints. This is not to imply that weak actors do not or should not push for 'better' rules, only to make sense of why they may work to strengthen international arrangements informed by 'bad' rules.

The fact that developed and developing countries all share a demand for institutions, and that the former will tolerate rules that fail to reflect the regnant distribution of resources as the price of securing compliance, provides developing countries with possibilities for exerting unexpected degrees of influence on regime outcomes, even in issue-areas marked by conflict. That is, developing countries may exploit the opportunities created by institutions and achieve more favourable outcomes than they might otherwise be able to secure. However, such a strategy may have decreasing returns if it destabilizes the institutions by diminishing developed countries' respect of and support for such institutions.[15]

In the remainder of this chapter I use these insights to shed light on North–South conflicts in the WTO over IP and investment.

3. POLITICS OF INTELLECTUAL PROPERTY

The management of IP is a critical component of development policy. National strategies for IP influence trajectories of industrial development and capacities to address humanitarian concerns. As pillars of national systems of innovation, IP regimes drive technological change; they affect trajectories of knowledge-creation and knowledge-diffusion. And by affecting access to technologically-intensive goods, such as pharmaceuticals, IP regimes contribute to national public health programs.

To understand the fundamental differences in approach toward managing IP, and hence the underlying conflict in the WTO, a quick review of the issue-area is in order. When governments create intellectual property rights ('IPRs'), they are granting actors rights of exclusion over knowledge and information. National policy responds to two objectives: encouraging the creation and commercialization of knowledge, and encouraging the dissemination and use of knowledge. Granting and protecting IPRs can accomplish the first objective by providing actors with the means – legally enforceable rights of exclusion – to appropriate the returns to their investments in innovation and knowledge production. The catch, however, is that the instrument to achieve the first objective can undermine fulfillment of the second objective, because IPRs – by their very nature – restrict use by converting knowledge into privately owned property where owners set the conditions over use.[16] In sum, IP regimes have two desirable – but unavoidably conflicting – objectives; that knowledge be generated and that knowledge be used.

Structural characteristics that distinguish developed and developing countries generate different perspectives on how to prioritize the quests for generating and using knowledge, thus leading to conflict over international IP rules.

---

15 In his analysis of North–South conflict in the 1980s, for example, Krasner showed that where institutional arrangements allowed developing countries to influence that which was disproportionate to their resources, developed countries simply stopped participating. See Krasner, above n 4. I return to this point in the conclusion.

16 To the extent that legal security derived from IPRs encourages owners to share (that is, license) their knowledge, IPRs may also contribute to knowledge dissemination. Yet where third parties can access knowledge without the help of the owner, the costs imposed on third parties for using knowledge is greater in the presence of IPRs than in their absence.

Wealthier countries, with higher levels of innovative capacity and where more research and development tends to produce new knowledge, have tended to opt for setting incentives to encourage and reward knowledge generation. Poorer countries, in contrast, with lower innovative capacities and where most new knowledge is that which is imported from abroad, have tended to opt for setting incentives to encourage dissemination and use of new knowledge. Thus, wealthier countries have historically offered stronger IPRs than poorer countries.

Prior to the 1980s, the international rules on IP permitted the sort of diversity described in the previous paragraph. In the 1980s and 1990s, however, the developed countries, pushed for a less flexible set of international regulations regarding national IP policies. Importantly, these more stringent regulations would be embedded in the international trade system, thus making developing countries' ability to export goods to developed countries' markets conditional on their treatment of IP.[17]

The hallmark of the effort to link higher standards of IP to trade was the inclusion of the TRIPS Agreement[18] in the Uruguay Round. Many middle-income developing countries were opposed to the integration of IPRs into the GATT and attempted to block negotiations on IP. Yet IP was a high priority for the developed countries (especially the US and European Community) in the Uruguay Round, and developing countries were unable to keep IP off the negotiating agenda.

In the course of negotiating the TRIPS Agreement, developing countries were able to exploit differences between the US, Europe, and Japan, and thereby prevent inclusion of some of the strictest and most egregious restrictions on national policy, but few could disagree with the conclusion that the developed countries prevailed in getting most of what they wanted out of the negotiations.[19] TRIPS dramatically alters the international environment for IP policy, precluding – or at least complicating – the use of many instruments that

---

17 See, among others, Peter Drahos, 'Global Property Rights in Information: The Story of TRIPS at the GATT' 1995 13 *Prometheus* 6; Duncan Matthews, *Globalising Intellectual Property Rights: The TRIPs Agreement* (Routledge, London, 2002); Susan K Sell, *Private Power, Public Law: The Globalization of Intellectual Property Rights* (Cambridge University Press, London, 2003); Kenneth C Shadlen et al., 'The Political Economy of Intellectual Property Protection: The Case of Software' (2003) 49 *International Studies Quarterly* 45.

18 *Marrakesh Agreement Establishing the WTO*, opened for signature 15 April 1994, 1867 UNTS 3 (entered into force 1 January 1995) Annex 1C (*Trade Related Aspects of Intellectual Property Rights*) ('TRIPS').

19 Matthews, above n 17; Jayashree Watal, *Intellectual Property Rights in the World Trade Organization: The Way Forward for Developing Countries* (Oxford University Press (India), New Delhi, 2001).

have historically been used to manage knowledge and technology. With regard to patents, for example, the agreement requires countries to grant patents in areas that many countries previously treated as ineligible for patent protection (for example, pharmaceuticals and chemicals) and places new restrictions on states' ability to issue compulsory licenses.

In the period since the conclusion of the Uruguay Round and the establishment of the WTO, the North–South conflict over IP has been most intense as regards access to essential medicines.[20] The reason for this is that there remained substantial uncertainty regarding just what measures countries were and were not allowed to take with regard to compulsory licenses and parallel imports, legal uncertainty that was exacerbated and compounded by developing countries facing considerable political pressure to *exceed* their new obligations in the area of IP. The principal source of pressure came from the US, which demanded accelerated implementation of TRIPS obligations (that is, forgo transition periods allowed by TRIPS) and discouraged countries from utilizing policy prerogatives (that is, forgo policy measures allowed by TRIPS). The 'TRIPS Plus' campaign is illustrated by considering the treatment of developing countries in the United States Trade Representative's ('USTR') annual Special 301 Reports on IPRs. Throughout the 1990s, developing countries were routinely placed on the Watch List and Priority Watch List for what the US regarded as 'insufficient' protection of intellectual property. In the seven years after the WTO entered into effect, more than half of the countries subject to this pressure were developing countries. Developing countries also accounted for nearly two-thirds of the countries identified on the Priority Watch List. Developing countries often found themselves under threat even when they were behaving in compliance with the Uruguay Round's IPR obligations. In pursuit of higher standards of intellectual property protection, the USTR singled out countries that were in compliance with TRIPS but that, in taking advantage of the agreement's flexibilities, had introduced IPR regimes that the US deemed objectionable. Thus, developing countries often found themselves subject to penalties not for violating TRIPS or even for being too slow in making their IPR regimes TRIPS-compliant, but rather for using the flexibility that TRIPS formally permits – for not adapting 'TRIPS Plus' regimes.

The focal point of the North–South conflict over IP was over compulsory licenses for essential drugs. A compulsory license ('CL') allows a public or private actor to use patented knowledge without the authorization of the owner.[21] Although TRIPS places conditions on countries' ability to issue

20 This discussion draws on Shadlen, above n 4.

21 Article 31 TRIPS addresses compulsory licenses.

compulsory licenses, the agreement does not prohibit the use of CLs. But external pressures certainly discouraged developing countries from taking TRIPS-acceptable measures. Many of the countries included on the USTR's Special 301 lists, for example, were there because of the provisions in their IPR legislation regarding compulsory licenses. And because the US and the major pharmaceutical companies expressed disapproval of the use of flexibilities, countries that took advantage of their rights under TRIPS feared retaliation.[22] Ultimately, this strong opposition to the use of CLs, and prominent statements regarding their alleged illegality, cast a shadow of doubt and uncertainty over an issue that is already marked by high levels of legal complexity. Indeed, as one developing country representative noted, the challenges presented by CLs' legal complexity was greatly exacerbated by external pressures and the uncertainty as to what falls outside TRIPS.[23]

Vulnerability to external pressures prompted developing countries to seek real, and not just formal, flexibilities in IP policy. Developing countries, thus, launched a campaign to secure political space to take advantage of their rights under the agreement.[24] The campaign came to the fore in 2001, with a joint WHO/WTO conference on affordable medicines, two Special Sessions of the TRIPS Council dedicated to the same topic, and the WTO's Fourth Ministerial Meeting in Doha. A coalition of more than fifty developing countries sought to use the Ministerial meeting to affirm their rights under TRIPS – to gain assurances that they could use the TRIPS flexibilities for public health purposes without having to worry about reprisals. To that end, they demanded a Ministerial Statement that would eliminate any outstanding ambiguities and

---

[22] South Africa is the most prominent case, of course, but a number of countries were punished by the USTR (for example, by loss of Generalized System of Preferences ('GSP') benefits) for failing to meet US standards' TRIPS Plus demands.

[23] Comments of Francisco Cannabrava, Brazilian delegate to TRIPS Council, at the meeting of the Commission on Intellectual Property Rights, 'How Intellectual Property Rights Could Work Better for Developing Countries and Poor People', Session 6: Medicines and Vaccines (22 February 2002).

[24] The June 2001 remarks of Thailand's delegate to the TRIPS Council are illustrative of the campaign's demands and the issues at play: '[w]e are all aware that TRIPS provides built-in flexibilities regarding measures WTO members can take to obtain medicines, both patented and non-patented, from the best and cheapest sources, both foreign and local. However, due to lack of clarity of certain provisions of the Agreement, developing countries seem to be reluctant to take measures that they are entitled to under the Agreement. This is very unfortunate, because one of the purposes of the Agreement was to establish an international benchmark for intellectual property protection and to prevent unilateral pressure, as stated in the Preamble [of the TRIPS Agreement]': *Special Discussion on Intellectual Property and Access to Medicines*, WTO Doc IP/C/M/31 (10 July 2001).

uncertainties in TRIPS, and thus shield countries from external pressures that challenged their use of TRIPS-acceptable flexibilities to secure access to essential medicines.[25]

The ensuing statement took the form of the *Doha Declaration on the TRIPS Agreement and Public Health*.[26] The Doha Declaration was brief, a seven-section statement, fewer than two pages long, that was designed to clarify members' obligations and rights under TRIPS. The fourth section, which noted that TRIPS 'does not and should not prevent members from taking measures to protect public health', includes as a separate paragraph the critical affirmation of developing countries' rights 'to use, to the full, the provisions in the TRIPS Agreement, which provide flexibility for this purpose'. The declaration also clarifies countries' rights under Article 31 TRIPS to issue compulsory licenses: 'Each member has the right to grant compulsory licenses and the freedom to determine the grounds upon which such licenses are granted.'

The Doha Declaration marks the culmination of a successful campaign to strengthen the multilateral system, in that it can protect developing countries from opportunistic behaviour of developed countries that pressure for TRIPS Plus.[27] To be sure, the Doha Declaration cannot directly constrain the USTR: nothing agreed at the WTO could guarantee that the US will not continue to subject countries unilaterally to its own TRIPS Plus standards. Yet the Doha Declaration potentially raises the associated political costs of this sort of opportunistic behaviour, for it makes it clear that when the US (or other developed countries) act in this way, they, and not the developing countries, are violating the WTO's rules.[28] It makes it more obvious that when the US pursues an aggressive TRIPS Plus agenda within the WTO, it is undermining and violating its own multilateral commitments. And while such violations may not be effectively punishable at the global level, they may impose reputation costs on violators. In addition, the agreement provides leverage for

---

25 The formal proposal for a declaration was made by the Africa Group in alliance with Bangladesh, Barbados, Bolivia, Brazil, Cuba, Dominican Republic, Ecuador, Haiti, Honduras, India, Indonesia, Jamaica, Pakistan, Paraguay, Philippines, Peru, Sri Lanka, Thailand, Venezuela: WTO Doc IP/C/W/296 (29 June 2001). A number of other developing countries articulated similar positions in the WTO Council without formally endorsing the Africa Group's proposal.

26 WTO Doc WT/MIN(01)/DEC/W/2 (14 November 2001) ('Doha Declaration').

27 Shadlen, above n 4.

28 The US makes the adoption of TRIPS Plus policies a condition for signing regional and bilateral trade agreements ('RBTAs'), for example, but at least in those agreements the US also makes 'WTO Plus' concessions in terms of market access: Shadlen, above n 10.

domestic political actors who attempt to hold government officials to their multilateral obligations.[29]

This analysis speaks to some of the key issues of this chapter regarding resources and rules in the international political economy. Developing countries' ability to push through the Doha Declaration is rooted in the WTO's consensus rule, which allowed them to make the clarifying Ministerial statement a condition for the formal launching of a new round of multilateral trade negotiations. Developing countries blocked the launching of a new round of multilateral trade negotiations in 1999 at the WTO's Third Ministerial in Seattle, and this history could have been repeated two years later in Doha. Consensus meant that developed countries could not proceed with a new trade round without the consent of the developing countries, and developing countries would not provide this consent without the Doha Declaration on TRIPS and Public Health.

Although the rules of the WTO clearly empowered developing countries in this regard, allowing them to secure the clarifying statement on the important issue of TRIPS and health, one must be careful not to overstate the degree of empowerment. After all, what, ultimately, developing countries accomplished was clarification and affirmation of a set of already-existing rules that they only grudgingly accepted in the Uruguay Round. It might very reasonably be suggested that genuine empowerment would allow actors to secure *new* rules that are more in line with their preferences. Indeed, many developing countries may wish to substantially revise – or even abolish – TRIPS, but doing so is clearly beyond their means.

The limits to developing countries' power and influence are illustrated by looking, briefly, at the aftermath of the Doha Declaration. TRIPS permits countries to issue compulsory licenses, a right reaffirmed by the Doha Declaration, but the remaining uncertainty regarded the export of drugs produced under CL. After all, few countries can produce their own pharmaceuticals, so a compulsory license, to be useful, must permit that drugs can be exported from the countries that do have such manufacturing capacity. Here TRIPS did indeed complicate matters, by requiring that compulsory licenses must be 'predominantly' for domestic use (Article 31(f) TRIPS). The Doha Declaration recognized this unresolved business and committed members to finding a solution, and for more than four years addressing this issue consumed the TRIPS Council. Space limitations preclude detailed discussion

29 Andrew P Cortell and James W Davis, Jr, 'How Do International Institutions Matter? The Domestic Impact of International Rules and Norms' (1996) 40 *International Studies Quarterly* 451.

of these negotiations,[30] though what is clear is that developing countries were much less successful here and, ultimately, had to settle for what many observers regard as an unsatisfactory resolution. The reason why is that, in contrast to the issues addressed in 2000–2001, which entailed clarifying TRIPS, to resolve the CL-for-export issue to their liking developing countries would have had to secure *substantive reforms* of TRIPS.[31]

4. POLITICS OF INVESTMENT

Managing inward foreign direct investment ('FDI') has historically been a key point of economic development policy. States regulate international investors, quite simply, because what is best for individual enterprises may not be best for all of society. Even states that are largely neoliberal in orientation, that is, guided by the principle that private actors' autonomous decisions regarding resource allocation are optimal, are likely to regulate international firms, because local subsidiaries of transnational firms do not make resource allocation decisions 'autonomously' but rather in coordination with (if not under control of) their parent firms.

As in the case of IP, the 'North–South' conflict over international investment regulation ('IIR') is rooted in economic structure. Most FDI (roughly eighty per cent) occurs among advanced, industrial economies. Developed countries, thus, approach the area of IIR as capital exporters *and* capital importers: Canada and France regulate foreign investors, for example, and Canadian and French firms are subject to regulations in other countries. Developing countries, in contrast, approach the area of IIR as capital importers: Argentina and Senegal regulate foreign investors but few Argentinean and Senegalese firms are subject to other countries' regulations.[32]

30 Frederick M Abbott, 'The WTO Medicines Decision: World Pharmaceutical Trade and the Protection of Public Health' (2005) 99 *The American Journal of International Law* 317; Duncan Matthews, 'WTO Decision on Implementation of Paragraph 6 of the Doha Declaration on the TRIPS Agreement and Public Health: A Solution to the Access to Essential Medicines Problem?' (2004) 7 *Journal of International Economic Law* 73; Duncan Matthews, 'From the August 30, 2003 WTO Decision to the December 6, 2005 Agreement on an Amendment to TRIPS: Improving Access to Medicines in Developing Countries?' (2006) 10 *Intellectual Property Quarterly* 91.

31 To reinforce the point about developing countries' inability to introduce changes to TRIPS, one could note ongoing – and thus far unsuccessful – efforts to make disclosure of origin in patent applications a requirement or to buttress the system of technical assistance.

32 This is beginning to change, of course, with the rise of trans-national

Furthermore, developed and developing countries' interests as capital importers are not the same either, because of the different roles that FDI tends to play in the local economy. Foreign investors tend to be concentrated in different sectors, use different modes of entry, and account for different shares of investment, production, exports, and so on.

Thus, similar to what we see in the case of IP, structural characteristics lead to differing perspectives on investment and, subsequently, persistent conflict in the area of IIR. Developed countries seek limited regulations on investors, while developing countries have historically sought the right to use policy instruments designed to harness the benefits of FDI. These instruments include, for example, local content requirements, screening entry of foreign investors, equity limitations (that is, making joint ventures compulsory), controls on repatriation of profits and export of capital, and requirements regarding technology transfer and the training of human resources.

Although there is little new about the basic observation that states seek to regulate inward investment and the claim that conflicts over IIR are rooted in structural differences between countries, a set of changes that have occurred since the 1980s have brought increased prominence to the issue-area. From the perspective of developing countries (that is, capital importers), we see a new orientation in the wake of debt and protracted economic crises in the 1980s and 1990s and, subsequently, widespread trade liberalization and privatization. Attracting FDI has become, in most if not all developing countries, one of the primary objectives of economic policy. Countries seek investors as exporters (and, hopefully, purveyors of skills and technologies); countries seek foreign investors as purchasers of privatized state enterprises and suppliers of public services (particularly when, as is often the case in poorer countries, local private actors lack the capital to take over the state's role). Most generally, whereas in the past many governments were wary of FDI and preferred the autonomy that came from borrowing from international banks,[33] in the current environment foreign investors have come to be regarded – and desired – as more stable and less mobile forms of capital inflow. Thus, as countries become more desiring of and dependent on FDI, they are more wary of frightening away potential investors with 'over-regulation', and this changes their approach to the area of IIR.

We also see a change from the perspective of developed countries (that is, capital exporters), in that the nature of FDI in developing countries has

corporations ('TNCs') from developing countries, but this phenomenon is fairly new and remains, in the grand picture, marginal.

33 Jeff Frieden, 'Third World Indebted Industrialization: International Finance and State Capitalism in Mexico, Brazil, Algeria, and South Korea' (1981) 35 *International Organization* 407.

undergone a shift since the 1980s. Whereas FDI had historically been in extractive industries or tariff-hopping manufacturing sectors, the contemporary environment is marked by the proliferation of 'efficiency-seeking' foreign investors seeking to use developing countries as export platforms, and by 'market-seeking' foreign investors taking over formerly state-reserved roles of public service and infrastructure provision. Linked to this change, especially the growth of FDI in public services, are new concerns on the part of investors as they move into sectors that are, by their very nature, more heavily regulated and more vulnerable to expropriation. Also worth noting here is that as *international* operations represent increased shares of some global firms' revenues, the subject of how subsidiaries are regulated becomes more important.

The upshot of these two sets of changes is that the issue of international investment, always a hot topic in 'North–South' international political economy, has gained increased importance. Capital importing countries have become more desiring of and dependent on FDI (and thus wary of potentially frightening investors with 'over-regulation'), and the interest of capital exporting countries has grown on account of the greater number and variety of firms with a stake in the rules of IIR.

Now let's turn to analysis of the North–South politics of IIR in the GATT and WTO. As in the case of IP, investment was a domain where countries historically retained a great deal of policy autonomy; and as in the case of IP, the 1980s would witness an effort by developed countries to embed a more restrictive set of rules on investment regulations in the international trade regime. Here too the Uruguay Round provided the setting, as developed countries (again, the US as lead demandeur) pushed for an agreement that would restrict countries' abilities to impose investment regulations on foreign firms.[34]

The history of the TRIMS Agreement[35] shares many features with the history of the TRIPS Agreement, in that developing countries first resisted inclusion of any negotiations at all (arguing that investment was not 'trade-related'), and second, when unsuccessful in keeping the issue off the Uruguay Round agenda, strongly resisted the content of an agreement that threatened to

---

[34] In fact, earlier in the 1980s, prior to the launch of the Uruguay Round, the US lodged a GATT dispute against Canada over the latter's foreign investment regulations. Specifically, the US claimed that Canada's local content requirements, which demanded that firms source a given percentage of their inputs from local suppliers, constituted a non-tariff measure that illegally restricted trade. The US won the case, and then sought to generalize the ruling with an agreement on investment in the Uruguay Round.

[35] *Marrakesh Agreement Establishing the WTO*, opened for signature 15 April 1994, 1867 UNTS 3 (entered into force 1 January 1995) Annex 1A (*Trade Related Investment Measures*) ('TRIMS').

impinge negatively on their autonomous economic policy prerogatives.[36] Where the two histories differ, however, is that in the area of investment, developing countries were much more successful at exploiting differences among developed countries and diluting the final agreement. To understand this, it is important to appreciate the breadth of the investment agreement that the US initially sought in the Uruguay Round: the US negotiating objectives extended significantly beyond local content requirements per se, and included binding regulations on a wide array of investment policies. Indeed, the US sought to restrict specific policies, regardless of their demonstrated effects on trade. Not surprisingly, developing countries actively resisted such a broad agreement, and the Uruguay Round's investment negotiations were marked by deadlock. Eventually a compromise was reached to limit the agreement to policies with direct effects on trade.[37]

The subsequent TRIMS Agreement is a fairly narrow agreement in that it addresses, as the name suggests, 'trade-related' investment measures, while leaving countries with significant degrees of latitude regarding investment regulation more generally. After all, the agreement does not offer a precise definition of what a 'trade-related investment measure' is, nor does it establish criteria for identifying such measures. The agreement simply provides examples of prohibited regulations in the form of an 'illustrative list' in the appendix, which countries are expected to identify and eliminate. Beyond the measures explicitly included in the appendix, however, TRIMS lets countries determine what is and what is not a 'trade-related investment measure', and, critically, which of their investment measures need to be retired. Investment measures that do not violate national treatment or impose quantitative restrictions on firms' imports and exports are legal. Thus, states can screen entry of foreign firms, for example, and demand joint ventures or require foreign firms to transfer technology to local firms. And states can regulate foreign investors' hiring practices, with the aim of enhancing development of human capital and skills. Even under the more restrictive international regime on investment, developing countries can continue to use standard and time-honoured investment regulations as instruments of industrial promotion.

---

36 Mohamed Ariff, 'TRIMs: A North–South Divide or a Non-Issue?' (1989) 12 *World Economy* 347; V N Balasubramanyam, 'Putting TRIMs to Good Use' (1991) 19 *World Development* 1215; David Greenaway, 'Why Are We Negotiating on TRIMs?' in David Greenaway et al. (eds) *Global Protectionism* (Palgrave Macmillan, London, 1991) 145; United Nations Development Program, *Making Global Trade Work for People* (Earthscan, London, 2003) Ch 12.

37 The compromise was based on a proposal made jointly by Colombia and Switzerland, which focused on assessing the direct trade effects of investment measures, and not the measures themselves.

To be sure, the agreement does outlaw key investment regulations that have been at the heart of many countries' development strategies, most importantly local content requirements, which demand investors to source their inputs locally, and also trade and balancing requirements, which oblige foreign investors to include sufficiently high levels of domestic inputs in exports to offset imported inputs. Both of these regulations aim to generate backwards linkages from foreign investors to local manufacturers, and outlawing them clearly takes away developing countries' ability to use important policy instruments to increase local value-added, employment, and industrial upgrading. Yet while it would be unwise and inappropriate to downplay the significance of these particular – and now prohibited – policy instruments, one cannot help but note that TRIMS is significantly less restrictive than its advocates originally sought (and certainly less restrictive and intrusive than TRIPS). In fact, some of these prohibitions enshrined in TRIMS actually predate the Uruguay Round. For example, it was under the GATT that local content rules were deemed illegal.[38]

Developed countries' dissatisfaction with the outcome achieved in the TRIMS negotiations could be seen in the immediate aftermath of the conclusion of the Uruguay Round. No sooner was the new WTO established, than developed countries sought to re-initiate negotiations in pursuit of a more broad-based international investment agreement. Developed countries (now the EU more than US) made investment a high priority at the WTO's Second Ministerial Meeting in Singapore in 1996. Once again, however, developing countries opposed this effort, and the North–South cleavage on investment that marked the Uruguay Round remained evident in the post-Uruguay Round setting. Developed countries sought a broad-based agreement, more akin to the investment chapter in the *North American Free Trade Agreement*[39] and the many bilateral investment treaties ('BITs') that were proliferating in the 1990s, which proscribe a wide range of investment measures; developing countries, seeking to hold the line at TRIMS, attempted to keep investment off the negotiating agenda. The compromise settlement was to create a WTO

---

38 The reference here is to the US challenge to local content requirements in Canada's sectoral automotive policy: above n 34. It is also worth noting that many developing countries, as part of their autonomous liberalization processes and efforts to attract FDI in new sectors for *export*, were already removing many regulations on foreign investors. In fact, some countries – independently of the WTO – now present investors with completely different sets of incentives in the form of preferential tax treatment on *imported* inputs. Thus, instead of regulating foreign investors to promote local suppliers, many countries now promote foreign investors' exports at the expense of local suppliers.

39 Opened for signature 17 December 1992, 32 ILM 289; 32 ILM 605 (entered into force 1 January 1994) ('NAFTA').

Working Group on Trade and Investment ('WGTI'), which would continue to study the issue.[40]

Before proceeding to a discussion of the deadlock's resolution (or not), it is worth underscoring some of the underlying factors that contributed to the North–South stalemate over investment. Most obviously and most directly, this was a disagreement over the policy flexibility and developing countries' rights and capacities to regulate inward FDI. The TRIMS agreement may have been inadequate from the perspective of capital-exporting countries, but few capital importers were likely to agree to a project that would make binding regulations more restrictive. Moreover, even developing countries that may have had few reservations regarding the substantive dimensions of such an agreement, that is, governments that are 'neoliberal' in orientation and unilaterally removing the sorts of provisions that would be prohibited by such an agreement, had ample reasons to oppose the inclusion of a broad-based investment provision in the WTO. Many countries complained of negotiation and implementation 'overload' and, critically, asymmetric risks of exposure to dispute settlement. Beginning negotiations on investment means yet another issue where countries need to find the resources to participate, and any subsequent agreement would lead to yet one more WTO standing body where countries would need to be represented. Moreover, since the subsequent rules would be binding on governments in capital-*importing* countries, what developing countries would be consenting to would be a legal framework in which they would find themselves more likely than not in the position of defendant.[41]

When the Doha Round was formally launched in November 2001, investment was included on the agenda (of the Ministerial Declaration, [20]–[22]). The declaration recognized countries' fundamental right to regulate investors and declared that were any negotiations to occur they would proceed on the basis of a 'positive list' (like the GATS),[42] meaning that countries put forward the sectors where they are prepared to negotiate. Yet, notwithstanding these substantive concessions, developing countries (for reasons alluded to in the previous paragraph) were not prepared to negotiate. Indeed, as a result of the strong resistance of a coalition of developing countries led by India and

---

[40] It was in response to the perceived inadequacy of TRIMS and the failure to launch new investment negotiations at the Singapore Ministerial that many came to regard the OECD as a more appropriate forum, and negotiations soon began in that forum on a 'Multilateral Agreement on Investment' ('MAI').

[41] Note that in 1997 India (and later, in 2002, a handful of other developing countries) did propose also regulating the behaviour of firms and TNCs' home governments, but these proposals had little traction and were not taken seriously.

[42] *Marrakesh Agreement Establishing the WTO*, opened for signature 15 April 1994, 1867 UNTS 3 (entered into force 1 January 1995) Annex 1B (*General Agreement on Trade in Services*) ('GATS').

Malaysia (the 'Like-Minded Group'), the Ministerial Declaration also stipulated that negotiations on investment would proceed only on the basis of 'explicit consensus'. That is, in contrast to ordinary WTO rules of implicit consensus, which requires a country to actively dissent to block consensus (and thus encourages negotiations in closed 'green room' sessions), the explicit consensus rule for investment required all WTO members to actively consent to taking negotiations forward.

By the time of the WTO's Fifth Ministerial Meeting in Cancún in 2003, the WGTI had received nearly fifty submissions,[43] but the precise mandate of Ministers remained unclear. Many developed countries (especially the EU) interpreted the Doha Ministerial Declaration such that the requirement was for explicit consensus on the 'modalities' (that is, the basic terms of agreement). To that end, the Canadian facilitator for negotiations on investment (and all the 'Singapore Issues'), attempted to push forward, on the basis of the submissions received by the WGTI, and reach agreement on modalities. Developing countries resisted both this interpretation of the Doha Ministerial Declaration and the efforts of the Canadian chair, insisting that without explicit consensus negotiations could not even proceed. Indeed, a coalition of sixty developing countries formally opposed negotiations in the absence of the 'explicit consensus', and, ultimately, refused to negotiate. This refusal, which is what Smythe refers to as 'just saying no', contributed to the end of the Cancún Ministerial and meant that investment was effectively removed from the Doha Round agenda.[44] While, at the time of writing (July 2008), the future of the Doha round as a whole is uncertain, whatever comes out of the negotiations will almost certainly not include investment. TRIMS, for better or worse, is and will remain the WTO status quo for the foreseeable future.

The ability of developing countries to block investment negotiations was a function of the WTO's rules. The Doha Round would not begin if any country objected (negative consensus rule), so India could condition its authorization of the 2001 Ministerial Declaration on the inclusion of what amounted to a 'poison pill' in the area of IIR. This is a clear instance of institutions providing actors with power and influence that are disproportionate to their underlying resources.

Yet, as 'victories' go, this is a rather limited outcome. From a development perspective, TRIMS only looks good when contrasted to what the developed countries sought in the Uruguay Round, sought in the MAI, included in many bilateral investment treaties (and investment chapters of RBTAs), and in

[43] Elizabeth Smyth, 'Just Say No! The Negotiation of Investment Rules at the WTO' (2003) 33 *International Journal of Political Economy* 70, Table 1.

[44] Ibid.

proposals made to the WGTI.[45] Developing countries have been able to ward off 'more unfavourable' outcomes, but they have not been able to secure outcomes in line with their preferences. They could not revise the TRIMS Agreement, as many sought, by placing binding obligations on investors and home countries and restoring the right to use some investment measures that were prohibited during the Uruguay Round. In short, they could prevent a bad situation (namely TRIMS) from getting worse, so to speak, but they remain unable to fashion an outcome that matches – or even approximates – their preferences. Developing countries lack the power to accomplish that goal.

5. CONCLUSION

In reviewing the North–South politics of IP and investment, I have shown how institutional arrangements – in particular the consensus rules of the WTO – can give weaker actors more power and influence than we might expect from simply reading off the underlying distribution of resources. After all, developed countries are stronger and, subsequently, a structuralist approach would lead us to expect them to be able to impose their preferences. Yet they have not: for all their efforts to rewrite the rules regarding IP and investment in the post-Uruguay Round period, they have not succeeded. Developing countries – weak as they may be – have seen to it that the WTO's rules on IP and investment are essentially the same in 2008 as they were at the conclusion of the Uruguay Round in 1994. This finding represents a clear tick in the institutionalists' column.

Yet all the power developing countries have exercised has been essentially 'blocking' power. In both instances, developing countries would like to introduce more substantive reforms, both to TRIPS and TRIMS, but have been unable to do so. Instead they settle for clarification of rules that most countries strongly objected to in the first place and for preventing the imposition of what many regard as even more unfavourable rules. Developing countries have been able to prevent (or at least limit) the imposition of rules that exceeded what they agreed to in the Uruguay Round, either by clarifying the rules and thus creating a check on unilateral pressures (IP) or preventing additional multilateral negotiations (investment). What they have been unable to do,

45 For another analysis of developing countries' blocking power in the area of international investment negotiations, see Eduardo Plastino, *Investments and the WTO* (MSc Dissertation, Development Studies Institute, London School of Economics, 2008).

however, is act proactively – to secure agreement on new WTO rules that are more to their liking.[46]

Of course, the ability of developing countries to block developed countries' initiatives in the areas of IP and investment only begs the more critical question of why, if they can do this now, they could not do it before and stop these agreements in the first place. Or to put it differently, if developing countries can prevent the unfavourable Uruguay Round agreements from being supplanted by a set of more unfavourable Doha Round agreements, why could they not prevent the more favourable Tokyo Round agreements from being supplanted by the unfavourable Uruguay Round agreements? After all, they did try: as discussed, developing countries opposed TRIPS and TRIMS in the Uruguay Round, just as they oppose developed countries' TRIPS-Plus and TRIMS-Plus initiatives in the contemporary environment. Why did they acquiesce to the former but block the latter? The answer to this question gets to the heart of the analysis, and in particular the interface between institutionalist and structuralist approaches. Addressing this question, then, sheds light on both the importance and limitations of international institutions.

The existence of a 'single undertaking' is frequently invoked as an explanation for why developing countries accepted TRIMS and TRIPS in the Uruguay Round. In previous rounds, countries chose whether or not to sign on to supplemental codes, but the single undertaking meant that the Uruguay Round was an all or nothing affair. But that explanation is unsatisfactory without considering the exercise of power that made the introduction of this institutional device feasible and, moreover, effective. After all, the single undertaking itself was new – an institutional reform introduced to gain developing countries' consent to agreements that they had resisted.[47]

The key to making the single undertaking work was to make the WTO the only game in town. That is, the way to get developing countries to accept a set of Uruguay Round agreements that they had fiercely rejected was to make the alternative to acceptance being excluded from the international trade regime. But how to do that? After all, many developing countries were already members of the GATT, which offered most-favoured-nation ('MFN') access to the developed countries' markets. Any tariff reductions made in the Uruguay Round, then, would have to be granted on a MFN basis to GATT members, even if they rejected TRIPS and TRIMS. Thus the key would be to eliminate the GATT from the shadows of the WTO.

---

[46] As I have argued elsewhere, bad rules may be better than no rules – but they are still bad rules! See Shadlen, above n 4; K. Shadlen, 'Intellectual Property, Trade, and Development: Can Foes be Friends?' (2007) 13 *Global Governance* 171.

[47] Richard Steinberg, 'In the Shadow of Law or Power? Consensus-Based Bargaining and Outcomes in the GATT/WTO' (2002) 56 *International Organization* 339.

At the end of the Uruguay Round, all countries who participated in the negotiations signed the 'Final Act' and thus became signatories to all the various WTO agreements. One of the texts included in the Final Act was the GATT 1994, a new agreement that incorporated – but superseded – the GATT 1947. The Uruguay Round's Final Act stipulates that GATT 1994 is 'legally distinct' from GATT 1947. Most importantly – and this is the frequently overlooked point – immediately upon joining the WTO (including GATT 1994) the US and EC both withdrew from GATT 1947, thus terminating their obligations under GATT 1947.[48] Any country that did not sign Uruguay Round's Final Agreement and join the WTO would, formally, retain their rights under GATT 1947, but since the largest countries with the most important markets were no longer bound by GATT 1947, non-joiners would be left with empty rights. The result of this is that MFN-based market access is only available to countries that joined the WTO, thereby consenting to TRIPS, TRIMS, GATS, the *Agreement on Subsidies and Countervailing Measures*,[49] and so on.

This review of how developed countries exercised power to create an institutional device (the single undertaking) that would secure a favourable outcome of the Uruguay Round remains relevant for the subsequent analysis of the Doha Round that I have discussed in this chapter. The case of IP and investment negotiations in the Doha Round shows how unweighted voting and the consensus system give developing countries unexpected power. The WTO's decision-making procedures inflate developing countries' power; institutions are endowing countries with influence that they would otherwise lack in the absence of these rules. Developing countries could condition the launch of a new round of multilateral trade negotiations, which developed countries had sought since 1996, on an agreement that would draw the line under TRIPS Plus demands, and they could make sure that the subsequent round did not include negotiations on investment.

The key point, however, is that we see this power-enhancing effect because the WTO already exists, and, in contrast to the early 1990s, no one is (yet – but see below) talking about effectively replacing the WTO with a new international trade institution. In other words, the 'power play' described by Steinberg is not being replicated.[50] In the Uruguay Round, developing countries were weakened because a new organization was created that supplanted the existing organization, which meant that the consequences of blocking conclusion would have been to be left out in the cold, not in the new WTO and

---

48 Ibid.

49 *Marrakesh Agreement Establishing the WTO*, opened for signature 15 April 1994, 1867 UNTS 3 (entered into force 1 January 1995) Annex 1A (*Agreement on Subsidies and Countervailing Measures*).

50 Ibid 360.

members of an old – and now essentially useless – GATT 1947. In the current environment, however, the consequences of blocking conclusion of the Doha Round is maintenance of the status quo. Developing countries' power, albeit only 'blocking power', is derived from the fact that they are in the WTO and cannot be excluded or expelled from it.

This discussion speaks to Gruber's insights that some countries might sign agreements that they do not like because the alternative is not the status quo but something worse than the status quo – and that more powerful countries with resources to 'go it alone' can present weaker countries with this new choice set.[51] Such dynamics help explain the conclusion of the Uruguay Round, and their absence helps explain the persistent deadlock in the Doha Round. Developing countries have less to fear in the current setting because developed countries are no longer exercising what Gruber refers to as their 'go it alone power'. As a result, obstinate resisters are not left facing something worse than the status quo.

To conclude, it is worth questioning the sustainability of the scenario. Developing countries' newfound influence in international trade negotiations is derived from the institutional setting, but for that very reason the power is extremely fragile. Institutions that generate outcomes that deviate far from what might be expected from the underlying distribution of resources are unstable.[52] Developed countries closed one institution and created another in the 1990s. Would they do that again? Legally they can: withdrawing from GATT 1994 is as simple as withdrawing from GATT 1947 was. Yet there is little evidence of any schemes to replace the existing international trading regime with a new one. Perhaps the proliferation of regional agreements is a movement in that direction, a de facto (if not explicit) effort to leave the WTO and create a new WTO-plus world that those developing countries on the outside will feel compelled to join – just as developed countries left GATT 1947 and created a new GATT-plus world that resisters to the Uruguay Round felt compelled to join. There are sound reasons to question the viability of regional and bilateral strategy, but just raising it as a possibility speaks to the fragility of rule-based power and the undying importance of the distribution of resources in the shaping of the international economic order.

---

[51] Gruber, above n 5.

[52] Krasner, above 4.

6. International economic justice: is a principled liberalism possible?

Patrick Emerton

Ted Honderich writes:

> What is a good life? For a start, a good life is one that goes on long enough [. . .] Some people, because of their societies, have average lifetimes of about seventy-eight years. Some other people, because of their different societies, live on average about forty years [. . .] [M]any people in the second group, those people who pull its average down to forty [. . .] have *half-lives at best* [. . .] The first group are in fact the populations of the United States, Canada, the United Kingdom, France, Germany, Italy, Spain, Denmark and Japan. The second group are the populations of the African countries of Malawi, Mozambique, Zambia and Sierra Leone.[1]

Honderich's figures are drawn from the *The World Guide 2001–2002*. The figures in the 2005–2006 edition show that those in the first group have average life expectancies of 78.6 years, those in the second group 36.2 years.[2] Less than half-lives.

Radical differences in life expectancy are not all there is to this radical inequality; Thomas Pogge, for example, draws our attention to the obvious cause of half-lives, and of much other suffering as well, namely, extreme poverty.[3] Whatever facts we take to best exemplify this inequality, such human suffering is plainly a matter of deep moral concern. But a consideration of life expectancies, or of inequalities of wealth and income, does not tell us exactly how, at the intellectual level, we should understand the problem in relation to

---

[1] Ted Honderich, *After the Terror* (Edinburgh University Press, Edinburgh, 2002) 1, 6.

[2] Life expectancy figures are found in the tables labelled 'Health', and population figures used to calculate an appropriately weighted average are found in the table labelled 'Demography': *The World Guide 2005–2006* (New Internationalist Publications/Institute del Tercer Mundo, Oxford, 2005) 602–6. The figures are attributed to *World Population Prospects – The 2002 Revision*, UN Doc ESA/P/WP. 180 (23 February 2003).

[3] Thomas W Pogge, *World Poverty and Human Rights* (Polity Press, Cambridge, 2002) 99–100.

our own circumstances and fields of action. *What sort of response (if any) does the problem demand from us?* This chapter addresses this question. Its central contention is that we cannot meet the moral challenge posed by the radical inequality between the inhabitants of different countries without addressing the international regime in which it arises, and asking whether this regime is consistent with the fundamental moral entitlements of the poor – what we shall see below can be characterised as their human rights. Given that the World Trade Organization ('WTO') is an important part of this international regime, its rules and practices are unavoidably implicated in this question of human rights satisfaction.

1. SUFFERING CAUSED BY POVERTY: A MORAL PROBLEM WITH POLITICAL DIMENSIONS

A. Singer's Argument

In his well-known 'Famine, Affluence and Morality', Peter Singer advances the following argument:[4]

S1 The average consumer in a developed country could give a substantial portion of his or her wealth and income for the relief of poverty without having to sacrifice anything of moral significance.[5]

S2 The relief of poverty would prevent many deaths among the world's poor from lack of food, shelter, and medical care.[6]

Therefore,

S3 It is within the power of the average such consumer to prevent many deaths without sacrificing anything of moral significance.

---

[4] Peter Singer, 'Famine, Affluence and Morality' (1972) 1 *Philosophy and Public Affairs* 229. The quasi-syllogistic rendering of Singer's argument in the text is mine.

[5] To support premise *S1*, Singer identifies as expendable expenditure meals in fine restaurants, beach holidays, cruises, home redecorations, new cars, new clothes not necessary for warmth, and 'spending on trivia' in general: ibid 235, 241; Peter Singer, 'Introduction' in P Singer, *Writings on an Ethical Life* (Fourth Estate, London, 2000) xvi; 'The Singer Solution to World Poverty' in P Singer, ibid 119, 123.

[6] Singer states premise *S2* for the special case of the 1971 Bengal emergency: Singer, above n 4, 229. The more general premise is implicit in the argument of his paper.

S4 To prevent these deaths would be to prevent something very bad from happening.

S5 If it is in a person's power to prevent something very bad from happening, without thereby sacrificing anything morally significant, that person ought, morally, to do so.[7]

Therefore,

S6 The average consumer in a developed country ought to give a substantial portion of his or her wealth and income for the relief of poverty.

As Singer notes, this simple argument nevertheless has radical implications.[8] If it is sound, then the consumer society that exists in developed countries is inconsistent with the bulk of its members' fundamental moral obligations: '[W]e would have to give away enough to ensure that the consumer society, dependent as it is on people spending on trivia rather than giving to famine relief, would slow down and perhaps disappear entirely'.[9]

Singer's argument turns on one factual premise and three moral ones. I do not think that premises *S2* (the factual premise) or *S4* are very controversial.[10] It is premises *S1* and *S5* that have been the subject of philosophical debate since Singer first put forward his argument, and this chapter will return to them.

First, however, we should note a certain respect in which Singer's conclusion is not radical. It states a moral obligation of each wealthy person to *give*, but says little about the *entitlements* of the poor. The very notion of 'giving' appears to presuppose an entitlement on the part of the giver, up until the point at which the property is actually transferred; only then would it become the

---

7 Premise *S4* and the crucial moral premise *S5* are stated ibid 231. *S4* is asserted without argument, but presumably none is needed – *S4* appears to be self-evidently true.

8 Ibid 236.

9 Ibid 241. Singer notes that wealthy countries would need to ensure that their economies do not slow down to such an extent that they fail to produce as much to give away as would stronger economies: ibid 241–2. This point is also noted by David Schmidtz, 'Islands in a Sea of Obligation: Limits of the Duty to Rescue' (2000) 19 *Law and Philosophy* 683, 701–2; Robert N Van Wyck, 'Perspectives on World Hunger and the Extent of Our Positive Duties' (1988) 2 *Public Affairs Quarterly* 75, 85.

10 Both appear to be presupposed by the Millennium Development Goals set forth in the *United Nations Millennium Declaration*, GA Res 55/2, UN GAOR, 55th sess, 8th plen mtg, UN Doc A/Res/55/2 (8 September 2000).

recipient's.[11] Thus, Singer does not seem to conclude that the wealthy's wealth is somehow illegitimate, nor that the wealthy in some manner deprive the poor of what is rightfully theirs. In a subsequent essay on the same topic Singer characterises the wealthy as 'not having initiated the chain of events imperilling' the poor,[12] apparently excluding the possibility that the wealthy in some active fashion deprive the poor.[13]

B. The Importance of Institutions

Singer's failure to reach a more radical conclusion is a little surprising, because in support of his own view he quotes Aquinas:

> [M]aterial goods are provided for the satisfaction of human needs. Therefore the division and appropriation of property, which proceeds from human law, must not hinder the satisfaction of man's necessity from such goods. Equally, whatever a man has in superabundance is owed, of natural right, to the poor for their sustenance [. . .] 'The bread which you withhold belongs to the hungry; the clothing you shut away, to the naked; and the money you bury in the earth is the redemption and freedom of the penniless'.[14]

Not only does Aquinas canvass the entitlements of the poor; having suggested that the wealthy are literally (and not merely metaphorically) stealing from the poor, Aquinas offers the following further remarks (not cited by Singer) canvassing institutional arrangements for the relief of poverty:

> But because there are many in necessity, and they cannot all be helped from the same source, it is left to the initiative of individuals to make provision from their own wealth, for the assistance of those in need. If, however, there is such urgent and evident necessity that there is clearly an immediate need of necessary sustenance – if, for example, a person is in immediate danger of physical privation, and there is no other way of satisfying his need – then he may take what is necessary from another person's goods, either openly or by stealth. Nor is this, strictly speaking, fraud or robbery.[15]

---

11 There is an obvious contrast here with 'returning', 'restoring' or 'making good'.

12 Singer, 'The Singer Solution', above n 5, p 120.

13 This contrasts markedly with Pogge's view: above n 3, 117, and see Part 2B below.

14 Thomas Aquinas, *Summa Theologica*, II-II, Question 66, Article 7, in A P d'Entrèves (ed.) *Aquinas: Selected Political Writings* (Basil Blackwell, Oxford, J G Dawson trans, 1970 edn) 171, cited in Singer, above n 4, 239 (Singer cites the 1948 imprint).

15 Aquinas, above n 14. It can be objected that the existence of multiple equally good claimants, not all of whose claims I can satisfy, makes it impossible to do my

In Aquinas's view, for reasons of efficiency, private control of wealth distribution is to be preferred. In extreme cases, however (including presumably the prospect of a mere half-life), self-help is legitimate.

By considering not only the moral obligations of the wealthy, but also the entitlements of the poor, and an institutional order which might satisfy these, Aquinas presents the problem of poverty as having a political dimension. Not that Singer is ignorant of the institutional implications of his own position, as the passage canvassing the end of consumer society illustrates. But he does not take these political matters to be relevant to the moral question. They are simply side-effects of individuals complying with their own moral obligations.

There are two reasons why Aquinas is right to present the problem of poverty as having an important political dimension, and Singer wrong to have ignored it. The first is itself a moral reason. As Aquinas notes, the existence of wealth and poverty is intimately bound up with the institution of property, which recognises entitlements to various things in various people (or, if you prefer, confers those entitlements upon them), while prohibiting others from accessing or using those very same things; this distribution of entitlements is the foundation of production, trade and consumption. As Aquinas's reference to 'human law' indicates, institutions are conventional, the products of human habit and decision. These habits and decisions, and the institutions to which they give rise, are proper subjects of moral inquiry. When it comes to the institution of property, the inquiry would ask whether the entitlements that *are* recognised (or conferred) are those which *ought to be*. When it comes to the institution of property, furthermore, the inquiry is mandatory: even if the wealthy do not have any doubts about the legitimacy of the current institutional regime – which at the international level includes the rules and practices of the WTO – the poor may well.

Focusing on the institution of property also avoids two standard objections to Singer's argument. Consider again premise *S5*, that a person who has the power to prevent something very bad from happening, without thereby sacrificing anything morally significant, ought to do so. It is often argued that, if the bad thing that will happen was not brought about by me, then while it might be admirable for me to try and prevent it, I have no obligation to do so,

---

duty, because in choosing to help one I sacrifice others whose claims are of equal moral importance: Karen Green, 'Distance, Divided Responsibility and Universalizability' (2003) 86 *The Monist* 501, 506–7. In such circumstances, however, determining who will benefit by drawing lots (or some equally impartial method) is surely sufficient: see J J C Smart, 'Extreme and Restricted Utilitarianism' in Michael D Bayles and Kenneth Henley (eds) *Right Conduct: Theories and applications* (Random House, New York, 1983) 107; J J C Smart, 'A System of Utilitarian Ethics' in J J C Smart and Bernard Williams (eds) *Utilitarianism: For and Against* (Cambridge University Press, Cambridge, 1973) 57.

or at least, no obligation of the sort that institutional arrangements might take up and enforce.[16] This argument against *S5*, coupled with the claim that the poverty of the poor was not caused by the wealthy, leads to the conclusion that there is no general obligation of the sort Singer asserts.[17]

A different argument to the same conclusion begins from the thought that I have no moral obligation to relieve the suffering of those distant from me.[18] Coupled with the (often asserted, if perhaps implausible) idea that the poor are far from the wealthy, this leads to the conclusion that the wealthy have no general duty to aid the poor.

But both of these objections to Singer presuppose the legitimacy of existing proprietary arrangements. Thus, suppose we concede that *S5* is, in general, false: there is no duty on *A* to aid *B* where *B*'s suffering was not caused by *A*, at least when *B* is far from *A*. It does not follow from such a concession that *A* has no duty to restore to *B* that which is in *A*'s possession, but which is rightfully *B*'s.[19] Until we have determined what sort of property regime is morally defensible, we cannot be certain what is *A*'s and what is *B*'s; in our case, that is, what properly belongs to the rich, and what to the poor.

The second reason for imputing a political dimension to the problem arises, initially, out of a practical consideration. As Singer himself notes, on the assumption that his argument is sound, it is likely that many people who have an obligation to devote a substantial part of their income to the relief of poverty will not do so:

> If it is the case that we ought to do things that, predictably, most of us won't do, then let's face that fact head-on [. . .] If we don't do it, we should at least know that we are failing to live a morally decent life – not because it is good to wallow in guilt but because knowing where we should be going is the first step towards heading in that direction.[20]

But it is no comfort to the suffering poor that the comfortable rich are aware of their moral failings, and resolving to do better in future – for a moral conclusion to have practical significance, it must be acted upon. It is no good

---

16 Robert Nozick, *Anarchy, State and Utopia* (Blackwell, Oxford, 1974) 28–34, 169–73, 265–68; Jan Narveson, 'We Don't Owe Them a Thing! A tough-minded but soft-hearted view of aid to the faraway needy' (2003) 86 *The Monist* 419, 420–1.

17 Ibid.

18 F M Kamm, 'Does Distance Matter Morally to the Duty to Rescue' (2000) 19 *Law and Philosophy* 655.

19 This point is made for the particular case in which *A* is in possession of property stolen from *B* by Van Wyck, above n 9, 79–80.

20 Singer, 'The Singer Solution', above n 5, 123–4. See also ibid, 122; Singer, above n 4, 238, 242–3.

waiting for the wealthy to act individual by individual: some sort of institutional solution is essential to systematise what would otherwise be the vagaries of individual behaviour.

This practical consideration connects to a moral one, namely, the truth (or otherwise) of Singer's premise *S1*. This claim, that the average consumer in a developed country could give a substantial portion of his or her wealth and income for the relief of poverty without having to sacrifice anything of moral significance, has been widely contested by those who defend an 'agent-centered' account of moral obligation and permissibility:

> It is commonly thought that one has a moral prerogative to give greater weight to one's own interests and projects rather than giving equal weight to oneself and to others . . . This prerogative, while agent centered, is not fundamentally egoistic [. . .] The prerogative gives us a permissible option, not a duty, to act from a non-impartial perspective.[21]

If this is correct, then a significant devotion of wealth and income to poverty relief might well entail the sacrifice of something of moral significance, namely, the wealthy person's living of his or her own life, and devotion of his or her efforts, as he or she chooses.[22] This thought becomes especially plausible when we note that no single person is able to solve the problem of poverty.[23] One can envisage a lifetime being spent working harder and harder, earning more and more money, to be used for the relief of poverty and not for the worker's own life beyond the provision of necessities.[24]

An institutional solution can meet this objection. Instead of wealthy individuals facing open-ended moral obligations, institutions can allocate responsibilities such that everyone contributes his or her fair share and no more,[25] and only those who wish to devote their lives to the problem of poverty need do so (as administrators, campaigners, etc). Singer rejects the notion that one's obligation stops at the provision of a fair share, on the grounds that if others who ought to contribute are not doing so, then more lives can be saved without anything of moral significance being sacrificed.[26] But an institutional solution

---

21 Kamm, above n 18, 675–6.

22 See Green, above n 15, 503–4; Schmidtz, above n 9, 690; Van Wyck, above n 9, 82; Narveson, above n 16, 425, 430 (who expresses the point in terms of others not being entitled to my time and effort).

23 It does not therefore follow that individual efforts are futile, as Green suggests: above n 15, 506, 514. At least some poor individuals would benefit from such efforts even if there were many others, equally in need, who did not.

24 Schmidtz, above n 9, 691–3.

25 Van Wyck suggests that one's individual obligation should be limited to a fair share of the burden: above n 9, 82.

26 Singer, above n 4, 233.

can bring it about that everyone who should contribute does so (typically by generating coercive incentives to comply, as illustrated by the levying of taxation to provide for public services and welfare). Of course, not every institutional order will achieve this; Aquinas's suggestion, for example, has no way of ensuring that everyone who ought to actually does contribute, and its response to the inadequacies this will engender is the completely ad hoc one of self-help on the part of the poor. This chapter will not canvass in any detail what an effective institutional solution might look like, but the next two sections will consider some of the constraints that an institutional order must meet – and in particular, what sorts of obligations and entitlements any such order must recognise (or, if you prefer, confer) – if it is to constitute a satisfactory solution to the moral problem of poverty.

2. COSMOPOLITAN VERSUS SOCIAL LIBERALISM: COMPETING THEORIES OF INTERNATIONAL JUSTICE

A. Why Liberalism?

It is natural to call this moral problem of poverty, understood as having an important political dimension, the problem of international economic justice: *international*, because it involves comparisons and dealings across national boundaries; *economic*, because it concerns the generation and distribution of wealth and income; *justice*, because it concerns the proper entitlements of both rich and poor.

There are many interesting and well-developed philosophical theories of justice – far too many for this chapter to canvass! For three reasons, this chapter will consider only *liberal* responses to the problem of international economic justice. The first reason is purely contextual: the majority of my audience likely hold political views of a broadly liberal character, and thus may be interested in the implications of those views for this problem.

This assumption about my audience is not ungrounded: liberal theories identify political commitments implicit in the existing international institutional order. Gerald Gaus characterises liberalism as 'first and foremost, about individual liberty',[27] while John Rawls characterises a liberal polity as one which assigns a special priority to certain familiar rights, liberties and opportunities, and which also includes measures to ensure that all citizens have

27 Gerald F Gaus, *Contemporary Theories of Liberalism* (Sage Publications, London, 2003) 1.

adequate means to make intelligent and effective use of their freedoms (in Rawls's view the absence of such measures would permit excessive and unreasonable inequalities to develop, undermining some citizens' capacity to take advantage of their freedoms, and thus undermining the reciprocity between citizens that is implicit in liberalism).[28] With these conceptions in mind, both the international human rights system and the international economic order can plausibly be seen as fundamentally liberal in character: the preambles to the *Universal Declaration of Human Rights*,[29] the *International Covenant on Civil and Political Rights*[30] and the *International Covenant on Economic, Social and Cultural Rights*[31] proclaim that 'recognition of the inherent dignity and of the equal and inalienable rights of all members of the human family is the foundation of freedom, justice and peace in the world,' while the preamble to the *Marrakesh Agreement Establishing the WTO*[32] expresses the desire to reduce barriers to trade, and resolves to build on past trade liberalisation efforts, for the purpose of raising standards of living. This, then, is a second reason to focus on liberal theories of international economic justice.

A third reason for such a focus arises from the international distribution of wealth and power. As things stand, with the exception of China the dominant countries in the world (and all those in the first of Honderich's two groups of countries)[33] profess to be liberal democracies. Liberal theories can therefore be seen as attempts to work out the commitments inherent in these societies' professed political values.[34] This is important if these societies, and their members, are to act consistently with those values. It is also important because the poor lack the power to compel the rich. Any institutional changes will have to be initiated by the rich themselves, who will be motivated only by arguments that speak to their own concerns and convictions.

Even within the confines of liberal theory there are numerous accounts of international economic justice.[35] The fundamental theoretical cleavage,

---

28 John Rawls, *Political Liberalism* (Columbia University Press, New York, rev ed, 1996) 5–6, 156–7; *The Law of Peoples, with 'The Idea of Public Reason Revisited'* (Harvard University Press, Cambridge, 1999) 14, 49.

29 GA Res 217A (III), UN Doc A/810, 71 (1948) ('UDHR').

30 Opened for signature 16 December 1966, 999 UNTS 171 (entered into force 23 March 1976).

31 Opened for signature 16 December 1966, 999 UNTS 3 (entered into force 3 January 1976).

32 *Marrakesh Agreement Establishing the WTO*, opened for signature 15 April 1994, 1867 UNTS 3 (entered into force 1 January 1995).

33 Above, text at n 1.

34 *The Law of Peoples*, above n 28 5–10; Pogge, above n 3, 25.

35 Charles R Beitz surveys recent thought in 'International Liberalism and Distributive Justice: A Survey of Recent Thought' (1999) 51 *World Politics* 269–96; 'Social and Cosmopolitan Liberalism' (1999) 75 *International Affairs* 515–29.

however, is between *cosmopolitan* and *social* liberalism.[36] Pogge is a leading exemplar of the former approach, Rawls of the latter, and this chapter will therefore consider only their competing accounts, using them to illustrate a deep tension in liberal thinking on the topic.

B. Pogge's Cosmopolitan Liberalism

Pogge characterises *moral cosmopolitanism* in the following way: 'every human being has a global stature as the ultimate unit of moral concern'.[37] *Cosmopolitan liberalism*, then, holds that each individual is entitled to live within a just liberal social order, with no moral distinction being drawn between the international and the domestic realm: questions of international justice are to be settled simply by a consideration of the claims and interests of each individual person affected.[38]

Cosmopolitan liberalism need not hold that individuals should conceive of themselves as citizens of the world, need not advocate abandonment of familial, national and other non-cosmopolitan loyalties and responsibilities,[39] and is consistent with the view that a division of the world into states is the best, or the only realistic, institutional structure through which international justice may be realised.[40] Its commitment is simply to individualism as the basis for the moral evaluation of institutions.

Pogge works out his cosmopolitan liberalism by starting with the UDHR,[41] and in particular Article 28 UDHR: 'Everyone is entitled to a social and international order in which the rights and freedoms set forth in this Declaration can be fully realized.' He derives from this an *institutional understanding* of what it means to enjoy a human right to some good *G*: Any institutional order

---

36 The terminology is Beitz's: 'Social and Cosmopolitan Liberalism', above n 35, 515; 'International Liberalism and Distributive Justice', above n 35, 272. The 'laissez-faire' liberalism identified by Beitz as a third and distinctive liberal conception of international distributive justice appears to be simply a species of cosmopolitanism, as it takes individuals, each possessing a right to an equal share of the world's resources, to be the pre-eminent rights-bearers at the international level: 'International Liberalism and Distributive Justice', above n 35, 280–6.

37 Thomas W Pogge, 'Cosmopolitanism and Sovereignty' (1992) 103 *Ethics* 48, 49.

38 Beitz, 'Social and Cosmopolitan Liberalism', above n 35, 519.

39 Ibid.

40 Ibid; Charles R Beitz, 'Rawls's Law of Peoples' (2000) 10 *Ethics* 669, 681.

41 As Beitz notes, 'Most cosmopolitan theories hold that a more or less expansive subset of the human rights of the declaration yields a reasonable proxy for standards of global justice': 'International Liberalism and Distributive Justice', above n 35, 288. Pogge is distinctive in drawing on the UDHR not only for the content of human rights thought, but for a theory of its structure.

should be designed so that all those whose conduct is constrained by the order in question enjoy secure access to *G*.[42]

Individuals and their governments thus have a correlative duty 'to work for an institutional order and public culture that ensure that all members of society have secure access to the objects of their human rights.'[43] Applied to economic rights, it follows that:

> [A] coercive order must not avoidably restrict the freedom of some so as to render their access to basic necessities [as set forth in Article 25 UDHR] insecure [. . .] If it does, then all human agents have a [. . .] duty [. . .] not to cooperate in upholding it unless they compensate for their cooperation by protecting its victims or by working for its reform [. . .] Each member of society, according to his or her means, is to help bring about and sustain a social and economic order within which all have secure access to basic necessities.[44]

This moral claim, together with the empirical claim that there exists an *international* economic order, entails that everyone (including every member of a wealthy society) is obliged to work towards an international institutional order in which everyone (including every member of a poor society) has secure access to basic necessities. Conversely, enjoying the benefits of institutions which have extreme poverty as the foreseeable outcome for many participants, without taking steps to redress that poverty, is a grave breach of moral duty.[45]

(The discussion above of Singer's premise *S5* suggested that, even if *A* has no obligation to relieve *B*'s suffering in general, *A* nevertheless may be under an obligation to *B* if *A* is either proximate to *B*, or the cause of *B*'s suffering, or in possession of that which is rightfully *B*'s. On Pogge's account of human rights, the latter two matters – that is, the causation of suffering and distributive justice – are intimately related, for on Pogge's account an institutional allocation of entitlements to *A* and *B* is just only if it does not involve *A* cooperating (via the mediation of institutions) in the deprivation of *B*, or vice versa).

---

[42] This summarises Pogge's four-step unpacking of Article 28 UDHR: above n 3, 64–5.

[43] Ibid 65.

[44] Ibid 67, 69.

[45] Ibid 67, 134, 170–1. The empirical claim is crucial, as 'the *global* moral force of human rights is activated only through the emergence of a *global* institutional order': ibid 171 (emphasis original). Pogge defends the claim that we live within 'a global scheme of social institutions' in 'Cosmopolitanism and Sovereignty', above n 37, 51. See also Thomas W Pogge, *Realizing Rawls* (Cornell University Press, Ithaca, 1989) 246–8, 250–1, 255–6; Charles R Beitz, *Political Theory and International Relations* (Princeton University Press, Princeton, 1979) 149–153.

Pogge has two arguments supporting the conclusion that our actual international economic order engenders a great deal of poverty. The first is that no one could, with any confidence, suggest that those poor who currently lack access to sufficient food, clean water, clothing and shelter would not be better off in a 'pre-institutional state of nature', in which all share equally in the world's natural resources, than subject to the current global economic order which forces them 'to observe the property rights that others assert over all the wealth of this world'.[46]

The second argument focuses on particular aspects of the international order.[47] For example, the international agreements that determine the distribution of the benefits of production and trade are slanted strongly in favour of wealthy societies and their members,[48] and not by accident, but because of imbalances in negotiating capacity resulting from inequalities both of expertise and of power.[49] Consistently with his cosmopolitanism, Pogge does not accept as a defence of such negotiating tactics that the governments of these countries have a special duty to their own citizens, or at least not one which permits violation of the rights of foreigners not to be burdened by unjust economic institutions.[50] (Pogge does not claim that it is inevitable that such imbalances of expertise and power must produce unjust consequences. Rather, and as we noted earlier in this chapter,[51] the existence of these imbalances means that justice is possible only if those with power refrain from using it to establish and uphold a regime that is unjust. In the context of international negotiations, that means not pressing every negotiating advantage in the pursuit of national self-interest when the foreseeable outcome of achieving marginal material benefits for the wealthy is the death and further impoverishment of many other human beings.)[52]

Pogge also notes that the international legal rules governing the recognition of governments are, on the whole, indifferent to the manner in which a government comes to or retains power: dictators as well as democrats may deal in the

---

46 Pogge, above n 3, 16, 138–39.

47 Ibid 15–23, 112–16, 124–6, 141–4.

48 Ibid 17–20 (referring to the WTO agreements, and in particular to the disparities in their treatment of the sorts of things typically exported by poor and by rich countries, such as agricultural goods on the one hand, and complex manufactures and intellectual property on the other), 125–6 (referring to the *Agreement Relating to the Implementation of Part XI of the United Nations Convention on the Law of the Sea of 10 December 1982*, opened for signature 28 July 1994, 33 ILM 1309 (entered into force 28 July 1996)).

49 Ibid 18–20, 187.

50 Ibid 129–39, 144–5.

51 See Part 2A above.

52 Pogge, above n 3, 18–20.

resources of their country and acquire debts in its name, spending the money acquired in their own interests (including the preservation of their own rule) rather than those of their people. This generates an incentive for coups and civil wars, deprives people of control over their own resources, and burdens them with liability for debts from which they never derived any benefit.[53] Pogge draws an explicit comparison to theft:

> A group that overpowers the guards and takes control of a warehouse may be able to give some of the merchandise to others, accepting money in exchange. But the fence who pays them becomes merely the possessor, not the owner, of the loot. Contrast this with a group that overpowers an elected government and takes control of a country. Such a group, too, can give away some of the country's natural resources, accepting money in exchange. In this case, however, the purchaser acquires not merely possession, but all the rights and liberties of ownership, which are supposed to be – and actually *are* – protected and enforced by all other states' courts and police forces [. . .] How can there be a moral difference between paying the Saudi clan or General Sani Abacha – the Nigerian strongman who kept the winner of the annulled 1993 election in jail and has executed numerous political opponents – and stealing the oil outright?[54]

In all these cases, the institutional order could be different – that is, the terms of international economic agreements, and the international legal rules pertaining to the recognition of authority to sell and borrow, could be other than what they are – such that less poverty would result.[55] It is thus grossly unjust, and all of us who participate in it have a duty to change it, and in the meantime to compensate its victims.

C. An Internal Objection to Cosmopolitan Liberalism

Pogge's argument has many attractive features. While agreeing with Singer that world poverty is a moral problem of the first order, Pogge, like Aquinas, presents poverty as not only a moral but a political problem, focusing on the institutional order that engenders widespread extreme poverty, and on the resulting political duties of individuals: it is not simply a matter of individual moral obligation, but of the sort of institutional order that the poor are entitled to and the wealthy obliged to support. This avoids what might otherwise be objections to Singer's premises *S1* and *S5*, by putting limits on what each wealthy individual owes the poor (namely, support for just institutions, and compensation in the meantime) and by explaining the relevant sense in which the wealthy cause the suffering of the poor (namely, by imposing an unjust

53 Ibid 112–15, 141–3.
54 Ibid 113, 142 (emphasis original).
55 Ibid 19, 115.

institutional order upon them). Furthermore, the account's grounding directly in the UDHR makes it apt to enjoy support among internationally minded members of wealthy societies, for many such persons hold the UDHR in high regard.

But what about those who do not share this regard, or who are not inclined to read the UDHR in Pogge's liberal, individualist way? Many people in the world are not liberals; many, indeed, see liberal individualism as a cultural threat. Many of the world's poor probably fit this description. Does it matter that they do not accept Pogge's argument, even though they might agree with his conclusion?

This question highlights a complexity in the link between liberalism and democracy. Rawls states that a liberal polity 'protects the familiar basic rights' of each member,[56] thus presenting liberalism as a democratic political ideal. But what grounds this ideal? One possibility is Locke's contention that individuals are naturally equal and free to act and to order their affairs as they wish, provided only that each respects the like liberty of others;[57] institutions are thus legitimate only to the extent that they help ensure this natural freedom.[58]

This account is democratic in one sense, positing as moral ideals the equality of all human beings, and the dependence of legitimate institutions upon preservation of their equal liberty. But these moral ideals are not themselves derived via any democratic route; rather, Locke infers them from (what he takes to be) our status as creations of the divinity: having been put here by God at His pleasure to do His work, we are obliged to preserve both ourselves and one another.[59] A polity founded on such theological considerations, which included atheists, or adherents of traditions very different from Locke's own, would therefore be *undemocratic* in one important respect: its constitutional foundations could not enjoy the support of those members, even if (as a practical matter) they accepted the liberties accorded to them. In this sense, it could not be *their* polity or *their* constitution. And such a polity would, in its very foundations, violate the liberal commitment to toleration of, and political neutrality as between, the diverse traditions and beliefs of its members.

---

56 Above n 28.

57 John Locke, *Two Treatises of Government* (Cambridge University Press, New York, Peter Laslett ed., 1963) 309, 311.

58 Ibid 395–99, 402–3, 406–7. Locke focuses particularly on the institution of government, which removes the need, if rights are violated, for each to be the judge and enforcer in his or her own case, a situation apt to produce rather than to resolve conflict: ibid 316–17, 395–7, 404–5. He also regards consent to government as a necessary condition of its legitimacy, and notes that an illegitimate government may be justly overthrown: ibid 374–5, 460–2.

59 Ibid 311.

Rawls's later writings are acutely aware of this issue, and attempt to ground liberalism not in controversial morality or metaphysics, but in the common commitments of the political culture of our actual existing liberal democracies. Rawls identifies as the core of these a commitment to the free equality of all members of society as participants in a reciprocal scheme of social co-operation. He describes this ideal as enjoying the support of an *overlapping consensus* of the various moral, religious and philosophical doctrines that are to be found within our liberal polities (a *consensus*, because it enjoys the support of these diverse views, but *overlapping* because while each doctrine supports the subject-matter of the consensus, the reasoning that constitutes that support is different for each).[60]

Unlike Locke's approach, this way of grounding liberalism gives effect to freedom and equality not only in its conclusions, but in the process whereby it reaches them. Rawls characterises it as 'appl[ying] the [liberal] principle of toleration to philosophy itself'.[61] But its democratic character means that it simply has nothing to say to adherents of doctrines which do not support the ideal of members of society as free and equal participants in a reciprocal scheme of social co-operation, and which therefore cannot participate in the overlapping consensus.

Rawls labels the adherents of such doctrines who are members of liberal societies *unreasonable*, because they refuse to accept the lesson that history has taught to members of liberal societies (whether that history be the Wars of Religion in early modern Europe, or the sectarian divide between Australian Catholics and Protestants that lasted much of last century), that in such polities, under conditions of freedom, doctrinal pluralism is inevitable (Rawls calls this *the fact of reasonable pluralism*). The unreasonable, who deny reasonable pluralism and are thus prepared to use state power to impose their doctrines upon others, cannot be accommodated within liberal democracy, and if liberal democracy is to endure and thrive they must be contained.[62]

But the same attitude cannot be taken towards members of non-liberal societies who adhere to doctrines that cannot participate in the overlapping consensus. For the fact of reasonable pluralism is a state of affairs whose recognition is historically emergent. For members of liberal societies, it is an

---

60 John Rawls, 'Justice as Fairness: Political not Metaphysical' in S Freeman (ed) *John Rawls: Collected Papers* (Harvard University Press, Cambridge, 1999); *Political Liberalism*, above n 28, 11–15, 49–50, 133–72.

61 *Political Liberalism*, above n 28, 10, 154.

62 Ibid, xviii–xx, 36–7, 50, 54, 60–1, 64, 136–7; Rawls, above n 60, 390, 412; John Rawls, *Justice as Fairness: A restatement* (Belknap Press, Cambridge, 2001) 33–4; Rawls, *The Law of Peoples*, above n 28, 16, 87, 124; 'The idea of public reason revisited' in *The Law of Peoples*, above n 28, 151–2.

undeniable truth revealed by a common history. But other societies have different histories. For them reasonable pluralism may not be a recognised truth at all.[63] In such societies, liberal arguments will be unable to gain purchase, and to impose liberal ideals upon them would be contrary to liberalism's own commitment to toleration (just as we saw Locke's theologically grounded liberalism to be). If liberalism is to honour its own commitments, it must therefore tolerate non-liberal societies.[64]

This recognition of the full implications of the liberal commitment to toleration is the starting point for Rawls's social liberalism, as worked out in *The Law of Peoples*. It also entails the rejection of Pogge's cosmopolitan liberalism, because an institutional order founded upon Pogge's principles would simply impose upon non-liberal societies a liberal individualist interpretation of the UDHR which does not enjoy the support of those societies' own political cultures. Let us therefore turn to Rawls.

D. Rawls's Social Liberalism

Whereas cosmopolitan liberals take the subjects of international justice to be individuals, social liberals advance a two-level conception of international society: the world is divided into a multiplicity of societies, and the aim of international justice is to establish conditions under which these can flourish. Individual societies, in turn, have primary responsibility for the well-being of their members.[65]

At first blush, social liberalism can appear conservative, even reactionary, especially if one reads 'states' in place of 'societies'. Many progressive international lawyers regard states as lingering anachronisms that are impediments to, rather than at the centre of, international justice,[66] and *The Law of Peoples* has been subject to extensive criticism of this sort: Rawls has been accused of paying an excessive regard to the existing claims of states and state sovereignty, of thereby both failing to recognise the realities of contemporary international relations and of paying insufficient regard to the moral claims of

---

63 David A Reidy, 'Rawls on International Justice: A defense' (2004) 32 *Political Theory* 291, 307–8.

64 Rawls, *The Law of Peoples*, above n 28, 11–12, 59–62, 82–4, 121–3.

65 Beitz, 'Social and Cosmopolitan Liberalism', above n 35, 515, 518; 'International Liberalism and Distributive Justice', above n 35, 272. Beitz regards Rawls as the pre-eminent exponent of social liberalism: 'International Liberalism and Distributive Justice', above n 35, 273; 'Social and Cosmopolitan Liberalism', above n 35, 518–19.

66 A recent example of an anti-statist theorisation of international law is Robert McCorquodale, 'An Inclusive International Legal System' (2004) 17 *Leiden Journal of International Law* 477–504.

individuals and of groups that are (or are apt to be) ignored by states.[67] But Rawls himself defends social liberalism as necessary to avoid ethnocentrism, and to show that a liberal account of international justice can accommodate a wide variety of human communities, animated by and exemplifying quite different values and communal ideals, including non-liberal, non-individualist ideals.[68]

In the previous sub-section, we noted that once the principle of toleration is applied to philosophy itself, the shared history and political culture of a society play a central role in any attempt to ground political ideals. In a liberal society these underpin the overlapping consensus in favour of free equality; and it is because of the different histories and cultures of non-liberal societies that it would be inconsistent with liberal commitments to impose liberal ideals upon them. But we did not explain what it means for the members of a particular society to share a common history and political culture. Rawls addresses this question in *The Law of Peoples*; the key concept he uses is that of a 'people'.[69]

Rawls has two reasons for identifying the subjects of international justice as 'peoples' rather than as 'nations' or 'states'.[70] First, he wishes to signal a departure from the Westphalian doctrine of sovereignty, and to avoid the attribution to these subjects of such aspects of Westphalian, pre-twentieth-century sovereignty as an unlimited right to wage war and an unlimited degree of state autonomy with respect to internal matters.[71]

---

67 The general tone of this criticism is best summed up by the title of Allen Buchanan's paper, 'Rawls' Law of Peoples: Rules for a Vanished Westphalian World' (2000) 110 *Ethics* 697. Other examples include Beitz, above n 40, 679–81; 'Social and cosmopolitan liberalism', above n 35, 521–5; Onora O'Neill, 'Bounded and Cosmopolitan Justice' in K Booth et al. (eds) *How Might We Live? Global Ethics in the New Century* (Cambridge University Press, Cambridge, 2001) 46, 50–1, 59; Thomas W Pogge, 'An Egalitarian Law of Peoples' (1994) 23 *Philosophy and Public Affairs* 195, 206; 'Rawls on International Justice' (2001) 51 *The Philosophical Quarterly* 246, 248; John Tasioulas, 'From Utopia to Kazanistan: John Rawls and the Law of Peoples' (2002) 22 *Oxford Journal of Legal Studies* 367, 377–9; Fernando R Téson, 'The Rawlsian Theory of International Law' (1995) 9 *Ethics and International Affairs* 79, 85.

68 *The Law of Peoples*, above n 28, 59–62, 121–2.

69 Unfortunately, Rawls's exposition and argument in *The Law of Peoples* is not always as clear as it might be. This sub-section should therefore be read as a reconstruction of the argument implicit in that work.

70 This use of 'peoples' is a departure from his earlier terminology of 'nations': *A Theory of Justice* (Harvard University Press, Cambridge, 1971) 377–9.

71 *The Law of Peoples*, above n 28, 25–9. As Rawls notes, this is consistent with the general trend of international law since World War II: ibid 27.

Second, and more importantly, Rawls attributes to peoples a moral character – a coherent personality and a capacity for moral conduct – that he believes cannot be attributed to (all) states.[72] A people is to be conceived of as having an internal government in a defined territory,[73] and as being united by common sympathies (whether derived from a common language, a shared political culture or shared historical memories).[74] The fundamental interests of a people therefore include the protection and conservation of its territory so it will sustain its members in perpetuity;[75] the safety, security and well-being of its members;[76] the preservation of its political independence, political institutions and political culture;[77] and self-respect, which depends upon a people's sense of its history and cultural accomplishments (that is, the same bases as its common sympathies), upon the justice and decency of its domestic institutions, and upon the receipt of proper respect, including a recognition of equality, from other peoples.[78] Importantly, and unlike a (Westphalian) state, a people is able to extend such respect to other peoples, and to recognise their equality.[79] A liberal democratic people, for example, achieves self-respect by living under a legitimate government, and is not swayed by 'the passion for power and glory', by the excitement or pride of conquest, or by the yearning for 'a place in the sun'.[80] Other peoples also have their sense of self-respect satisfied by the endurance and example of their own institutions, and do not seek conquest or domination.[81]

Not every society, and not every state, will constitute a people in this sense, because only under certain sorts of governmental arrangements will it be the case that social cohesion rests not on force or other compulsion, but rather upon common identity and sympathies, manifested in a common political

---

72 Ibid 23, 27.

73 Ibid 3, 38–9.

74 Ibid 24–5.

75 Ibid 8, 29, 34, 38–9.

76 Ibid 29, 34, 69.

77 Ibid 29, 34, 69. Rawls does not use the phrase 'political culture', but simply describes the political cultures of liberal and non-liberal peoples: ibid 29, 34, 69.

78 Ibid 34–5, 47–8, 61–2. The phrase 'justice and decency' must be read distributively and not collectively across peoples: the self-respect of liberal peoples rests upon the justice of their institutions (*justice*, in Rawls's view, being the pre-eminent virtue of liberal political institutions), while the self-respect of non-liberal peoples rests upon the decency of their institutions (*decency* being used by Rawls to characterise the type of legitimacy enjoyed by the domestic institutions of non-liberal peoples: below, text at n 85ff). The self-respect of a liberal people also rests upon the freedom and integrity of its citizens: ibid 47.

79 Ibid 35.

80 Ibid 47.

81 This is implied by Rawls, if not expressly stated: ibid 64, 69.

culture and sense of self-respect. Furthermore, and conversely, it may be possible for a people to exist in this sense although it does not enjoy statehood at international law.[82]

Rawls himself identifies two different categories of peoples: liberal and decent but non-liberal. 'Liberal peoples', he says,

> [H]ave three basic features: a reasonably just constitutional democratic government [that is, one that conforms to Rawls' account of liberalism[83]] that serves their fundamental interests; citizens united by [. . .] 'common sympathies'; and [. . .] a moral nature [that is, they are prepared to offer fair terms of co-operation to other peoples, and to honour those terms when assured that others will do likewise].[84]

Rawls's characterisation of decent non-liberal peoples is more sketchy. He offers only the example of a decent hierarchical society,[85] in which citizens are recognised as members of groups that play particular roles in the overall system of social co-operation, and public life is conceived of in terms of membership of and interaction among these groups.[86] The institutional order of such a society encourages pursuit of certain professed aims or special priorities (whether religious or secular),[87] but it also includes a decent consultation hierarchy in which each group is represented,[88] which tempers the controlling and directive force of the other institutions. (Rawls describes the ideal behind such an institutional arrangement as a 'common good idea of justice'.[89] He also emphasises the importance of participation in the consultation hierarchy of historically oppressed groups such as women.[90]) A decent consultation hierarchy allows different and dissenting voices to be heard. The officials overseeing the hierarchy respect the right of dissent, and conscientiously reply to dissenting views from the reasonably and sincerely held position that the law that they administer is indeed guided by the society's common good idea of justice.[91]

---

82 Reidy, above n 63, 314 (FN14), suggests as examples the Palestinians, the Kurds and the Navajo. Whether or not one accepts these particular examples, they show that it is wrong to say, as for example O'Neill does, that 'in reality the only peoples who have well-defined and controlled boundaries and capacities to negotiate with outsiders on a sustained and reasonable basis are peoples with states': above n 67, 51.

83 Above n 28.

84 *The Law of Peoples*, above n 28, 23, and see also 24–5.

85 Rawls canvasses the possibility of other decent political arrangements, but does not identify any: ibid 63–4.

86 Ibid 64, 66, 71–3.

87 Ibid 64, 71, 77.

88 Ibid 63–4, 71–3, 88.

89 Ibid 65, 71, 88.

90 Ibid 75, 110.

91 Ibid 66–7, 72, 88. A decent hierarchical society regards its members as rational moral agents: ibid, pp 66, 71.

In part because they are adopted within this consultative framework, the laws of a decent hierarchical society are not experienced by its members as commands imposed by force, but are accepted as fitting with the society's common good idea of justice.[92] And a decent hierarchical society does not have aggressive aims. However much it may seek international influence in order to spread its own idea of justice, it recognises and respects the independence of other societies, including their religious and civil liberties.[93]

According to Rawls both liberal peoples and non-liberal decent peoples respect human rights.[94] *Human rights* he defines as a special class of urgent rights that are the necessary conditions of any system of genuine social co-operation,[95] including:

- The right to life (including the right to the means of subsistence, to minimum economic security, and to security against genocide);[96]
- The right to freedom from torture and cruel, degrading treatment or punishment;
- The right to freedom from slavery, serfdom, and forced occupation;
- The right to personal property;
- The right to sufficient (but not necessarily equal) liberty of conscience to ensure freedom of religion and thought, including the peaceful practice of minority religions free from fear;
- The right to formal equality (that is, similar cases are treated similarly);[97]
- The right of peoples to self-determination;
- The right to emigrate (with assistance provided where feasible, at least to members of religious minorities) and to seek asylum;
- The right to personal privacy;
- The right to be governed by laws that are not mere commands imposed

---

92 Ibid 65–7, 71, 77, 88.

93 Ibid 64, 88.

94 Ibid 5, 65, 68–9.

95 Ibid 68, 79. Their regular violation is described as 'command by force' and slavery: ibid 65, 68.

96 John Tasioulas suggests that a society might be decent, and yet distribute its wealth such that, for some of its members, it satisfies the right to subsistence only to the most minimal level; but he himself notes that this would likely be inconsistent with the society being animated by a common good idea of justice implemented via a decent consultation hierarchy: 'Global Justice Without End?' (2005) 36 *Metaphilosophy* 3, 17. See also Reidy, above n 63, 313 (FN7). Further reason to think that the possibility that Tasioulas canvasses is not a real one is provided by Rawls's account of the duty of assistance between peoples, discussed in the text at n 112, below.

97 The above six human rights are all expressly identified by Rawls as such: *The Law of Peoples*, above n 28, 65–6, 74, 79, 80 (FN23).

by force, but can be embraced as fitting with one's conception of justice;[98]

- The right to participate in government; this includes the rights of historically oppressed groups, such as women, to have their claims taken into account.[99]

Rawls excludes certain other rights that are typically regarded as human rights as mere 'liberal aspirations', or as presupposing specific institutional arrangements:[100]

- The universal equality of human beings, in relation to freedom, dignity and rights;
- The rights to freedom of association and to freedom of expression;[101]
- The rights to political equality and to equal liberty of conscience;[102]
- The rights to social security and to education;
- The rights to equal pay for equal work, and to paid leave.

---

[98] Rawls expressly mentions both the right to emigration and the right of peoples to self-determination, without explicitly identifying them as human rights: ibid, 61, 71–2, 74, 85, 111. The latter right is also built into the fundamentals of the law of peoples: below, text at n 109.

The right to personal privacy and the right to seek asylum are both characterised by Rawls as genuine human rights: *The Law of Peoples*, above n 28, 80 (FN23), endorsing Articles 12 and 14 UDHR.

The right to be governed by legitimate laws is expressly mentioned by Rawls: ibid 65–7. It is also implicit in his endorsement of Articles 6, 7, 8, 9, 10 and 11 UDHR: ibid 80 (FN23). It is also a natural extension of his suggestion that command by force amounts to a slave system which provides grounds for resistance and rebellion: ibid 66, 68.

[99] This follows directly from the way that peoples guarantee the right to live under legitimate laws (liberal peoples through civil and political rights together with a guarantee of adequate means to make use of these freedoms, non-liberal decent societies through their political practices, such as a decent consultation hierarchy).

[100] The exclusion of some of these is implicit in the contrast between liberal democracy and the political structure of decent non-liberal peoples. Others are expressly excluded, or are found in the articles of the UDHR that Rawls denies set forth genuine human rights: ibid 80 (FN23). Of course, nothing in Rawls's account of international justice prevents like-minded peoples from covenanting with one another to uphold a more extensive list which includes such rights: Reidy, above n 63, 311, 318–9 (FN52).

[101] A certain degree of freedom of association will be an element of freedom of conscience: John Rawls, 'The Law of Peoples' in S Shute and S Hurley (eds) *On Human Rights* (Basic Books, New York, 1993) 68.

[102] Rawls expressly notes that a decent hierarchical society may have a favoured religion, and may confine certain positions of political authority to the adherents of that religion: *The Law of Peoples*, above n 28, 75.

Rawls's list of human rights has therefore been criticised for being unduly truncated.[103] But such a judgement cannot be made until we understand the reasons behind it. Unfortunately, Rawls does not make these entirely clear.[104] I take the underlying thought to be that a society in which human rights were not respected – and which was therefore neither liberal nor decent – could not constitute a *people* at all, because, in virtue of the oppression taking place within it, it would lack the common identity and political culture, and consequently the sense of self-respect and entitlement to the acknowledgement and respect of other peoples, that constitute the moral character of a people.[105] Conversely, a society in which the rights on Rawls's list were respected, which was bonded by common sympathies and which occupied a governed territory would be apt to be a people even if it lacked (for example) guaranteed education and social security.[106] Furthermore, it is plausible to suppose that any society which honoured these human rights would have the commitments to non-aggression and reciprocal dealings that Rawls takes to be inherent in any people.[107]

It is peoples in this sense, characterised by the sort of respect for human rights that makes a shared history and political culture possible, that Rawls takes to be the subjects of international justice. Some are liberal, and some are not; indeed, 'decent' in the phrase 'decent non-liberal peoples' is in a sense redundant, because all non-liberal peoples are nevertheless decent. This is not a matter of definition or stipulation, however, but a consequence of the general truths of sociology and politics stated in the previous paragraph. Inclusion of 'decent' therefore reminds us of the (empirically) necessary conditions for a society being a people at all.

The diversity among peoples, with their varying and mutually inconsistent conceptions of domestic justice, is analogous to the fact of reasonable plural-

---

103 See, for example, Beitz, above n 40, 683–8; Pogge, above n 67, 214–15; Tasioulas, above n 67, pp 380–90; Téson, above n 67, pp 91–7.

104 At one point Rawls defends it as 'sufficiently liberal' (*The Law of Peoples*, above n 28, 78–9), but the only express argument is an appeal to the intuition that liberal persons will agree that decent non-liberal societies are able to be accepted as members of the society of peoples: ibid 60, 67, 78. I therefore prefer the argument to be given in the text, which I take to be implicit in Rawls's own text.

105 Chris Naticchia recognises that Rawls regards respect for human rights as a precondition for peoplehood, but (in my view wrongly) suggests that this precondition is unargued: 'Human Rights, Liberalism, and Rawls's Law of Peoples' (1998) 24 *Social Theory and Practice* 345–74, 351–62, 366–9.

106 Reidy emphasises the independence of peoplehood from compliance with these 'liberal aspirational' rights: above n 63, 296, 311, 318 (FN52).

107 *The Law of Peoples*, above n 28, 25. Rawls argues in favour of the theory of 'democratic peace', and expresses the belief that decent non-liberal peoples can also participate in such a 'peace by satisfaction': ibid 45–54, 124–5.

ism. It is not going to go away. Consequently, principles of international justice, to be legitimate, must not be such as to call into question the legitimacy of these diverse conceptions of justice, and the communities in which they are realised.[108] But to impose upon non-liberal peoples institutions grounded in individualist cosmopolitanism would be to do just that, and would therefore be inconsistent with liberalism's own recognition of pluralism and concomitant commitment to toleration.

Given that all peoples are committed to non-aggression and the peaceful development of their own forms of life, however, what would be consistent with all their political cultures would be a body of principles under which all agreed to respect the freedom, equality and independence of other peoples, and to deal with one another on a basis of mutual respect. Just as in a liberal polity the values of freedom and equality enjoy the support of an overlapping consensus of the various moral, philosophical and religious doctrines that are found within the community, so such a *law of peoples* is able to enjoy the support of an international overlapping consensus: each liberal or decent non-liberal society, starting from the viewpoint of its own political culture but reasoning towards a common destination, is able to support the principles of freedom, equality, independence and mutual respect among peoples.[109] It is an ideal of the law of peoples, furthermore, that all societies should come to be members of the society of peoples in accordance with its principles.[110]

---

[108] Ibid 11–12, 59–60, 121–3.

[109] 'Able' here does not signal a prediction of the willingness of peoples to affirm these principles; rather, it signals that each people's political culture commits them to these principles: see Onora O'Neill, 'Political Liberalism and Public Reason: A Critical Notice of John Rawls, *Political Liberalism*' (1997) 106 *The Philosophical Review* 411–28, 415–6.

Rawls specifies the law of peoples in terms of eight principles supported and given shape by the fundamental interests of peoples: above n 28, 23, 37. The first, fourth and fifth establish independence, non-intervention and mutual respect as the pre-eminent values among peoples, the sixth recognises the constitutive role that respect for human rights plays in peoplehood, and the second and third establish the regime for co-operation among peoples as one of binding agreement among equals, that is, a system of just treaties. The other two establish rules for dealing with societies that are not peoples, either because they are aggressors, human rights violators, or impoverished. This chapter will not discuss Rawls's theory of armed conflict; his account of international economic justice will be taken up in the next section.

[110] Ibid 89, 93, 106. By 'society of peoples' Rawls means those peoples who accept and adhere to the law of peoples: ibid 3. Rawls does not expressly identify the basis for this ideal, but he does state that support for human rights is part of a just or decent people's foreign policy (ibid, p 65 n 4). It can readily be seen as flowing from this commitment of all peoples to respect human rights.

Contrary to the accusations of its critics, therefore, Rawls's law of peoples is not a doctrine of state sovereignty. Rather, grounded in a recognition of the reality of diversity, and in the liberal commitment to toleration, it is an argument for the self-determination of, and mutual respect among, the diverse peoples of the world.

3. THE SOCIAL LIBERAL ACCOUNT OF INTERNATIONAL ECONOMIC JUSTICE

A. A Tension in Rawls's Account of International Economic Justice

In the social liberal ideal there would be no need for principles of international economic justice. Each people would pursue its own course free from interference by other peoples, its history unfolding in accordance with its own political culture and self-conception.

The world is not ideal, however. Societies are not always able to satisfy their members' subsistence needs and to ensure a minimum economic security. But these are necessary conditions of the sort of social cohesion that constitutes peoplehood, and poverty therefore poses a threat to any society's membership of the society of peoples. Furthermore, in addition to liberal peoples and other decent peoples the world contains what Rawls calls 'burdened societies', that is, societies which cannot establish liberal or otherwise decent institutions because of unfavourable conditions, whether economic or cultural.[111] These societies cannot be said to be committed to the ideals of the law of peoples, but nor are they opposed to them. Lacking the institutions necessary to generate the requisite degree of social cohesion for peoplehood, they cannot be said to have any common political culture at all.

We saw above that peoples are committed to an inclusive society of peoples. This requires ensuring, over time, that all societies are able to realise the degree of common identity and political culture necessary to peoplehood. It therefore gives rise to a duty of assistance, both between peoples, to provide relief in the event of natural disaster and to ensure to the extent that is possible the satisfaction of individuals' basic needs,[112] and to burdened societies, in order to enable the expansion, over time, of the society of peoples.[113]

---

111 Ibid 5, 63, 90, 106.

112 Ibid 38.

113 Ibid 5, 106, 111, 118. Although Rawls words the duty of assistance as one of peoples to other peoples (ibid 37) this is clearly an error: his discussion of the duty of assistance makes it clear that its principal beneficiaries are to be burdened societies.

The purpose of assistance means that conditional assistance is permissible, provided

This duty of assistance is not open-ended, however. Once the cut-off level is reached – that is, once a society's status as a people is secure – there is no duty of continued assistance, even if significant inequality between peoples remains.[114] Rawls rejects a more expansive duty of international economic justice, advancing four reasons why it would be inconsistent with the fundamental interest of peoples in securing independence and mutual respect: that economic well-being is primarily a function of domestic political culture;[115] that in any event, wealth above a certain minimum is not necessary for the establishment and endurance of just or decent institutions;[116] that it would be unfair to require productive peoples to subsidise less-productive peoples;[117] and that the fundamental interests of peoples are satisfied when equality and mutual respect are established, regardless of economic differences.[118]

As Pogge has forcefully argued, these reasons are unpersuasive, and would grant international boundaries a significance in relation to wealth and poverty that they do not deserve.[119] It is simply false to suppose that economic well-being is not significantly influenced by global factors.[120] Furthermore,

---

that the conditions are consistent with the law of peoples: ibid 111. Peoples who provide assistance have good reasons, however, to provide it in such a way that local culture and capacity are not undermined, nor dependency generated: Schmidtz, above n 9, 685–6; Van Wyck, above n 9, 85.

Beitz doubts that the duty of assistance fits within the framework of the law of peoples, because burdened societies seem to pose little threat to the self-determination of other peoples: above n 40, 688–9. He fails to notice its support by the inclusive ideal of the law of peoples. This extension of the law of peoples from its central role of regulating relations among peoples is analogous to the extension of justice as fairness that Rawls envisages, from its central role of regulating relations among competent members of a polity to the case of health care for those who are incapacitated: *Political Liberalism*, above n 28, 21, 244–5.

114 Rawls, *The Law of Peoples*, above n 28, 106, 118.

115 Ibid 39, 108–10, 112.

116 Ibid 106–7, 119.

117 Ibid 117–18.

118 Ibid 114–15. In an earlier essay, Rawls offers as a fifth reason that non-liberal societies cannot be expected to agree to a more egalitarian standard of distributive justice, and that even different liberal societies adopt different principles to govern economic justice within their domestic institutions: above n 101, 75. But as Buchanan notes, this would not preclude the adoption of non-individualist principles for economic justice among peoples (as opposed to individuals): above n 67, 712. Furthermore, as Pogge points out, given the present international distribution of wealth it is non-liberal peoples who would benefit the most from increased egalitarianism: 'An Egalitarian Law of Peoples', above n 67, 218.

119 Pogge, 'An Egalitarian Law of Peoples', above n 67, 198–9; 'Rawls on International Justice', above n 67, 252–3.

120 Pogge, 'Rawls on International Justice', above n 67, 252–3; Thomas W Pogge, 'The Incoherence Between Rawls's Theories of Justice' (2004) 72 *Fordham Law Review* 1739–60, 1753–4. Pogge, above n 3, 15–23, 112–16, 141–4.

extreme differences in the wealth of peoples are apt to undermine equality between peoples, just as in the domestic case they can undermine equality between persons. They are apt to lead to a distortion of institutional arrangements in favour of the wealthy, and also allow wealthy societies to use their greater wealth to corrupt the institutions of poorer societies, not only via the direct corruption of the political process, but also via the subordination of the productive imperatives of poorer societies – which ought to be concerned first and foremost with their own domestic economic needs – to the interests of purchasers in wealthy countries (for example, by encouraging the production of luxury exports over production for domestic consumption).[121]

There is, therefore, a tension between a commitment to equality and mutual respect on the one hand, and the absence of principles to prevent economic domination on the other. If this tension is not resolved, then the law of peoples becomes essentially unstable: its claim to enjoy the support of an overlapping consensus of all peoples is cast into doubt, and its status as a coherent liberal position, consistent with the recognition of pluralism, is threatened.

Of course, if wealthy peoples conducted themselves consistently with a very expansive interpretation of their obligations of non-intervention and mutual respect, then they would refrain from actually exercising their capacity for economic domination, thereby resolving the tension without alteration to the law of peoples. Unfortunately, there is nothing in the law of peoples that would ensure such self-restraint, and the realities of international life mean that even the best-intentioned actors are apt on occasion to take advantage of opportunities that present themselves. It is precisely the purpose of principles to put limits on this sort of self-interested behaviour.[122] It therefore seems that what is

---

121 Pogge, 'An Egalitarian Law of Peoples', above n 67, 213–14; Pogge, 'Rawls on International Justice', above n 67, 250–2; Pogge, 'The Incoherence Between Rawls's Theories of Justice', above n 120, 1750–1. Similar arguments to Pogge's second objection are advanced by Buchanan, above n 67, 711–12, 714. Reidy argues in defence of Rawls that a society could exist entirely independently of other societies and yet still be a properly-constituted people, and thus that that peoples have no compelling reason to regard the international economic order as anything other than (in principle) voluntary: above n 63, 298–301, 316–17 (FNN27, 30). As Pogge emphasises, however, an economic order that is voluntary in principle is apt to be corrupted if excessive differences in wealth are permitted to accumulate.

Pogge also argues that there is no reason to suppose that the fundamental interests of a people might not also include a preference that, everything else (such as mutual respect and equality) being equal, its members be economically better off: 'An Egalitarian Law of Peoples', above n 67, 208–11; 'The Incoherence between Rawls's Theories of Justice', above n 120, 1744–5. This may be true, but is as true of wealthy as of poor peoples, and therefore does not argue strongly in favour of the law of peoples containing a more robust principle of redistribution.

122 The principle Lockean argument for the legitimacy of government is that it

needed, to render the law of peoples coherent, is to introduce into it principles expressly preventing the abuse of economic power. (Somewhat at odds with the main thrust of his argument, in a couple of passages Rawls apparently agrees with this: he canvasses the possibility, even the necessity, of principles for maintaining fair background conditions of international trade, and for correcting unjustified inequalities among peoples that result from the operation of international markets.[123] But he does not spell out any such principles.)

B. Obstacles to a Principled Solution

One possible way of meeting this need for principles of economic justice might be to include within the law of peoples a requirement that compensation be paid to those peoples who suffer as a result of the effect that economic inequalities have upon the framework governing international investment and trade.[124] Or, in order to avoid the constant need for corrective redistribution, principles could be adopted that would prevent gross inequalities from arising in the first place.[125] In the abstract, at least, no people could have a reason to reject such a principle, as no people (consistently with its moral character as a people) would have an interest in trying to derive unfair benefits out of its enjoyment of an economic position superior to that of other peoples.

Precisely stating and implementing any such principle would raise many difficult technical issues. But such a principle also has the potential to clash with one particular aspect – let us call it *principled territoriality* – of the general principle of independence and self-determination of peoples. To appreciate the importance of principled territoriality, recall that in our consideration of Singer's premise *S5* we noted that questions of entitlement, and of proper institutional arrangements, are settled together.[126] In the case of the law of peoples, however, that is not quite true, because, prior to the establishment of the institutional order that is to govern peoples, we have already acknowledged that each people lives in a defined territory, and that one of its interests is to ensure the capacity of that territory to sustain its

eliminates such problems of self-interest: above n 58. Rawls describes the role of principles in constraining an actor's pursuit of his or her (or its, if a people) goals as the *reasonable* constraining the *rational*: *Political Liberalism*, above n 28, 48–54.

123 *The Law of Peoples*, above n 28, 42–3, 115. These passages are ambiguous as to whether Rawls regards the duty of assistance as a sufficient corrective for the effects of unfair conditions of trade (as ibid 43 suggests) or not (as ibid 115 suggests).

124 Consistently with Pogge's requirement above, text at n 44.

125 This might involve the use of the Tobin tax, or a global resource dividend, to generate a pool of money to be used to support global social welfare: Green, above n 15, 509, 513–14, Pogge, above n 3, 23, 111 and Ch 8.

126 Above, text at n 19.

people in perpetuity.[127] It follows from this that the law of peoples must recognise that a people has some sort of entitlement to the wealth that it produces on its own territory.[128]

Principled territoriality creates problems for any principle of corrective redistribution, because it complicates both the determination of what is to count as the derivation of an unfair benefit, and the determination of what assets a people could be obliged to transfer in order to meet another people's demand for compensation. It also creates problems for any principle intended to prevent gross inequality from arising, for the possibility would always seem to be present that a people, simply by exploiting the territorial resources to which it is entitled, might build up sufficient wealth to give rise to such inequalities.

It does not follow that no resolution is possible.[129] And in practical terms, Rawls's duty of assistance is in any event not far from Pogge, or even Singer, in it implications. After all, peoplehood depends upon the satisfaction of subsistence rights,[130] and the duty of assistance between peoples requires ensuring that people's basic needs are met, so that peoplehood is not threatened.[131] Compliance with the duty would therefore go a long way towards the elimination of the extreme poverty with which Pogge and Singer are

---

127 *The Law of Peoples*, 8, 29, 34, 38–9.

128 Pogge objects to Rawls' contention that it would be unfair to require productive peoples to subsidise the less productive, on the grounds that this assumes entitlements which have not yet been established: 'An Egalitarian Law of Peoples', above n 67, pp 211–13. The same objection is put by Buchanan, above n 67, 714–15. Both fail to notice the significance of principled territoriality.

129 Pogge's global resource dividend (above n 125) might appear satisfactory, because it does not oblige a people to exploit its territory, but simply to make a certain proportion of the economic benefits of such exploitation available for international redistributive purposes. The difficulty facing this suggestion, however, is that it presupposes that the benefits that a people derive from the exploitation of its resources are of a purely commodified character, whereas it is quite possible that many peoples may have political cultures in which their relationship to their territory and its resources precludes such commodification. In conversation with the author, Pogge has suggested that in such cases these non-commodified benefits could simply be excluded from the reach of the global resources dividend. This would be at odds with a general Rawlsian requirement, however, that the principles that are to govern an institutional order must be publicly knowable (*Political Liberalism*, above n 28, 66–9, 137, 215–16; *The Law of Peoples*, above n 28, 19, 56–7); for only the members of a particular political culture could know the genuine limits on commodification imposed by that culture (it is not uncommon for such claims to be met with scepticism by outsiders, whether they be made by indigenous peoples about their fishing practices or by French or Japanese farmers about their agricultural practices).

130 Text at n 96.

131 Text at n 112.

concerned.[132] It might also require some of the institutional changes for which Pogge argues,[133] if these are necessary to remove the burdens that prevent the emergence of just or decent regimes.

Until such a resolution is devised, however, we have no principled liberal response to the problem of international economic justice. Nothing about this conclusion prevents wealthy liberal societies, and their members, from proceeding in an ad hoc fashion to do what they can to alleviate extreme poverty, including by agreeing to changes to the rules and practices of the WTO so as to reduce international poverty. But unless such changes themselves amount to an institutional solution to the problem of international economic justice – a solution that is truly principled by the lights of both liberal and non-liberal political cultures – then this sort of response differs in only one important respect from Aquinas's suggestion that each wealthy individual should determine privately the extent of his or her obligation to the poor:[134] few wealthy societies, and few individuals today, acknowledge the right of the poor to self-help. But the resort to self-help is one of the most predictable consequences of a continuing failure to satisfy the human rights of the poor. As the means required to prevent self-help by the world's poor become increasingly harsh, we will therefore learn which wealthy liberals value more dearly – wealth, or principles.

---

132 Rawls and Beitz both note this tendency towards practical (if not theoretical) convergence: *The Law of Peoples*, above n 28, 118–19; 'Social and Cosmopolitan Liberalism', above n 35, 520; 'Rawls's Law of Peoples', above n 40, 694.

133 Above, text at n 48ff.

134 Above n 15.

7. Inter-regime encounters

Andrew T. F. Lang

Human rights have, over the last two decades, emerged as one pillar of progressive critiques of the contemporary international economic order. As a result, human rights actors have emerged as important critical and reformative voices in debates about global economic governance generally, and about the global trade regime in particular. Since the late 1990s, there have been significant efforts on the part of human rights actors to engage with the global trade regime – to elaborate human rights-based critiques of the WTO, to define a 'human rights approach' to trade, and to facilitate cooperation between the international trade and human rights regimes. This encounter – what I will call the 'trade/human rights encounter' – has come to be a significant domain of contestation and discussion over the shape and future of the global trading system.

This chapter seeks to highlight and reflect on the terrain over which this encounter has so far occurred – the framings in which it has operated, and underlying narratives which have helped to give it its shape. In Part 1, I give some history of the development of the trade and human rights debate, focusing in particular in the period from the late 1990s to roughly 2005, which I see as its key formative period. In Part 2, I draw attention to two discursive frameworks or narratives which have been important in the evolution of this debate. First, I show that, through the narrative of 'inter-regime encounters', political contestation over the purpose and shape of the global trade regime has been recast as a conflict between specialised international regimes, and as the outcome of a fragmented international order. Second, I argue that, through the narrative of 'state erosion', such contestation has come to be understood as a struggle over the appropriate allocation of decision-making authority between international and domestic levels of governance. I show how both frameworks continue to structure and shape positions taken in the trade and human rights debate, and draw attention to the risks that I see associated with each.

1. THE ENCOUNTER

A. Human Rights and Trade in Seattle

In the years between roughly 1997 and the end of the millennium, a new network of political actors – and, perhaps, a new social movement – crystallised, drawn together by a common opposition to the perceived expansion and entrenchment of neoliberal global economic policies over the previous two decades. One catalyst for the coming together of this network was the civil society campaign against the Multilateral Agreement on Investment, which resulted in a sustained period of intense collaborative effort on investment issues between a variety of progressive advocacy groups from the second half of 1997 through to the end of 1998.[1] After the collapse of the Multilateral Agreement on Investment ('MAI') negotiations – and to some extent even during them – this network began also to focus its attention on trade issues – first, in the context of opposition to the renewal of 'fast track' authority for US President Clinton in the middle of 1998, but then, more importantly, in the context of protests around the Ministerial Conference of the World Trade Organisation, held in Seattle in November and December of 1999.[2]

As is well known, and as has been chronicled extensively elsewhere, the Seattle Ministerial was a watershed moment in the development of progressive critiques of the global economic order.[3] Civil society protests at that

[1] For information on the conduct of the MAI negotiations, including the role of civil society in them, see Charan Devereaux et al., *Case Studies in US Trade Negotiation: Making the Rules* (Peterson Institute, Washington DC, 2006) Ch 4, 139–76. For documents related to the negotiations, see also the OECD website: http://www1.oecd.org/daf/mai/toc.htm at 25 November 2008.

[2] Jackie Smith, 'Globalizing Resistance: The Battle of Seattle and the Future of Social Movements' in J Smith and H Johnston (eds) *Globalization and Resistance: Transnational Dimensions of Social Movements* (Rowman and Littlefield, Lanham, 2002) Ch 12, 207–8.

[3] This account draws on a number of published accounts of the Seattle campaign, as well as information from a number of interviews conducted with individuals involved in NGOs working at the interface of trade and human rights during the period 1999–2005. See, for example, Gillian Murphy, 'The Seattle WTO Protests: Building a Global Movement' in R Taylor (ed.) *Creating a Better World: Interpreting Global Civil Society* (Kumarian Press, Bloomfield, 2004) Ch 3; Stephanie Guilloud (ed.) *Voices from the WTO* (Evergreen, Washington DC, 2000); Alexander Cockburn et al., *Five Days That Shook the World: Seattle and Beyond* (Verso, London, 2000); Margaret Levi and David Olson, 'The Battles in Seattle' (2000) 28 *Politics and Society* 309; Marc Williams, 'Contesting Global Trade Rules: Social Movements and the World Trade Organization' in L Benería and S Bisnath (eds) *Global Tensions: Challenges and*

Ministerial brought together for the first time a famously diverse range of non-governmental groups sharing little more than common concerns about what they saw as the socially regressive character of contemporary forms of economic globalisation. One key actor was an organisation called People for Fair Trade ('PFT'), which was a loose network of largely US-based labour, environmental and consumer groups who had been energised around trade issues from at least the time of the *North American Free Trade Agreement*[4] ('NAFTA') negotiations.[5] This network's substantive agenda covered at least three broad areas. First, on the environmental side, concern focused on the recent GATT/WTO disputes in *Tuna/Dolphin*[6] and *Shrimp/Turtle*,[7] which some saw as undermining global environmental objectives in the name of free trade. Second, consumer groups within this network focused primarily on the WTO's *EC – Hormones*[8] decision, which was taken as emblematic of the tendency for progressive trade liberalisation gradually to erode health and safety and other consumer protection regulation. The third theme was labour standards: the headline issue had always been the phenomenon of sweatshop labour in developing countries, but more generally there was the concern that the competitive pressures associated with neoliberal globalisation were helping erode labour conditions even in the industrialised world.

On labour issues, the PFT network overlapped with another important actor behind the Seattle protests, namely organised labour.[9] The agenda of organised labour was also focused on the inclusion of core labour standards within the WTO. In fact, this was by no means the first time such groups had engaged in international trade negotiations directly – even apart from their involvement in the NAFTA negotiations in the early 1990s, organised labour

Opportunities in the Global Economy (Routledge, New York, 2003) Ch 11; Jeffrey Ayres, 'Transnational Political Processes and Contention Against the Global Economy' (2001) 6 *Mobilization* 55; Janet Thomas, *The Battle in Seattle: the Story Behind and Beyond the WTO Demonstrations* (Fulcrum, Golden, 2000); Smith, above n 2.

4 *North American Free Trade Agreement Between the Government of Canada, the Government of Mexico and the Government of the United States*, opened for signature 17 December 1992, 32 ILM 289 (entered into force 1 January 1994).

5 See, for example, Murphy, above n 3, 31.

6 *United States – Restrictions on Imports of Tuna*, GATT Doc DS29/R (16 June 1994) (Report of the Panel) ('*Tuna/Dolphin*').

7 *United States – Import Prohibition of Certain Shrimp and Shrimp Products*, WTO Doc WT/DS58/AB/R (12 October 1998) (Report of the Appellate Body) ('*Shrimp/Turtle*').

8 *European Community – Measures Concerning Meat and Meat Products (Hormones)*, WTO Doc WT/DS26/AB/R; WT/DS48/AB/R (13 February 1998) (Report of the Appellate Body).

9 Specifically, the AFL–CIO, and King County Labor Council, see, for example, Murphy, above n 3, 32ff.

had already played an important role in bringing the issue of labour standards to the WTO at its Ministerial Conference in Singapore three years earlier in 1996.[10]

In addition to these labour, environment and consumer groups, the Seattle protests also incorporated other NGOs with interest and expertise in development issues. Some, for example, were energised about the adverse social consequences of agricultural liberalisation in developing countries.[11] Others focused on the extent to which WTO rules appeared to limit the ability of developing countries to pursue interventionist industrial policy in pursuit of development. More generally, these groups shared concerns about recent experiences with trade liberalisation in developing countries, and with the ways in which a neoliberal economic agenda was in their view being exported to the developing world through global institutions such as the WTO.

Despite the diversity of specific issues, it is possible to read this network's broad agenda as expressive of a single core concern: namely, that the social dimension of trade liberalisation is systematically deprioritised in the making of trade policy. In Williams's words, the concern was that the version of liberal trade currently propagated 'privileges trade over non-trade issues, and economic issues over noneconomic ones . . . [it] relegates distributional issues to secondary importance, and neglects the social consequences of trade'.[12] The WTO itself – as opposed to other forums of trade policy-making – became the target of such criticisms in part because of a perception that it was the single institution with the most powerful influence over practices and processes of global trade policy-making, and that it set the fundamental 'rules of the game' of the global trading system.

While the language of human rights was not always prominent in the arguments made and literature disseminated by the Seattle protestors, nor uniformly embraced by all actors in the network, a strong link was certainly made at this time between human rights and the emerging progressive critique of the global economic order.[13] In part, human rights language was introduced

10 See, among a very large literature, Virginia Leary, 'The WTO and the Social Clause: Post-Singapore' (1997) 8 *European Journal of International Law* 118.

11 See, for example, John Madeley, *Hungry for Trade: How the Poor Pay for Free Trade* (Zed, London, 2000).

12 Williams, above n 3, 198.

13 It is interesting to note that a seminal piece of literature in the trade and human rights debate, which catalysed a good deal of other work, was presented to NGOs for the first time during the Seattle Ministerial. See Robert Howse and Makau Mutua, *Protecting Human Rights in a Global Economy: Challenges for the World Trade Organisation* (International Centre for Human Rights and Democratic Development, Montreal, 2000).

by labour groups, who had for some years sought to (re)integrate labour rights into the broader corpus of human rights. But the language of human rights was also found prominently in and around the work of those development-oriented groups in the network. Many of these groups, particularly those with a religious affiliation such as CAFOD, Christian Aid, Brot für die Welt, Lutheran World Federation and others, were used to talking in human rights terms. As early as the 1980s, they had been involved in other campaigns on global economic governance – related to International Monetary Fund structural adjustment lending, the social consequences of World Bank major project lending, and Third World debt, among other issues.[14] Human rights language had been strongly present in all of these campaigns and debates and indeed the Geneva human rights institutions themselves had been a voice in many of them.[15] At the time of the Seattle Ministerial, then, human rights had already been associated with critical projects of global justice directed at international economic institutions, many development actors involved were already comfortable with human rights concepts and forms of argumentation, and inter-personal ties already existed between the relevant NGO networks and personnel within the UN human rights system. In this context, it is no surprise that the language of human rights came to be deployed in the criticisms of the WTO aired in Seattle.

But the introduction of human rights norms into debates about trade was also the result of more targeted action on behalf of specific groups and individuals. There was, for example, a small network of NGOs called the International NGO Committee on Human Rights in Trade and Investment ('INCHRITI'), which was created around the MAI negotiations, and which actively encouraged the adoption of a human rights framework for progressive critique of the global economic order. In 1998, for example, they produced a policy paper entitled 'Investment, Trade and Finance: The Human Rights Framework', which focused on the Multilateral Agreement on Investment, and argued that the promotion of human rights ought to be the objective of all trade and investment agreements.[16] When this group began to focus their attention

---

[14] Smith, above n 2, 210.

[15] See, for example, the work of the Danilo Türk, Special Rapporteur on Economic, Social and Cultural Rights, and Resolution 1995/32 of the Sub-Commission on the Prevention of Discrimination and the Protection of Minorities, *Effects on the full enjoyment of human rights of structural adjustment programmes*, UN Doc E/CN.4/Sub.2/RES /1995/32 (24 August 1995).

[16] See http://www.pdhre.org/involved/policy_statement.html at 25 November 2008. This statement is signed by the following human rights organisations: Habitat International Coalition ('HIC'); People's Decade for Human Rights Education ('PDHRE'); The Lutheran World Federation ('LWF'); Latin American and Caribbean Committee for the Defense of Women's Rights ('CLADEM'); Food First Information and Action Network ('FIAN').

on the WTO during the course of 1999, they again adopted the language of human rights to frame their work. In the lead-up to the Seattle Ministerial, they launched a book entitled *Human Rights and Economic Globalisation: New Directions for the WTO*[17] – the first book-length treatment of trade and human rights, and one which highlighted the development dimension of the trading order – and organised a 'human rights teach-in' on WTO-related issues during the Ministerial itself.[18] Furthermore, in the months leading up to and beyond the Seattle Ministerial, the individuals involved in this network acted as an important point of connection between the civil society protestors and UN human rights bodies. Indeed, it was in part in collaboration with this network that these bodies initially came to develop an interest in and a work program on trade issues. From 1998 to 2000, for example, individuals involved in INCHRITI, as well as associated NGOs, and the UN Committee on Economic, Social and Cultural Rights ('CESCR') collaboratively organised a number of workshops on trade and human rights issues, bringing together NGOs and UN personnel.[19] And in November 1999, just four days before the beginning of the Seattle Ministerial, the CESCR issued a statement, calling on delegates to the WTO to take heed of the human rights consequences of their decisions, and arguing for greater collaboration between the WTO and human rights bodies[20] – a statement which was then incorporated into INCHRITI's own advocacy efforts.[21] As we shall see, this was the beginning of a sustained period of work on trade issues by a variety of different bodies within the UN human rights system.

There were many reasons for this turn to human rights. At the most fundamental level, of course, it had to do with the convictions and values of the

---

[17] Malini Mehra (ed.) *Human Rights and Economic Globalisation: New Directions for the WTO* (Global Publications, Uppsala, 1999).

[18] See http://www.pdhre.org/involved/wto.html at 25 November 2008.

[19] The 11 May 1998 day of discussion is referred to in CESCR, *Globalization and Economic, Social and Cultural Rights*, UN Doc E/C.12/1998/SR.49; E/C.12/1998/SR.50 (May 1998) http://www2.ohchr.org/english/bodies/cescr/docs/statements/Globalisation-1998.doc at 25 November 2008. For a record of the May 2000 meeting, see http://www.unhchr.ch/tbs/doc.nsf/0/11d06750ac4e7acbc125691f002f01f0?Opendocument at 25 November 2000. In addition, a further Day of Discussion, organised by the CESCR, involving similar participants, and covering issues around the TRIPS agreement and access to medicines, was held on 27 November 2000.

[20] CESCR, *Statement of the UN Committee on Economic, Social and Cultural Rights to the Third Ministerial Conference of the World Trade Organization*, UN Doc E/C.12/1999/9 (26 November 1999).

[21] INCHRITI, 'United Nations Human Rights Body Calls for Urgent Review of WTO Rules' (Press Release, 2 December 1999) http://www.pdhre.org/involved/ICHRITI.html#1 at 25 November 1999.

individuals concerned, who all shared a passion for the promotion of human rights generally. Discursively, the rearticulation of political claims in human rights terms offers familiar advantages, not only lending moral weight and an air of incontestability to such claims, but also offering the promise of an already-agreed, shared basis for global collaboration. In addition, of course, the active support of human rights institutions adds significant authority and legitimacy to any political argument.

But there were more specific reasons as well why the human rights framework appeared (and appears) as an attractive one in the particular context of debate about the WTO and global trade. I noted above that the Seattle network was made up of groups representing a huge diversity of issues and interests, which seemed to share only a common antipathy to existing forms of economic globalisation. To some, this raised the problem of ideological incoherence, a problem which human rights promised to solve. Human rights, in other words, might provide a ready-made, well-accepted framework of principles for a movement sorely in need of a secure normative foundation: 'the regime of human rights provides the nearest thing to a coherent challenge to economic globalisation.'[22]

In addition, the language of human rights was attractive because it was a *legal* language. As a legal language, human rights law seemed particularly well suited to the task of resisting the WTO, which itself worked (according to the protestors) primarily by the imposition of international legal obligations. Instead of arguing that WTO rules ought to be different, it became possible to argue that they conflicted with obligations imposed by human rights law – the problem, therefore, was one of systemic fragmentation and incoherence, rather than simply political disagreement. This strategy was in fact partly borrowed from similar strategies which had already been deployed in the trade and environment debate, and was in that sense in part a product of the transmission of ideas occurring through the new social movement. In the trade and environment context, a number of NGOs had seen in international environmental law a promising tool for resisting the obligations imposed by trade law: if trade law pointed in one direction, in other words, it was useful to have an alternative body of international law which pointed in another. This kind of thinking had led many environmental groups to seek new legal instruments (and new interpretations of existing instruments) to counter the disciplines of trade law. The turn to human rights was in part born of exactly the same impulse – the search for other bodies of international law which could be developed and utilised as a counterweight to the obligations imposed by the WTO.

---

[22] See Miloon Kothari, 'Globalisation, Social Action and Human Rights' in Mehra, above n 17, Ch 3.

B. Developing a 'Human Rights Approach to Trade'

That, then, was the primary context in which the UN human rights bodies began to develop their work programs on trade and the WTO. These programs rapidly developed momentum. As early as August 1998, the UN Sub-Commission on the Promotion and Protection of Human Rights[23] passed a resolution entitled *Human rights as the primary objective of trade, investment and financial policy*, and requested a series of reports from two independent experts on issues around the impact of economic globalisation on the enjoyment of human rights.[24] This resolution, and the initial working paper produced by those experts in June of the following year, focused primarily on the World Bank, the IMF and issues around investment – trade agreements were mentioned, but not in any detailed way. But by August 1999, the focus had begun to shift squarely onto the WTO. The Sub-Commission, clearly with a view to the upcoming Seattle Ministerial, passed a new resolution specifically calling on trade policy-makers to take human rights concerns into account.[25] The UN High Commission for Human Rights, at that time under the leadership of Mary Robinson, began to integrate consideration of the international trade regime in her statements and public appearances.[26] The next progress report of the independent experts appointed by the Sub-Commission concentrated on trade issues, and presented a highly critical picture of the WTO.[27]

---

23 Known at that time as the Sub-Commission on the Prevention of Discrimination and Protection of Minorities.

24 OHCHR, *Human rights as the primary objective of trade, investment and financial policy*, UN Doc E/CN.4/Sub.2/RES/1998/12 (20 August 1998). This resolution also appointed the two Special Rapporteurs on globalization and its impact on the full enjoyment of human rights, who subsequently produced three reports on a number of issues around that topic.

25 See OHCHR, *Trade liberalization and its impact on human rights*, UN Doc E/CN.4/Sub.2/RES/1999/30 (26 August 1999).

26 See, for example, Mary Robinson, 'Constructing an International Financial, Trade and Development Architecture: The Human Rights Dimension' (Speech delivered at the Swiss Federal Institute of Technology, 17th Presidential Lecture, Zurich, 1 July 1999) http://www.unhchr.ch/huricane/huricane.nsf/0/0F71A933C5C3673F802567A100581224?opendocument at 25 November 2008 and Mary Robinson, 'Shaping Globalization: The Role of Human Rights' (Speech delivered at the American Society of International Law 97th Annual Meeting, Fifth Annual Grotius Lecture, Washington, DC 2 April 2003) http://www.realizingrights.org/index.php?option=content&task=view&id=118 at 25 November 2008.

27 See Joseph Oloka-Onyango and Deepika Udagama, *Globalization and its impact on the full enjoyment of human rights*, UN Doc E/CN.4/Sub.2/2001/10 (2 July 2001).

An important step was taken the following year, in August 2000, when the Sub-Commission requested the High Commissioner to prepare a report on the impact of the TRIPS[28] agreement on human rights, which was duly produced and received in June 2001.[29] This proved to be the first of a series of six influential reports drafted by the High Commissioner's office, dealing with a range of issues around international trade and investment, including agricultural liberalisation and the right to food, the liberalisation of trade in services, investment liberalisation, and the principles of non-discrimination and participation as they apply in the context of trade policy.[30] These reports were then submitted to the Sub-Commission, and their conclusions were invariably reflected in subsequent resolutions of that body. In addition, for some years both the Sub-Commission and the Human Rights Commission (and indeed, the General Assembly itself) produced numerous resolutions addressing these issues.[31]

Among the treaty bodies, the CESCR has been most active. As noted earlier, the CESCR was intimately associated with the activity of NGOs organising around the MAI and WTO during 1998 and 1999. It organised a day of discussion in the middle of 1998, worked with the INCHRITI network in the build-up to the Seattle Ministerial, and released a public statement to the WTO at the time of the ministerial itself.[32] Since then, it has on occasion continued the practice of releasing a statement to the WTO just prior to important WTO Ministerials.[33] It also began the (still-ongoing) practice of

---

[28] *Marrakesh Agreement Establishing the World Trade Organization*, opened for signature 15 April 1994, 1867 UNTS 3 (entered into force 1 January 1995), annex 1C (*Trade Related Aspects of Intellectual Property Rights*) ('TRIPS').

[29] CESCR, *The impact of the Agreement on Trade-Related Aspects of Intellectual Property Rights on human rights*, UN Doc E/CN.4/Sub.2/2001/13 (27 June 2001).

[30] In addition to the TRIPS report cited above n 29, this series also includes: CESCR, *Globalization and its impact on the full enjoyment of human rights*, UN Doc E/CN.4/2002/54 (15 January 2002); *Liberalization of trade in services and human rights*, UN Doc E/CN.4/Sub.2/2002/9 (25 June 2002); *Human rights, trade and investment*, UN Doc E/CN.4/Sub.2/2003/9 (2 July 2003); *An analytical study on the fundamental principle of non-discrimination in the context of globalization*, UN Doc E/CN.4/2004/40 (15 January 2004); *Analytical study of the HCHR on the fundamental principle of participation and its application in the context of globalization*, UN Doc E/CN.4/2005/41 (23 December 2004). See also more recently, OHCHR, *Human Rights and World Trade Agreements: Using general exceptions clauses to protect human rights* (United Nations Press, New York, 2005).

[31] A list of many of the most important resolutions can be found at http://www.unhchr.ch/html/menu2/trade/otherdoc.htm at 25 November 2008.

[32] See above nn 19–20.

[33] In relation to Doha, see CESCR, *Human Rights and Intellectual Property*, UN Doc E/C.12/2001/15 (26 November 2001).

systematically raising international trade-related matters in the context of some country-review processes.[34] In addition, on a number of occasions the General Comments of the CESCR have specifically directed attention to the activity of international economic institutions such as the WTO.[35]

The period between roughly 2000 and 2005, then, saw the emergence and rapid flourishing of a discourse on 'trade and human rights', fuelled in large part by this intense activity on the part of UN human rights bodies. These were the key formative years of the present trade/human rights encounter, during which human rights actors and institutions positioned themselves within broader debates about economic globalisation and international trade. It is true, of course, that there was – and still is – no single 'human rights voice' on trade issues: the human rights movement is a diverse one, and a wide variety of different trade agendas have claimed to find support in human rights principles. Nevertheless, some common themes seemed to have emerged during this period.

First, there is a set of claims commonly heard from human rights actors about the aims and outcomes of trade liberalisation. In a move similar to those found in debates over human rights and development, a 'human rights approach to trade liberalisation' is commonly understood to imply a reorientation of the fundamental goals and objectives of trade liberalisation – away from increasing economic growth, aggregate wealth or national economic welfare (or even trade as an end in itself), and towards the broader range of social goals represented in the corpus of international human rights. A human rights approach to trade, it is said, implies a different normative standpoint in choosing between different kinds of trade policy: in a human rights approach, the imperative is not to choose the policy which maximises growth or wealth, but rather that which maximises the enjoyment of human rights. At the level of process, a human rights approach is also commonly said to imply that the social impacts of trade policy ought to be considered more seriously throughout the policy-making process. Many have, for example, advocated 'human rights impact assessment' as a mechanism to achieve that goal.[36] Furthermore,

---

34 See CESCR, *Concluding Observations of the CESCR: Ecuador*, UN Doc E/C.12/1/Add.100 (7 June 2004). See also the opinion of the Committee on the Rights of the Child, *Concluding Observations: Ecuador*, UN Doc CRC/C/15/Add.262 (13 September 2005).

35 See, for example, CESCR, *General Comment 15: The right to water (Arts 11 and 12 of the International Covenant on Economic, Social and Cultural Rights)*, UN Doc E/C.12/2002/11 (20 January 2003) [35].

36 See, for example, CESCR, above n 29, 15; CESCR, above n 30 (*Globalization and its impact on the full enjoyment of human rights*) [46]; above n 30 (*Liberalization of trade in services and human rights*), [72]. See also the more recent work of Rights and Democracy: http://www.dd-rd.ca/site/publications/index.php?id=2094&subsection=catalogue at 25 November 2008.

a human rights approach, it is commonly claimed, combines this reorientation and expansion of the goals of trade policy with a special concern for the poorest and most marginalised groups, both as beneficiaries of and participants in, trade policy-making. A human rights approach to trade policy, in other words, requires the choice of trade policies which provide the greatest benefit to these most vulnerable groups, as well as the inclusion of such groups in the policy-making process, at both domestic and international level.

Second, a common (if still contested) set of propositions have also emerged about the appropriate allocation of responsibility for achieving these normative outcomes. For a variety of reasons – some of which no doubt have to do with the traditional state-centrism of international human rights law – many human rights actors in debates about trade tend to share the starting point that it is primarily the responsibility of the state (with appropriate consultation) to ensure that trade liberalisation is carried out in a way which promotes rather than undermines human rights protections. Thus, for many, a 'human rights approach' to the global trade regime is one which seeks to strengthen the capacity and willingness of the state to implement appropriate policies to ensure that that state's terms of engagement in the global economy work for, not against, the human rights of its people. To be clear, this is by no means the exclusive focus of human rights interventions. It is also true that human rights actors often stress duties of international cooperation, and argue that a concern for human rights ought to be integrated into the activities of international organisations. But, as will be discussed further below, the general claim that international institutions like the WTO ought to take human rights into account in its work has come to mean that the WTO ought not to overly constrain the policy choices available to states, ought where necessary to build the ability of states to make better and more socially responsible policy choices, and ought through its rule-making function to create an international environment which provides opportunities for states themselves to take advantage of. The emphasis remains, in other words, on a reinvigorated state as the primary mechanism for the protection and promotion of human rights in the contemporary global trading system.

The content of this emerging human rights agenda on trade issues has been shaped by a number of factors. Inevitably, it bears the imprint of the political context of its birth – the rise, that is, of a broad-based progressive movement within civil society, united by its opposition to what has come to be called neoliberal globalisation. Many of the critiques marshalled by that movement were ultimately reflected in some form in the work of UN human rights institutions. Even the choice of specific issues addressed by human rights bodies followed to some extent the evolving interests of civil society. Their work on the health impacts of the TRIPS agreement, for example, tracked closely the rise of civil society activism on the same issue, in the wake of the South African attempts to open a space for generic drug production during 1999–2000. Similarly, work on the human rights implications of agricultural liberalisation in developing countries grew out of, and in association with, a good deal of civil society research and advocacy on the same issues.[37] In some cases, the choice of issues addressed quite clearly reflected at some deep level the need to keep disparate elements of this civil society network together – advocacy around the GATS and its potential impact on water privatisation in the developing world, for example, seems to have gained traction in part because it brought together themes of interest to a variety of different groups: labour unions (already energised and mobilised by privatisation issues), the MAI network (keen to develop and refocus attention on investment not just trade), and development NGOs (for whom this fit into the broader narrative of the imposition of a neoliberal economic agenda on the Third World).

At the same time, however, it is abundantly clear that neither the human rights institutions, nor the human rights movement more generally, functioned simply as mouthpieces for anti-globalisation activists. First, human rights voices in trade debates have tended to carve out an explicitly and self-consciously moderate position, in contrast to the more radical positioning of some civil society actors. Thus, human rights actors are more likely to claim that trade liberalisation is neither positive nor negative in itself, but instead has potential costs to which we must pay greater attention; and that there is no conflict as such between trade liberalisation and human rights, merely a set of more specific concerns requiring remedial action. This is made clearest in the series of reports produced by the OHCHR referred to above.[38] There is no single reason for this, though no doubt some part of it reflects a desire to avoid a repetition of the heavy criticism to which the earliest (and most radical) human rights reports on the WTO were subject.[39] Second, there has clearly been an attempt on the part of human rights institutions to craft a *pro-development* trade agenda, and this has shaped the kinds of issues which human rights bodies have been readiest to support. This is in part because, within the political organs of the human rights system, a number of developing countries were the initial sponsors of efforts to develop work programs on trade, and in part to counter the perception (described below) in some circles that the trade and human rights debate represented little more than an

---

37 See CESCR, above n 30 (*Globalization and its impact on the full enjoyment of human rights*); Madeley, above n 11.

38 Above nn 29–30.

39 For one account of this response, see Padideh Ala'i, 'A Human Rights Critique of the WTO: Some Preliminary Observations' (2001) 33 *George Washington International Law Review* 537.

excuse for developed countries to impose further trade restrictions on export from developing countries. As a result, issues with greater political salience for developing countries have tended to be the focus of human rights activism on trade, while issues around labour rights and so-called trade conditionality have been clearly marginalised and de-emphasised.[40] Third, there was a perception among many involved in the early stages of the trade and human rights debate, that it was in some sense a successor to the literature on trade and environment – as 'two steps behind' the trade and environment debate. This has also left its mark on the trade and human rights debate, most notably in the way that human rights actors have borrowed arguments used and strategies deployed in environmental circles – focusing, for example, on claims that international trade law constricts the regulatory autonomy of members, and thus constrains their ability to promote human rights through regulatory means. In part as a result, one of the most important foci of attention to arise during these early years of the debate was the use of human rights law as a mechanism to open up so-called 'policy space' – a topic which had received a great deal of attention in the trade and environment literature.

C. The Uneven Spread of Human Rights Language

The elaboration of a distinctive human rights voice in debates about the global trading order has helped to entrench human rights as an accepted and recognisable part of normative discourse around international trade and economic globalisation. Within civil society, connections and networks between development and human rights actors working on trade issues have become increasingly dense. Through such networks, trade policy analysis carried out primarily by large development NGOs is circulated and transmitted throughout the human rights community, policy proposals are translated and recast in human rights terms and inserted into existing human rights advocacy mechanisms, and to a certain extent human rights language has come conversely to be deployed in the work of certain development NGOs. A number of intergovernmental organisations have also begun to incorporate human rights norms and standards in their work on trade issues. In close cooperation with human rights institutions, the FAO, WHO and UNCTAD have, to differing degrees, begun to incorporate human rights approaches into their programs,

---

40 In this respect, the Bossuyt report has been highly influential in reflecting positions within the human rights community on economic sanctions: Marc Bossyut, *The Adverse Consequences of Economic Sanctions on the Enjoyment of Human Rights*, UN Doc E/CN.4/Sub.2/2000/33 (21 June 2000).

including those on trade issues.[41] In addition, 'trade and human rights' has firmly taken root within international legal scholarship, as perhaps the primary framework within which such scholars seek to engage with many civil society critiques of the international economic order.[42] Since 2000, the number and variety of publications in this area has expanded dramatically and gathered considerable momentum – a development which in turn plays a very significant role in framing, guiding and sustaining the debate more generally.

Inevitably, of course, the uptake of human rights language has been less enthusiastic in some venues. The most conspicuous absence is the WTO itself. At the inter-institutional level, relations between the trade and human rights regimes have proven so far to be both rare and difficult. In large part, this difficulty is the legacy of acrimonious debates about the incorporation of labour standards into the WTO framework which occurred around the time of the Singapore Ministerial in 1996. As noted earlier, labour groups (particularly though not exclusively in the US) had become concerned about the extent to which global trade liberalisation was leading to the degradation of labour standards in the export industries of developing countries – and the consequent 'unfairness' of competition between such products and those made in the context of more stringent labour regimes. Labour groups had, for example, succeeded in persuading the US, Mexico and Canada to incorporate a labour 'side agreement' to NAFTA, and very soon after the conclusion of the Uruguay Round, the US sought to achieve a similar result at the multilateral level, by arguing for the inclusion of minimum labour standards in some unspecified form within the WTO agreements.[43] As is well known and well documented, developing countries strongly objected to this effort – seeing it as little more than disguised protectionism – and voiced these

---

41 For an interesting discussion of the integration of a human rights agenda into the FAO's work, including its work on agricultural trade, see I Rae et al., 'The Right to Food as a Fundamental Human Right: FAO's Experience' in B Guha-Khasnobi et al. (eds) *Food Insecurity, Vulnerability and Human Rights Failure* (Palgrave Macmillan, Basingstoke, 2007) Ch 10.

42 Most of this literature is referenced in Andrew Lang, 'Rethinking Trade and Human Rights' (2007) 15 *Tulane Journal of International and Comparative Law* 335–413. See also, more recently, James Harrison, *Human Rights Impact of the World Trade Organisation* (Hart, Oxford, 2007); Holger Hestermeyer, *Human Rights and the WTO: The Case of Patents and Access to Medicine* (Oxford University Press, Oxford, 2007); Susan Aaronson and Jamie Zimmerman, *Trade Imbalance: The Struggle to Weigh Human Rights Concerns in Trade Policymaking* (Cambridge University Press, Cambridge, 2008); and Wolfgang Benedek et al. (eds) *Economic Globalization and Human Rights* (Cambridge University Press, Cambridge, 2008).

43 See above n 11.

concerns vociferously at the Singapore Ministerial in 1996.[44] Because of the close association at the time between labour rights and human rights – and because efforts to craft a pro-development human rights agenda only came some years later – the legacy of this episode has been a profound and lasting suspicion by developing countries of all 'human rights talk' in the context of the WTO, and a resistance to discussion of all human rights issues within the trade regime.

These political sensitivities were no doubt augmented by the publication in 2000 of the preliminary report of the UN Sub-Commission's Special Rapporteurs on Globalisation and its impact on the full enjoyment of human rights, described earlier.[45] The report was highly critical of the WTO, and used strong language to express its concerns. It provoked severe criticism from officials within the WTO system, in part because of its substantive criticisms, and in part because of the lack of sustained consultation with the WTO itself prior to its publication.[46] This episode may have strained relations somewhat between officials in the two regimes, and thus retarded engagement between them. Perhaps more importantly, however, it meant that human rights voices came initially (though, as it turns out, unfairly) to be seen by some within the trade regime as unconstructive and radically critical, making dialogue appear difficult if not impossible. In more recent years, another reason for a lack of enthusiasm for engagement between the two regimes has appeared, this time on the human rights side. Although the claim that the WTO ought to take human rights concerns into account remains as strong as it ever was, it seems now to be conventional wisdom among many human rights actors that incorporating human rights into the WTO – in the sense of including human rights obligations in WTO texts, requiring the WTO's Appellate Body to consider the implication of human rights norms, giving the WTO oversight of human rights mechanisms, and so on – would be a strategic mistake. The argument is that this would cede a degree of control over the evolution of human rights norms to trade institutions – with potentially negative results, in the view of many in the human rights community. While of course this position in no way precludes other forms of engagement between the trade and human rights regimes, it does seem to have redirected attention to some degree away from the broader

---

44 Ibid.

45 Joseph Oloka-Onyango and Deepika Udagama, *Globalization and its impact on the full enjoyment of human rights: preliminary report*, UN Doc E/CN.4/Sub.2/2000/13 (15 June 2000).

46 See, for example, UN Wire, *Trade Body Protests 'Nightmare' Report*' (2000) UN Wire, http://www.unwire.org/unwire/20000825/10574_story.asp at 25 November 2008.

project of integrating human rights concerns and issues into the day-to-day operation and activities of the WTO.

That said, there have been some isolated instances of communication and cooperation between the two regimes.[47] In July and August of 2003, the UN Special Rapporteur on the Right to Health conducted a mission to the WTO itself, meeting with directors of various divisions within the WTO, and producing a report on the right to health implications of various elements of the global trade regime.[48] In 2008, the Special Rapporteur on the Right to Food conducted a similar mission. In at least one instance, a Geneva trade representative attended the review process carried out by the CESCR of [his] country, in which a variety of trade-related issues were raised.[49] In addition, some informal seminars and workshops involving personnel from the two regimes have been organised on occasion – though even in such informal contexts, it has proven politically infeasible to hold these sessions within the facilities of the WTO itself.

2. TWO FRAMES, TWO RISKS

So far, I have tried to tell a story of the origins and evolution of today's trade and human rights debate, from the emergence of resistance to the neoliberal ideology which is perceived to underpin the existing economic order, to the attempt to construct alternative visions of economic order, to the establishment of human rights as one pillar around which such alternative visions are beginning to sediment. In this account, the 'trade/human rights encounter' arises out of a conflict between different visions of what a fair, legitimate, appropriate and desirable international economic order looks like. In this section, I want to examine and reflect on the discursive terrain over which this contest is being fought – that is, the ways in which the contest is framed, and the way in which different positions in the debate are articulated and understood. In my view, this terrain has had an important shaping influence on the direction which the debate has taken and is likely to take in the future. In what follows, I highlight two distinct framings that I see at work within the debate, and draw attention to the risks that are associated with each.

47 See Susan Aaronson, 'Seeping in Slowly: How Human Rights Concerns are Penetrating the WTO' (2007) 6(3) *World Trade Review*, 413–449.

48 Special Rapporteur on the Right to Health, *The right of everyone to the enjoyment of the highest attainable standard of physical and mental health: Addendum*, UN Doc E/CN.4/2004/49/Add.1 (1 March 2004).

49 See Ecuadorian example, referred to above n 34.

A. Inter-Regime Encounters[50]

I noted above that one of the common threads of progressive critiques of neoliberal globalisation emerging during the late 1990s (and since) has been a concern that existing trade policy practices and processes tend to give greater weight and emphasis to the economic consequences of trade, and insufficient attention to its social consequences. It is, conversely, a fundamental goal of such critiques to imagine a new kind of global trade regime, and a new way of making trade policy, which take greater account of the social consequences of liberal trade. In the context of the trade and human rights debate, this fundamental desire has often come to be embedded within a narrative of *inter-regime conflict*, and has been recast and reconceived in terms of this narrative.

What do I mean by a narrative of inter-regime conflict? To simplify somewhat, this narrative sees the trade and human rights debate as expressive of a conflict between competing social goals. Trade liberalisation, with its potential to create wealth, is one social good – and it is by and large the specialised role of the international trade regime to help to produce that social good. The human rights regime, on the other hand, is concerned with another set of social objectives – broadly the promotion and protection of human rights, specifically the promotion of equality, health, access to food, and so on. Difficulties arise, according to this story, when the two social projects come into conflict. In such cases, it is necessary to have some kind of mechanism to ensure coherence between our respective social goals, and to ensure cooperation between the two regimes designed to further them. The problem with the current international system is that there is no adequate balancing mechanism, no systematic way to ensure that the operation of the trade regime does not undermine the objectives and goals of the human rights regime. When it is said that the trade regime ought to take into account human rights concerns, what is often meant is that some such balancing mechanism ought to be instituted.

Wherever this framework is deployed – and though it is by no means universal, I would argue it represents one of the dominant frameworks in the debate – arguments between the different participants in the trade and human rights debate come to take on a different character. As I have written elsewhere,[51] the struggle to re-imagine the ideological foundations of the global economic order, to redefine the social purposes of trade policy-making, is recast as a confrontation between two different sets of legitimate objectives of

---

50 For a fuller elaboration of this argument, see Lang, above n 42.

51 Ibid. See also Andrew Lang, 'Reflecting on "Linkage": Cognitive and Institutional Change in the International Trading System' (2007) 70 *Modern Law Review* 523.

the international community,[52] two international regimes with different functional specialisations, two domains of policy and expertise. Participants come to confront one another and talk with one another as representatives of precisely these different social objectives, regimes, and domains of expertise. As a result, the fundamental political confrontation underlying the trade and human rights debate is subtly displaced, and is redescribed or re-imagined as a structural problem of a fragmented international legal order.

As a result, this framing shifts the ground of debate in a number of ways. Most significantly, it changes the debate from one which is solely internal to trade policy (what kinds of trade policy enhance growth and welfare in what circumstances?) to a debate between trade policy experts and human rights experts. This seems to be useful for a number for reasons. First, on this basis, human rights actors can engage in debates about international trade not as laypersons, but rather as equals in expertise – albeit a different form of expertise, representing a different domain of policy-making, and pursuing a different set of objectives. As a result, the nature of the debate changes: the ground shifts from questions internal to trade policy, and the objective of debate comes to be to facilitate dialogue and mutual learning between experts in two different policies. Second, and related, human rights actors can engage in trade policy debates without first demonstrating their relevance. If the debate is about the ways in which the trading system interferes with the activities and objectives of the human rights regime, the relevance of human rights voices is presupposed from the beginning. Third, this framework appears to be useful by presupposing a broad domain of agreement among participants to the debate. We all agree, so the argument runs, that the promotion and protection of human rights is desirable, that the liberal trade project ought not to undermine such protection, and that therefore some mechanism ought to be put in place to ensure coherence between the two regimes. We may disagree about the precise balance which ought to be struck between the promotion of trade and the protection of human rights, but at least we can agree that a balance of some sort has to be struck.

In my view, these advantages are more apparent than real. There are a number of risks associated with the narrative of inter-regime conflict which make me sceptical of it as a useful terrain on which to play out the trade/human right encounter. First, to redescribe the underlying problem as one of fragmentation and incoherence between different international regimes

---

52 By saying that, in this debate, the confrontation is between 'two legitimate objectives of the international community', I am not saying that participants in the debate agree that equal weight ought to be given to each. On the contrary, of course, for many, human rights concerns ought to be given inherently greater weight.

seems to me to be an invitation to imprecise thinking. It induces a tendency to argue in some broad sense for 'balancing' and 'coherence', even when we all know that everything hangs on the kind of balance struck, and the sense in which coherence is understood. After all, the present international order embodies its own kind of balance, and its own vision of coherence. Similarly, this framework leads on occasion to vague calls for 'dialogue' and 'cooperation' between trade and human rights experts, as if such processes can in themselves lead mystically to the resolution of profound political disagreement. Second, framing the debate in terms of inter-regime conflict can serve to narrow the range of questions asked, reduce the domain of contestation – thus in fact, excluding significant aspects of the international economic order from discussion. This is because if the debate is about the appropriate way of resolving conflicts between trade and human rights objectives, it is predicated on the prior identification of a particular conflict between trade liberalisation and the protection of human rights. Where 'conflict' is understood – as it often is, particularly in legal circles – in narrow terms as a formal conflict between legal norms, the result can be a very significant reduction in the terrain of contestation. After all, specific legal conflicts are rare, and invariably ambiguous. Even where conflict is understood in broader terms, the result of this framework can be to refocus the debate on compiling and discussing a list of conflicts and potential conflicts, rather than directly addressing the key goal of re-embedding the liberal trade project within a re-imagined ideological framework.

The third risk associated with the narrative of inter-regime conflict – and perhaps the most pressing one – relates to the way that it risks inadvertently reinforcing precisely the kinds of insularity in trade policy-making circles which it seeks to contest. If it is true that certain kinds of social concerns are systematically deprioritised in the trade policy-making process, the primary reason is unlikely to be that individuals involved in trade policy-making tend not to care greatly about human rights protection. It is much more likely to be that trade officials see such social concerns as outside their domain of expertise and responsibility, and more appropriately addressed to others more qualified to deal with them. In what universe is it acceptable for any decision-maker not to explicitly accept the consequences of her decisions for working conditions, for environmental protection, or for distributional equity? Only in the universe in which those consequences are understood as part of a conceptually distinct policy domain: as 'labour issues', 'environmental issues' and 'human rights issues', and therefore not as 'trade issues'. The reason that social concerns are deprioritised in trade policy-making, in other words, is not the values of trade officials themselves, but rather the particular views they share about the appropriate domain of trade policy and appropriate role of trade policy-makers. It is these views which ultimately constitute the mechanism by which the authority to take trade policy decisions is divorced from responsibility for some of their social consequences – and by which such a separation is made to appear normal and desirable.

My concern, of course, is that to frame the trade/human rights encounter as a conflict between regimes or policy domains, risks reinforcing precisely these narrow conceptions of the proper domain of 'trade policy'. I described earlier the way in which certain NGOs who were critical of prevailing trade policy and the current international economic environment turned to human rights bodies to articulate and reinforce their concerns. I described the processes by which these human rights bodies developed an agenda and a voice of their own on trade issues. This is a process of constitution: certain issues and values and normative perspectives came to be constituted as 'human rights' issues, and 'human rights' values, and 'human rights' perspectives. The more that oppositional voices in trade debates framed their claims in human rights language, the more that their values came to appear as *human rights values* (not 'trade values') and the issues that they raise come to be seen as *human rights issues* (not 'trade issues'). In other words, the trade and human rights debate is not just about ensuring that the trade regime takes into account human rights concerns; it is first of all (and perhaps most importantly) about defining certain concerns as 'human rights concerns' and others as 'trade concerns'. This is important because characterising particular concerns as human rights concerns makes it *more* difficult for trade policy-makers to take them into account, and *less* likely that they will do so. This is because characterising them in this way enables a whole series of new arguments against considering them: 'we already have a human rights regime to deal with those issues'; 'that is not our area of expertise'; 'we are a trade institution, not a human rights institution'; 'expanding the mandate of the trade regime to include non-trade issues risks spreading it too thin, and diluting its resources'; and so on.

It is true, of course, that the human rights actors in the debate argue explicitly against insularity in trade policy-making. It is precisely their point that human rights concerns *are* relevant to trade policy-makers. The trade and human rights debate is in some sense all about coherence and 'joined-up' policy-making. My point is that, despite this, the actual effect of the framing of the debate is to work against these arguments, to *enable* and *legitimate* precisely the form of thinking which excludes certain social concerns from trade policy – by constructing concerns as human rights concerns, and therefore reinforcing the view that they properly fall within the purview of the human rights regime. Furthermore, even if human rights actors win a concession that the trade regime ought to pay attention to 'human rights objectives', the very fact that they have been constructed as human rights objectives limits the ways they can be taken into account. Trade policy-makers can relatively easily agree that their work should not conflict with such objectives, and provided no such conflict can be shown to exist, then the pursuit of such objectives ought still to be handled by the human rights regime, not the trade regime. By their nature, they cannot be *core* objectives of the trade regime – the mandate of the trade regime is to liberalise trade. The trade regime can't do everything, so the argument runs – it is a *trade* regime, not a human rights regime.

Indeed, we have seen precisely this dynamic at work within the other 'trade and' debates – trade and labour, trade and environment, even to some extent trade and development. For example, consideration of the impact of international trade on working conditions was excluded from the WTO's agenda on the basis that the WTO ought not to stray from its trade vocation, and that the ILO was the appropriate venue for such concerns. The environmental impact of international trade (though not the trade impact of environmental measures) was excluded from the mandate of the original GATT Group on Environmental Measures and International Trade, on the basis that the GATT/WTO should limit itself to its core competence, namely 'trade issues'. Presumably the environmental impact of international trade is a matter for environmental experts, and not something on which trade officials have particular competence. The point is that the framing of these debates has itself contributed to the construction of these social issues as belonging to separate domains of policy, or separate international regimes, and has thus enabled their practical exclusion from the trade regime.

That said, I have deliberately described it as a *risk* that the trade and human rights debate may ultimately serve to reinforce existing conceptions of the role and domain of trade experts and policy-makers, rather than the opposite. It is a tendency built in to the terrain of the debate, rather than as a necessary or inevitable outcome. It is true of course that the discursive terrain of the trade/human rights encounter does not fully determine the evolution of that encounter, and that the framework of inter-regime conflict is not the only framework at work in the trade and human rights debate. It is true also that the explicit arguments advanced by human rights actors work in precisely the opposite way, and may in fact overcome this risk.[53] My argument is probably best understood, then, as a warning and an exhortation. A warning to deploy the framework of inter-regime conflict sparingly and with caution, and an exhortation to focus attention on those forms of argument and practice which expose the contingent nature of existing perceptions of what counts as the proper domain of trade policy and expertise, and which seek to reorient those perceptions by contesting the sedimented ideological frameworks which give them their shape.

---

53 See, for example, Howse, above n 13 [20].

B. The Erosion of State Autonomy

Let me turn now to the second dominant framework which I see at work within the trade and human rights debate. In this second framework, the trade/human rights encounter is embedded within a narrative not about inter-regime encounters, but about the erosion of state power. The dominant image is not that of a fragmented and incoherent international order, but rather an overly intrusive international system, which is contributing to the erosion of the state as the primary centre of political authority by drawing decision-making authority upwards away from the state, constraining state action, and propagating or imposing globally a neoliberal model of minimal state intervention and maximum market freedom. This is of course a very familiar narrative, and one which has by now been analysed, qualified and critiqued from a number of perspectives. Despite this, it still retains its importance as a structuring heuristic for much contemporary debate about economic globalisation. That is to say, it is still the case that contemporary political struggles over economic globalisation often tend to be played out as conflicts over the appropriate allocation of authority between the international and the domestic spheres.

Given its prevalence generally within debates about globalisation, it is not surprising that the 'state erosion' frame is also strongly present in the trade and human rights debate. The international trade regime, it is said, has imposed new constraints on states' policy choices, so that they are now less able to intervene in the economy to fulfil their human rights obligations. The primary mechanism by which the human rights system achieves its objectives, the story goes, is losing its efficacy in the face of a newly powerful and newly dominant neoliberal international economic order. As noted earlier, this naturally has led many to focus on mechanisms for strengthening the state, rebuilding its governance capacity, reasserting and expanding its freedom and authority in the face of a constraining international order.

This emphasis on restrengthening the state has deeply shaped the kinds of issues which human rights actors have tended to raise. On one side, there is a cluster of issues around the idea of freedom from substantive constraint, or policy space. Concerns about the erosion of health and safety laws, affirmative action programs, social policies, development policies and 'regulatory autonomy' generally have loomed large for human rights actors, particularly from 2000 to 2005.[54] The High Commissioner's report on the general exceptions provision of the GATT,[55] and the emphasis in the debate more generally

---

54 See Lang, above n 42.

55 CESCR, above n 29.

on the potential use of human rights obligations as a 'shield' against overly constraining trade rules, also emanate from the same fundamental concern to maintain and expand states' freedoms to take action to fulfil their human rights obligations. On the other side is a range of issues which focus broadly on strengthening the state. Ongoing work to develop tools and methodologies for 'human rights impact assessments' to be carried out by states in the context of trade negotiations is a good example.[56] The strong emphasis, at least since the launch of the Doha Round, on expanding the role of 'technical assistance' and 'capacity building' in the trade regime, is another.[57] Indeed, it is interesting how quickly and how strongly technical assistance and capacity building have come to be promoted by progressives involved in debates about global economic governance, including human rights actors.[58] The recent development of 'aid for trade' – and more generally the push to help developing countries integrate into the world trading system in which they have historically been marginal players – is yet another aspect of this emphasis on restrengthening the state as the key actor in the promotion and protection of human rights.[59]

In part by way of response to these claims, we may be beginning to see changes occurring within the trade regime itself. Specifically, what we may be seeing is the emergence of a new understanding of the role and purpose of the trade regime, organised around these twin pillars of freedom and capacity. As a result of widespread consensus that the trade regime ought not to impose or project a particular economic ideology on its Members, there is growing agreement that the WTO ought to de-emphasise, or even roll back, rules which aim to restructure Members' domestic markets or harmonise their regulatory frameworks. Instead, a new role for the trade regime has emerged, following at least a decade behind its Bretton Woods counterparts, as an enforcer and overseer of 'good governance' norms in the field of trade policy – not so much imposing a substantive economic agenda, but rather seeking to ensure transparency, non-discrimination, procedural rationality, efficiency, and so on, in the making of trade policy. We see this trend in a number of provisions of WTO law, which focus on ensuring the international transparency of trade policy measures, and on ensuring the ability of negatively affected foreign actors to have some input

---

56 Above n 36.

57 A reasonable overview of the WTO's activities can be found at: WTO, *Building Trade Capacity* (2008) WTO, http://www.wto.org/english/tratop_e/devel_e/build_tr_capa_e.htm at 26 November 2008.

58 See, for example, Howse, above n 13.

59 See Dominique Njinkeu and Hugo Cameron (eds) *Aid for Trade and Development* (Cambridge University Press, Cambridge, 2008), for an excellent summary and evaluation of WTO (and other organisations') activities in this role.

into the process by which such measures are established.[60] We also see a similar focus on good governance in norms in some recent trends in WTO jurisprudence, particularly in the context of disputes over regulatory measures. The *Shrimp/Turtle* case was a watershed in this regard, interpreting the Article XX *chapeau* in ways which clearly encouraged cooperative endeavours and requiring disadvantaged actors to have the ability to comment on proposed regulatory actions.[61] More recently, the Appellate Body in *Brazil – Retreaded Tyres* demonstrated a strong disinclination to substantively second-guess the Brazilian government in the context of health- and environment-related trade restrictions.[62] Similarly, the Panel in *EC – Biotech* preferred to base its judgment on the (essentially procedural) ground that the EC had taken too long in making decisions about marketing certain biotech products, rather than wading into the more treacherous waters of the substantive legality of restrictions on biotech foods under WTO law.[63] Of course, this emphasis on good governance norms reflects the belated adoption by the WTO of the broader 'good governance' agenda which has over the past decade or so become such a significant feature of the landscape of international economic governance.

In addition, another new role is in the process of being created for the WTO, a role which involves *empowering* and *enhancing* the ability of its Members to integrate into the global trading system. This is focused of course on helping to provide developing countries with the capacity and resources necessary to engage productively in trade, trade negotiations, and trade dispute settlement. It is most evident in the swift and relatively uncontested expansion of the WTO's work in the areas of capacity-building, aid for trade

---

60 For example, *Marrakesh Agreement Establishing the World Trade Organization*, opened for signature 15 April 1994, 1867 UNTS 3 (entered into force 1 January 1995), annex 1B (*General Agreement on Trade in Services*) Articles III, VI; *Marrakesh Agreement Establishing the World Trade Organization*, opened for signature 15 April 1994, 1867 UNTS 3 (entered into force 1 January 1995), annex 1A (*Sanitary and Phytosanitary Measures*) Article 7 and Annex B; *Marrakesh Agreement Establishing the World Trade Organization*, opened for signature 15 April 1994, 1867 UNTS 3 (entered into force 1 January 1995), annex 1A (*Technical Barriers to Trade*) Articles 2.5, 2.9–2.12, among many others.

61 *United States – Import Prohibition of Certain Shrimp and Shrimp Products*, WTO Doc WT/DS58/AB/R (12 October 1998) (Report of the Appellate Body).

62 See *Brazil – Measures Affecting Imports of Retreaded Tyres*, WTO Doc WT/DS332/AB/R (17 December 2007) (Report of the Appellate Body).

63 See *European Community – Measures Affecting the Approval and Marketing of Biotech Products*, WTO Doc WT/DS293/R (21 November 2006) (Panel Report) ('*EC – Biotech*'). On the interpretation of WTO regulatory provisions in a procedural framework, see generally Robert Howse, 'Democracy, Science and Free Trade: Risk Regulation on Trial at the World Trade Organization' (2000) 98 *Michigan Law Review* 2329.

and technical assistance.[64] Again, the WTO is a relative late-comer to this game. It is probably more fully and more clearly reflected in the practice of other major institutions of international economic governance, including the World Bank, International Monetary Fund, the United Nations Conference on Trade and Development, and so on, as well as in many activities facilitated at the bilateral level. The work of the WTO in this respect should therefore be understood as one part of a much broader system working through a variety of multilateral and bilateral channels and processes.

This transformation in shared ideas about the role and purpose of the trade regime potentially marks a profound historical shift. We have learnt from Ruggie and others that prior transformations of the international trading regime (and international economic order more generally) have been associated with changes to prevailing beliefs about the trade regime's role and 'social purpose'.[65] In the postwar era of 'embedded liberalism', for example, the trade regime sought to strike a compromise between domestic and international stability – taking action to prevent a repeat of the protectionist race to the bottom of the interwar years, while at the same time enabling various forms of domestic intervention in the pursuit of stability.[66] This gave a particular character to the postwar trade regime: it pursued a limited and progressive form of liberalisation, domestic regulation was disciplined primarily by the norm of non-discrimination, and developing economies remained largely peripheral to the trading system. During the 1980s and 1990s, 'embedded liberalism' became 'neoliberalism', and with it came a new conception of what the trade regime was for, and what it did. During this period, the trade regime came (in part) to see its project as the creation of a global market, and its role as a guardian of market freedoms. The postwar project of limited trade liberalisation became a nearly universal one, at least in aspiration. In relation to domestic regulation, the norm of non-discrimination moved somewhat closer to a norm of deregulation, and was augmented by first steps towards harmonisation. International trade law came at times to look like a mechanism for the

---

64 See Njinkeu and Cameron, above n 59.

65 See John Ruggie, 'International Regimes, Transactions, and Change: Embedded Liberalism and the Postwar Economic Order' (1982) 36 *International Organization* 379.

66 Ibid; see also Dunoff, 'The Death of the Trade Regime' (1999) 10 *European Journal of International Law* 733; Robert Howse, 'From Politics to Technocracy – and Back Again: the Fate of the Multilateral Trading Regime' (2002) 96 *American Journal of International Law* 94, Andrew Lang, 'Reconstructing Embedded Liberalism: John Gerard Ruggie and Constructivist Approaches to the Study of the International Trade Regime' (2006) 9 *Journal of International Economic Law* 81.

transborder projection of the neoliberal imagination.[67] What we are beginning to see now is the third chapter of this story – the emergence of a new 'social purpose' and a new compromise. While the outline remains vague, its key elements include a shift away from the propagation of a particular economic ideology, a new emphasis on procedural and 'good governance' disciplines, and a new focus on positive action to build the governance capacity of developing and least developed states.

There is no doubt much to be desired in a new social purpose of this type. But at this point, I want simply to register one concern, namely that a new international economic order based on 'governed liberalism' risks in practice becoming simply a continuation and entrenchment of the existing international economic order under another guise, and risks becoming complicit in (rather than a counter to) the projection of Western models of state action around the globe. This is for two reasons.

First, as Adler and Bernstein have already suggested, mechanisms of capacity-building – which include the provision of advice on the formulation of appropriate trade policy, targeted assistance to facilitate integration into the trading system, support in conforming legislation to international legal obligations and 'best practice', and so on – can be understood as mechanisms of socialisation, by which states come to accept existing trade policy norms.[68] Depending on who carries them out, what they are understood to mean, exactly how they are done, and what policy templates are circulated through them, mechanisms of technical assistance and capacity-building may end up being just another venue for the dissemination of the existing range of policy options, and just another mechanism for the disciplining of marginal states and the projection of Western models of state action.

Second, even the opening up of legal freedom – what looks on its face like a reduction of international legal constraint – can in some circumstances itself end up producing and perpetuating a particular kind of state, rather than encouraging experimentation with alternative forms of state-society relations. In particular, the creation of new exceptions and flexibilities within WTO law can positively encourage forms of state behaviour specifically designed to take advantage of these flexibilities. This is especially the case where they are accompanied by technical assistance programs educating policy-makers on the content of WTO law, and powerful desire on the part of many policy-makers to use such flexibilities to the full. It is significant, then, that a good deal of

---

67 Whether, and to what extent, it actually functioned as such a mechanism is another question.

68 Emanuel Adler and Steven Bernstein, 'Knowledge in Power: the epistemic construction of global governance' in M Barnett and R Duval (eds) *Power in Global Governance* (Cambridge University Press, Cambridge, 2005) Ch 13.

existing trade law – on subsidies, safeguards, anti-dumping measures, intellectual property, and so on – has been designed with the policies of a small group of developed states in mind. It is also significant that many of the legal flexibilities which are the subject of debate among human rights advocates and other progressive actors – namely, the flexibility to establish strong regulatory regimes for health and safety, environmental protection, affirmative action, and so on – have been elaborated in the context of concern about the erosion of the key features of the (Western) welfare state by international legal discipline. Very often, therefore, the use of such flexibilities will necessarily involve mimicking existing policy tools and institutional forms already in place in advanced industrialised countries. This risk is especially strong where few alternative templates of state action are available to policy-makers to guide their choices. My concern, then, is that contemporary contests over the appropriate degree of regulatory autonomy which ought to be granted to WTO Members risk, ultimately – and paradoxically – becoming another mechanism by which a particular set of policy choices is projected globally as representing the limits and domain of possible action.

3. CONCLUSION

I have tried in this chapter to paint a picture of the trade and human rights debate as one domain of struggle over the nature and purpose of the liberal trade project. My focus has been on the ways that this debate has been framed, and the influence these framings may have had on the evolution of this debate over the past decade or so. The historical material presented in the first part sought to put the existing debate in its early political context, and to explain the origins of the discursive frameworks which have structured it since. In the second part, I made two core arguments. First, I suggested that through the narrative of 'inter-regime coherence', contemporary struggle over the heart of the liberal trade project has been recast as a conflict between the goals of the trade regime and those of the human rights regime. As a result, there is a risk that questions about the purpose of the liberal trade project may be pushed to one side, and existing narrow understandings of the role of the trade regime and trade policy-makers will be reinforced and perpetuated. Second, I argued that the narrative of 'state erosion' *has* led to the re-imagining of a new role for the trade regime – but that this process is incomplete in crucial ways. Because of this incompleteness, there is a risk that this turn may ultimately do as much to constrain state action, and to project Western models of state action globally, as the existing international economic order.

8. Games within fragmentation: the Convention on the Protection and Promotion of the Diversity of Cultural Expressions

Hélène Ruiz Fabri

Once upon a time, there was the *Convention on the Protection and Promotion of the Diversity of Cultural Expressions*[1] ('the Convention'). This is not a fairy tale but the story of a legal policy that one could call 'games within fragmentation', such is the accuracy of the picture it gives of the itineraries one can explore during the journeys through the archipelago of international law, sometimes no more than steered by the stars. It is not a fairy tale because the Convention not only exists – it was adopted on 20 October 2005 by the 33rd General Conference of the United Nations Education Scientific and Cultural Organization ('UNESCO') – it has entered into force. One would like to see it as the younger sister, alive and viable, of the cultural exception whose death had left too many hopes unfulfilled. Yet, at once it is tempting to question whether the Convention is or will be of any utility and if it can be considered effective. Should one tend toward an elegant cynicism (though perhaps a better term would be realism), a prudent idealism, or maybe even a militant voluntarism?

Such questions already reveal one characteristic of the Convention, to have been and to remain a source of controversy, as an object of legal discourse and as an instrument of legal policy. On the one hand, the perspectives concerning the Convention do not seem overly encouraging, be they doubts relating to States' willingness to apply it or, more simply, to the Convention's ability to truly influence the course of things through its content or scope of application. Yet, this is the fate to which it was destined: to thwart or influence the implementation of other norms of international law, particularly international trade norms. On the other hand, it is unduly simplistic or

[1] Opened for signature 20 October 2005, UNESCO Doc CLT-2005/CONVENTION DIVERSITE-CULT REV (entered into force 18 March 2007).

reductive to measure the effects of a convention exclusively by the relatively low binding force of its contents. This would equate to giving in to the temptation of a singularly formalistic analysis that would do justice neither to the importance of the role played by the Convention's negotiation itself, whose effects ranged far beyond the sphere in which it took place, nor to the fact that the influence, and even the effectiveness, of a rule is not exclusively linked to the binding character of its formulation or its formal support.

There is no precedent of a UNESCO convention being elaborated, adopted and entering into force so quickly as the subject of this chapter. The Convention's relatively short history, of less than a decade, easily allows for reconstitution of its genealogy and an understanding of the project that carried it. From this perspective, the Convention would even testify to a certain exemplarity, as a sort of laboratory of legal issues linked to globalisation.[2] From a cultural perspective, globalisation admittedly fosters the diffusion of diversity through increased trade and communications, but it equally threatens it, since this increase of trade and communications is essentially of benefit to dominant cultures at the expense of subservient cultures. This in turn carries the threat of homogenisation, which is quite doubtfully a source of human happiness, should this be used as a measurement standard, as well as the threat of retreats into nationalism that forecast more or less violent reactions. In other words, one of the most important issues that arises from globalisation is the possibility to preserve a distinct cultural expression or, translated into cruder but concrete words, to preserve cultural expressions other than American, for the American domination is overwhelming. From this perspective, the idea of a necessary balance in trading relations is not new. Traces of this can be found as far back as the 1920s.[3] But the originality and the plurality of identities characterising groups and societies, which are the spring of cultural diversity, are more and more rapidly called into question by the process of trade liberalisation. This process is essentially focused on competition and tends to enforce a sole and reducing economic approach, mismatching the plurality of expectations of the public, the plurality of traditional technical and behavioural habits, and the plurality of values shared by groups or societies. The logic behind trade liberalisation correlatively tends to prevent States from adopting measures that could limit directly or indirectly the circulation of cultural goods and services, or from intervening in the sector of cultural industries by means such as subsidies, quotas, restrictions on foreign investment, regulatory measures, and so on.

---

2 J Smiers, *Arts under Pressure – Promoting Cultural Diversity in the Age of Globalisation* (Zed Books Ltd, New York, 2003).

3 M Hahn, 'A clash of cultures? The UNESCO diversity convention and international trade law' (2006) 9 *Journal of International Economic Law* 520.

This problem is not a problem of developed countries only, who struggle to secure the competitiveness of their cultural sector in international trade. According to the studies initiated in the 1970s and pursued ever since, the problem mostly concerns developing countries, since culture makes an important contribution to economic development, not only because it helps refocus the finality of development on the human, but also because cultural diversity acts as an important lever for economic development.[4] Indeed, cultural diversity fosters and enhances creativity that permeates not only the cultural sector but all sectors, including the economic sector. It also appears as a source of wealth, in the sense that cultural heritage and productions of different social groups represent a genuine capital that can and must be valued. And of course, cultural rights are well-recognised human rights.[5]

And yet, as is well known, there is no global approach to the problems to which the regulation of globalisation gives rise. While there exists a strong economic pillar, consolidated and of rapid potential development, the construction of a globalised law lacks a cultural pillar capable of rebalancing the trend. In other words, there are asymmetries in the normative developments relating to issues that one could, however, consider as being, in principle, of equal dignity. One could of course object that this only reflects the hierarchy according to which States have chosen to classify their interests, even though they would not expressly admit this. Although this harmoniously suits the reality of an international society operating in a horizontal and intersubjective mode, it also quite happily acknowledges the fatality of the fact that it is always easier to favour short-term profits rather than to anticipate long-term costs in order to reduce them. Yet, the development of globalisation precisely raises awareness of these medium- or long-term costs, implying that they can less easily be concealed, while also raising awareness of the absence or the shortcomings of mechanisms capable of relating the longer-term costs to more immediate concerns. Although this is in part concealed in the political field, where giving a normative answer appears to address this relationship – and States never hesitate to make use of this assimilation of rule-making and action – it is, however, unveiled in the legal field, where the

4 J Pérez de Cuéllar, *Our Creative Diversity: Report of the World Commission on Culture and Development*, (UNESCO Publishing/Oxford and IBH Publishing, Paris, 1996); K Stenou and C Keitner, *L'UNESCO et la question de la diversité culturelle – Bilan et stratégies 1946–2000* (UNESCO, Paris, 2000).

5 See for example Article 15 of the *International Covenant on Economic Social and Cultural Rights*, opened for signature 16 December 1966, 999 UNTS 3 (entered into force 3 January 1976); Article 27 of the *International Covenant on Civil and Political Rights*, opened for signature 16 December 1966, 999 UNTS 171 (entered into force 23 March 1976).

discourse is unable to compensate for the absence (that is, the rusticity or the embryonic character) of articulation or coordination mechanisms between normative systems. Yet, these normative systems are bound to interfere more and more frequently, and the expansion of international law only highlights the *normal*[6] phenomenon of the superimposition of norms from different origins but relating to the same subject, situation, or activity. This is precisely what the reflection on the fragmentation of international law aims to point out.[7] Concretely, as the elaboration of the Convention illustrates, this means that a normative answer is not only sought, but that it is conceived with regard to its interference with other normative systems. One of the most striking aspects of the negotiation has been the fact that the definition of the rules concerning the relationship between the Convention and international law at large has been extremely painful, far more so than the formulation of the substantive rules. Shifted from the status of a technical question to that of a political issue, this shows that the actors have acknowledged and understood the functioning of the system. Indeed, as another correlative fact of globalisation, this negotiation involved not only States, but, as described below, the entire constellation of actors that feel concerned and want to express their opinion directly or indirectly.

As the logical outcome of an interest that was never denied, the text born from the negotiation received broad support. Nevertheless, the rapidity of this elaboration, which in itself evidences the determination that accompanied the objectives that the text aims to realise, must not lead one to forget the opposition displayed during the negotiation, nor that its future effectiveness depends not only on a large number of ratifications by UNESCO Member States but also on effective implementation. Furthermore, the text needs to be assessed in its final version, with regard to the same objectives, in order to appreciate whether it can adequately further their achievement.[8] Indeed, the peculiarity of any negotiation is to force the actors to accept compromises that tend to weaken more or less substantially the provisions, or even to deprive them of any efficiency at all – the negotiation of this Convention being no exception. Thus, the formal success of achieving an adopted text does not necessarily coincide with the substantial success of achieving a text able to effectively

---

6 There is nothing new in observing that one 'object' can have different qualities and is henceforth subject to norms of different origin and logic.

7 M Koskenniemi, 'Fragmentation of international law: difficulties arising from the diversification and expansion of international law' [2006] II *Yearbook of the International Law Commission*, UN Docs A/CN.4/L/682 and A/CN.4/L/682/corr 1.

8 S Regourd, 'Le projet de Convention sur la diversité culturelle : Vers une victoire à la Pyrrhus' (2005) 226 *Légipresse* 115.

realise the stated objectives. Almost inevitably, the legal analysis leads to a more nuanced appraisal than that set forth in the political discourses, whether they supported the Convention or argued against it.[9] Nevertheless, the means by which the project came into being, as well as its implementation and outcome, account for an interesting story of legal policy.[10]

1. THE EXISTENCE OF A PROJECT: IMAGINING A CONVENTION ON THE PROTECTION OF CULTURAL DIVERSITY

A quick look back is enough to show that the development of the topic of cultural diversity and the reflection on the formulation of a corresponding body of rules was largely linked to the failure of the 'cultural exception' during the negotiations that led to the establishment of the World Trade Organization ('WTO'). This prompted a shift away from the WTO in favour of an external, fully fledged international convention capable of exerting an influence on WTO law.[11]

First Step: Resetting the Perspective

The failure of the cultural exception brought up the challenge of exceeding it, yet without giving up its objectives. The change was not only one of vocabulary – evolving from cultural exception to cultural diversity[12] – but also of perspective – evolving from the defensive logic underlying the exception to the positive approach of the concept of specificity, and thus evolving, from a legal standpoint, from a regime of isolation to a regime of articulation.

---

[9] H Ruiz Fabri, 'Reflections on possible future legal implications of the Convention' in N Obuljen and J Smiers (eds) *UNESCO's Convention on the Protection and Promotion of the Diversity of Cultural Expressions: Making It Work* (Interlink/IMO, London, 2006) 73; H Ruiz Fabri, 'Naissance d'une convention' in M Johannsen (ed.) *Mélanges offerts à J. Salmon* (Bruylant, Brussels, 2007) 547; H Ruiz Fabri, 'Culture seized by globalisation: can international law be of any help? Reflections on possible future legal implications of the UNESCO Convention on the protection and promotion of the diversity of cultural expressions' in A Reinisch and U Kriebaum (eds) *The Law of International Relations: Liber Amicorum Hanspte Neuhold* (Eleven International Publishing, Utrecht, 2007) 281.

[10] All the documents relating to the elaboration of the Convention have been listed and gathered by the Francophonie: http://www.francophonie.org/diversiteculturelle/recueil.cfm#francophonie at 30 June 2008.

[11] C Beat Graber, 'The new UNESCO Convention on Cultural Diversity: a counterbalance to the WTO?' (2006) 9 *Journal of International Economic Law* 563.

[12] D Atkinson, 'De 'l'exception culturelle' à la 'diversité culturelle': les relations internationales au coeur d'une bataille planétaire' (2001) 2 *AFRI* 663.

Outgrowing the approach in terms of exception was essential not only because it had failed, but also because it was inadequate. The 'cultural exception'[13] would have mainly consisted of keeping the cultural services sector unchallenged by the new provisions on trade in services (GATS), through an *a priori* exclusion. It is known to have failed from a legal standpoint, although the formula lives on as a political slogan. A compromise was eventually reached, according to which the very design of liberalisation of trade in services, allowing each WTO member to choose the level of market openness and therefore to choose not to open it at all, was in itself a satisfactory guarantee since any liberalisation would thus have to be agreed to.[14] While this was formally correct, this did not suppress the fears of the supporters of the cultural exception. But, it was quite quickly realised that the status of the exception was not only out of reach, but that it might well be inadequate.

The inadequacy of the 'cultural exception' regime is largely due to underlying misunderstandings. It wrongly leads to the assumption that the aim is to interrupt trade, when in fact trade is not only already highly developed but is also essential, regardless of any economic perspective. Still, opening up trade has always caused States to fear that national industries might suffer drawbacks from this phenomenon, which has given rise to the concern to preserve a space for national industries. In a way, the cultural exception aimed to address the same concern but failed to do so because of its general character, and also because of its maximising character. Thus, the cultural exception was unable to solve the real problem at hand, linked not to the mere existence of trade, but to its imbalance, emphasised by the dominant position of American cultural goods and services, especially in the audiovisual field. More fundamentally, the fear has become that the imbalance might lead to a problematic acculturation, considering the 'central role' of the audiovisual media 'in the

---

[13] J-M Baer, 'L'exception culturelle – Une règle en quête de contenus' *En Temps Réel*, Cahier 11, October 2003; S. Regourd, *L'exception culturelle*, PUF, Que sais-je? no 3647, 2004, p. 128; *De l'exception à la diversité culturelle*, La documentation française, 2004; B Gournay, *Exception culturelle et mondialisation* (Presses de Sciences Po, Paris, 2002); A Mattelart, *Diversité culturelle et mondialisation* (La Découverte, Paris, 2005); A Mattelart, *La mondialisation de la communication* PUF, Que sais-je? no 3181; J-P Warnier, *La mondialisation de la culture* (La Découverte, Paris, 2004); T Bishop, 'France and the need for cultural exception' (1996–1997) 29 *New York University Journal of International Law and Politics* 187; F Dehousse and F Havelange, 'Aspects audiovisuels des accords du GATT – exception ou spécificité culturelle?' in C Doutrelepont (ed.) *L'Europe et les enjeux du GATT dans le domaine de l'audiovisuel* (Bruylant, Brussels, 1994) 99.

[14] The 'positive list' approach dictates that only the sectors and modes of supply that are specifically mentioned need to be liberalised, and only then to the extent specified in the list.

functioning of modern democratic societies and in the development and transmission of social values. They have major influence on what citizens know, believe or feel'.[15] Clearly, the issue was not only one of markets, but a political and social one, with governments and elites themselves feeling threatened by the loss of control over instruments essential for the development of public discussions. This circumstance pinpoints the reasons why the role of States would become an essential concern and how the theme of cultural diversity could thus positively develop, having emerged in the political discourse since 1997–1998. This did not imply that nothing would happen within the WTO, quite the opposite actually,[16] but in order to achieve any progress, the idea of a legally grounded specificity of cultural goods and services needed to be autonomously and generally substantiated. The discussion thus no longer focused on the means of excluding the cultural issue from trade negotiations but rather on the idea of an international instrument specifically devoted to cultural diversity, which would acknowledge the legitimate role of domestic cultural policies in preserving and even developing it. This induced a radical change of perspective, the issue henceforth being addressed through a positive approach.

By connecting the concern, which had long been expressed via the cultural exception, to the new conceptual foundation of cultural diversity, a new legal approach based on the idea of specificity was promoted.

Although the notion of cultural diversity was not entirely new, it was very broad. This was all the more true since it was first used as a political slogan before being given an intellectual content, and finally being legally substantiated.[17] Supposed to promote an open and dynamic interpretation of the concept, its promoters seem to have realised this threat. Considered as such, the notion of cultural diversity is indeed ambivalent. In fact, the discourse competing with that of the Convention's promoters skilfully made use of this ambivalence, as the report published by the United Nations Development Programme during the early summer of 2004 and devoted to 'cultural liberty in today's diverse world' demonstrates quite clearly.[18] Admittedly, this report

---

15 Communication from the Commission, 'The Future of European Regulatory Audiovisual Policy' (Press release, 15 December 2003) 3; quoted by M Hahn, above n 3.

16 C Beat Graber et al. (eds) *Free trade versus cultural diversity* (Schulthess, Zürich, 2004).

17 F de Bernard, 'Pour une refondation du concept de diversité culturelle' in G Gagné (ed.) *La diversité culturelle: vers une convention internationale effective?* (Éd Fides, Saint Laurent, 2005) 21; M-F Labouz and M Wise (eds) *La diversité culturelle en question(s)* (Bruylant, Brussels, 2005); P Lemieux (ed.) *La diversité culturelle* (Les Presses de l'Université de Laval, Laval, 2006).

18 H Ruiz Fabri, *Le Rapport du PNUD sur la liberté culturelle: les mots et les*

insisted on the danger that cultural diversity might be used as an excuse for cultural conservatism and a fallback on traditions of which some are incompatible with the requirements of human rights. Therefore, cultural diversity should not be an end in itself, but rather a means to achieve the blossoming of cultural liberty, a notion that should be preferred and which implies above all the freedom of choice of individuals. Its achievement in turn implies a broadening of the range of choices, which is best accomplished by opening up markets. Admittedly, market openness could induce perverse effects of homogenisation in favour of the financially most powerful cultures. Yet, first and foremost, a decrease of diversity seemed perfectly acceptable as long as it resulted from the choice of the consumers, and secondly, the issue could not satisfyingly be addressed by limiting trade, but by public policies positively supporting and thus enhancing the development of local or national cultural industries capable of participating in a competition deemed to be a source of liberty.

The promoters of the Convention realised that, in order to avert such arguments in favour of free flow and to emphasise the relevance of preserving and promoting cultural diversity, the antagonistic aspect associated with the issue needed to be erased and that it had to be linked to other clearly identified values that would specify its content and legitimise it. On the one hand, they have thus linked the issue to those of cultural pluralism, development, human rights, peace, democracy, free circulation of ideas and national and international diffusion of cultural goods and services, among others, thus highlighting an open and dynamic approach to cultural diversity. On the other hand, they linked the concept of cultural diversity to several other highly symbolic notions, such as sustainable development or the common heritage of mankind, whose symbolic values were intended to be conveyed to that of cultural diversity.[19] Yet, while cultural diversity remained the slogan throughout the entire process, it could never be, in itself, more than the line of sight and needed to be dissected into more operative concepts, suiting the more precise purposes fuelling the process.

Therefore, the process focused on the diversity of cultural expressions[20] and addressed the 'recognition' of the 'distinctive nature of cultural activities,

---

conceptions (2004) at http://agence.francophonie.org/diversiteculturelle/fichiers/aif_note_ruiz_fabri_septembre2004.pdf on 30 June 2008.

19 A Kolliopoulos, 'La Convention de l'UNESCO sur la promotion et la protection de la diversité des expressions culturelles' [2005] *AFDI* 487.

20 These are defined as 'those expressions that result from the creativity of individuals, groups and societies, and that have cultural content' (Article 4.3 of the Convention), cultural content being itself defined as referring 'to the symbolic meaning, artistic dimension and cultural values that originate from or express cultural identities' (Article 4.2 of the Convention).

goods and services as vehicles of identity, values and meaning',[21] which was mentioned among the Convention's objectives. It forms a basis for countering an exclusively economic approach. The distinct nature thus acknowledged is 'both an economic and a cultural nature, because (cultural activities, goods and services) convey identities, values and meanings, and must therefore not be treated as solely having commercial value'.[22] This last value is therefore not erased, but needs to be associated with other issues. The concept of specificity operates as a justification on two levels. First and foremost, it enables States to continue using various means and methods essential in order to adequately ensure their cultural policies, which are henceforth acknowledged as being at the service of the protection and the promotion of cultural diversity. Secondly, it justifies the possibility of producing an international instrument outside the WTO, whereas the cultural exception, as an exclusion clause, was bound to be addressed within the WTO.

Second Step: Building the Process

Retrospectively, one can have the impression of a cacophony since the theme of cultural diversity seemingly surfaced in different locations and forums. Yet, there definitely was a project that combined objectives and methods in order to acknowledge cultural diversity as an essential value and to substantiate the need for an international instrument devoted to its protection, which was eventually decided to be negotiated in UNESCO. After the scattering comes a time of gathering.

The scattering

The theme of cultural diversity was not entirely new, which possibly accounts for the relative readiness with which UNESCO was designated as the forum where it should be addressed. UNESCO had long been concerned with the diversity of cultural identities[23] and, in a way, the World Decade for Cultural Development, concluded in 1998,[24] had prepared UNESCO for addressing the

---

21 The 'double nature' already appeared in the Universal Declaration on Cultural Diversity (UDCD) in Article 8, and Article 2 of the Convention echoes this by stating that 'the cultural aspects of development are as important as its economic aspects'.

22 Preamble of the Convention [18].

23 UNESCO, *UNESCO and the Issue of Cultural Diversity: Review and Strategy, 1946–2004* (2004) http://portal.unesco.org/culture/en/file_download.php/47cc07ba56443cb277023a75b5786DivCult-BilanStrategies-ENG-sept04.pdf at 30 June 2008.

24 Intergovernmental Conference on Cultural Policies for Development (Stockholm, 1998) UNESCO Doc CLT-98/Conf.210/CLD.19.

ties between the preservation of cultural diversity and globalisation when this issue became a serious challenge.[25] The first stage consisted of the work of experts,[26] before entering a more political stage. The Member States were even more inclined to consider addressing the challenge since the process within UNESCO did not appear to be isolated. Various reflection processes had in fact been triggered, at first concerning the feasibility of a legal instrument,[27] then concerning the formulation and the content it could be given.[28] This strategy was carried out on various fronts in order to trigger a significant mobilisation of support, including from experts in the field, the pedagogical and diplomatic impact of which was aimed at those States less involved in the genesis of the process and the preparation of the negotiation. They also used several institutional networks such as that of the Francophonie, and even set up such networks, such as the International Network on Cultural Policies initiated by Canada.[29] In addition, the Council of Europe adopted a Declaration on cultural diversity in 2000,[30] followed by the Francophonie in 2001.[31] The process thus truly set a trend, while other more informal groups started to circulate draft projects for a possible convention.

Thus, although the United States ('US'), while not being a Member of UNESCO at the time, fiercely tried to counter it, the UNESCO Universal Declaration on Cultural Diversity[32] ('the Declaration') was adopted with an enthusiastic unanimity[33] by the 31st General Conference on 2 November 2001. This Declaration was completed by an Action Plan aimed at 'taking

---

25 UNESCO, Report of the World Commission on Culture and Development, *Our Creative Diversity* (UNESCO, Paris, 1997).

26 UNESCO, *Culture: a form of merchandise like no other? Symposium of experts, 14–15 June 1999* (UNESCO, Paris, 1999).

27 See I Bernier and H Ruiz Fabri, *Evaluation of the Legal Feasibility of an International Instrument Governing Cultural Diversity* (Bibliothèque Nationale du Québec, Montreal, 2002) http://www.mcc.gouv.qc.ca/international/diversite-culturelle/pdf/106145_faisabilite.pdf at 30 June 2008.

28 See, for example, the projects of the International Network for Cultural Diversity ('INCD') http://www.incd.net/encdfr.html at 10 November 2008.

29 See http://www.incp-ripc.org/ (22 October 2008).

30 *Declaration adopted by the Committee of Ministers on December 7 2000 at the 733rd Meeting of Ministers' Deputies*, CDMM (2000) 44 http://www.ebu.ch/CMSimages/en/leg_t_gats_coe_decl_cultural_diversity_071200_tcm6-4311.pdf at 30 June 2008.

31 *Cotonou Declaration adopted on 15 June 2001 during the 3rd Francophonie Ministerial Conference on Culture* http://www.coe.int/T/E/Com/Files/Ministerial-Conferences/2003-Culture/declaration.asp at 30 June 2008.

32 *UNESCO Universal Declaration on Cultural Diversity*, UNESCO Doc CLT-2002/WS/9 http://portal.unesco.org/ci/en/ev.php-URL_ID=16730&URL_DO=DO_TOPIC&URL_SECTION=201.html at 30 June 2008.

33 There were 185 Member States present to vote on the Declaration.

forward notably consideration of the advisability of an international legal instrument on cultural diversity'.[34] From a symbolic and political standpoint, a significant threshold was thus crossed. The process, by which the challenge was first addressed through a declaration, whose subject matter was far wider than that intended for a convention, was not a useless deviation but rather the opportunity to test, by means of a non-binding instrument, whether it was possible to push the initiative further.

The gathering

Setting up the negotiation required an aggregation of indispensable actors. In order to have an impact, it was obvious that the process needed first to involve a sufficient number of States, as well as a sufficient number of representative States. The stage for this thus needed to be a multilateral forum. In addition to the Declaration's success, three reasons explain the attraction of UNESCO: the global feature of the organisation, which promised the participation of a maximum number of States in the negotiation; its field of competence, which rendered it particularly appropriate for a global approach to cultural diversity; and the advantage of having a codified procedure, since UNESCO was a usual forum of negotiations, which facilitated planning the process.[35]

These arguments prevailed. However, it may be noted that the US was absent at the time that this decision was made. The US's interest in returning to UNESCO precisely on the occasion of the Convention was obviously underestimated. Admittedly, its return to an organisation it left twenty years earlier constituted part of its renewed (if short-lived) multilateral re-engagement after the 9/11 attacks. Nevertheless, it coincided with the project of a convention considered, wrongly or rightly, as a potential harm to the American film industry. In other words, considerable issues and the interests at stake account for a coherent and constant negative attitude by the US, basically founded on the *leitmotiv* of liberty and on the idea that the Convention truly aimed at commercial protectionism.

The US was not the only State interested in the matter, since some 150 Member States of UNESCO participated, at one stage or another, in the

---

[34] Above n 32 [Action Plan, 1]. In Article 12(c), the Declaration itself suggests UNESCO should 'Pursue its activities in standard-setting, awareness-raising and capacity-building in the areas related to the present Declaration within its fields of competence'.

[35] Rules of Procedure concerning recommendations to Member States and international conventions are covered by the terms of Article IV, paragraph 4, of the Constitution of UNESCO. See UNESCO, *Manual of the General Conference* (2002), http://unesdoc.unesco.org/images/0012/001255/125590e.pdf at 6 July 2008.

preparation of the Convention and expressed their views via their regional groups,[36] whose role in the elaboration process thus became visible. In this regard, the European Community possibly operated as a driving force throughout the negotiation, without ever being isolated since it was rapidly joined by States that were candidates for EU adherence, but also by Canada, Brazil, India, China, and Switzerland, among others.

Furthermore, like many contemporary multilateral negotiations, this one would be closely watched by NGOs, primarily the professional organisations from the cultural milieu, of whom some had already fought for the cultural exception before being closely involved in the setting-up of an alternative, notably by establishing coalitions for cultural diversity aimed at federating those working in the cultural milieu, through national and international networks.[37] They had mobilised substantial financial means in order to organise, in different parts of the world,[38] successive international meetings of professional organisations concerned with culture. Their promotion through the media prompted the participation of political personalities and led them to publicly commit to support the future Convention, while experts were solicited in order to elaborate legally and economically argued studies. In short, a very active lobby had been set up, at first and quite unsurprisingly in France and in Canada, where the professional organisations in the cultural milieu had been associated with the reflection and the preparation of projects from the beginning, and then more widely. Admittedly, this domination by corporatist interests was only the outward expression of ambiguities from which none of the actors were exempt, and the represented interests were less homogeneous than what the discourse of the coalitions let appear. Nevertheless, this corporate domination remains a key to reading the Convention.

Finally, as a location but also as an actor, there was UNESCO, which was not prepared to carry a negotiation involving so many issues, particularly one as highly polarised as this. However, UNESCO was not the only international organisation involved in the process. The concern expressed from the very beginning about the Convention's relationship to other international agreements motivated a request that the Director-General consult with the other international organisations that had thorough knowledge of or were in charge of the international legal instruments most likely to interfere with the normative action within UNESCO, namely and quite obviously the WTO. Since it

---

36 Such groups included the Group of 77, the Group of Latin America and Caribbean Countries (GRULAC), the African Group, and the Arab Group.

37 Thirty-seven coalitions exist as of today and have recently launched an International Federation of Coalitions for Cultural Diversity.

38 Annual meetings were successively organised in Canada, France, Korea, and Spain during the preparation and negotiation of the Convention.

could not be mentioned alone, the World Intellectual Property Organization ('WIPO') and the United Nations Conference on Trade and Development ('UNCTAD') were included as well. The process was quite unusual, but what was quite clear was that, independently from their legal value, adverse or even non-committal comments would cast a shadow. Thus, when the core of the subject was reached, that is, the negotiation was launched and the WTO and WIPO intended to send their observers, quite unsurprisingly every possible action was taken on the one side to trigger, and on the other side to prevent, comments emanating particularly from the WTO.[39]

2. THE IMPLEMENTATION OF A PROJECT: ELABORATING THE CONVENTION ON THE PROTECTION AND PROMOTION OF THE DIVERSITY OF CULTURAL EXPRESSIONS

In the end, the elaboration process went quite quickly. The outcome was due to a strong will to tighten the schedule, which was prompted by the fast polarisation of the negotiation.

The Dynamics of the Negotiation

The projected calendar of trade negotiations, which the promoters of the project had to take into consideration, was well known, especially the conclusion of the Doha Round, initially scheduled for the end of 2005. Therefore, time pressure was great since UNESCO's procedures are to submit the decision to elaborate and to adopt conventions to the General Assembly, which only gathers every two years, and also to provide for multiple stages backed up by time limits which considerably restrain the manoeuvring margin if a speedy process is being sought. Even by compressing the procedure to its shortest extent, it was impossible to adopt the Convention before the General Assembly of 2005, and even that remained a considerable challenge since such

[39] Even though a debate took place at the WTO, it did not lead to an aggregated standpoint imputable to the organisation. See the *WTO Annual Report 2004*, WTO Doc WT/GC/86 (2004) 20; General Council, *Minutes of meeting held 20 October 2004*, WTO Doc WT/GC/M/88 (2004) §64–85. Furthermore, upon invitation from the Director-General, UNESCO participated in an informal consultation with the delegates from the Members of the organisation, in Geneva on 11 November 2004, of which a summary of the expressed standpoints has been communicated to the Director-General of UNESCO and made accessible to UNESCO Member States (UNESCO Doc CLT/CPD/2004/CONF.607/1 (2004) Part IV, 22–6).

swiftness was unprecedented in an organisation whose activities do not usually call for urgency. Obviously, it did not seem wise to put this possibility into practice for a convention whose very subject matter already aroused great controversy. Thus, the attempt to speed up procedures was – successfully – made first with regard to the *Convention for the Safeguarding of the Intangible Cultural Heritage*.[40] In the end, the preparatory stages and the negotiation of the Convention took barely more than two years.

The Preparatory Stages

Preparation included a *Preliminary Study on the Technical and Legal Aspects relating to the Desirability of a Normative Instrument on Cultural Diversity*[41] submitted by the Director-General in 2003. On this basis, the General Conference invited the Director-General to submit, in 2005, a preliminary draft convention. In spite of the resistance displayed by the US, who re-entered UNESCO on this occasion, the adoption of the resolution deciding in favour of such a draft was completed with an enthusiasm uncommon at UNESCO. The only point of compromise granted to the reluctant actors was the demand for consultations with the WTO, WIPO and UNCTAD. Thus, the sensitive issue of the relationship between the future convention and other instruments of international law was forecast.[42] Moreover, considering that the States' representatives would need to be given a basis for discussion when they met, the Director-General of UNESCO decided to set up an international drafting group of independent experts working only for him. These experts[43] worked out a complete draft text. Their text mapped out single and consensual formulations of the drafted Articles, except (quite significantly) for the provision concerning the relationship between the Convention and other international instruments.[44]

---

[40] Opened for signature 17 October 2003, UNESCO Doc MISC/2003/CLT/CH/14 (entered into force 20 April 2006).

[41] This study acknowledges the totality of the texts actually in force or in the process of elaboration concerning cultural diversity, and which display several tracks of reflection concerning the advisability, the nature and the scope of a new instrument on cultural diversity: UNESCO Doc 166 EX/28 (2003).

[42] H Ruiz Fabri, 'Sur les enjeux juridiques et institutionnels liés à l'élaboration d'une convention sur la diversité culturelle par l'UNESCO' (May 2004) http://www.francophonie.org/diversiteculturelle/fichiers/aif_etude_ruiz_fabri_2004.pdf at 6 July 2008.

[43] The group met three times between autumn 2003 and the end of spring 2004; see UNESCO Docs CLT/CPD/2003-608/01, CLT/CPD/2004/602/6, CLT/CPD/2004/603/5.

[44] H Ruiz Fabri, 'Analyse et commentaire critique de l'avant-projet de conven-

The First Meeting

It could not reasonably be expected that the negotiation would truly be launched at the first meeting of the 'governmental experts' in September 2004, since the governments' written commentaries were due in November.[45] However, it was not until after the work of the drafting committee, in December 2004, that the coalition with which the US would be confronted started to emerge. This coalition was even fuelled by the attitude of the US, during a process that sometimes appeared as a counter-hegemonic battle, with the coalition being joined by almost all developing countries. The committee's work enabled States to assess the ease with which the negotiation could get stuck on apparently technical matters which nevertheless belied significant issues, which brought with it the threat that the schedule projected by the promoters of the Convention would not be complied with. Thus many issues of working methods and procedure still needed to be addressed during the second plenary session, with discussions often turning into a cacophony or a dialogue of the deaf. Also constantly tangible throughout the negotiation was the dilemma faced by many States who remained doubtful about the outcome of the project and thus did their best not to fall out too significantly with the US, resulting in apparently minor successive concessions of, however, a symbolic dimension.[46] If, by the end of the second session at the beginning of February 2005, more than half of the Convention had already been negotiated, the drawback was that the most sensitive arguments had been postponed, particularly the discussion on the definition of the essential terms of the Convention.[47] The third

---

tion sur la protection de la diversité des contenus culturels et des expressions artistiques dans la version soumise pour commentaires et observations aux gouvernements des Etats membres de l'UNESCO' (August 2004) http://www.francophonie.org/diversiteculturelle/fichiers/aif_etude_ruiz_fabri_aout2004.pdf at 6 July 2008.

[45] I Bernier, 'La première réunion d'experts gouvernementaux sur l'avant-projet de convention sur la protection de la diversité des contenus culturels et des expressions artistiques de l'UNESCO: Les implications pour la suite de la négociation' (December 2004) http://www.mcc.gouv.qc.ca/international/diversite-culturelle/chronique.html at 6 July 2008.

[46] An example was the discussion on the opportunity to incorporate in the Convention a definition of the term 'protection', which the US automatically associated with protectionism, thus supporting its denunciation of the truly economic aims of the negotiated text.

[47] I Bernier, 'La seconde session de la réunion des experts gouvernementaux sur l'avant-projet de convention sur la protection de la diversité des contenus culturels et des expressions artistiques de l'UNESCO' (May 2005) http://www.mcc.gouv.qc.ca/international/diversite-culturelle/chronique.html at 6 July 2005.

session[48] worked on a 'consolidated' text,[49] that is to say without brackets and options, which had been prepared by its President and imposed as the basis for discussions by an intense diplomatic battle. A directive presidency and a dilution of the most sensible discussions in many working groups enabled States to complete the negotiation quite efficiently. The debates flared up when the issue of the Convention's relationship to other international instruments was addressed. A provision on this matter was not mandatory and many conventions operate well without one.

Everyone was aware, though, that the existence of such a provision would greatly contribute to giving a meaning to the project. This was the turning point upon which the battle of the negotiation would be won or lost. Once the relationship issue had been acknowledged but also isolated in the process, the rest of the negotiation could be carried out, possibly at the price that some issues, such as the dispute settlement provisions or the existence of a federal clause, were settled too rapidly.

While the negotiation was successfully completed at the beginning of June 2005, the US did not 'surrender' without a public statement denouncing the 'deeply flawed' character of a text which it considered truly to be about international trade and not culture and whose adoption would put at stake UNESCO's reputation. Moreover, it had in fact not yet given up. It first fought back in the forum of the WTO, seeking and obtaining from its Director-General approval for an informal meeting to be called, in August 2005, in order to address the issue of the Convention. Several States opposed to the text of the draft Convention argued that the minutes of the meeting should be sent to the Secretariat of UNESCO in order to inform it that the text approved of in June still raised many difficulties for several WTO Members. The majority of the participating States were however opposed to a procedure which consisted of communicating an unsolicited standpoint. However, probably hoping for a surge in the opposite direction, triggered by the letter sent by Condoleezza Rice to the Foreign Affairs ministers of UNESCO Members in which the US concerns about the text were reiterated at a more official level, the US took up the battle in UNESCO. It fiercely fought using procedural arguments. For

[48] I Bernier, 'La troisième session de la réunion intergouvernementale d'experts sur l'Avant-projet de Convention sur la protection et la promotion de la diversité des expressions culturelles et l'examen du Projet de Convention par la Conférence générale de l'Unesco' (January 2006) http://www.mcc.gouv.qc.ca/international/diversite-culturelle/chronique.html at 6 July 2008.

[49] H Ruiz Fabri, 'Analyse du texte consolidé d'avant-projet de convention sur la protection de la diversité des expressions culturelles établi par le Président de la Réunion intergouvernementale' (May 2005) http://www.francophonie.org/diversiteculturelle/fichiers/aif_note_ruiz_fabri_mai2005.pdf at 6 July 2008.

example, it came up with a new practice, which it repeated consistently until the end of the General Conference, whereby it would ask for a vote to be taken, first to prevent the Executive Board from recommending to the General Conference that it convert the preliminary draft into a formal draft and adopt it immediately, and then to slow down the adoption process by proposing numerous amendments for which it sought, as it was entitled to, a vote for every single one of them. UNESCO, where agreements are usually reached by consensus, was not equipped for electronic votes so the votes took place by show of hands: the votes supporting the amendment were never more than three and the abstentions never more than five, with the US positions being systematically rejected by overwhelming majorities. Later, the Convention was approved by the same majority. Commission IV could thus suggest that the General Conference adopt the Convention, which it did on 20 October 2005, again by an overwhelming majority of 148 to 2,[50] with 4 abstentions.[51]

The Outcome of the Negotiation

The text eventually adopted may have a limited subject matter, but it is matched by the wide scope in which the States' rights are firmly asserted while the obligations weighing on them appear only to be hinted at.

The Convention applies 'to the policies and measures adopted by the Parties related to the protection and promotion of the diversity of cultural expressions'.[52] In other words, the text is mainly aimed at the means of action of States. Thus focused, the Convention is not intended to regulate various other matters, even subsidiarily. Its purpose is not to proclaim cultural rights, and the appearance of the notion of human rights is only to recall that the protection and promotion of the diversity of cultural expressions are inseparable from respect for human rights. Thus, it is a question, on the one hand, of ensuring that the Convention is not invoked to justify, on the pretext of protecting cultural diversity, measures that infringe internationally guaranteed human rights, and, on the other, of affirming that the diversity of cultural expressions cannot be effective if human rights and fundamental freedoms, such as freedom of expression, information and communication, and the possibility of choosing cultural expressions are not guaranteed. Moreover, the text is not intended to clarify the legal status of authors and artists or to grant prerogatives to civil society in general. At most, these actors are mentioned as stakeholders whose important contribution to the protection and promotion of

50 Only the US and Israel rejected the draft.

51 Australia, Honduras, Liberia and Nicaragua abstained.

52 Article 3.

the diversity of cultural expressions States should recognise,[53] which is no more than they deserve but of little normative significance. Last but not least, the text does not deal with certain issues essential to the diversity of cultural expressions such as intellectual property rights or the rules governing the economic structuring of the cultural industry sector. However, the decision to leave them out, which is understandable in terms of relative effectiveness, since the negotiation of an instrument incorporating these dimensions was doubtless out of reach, should not be allowed to obscure the fact that if the protection of the diversity of cultural expressions is to be effective, it will not be possible to elude them for very long,[54] especially as this is a matter of particular concern for developing countries. Moreover, among its objectives the Convention includes a reaffirmation of the link between culture and development and, similarly, proclaims a principle of 'the complementarity of economic and cultural aspects of development' and a principle of international solidarity and cooperation, which envisages, in particular, the need to enable developing countries to create and strengthen their cultural industries. Clearly, then, the cultural industry issue is a vital one, considering the nature of the present modes of production and dissemination in the cultural sphere.

More than rights and obligations, the text formulates rights and incentives. The normative heart of the Convention lies in the reaffirmation of the 'sovereign right to formulate and implement their cultural policies and to adopt measures to protect and promote the diversity of cultural expressions and to strengthen international cooperation to achieve the purposes of this Convention'.[55] This gives ground for a rather comprehensive approach, so as to ensure that States do not inadvertently depart from it in favour of liberalisation commitments whose extent they may have failed to appreciate. Indeed it is within this context that the reaffirmation of the 'sovereign right' of States acquires its full significance. In any event, it does not prevent them from choosing to limit or waive this sovereign right, for example by entering into commitments to liberalise trade, the assumption of which itself corresponds to

---

[53] Articles 7.2 and 11.

[54] See Smiers, above n 2; L Richieri Hanania, *La diversité culturelle et le commerce des produits et services culturels* (Thèse Université Paris 1 Panthéon-Sorbonne, Paris, 2007); J Smiers, 'Regulating the Cultural Market in Favour of Cultural Diversity at the Same Time Cherishing the Freedom of Communication' in *La diversité et les échanges culturels dans le cadre de la globalisation* (CGRI, Brussels, 2005) 85–101; R Wallis, 'Trade and Cultural Diversity. Technological Opportunities, Legal Regimes and Threats from Collective Dominance' in *La diversité et les échanges culturels dans le cadre de la globalisation* (CGRI, Brussels, 2005) 65–77.

[55] Article 5(1) of the Convention.

the exercise of sovereignty.[56] It is therefore more a question of drawing the attention of States to the future consequences of such commitments, insofar as in practice they prove to be more or less irreversible.

The text does not offer a general definition of the measures that Parties can take in this respect, which leaves them free to choose their own, but it avoids the trap of being simultaneously too vague and too restrictive by giving an illustrative list. The importance of this list is obvious. It sets out, with variable clarity, the principal types of measures that Parties may use. These include, in particular, support measures, which enable the economic dimension of cultural diversity to be taken into account, and, under cover of a rather abstruse formula, quotas. There is also an explicit reference to public institutions, which may be established and supported and be a means of enhancing diversity of the media. Finally, there are references to measures on behalf of domestic independent cultural industries and the informal sector, aimed at providing them with effective access to the means of production, dissemination and distribution, as well as measures aimed at supporting artists. Thus, all the measures listed gain in legitimacy, subject to their being applied in a manner consistent with the objectives of the Convention. However, there can be no denying that in some respects the text gives rise to uncertainty.

There is no trace of any truly binding formula in the final text, as far as positive measures to be taken are concerned. On the measures taken, it is always a question of 'endeavouring', 'fostering', or 'encouraging', that is to say, formulas typical of soft law in the substantive sense of the term, even where intervention on behalf of threatened cultural expressions is involved. The argument invariably put forward to justify this kind of formulation, and one which could therefore be used in defence of the Convention, is that account has to be taken of the fact that not all Parties have the same resources and, if the obligations are too strict, they could discourage those economically less well endowed from acceding to a Convention that required them to assume commitments beyond their means. However, it is not certain that this is the real or principal cause of the softening of the Convention. The Convention promoters were not particularly keen on having overly strong commitments.

The provisions relating to international cooperation are fairly well developed. Special emphasis is placed on cooperation with and assistance for developing countries to enable them to strengthen their cultural industries. This cooperation may take various forms (for example information sharing,

---

56 According to the Permanent Court of International Justice 'the right [to enter] into international engagements is an attribute of State sovereignty': *Case of the SS Wimbledon* [1923] 1 PCIJ Ser A 5, 25.

technology transfer, capacity building in the public sector, conclusion of co-production and co-distribution agreements) and may include financial assistance. In particular, the text encourages developed countries to grant preferential treatment to developing countries in connection with cultural exchanges and, more especially, proposes, as a means of cooperation, 'innovative partnerships' between States and their private partners. This type of arrangement is designed to ensure effective assistance with the development and strengthening of the cultural sector in developing countries. Secondly, the Convention provides for the establishment of an International Fund for Cultural Diversity and for mechanisms for the exchange, analysis and dissemination of information, to be managed by UNESCO. Nevertheless, although innovative cooperation formulas are certainly identified and it is useful to list the ways and means of achieving effective cooperation, from the normative point of view, it is still a question of 'endeavouring', 'encouraging', and so on. Moreover, the International Fund for Cultural Diversity depends on voluntary, and hence uncertain, contributions. The enthusiasm of a number of developing countries for such a fund overcame the doubts about the usefulness of an arrangement of this type but never completely dispelled the fairly widely shared conviction, especially on the part of potential donors, that other modes of cooperation were preferable. All in all, the fact remains that the question of the resources needed to implement genuine policies for the protection and promotion of the diversity of cultural expressions by the developing countries is by no means settled, although it is essential to show that their involvement in the negotiations was not solely intended to obtain their support for a text that was subsequently confined, in practice, to protecting the right to support cultural industries which they themselves often lack.

Just as they stripped the text of its normative constraints, the negotiators did everything they could to rid it of as many institutional and procedural constraints as possible. True, the Convention has organs, notably a Conference of Parties, which meets, in principle, every two years, and an Intergovernmental Committee, which will be the executive organ, with the UNESCO Secretariat providing the necessary administrative assistance. Moreover, the Intergovernmental Committee has a number of functions (such as establishing procedures for consultation between the parties and preparing operational guidelines for the implementation of the Convention) which could put it in a position to contribute to some fairly effective monitoring of the implementation of the Convention. This should not be ignored, particularly as it is known that, in general, follow-up and/or dispute settlement arrangements – though in most cases non-binding, which means that States are more inclined to accept them – make a positive contribution to the effectiveness of the commitments contained in the agreements or accompanying recommendations.[57] However, as we shall see, everything depends not only on when they are set up but also, and above all, on the firmness of the intention to make them work.

As for the dispute settlement mechanism, during the course of the negotiations it became particularly 'lightweight' since, should negotiation and/or mediation fail, it merely provides for possible recourse to conciliation in accordance with a procedure laid down in an Annex to the Convention. This is far from being a mechanism as powerful as that to be found, for example, in the WTO, if only because, like all conciliation, the outcome is not binding on the parties to the dispute. However, we should refrain from judging it too harshly. Indeed, one might wonder what disputes are likely to arise out of a Convention with so few obligations. For all that, the mechanism has the virtue of existing, albeit at the price of an opt-out clause that allows any party to refuse to recognise it. It also has the merit of being a compulsory conciliation, that is to say, one that can be activated unilaterally, while providing for a possible disagreement to be reviewed by a body composed of specialists in cultural matters. Their decisions, even though not legally binding, may still be useful, in particular for proposing interpretations of a text which, like all international conventions, has its share of ambiguities. This could be all the more important in that the Convention has to fit in with the rest of international law.

3. THE ACHIEVEMENT OF THE PROJECT: INSERTING THE CONVENTION INTO THE INTERNATIONAL LEGAL ORDER

The Convention has never been thought of as an isolated project. On the contrary, it was conceived to produce effects on other international norms, particularly on WTO law. The negotiation has displayed quite clearly that this has been a central issue. However, this does not answer the question as to whether the Convention can truly measure up to this challenge. Indeed, this implies an effective implementation, whose terms will inevitably put pressure upon the ways in which these relationship issues can be resolved.

The Relationship between International Norms

A harmonious relationship between international norms cannot be granted by the sole existence of a provision in the Convention, but also depends on other triggers.

---

[57] See H Ruiz Fabri et al. (eds) *L'effectivité des organisations internationales – Mécanismes de suivi et de contrôle* (Athènes/Paris, Sakkoulas/Pedone, 2000).

Regarding the relationship according to the Convention, it should be recalled that international conventions do not necessarily contain provisions for regulating this situation, the lack of which triggers an implicit referral to the rules of general international law contained in Article 30 of the *Vienna Convention on the Law of Treaties*,[58] although these concern only treaties relating to the same subject matter. However, it is hard to see how the Convention could have remained silent on this point. Indeed, a clause was deliberately included not just for legal reasons but also, and above all, for political and symbolic reasons. More particularly, it forms the subject of Article 20, which was bitterly negotiated and supplemented by Article 21. To put it briefly, Article 20 declares that the convention is not subordinated to any other treaty while it is not intended to modify any other treaties. This is a perfectly schizophrenic formula[59] which calls, at the end of the day, for mutual supportiveness between the Convention and other treaties. Of course, while this is the intention, it does not shield this meaning from competing and adversarial interpretations. However, it is also possible to envisage forestalling this type of effect by means of more political and preventive articulation procedures. In particular, this is the objective of Article 21 according to which 'Parties undertake to promote the objectives and principles of this Convention in other international forums. For this purpose, Parties shall consult each other, as appropriate, bearing in mind these objectives and principles'. This type of provision has the advantage of refocusing attention on the real challenges of fitting the Convention into the rest of international law. Indeed, the question is not so much one of knowing whether, in itself, the Convention is going to prevail over other treaties, in a spirit of competition, as of making sure that its objectives will not be sacrificed or indeed forgotten but are and will be positively taken into account, in a spirit of complementarity. In other words, it is a question of acting in such a way that the effort to reconcile the various aspects and implications of cultural diversity made in the text does not remain confined to the text but spills over into other forums in which the issue might be dealt with directly or indirectly. From this point of view, responsibility for the articulation of the Convention with the rest of international law lies essentially with the Parties, who must not only be consistent in their commitments

58 *Vienna Convention on the Law of Treaties*, opened for signature 23 May 1969, 1155 UNTS 331 (entered into force 27 January 1980).

59 The same kind of juxtaposition of two formulas on non-subordination and non-prejudice, which inspired the reflection for the Convention, appears for example in the Cartagena Protocol. See H Ruiz Fabri, 'Concurrence ou complémentarité entre les mécanismes de règlement des différends du Protocole de Carthagène et ceux de l'OMC?' in J Bourrinet and S Maljean-Dubois (eds) *Le commerce international des organismes génétiquement modifiés* (La Documentation française, Paris, 2002) 149–76.

but also endeavour to promote the principles and objectives of the Convention in other forums. To assist them in this, the text proposes consultations between Parties. Thus, it expresses the realistic and pragmatic view that collective positions will carry more weight and be more effective, by virtue of being common and shared. It also reflects a positive and conciliatory approach capable of preventing competition by acting upstream of the processes of discussion. However, at the present stage, these conciliatory intentions concern only the Parties to the Convention and the terms in which they are expressed are only weakly binding. Thus, the threat of conflict is not averted, as far as the point of view of other normative spaces is concerned, and in particular that of WTO law.

Regarding the relationship viewed from outside the Convention, quite naturally, there remain several uncertainties with regard to the possible effects of the Convention in other normative spaces, such as the WTO, whether the matter is considered through the perspective of Article 20 or more broadly.[60] Although Article 20 has been fiercely negotiated, one problem which has not been solved (and which the Convention could not solve) is that of the extent to which such an approach might usefully be adopted in a forum other than that of the Convention; for example, before a WTO Panellist or Appellate Body member. The issue whether he or she can apply norms other than those of WTO law and which would not be expressly mentioned by WTO law remains highly controversial and it seems rather unlikely that the Convention would be used directly and autonomously as a means of defence in order to justify non-compliance with a WTO obligation. The question is more likely to arise in terms of interpretation, in cases where Articles 31 and 32 of the *Vienna Convention on the Law of Treaties* are being assessed.[61] Indeed, one might reasonably seek to claim the use of Article 31(3)(c) of the *Vienna Convention on the Law of Treaties*, according to which 'there shall be taken into account, together with the context [. . .]: (c) any relevant rules of international law applicable in the relations between the parties'. It is well known that this provision is now more frequently used before international courts. The WTO Appellate Body, since its earliest cases, has itself taken position against the 'clinical isolation'[62] of WTO law from the rest of international law and has, ever since, adopted an approach of complementarity and mutual support between WTO law and exterior treaties, by interpreting the former in light of

---

60 T Voon, 'UNESCO and the WTO: a clash of cultures?' (2006) 55 *International and Comparative Law Quarterly* 635.

61 H Ruiz Fabri, 'Le juge de l'OMC: ombres et lumières d'une figure judiciaire singulière' [2006] *Revue Générale de Droit International Public* 39.

62 *United States – Standards for reformulated and conventional gasoline*, WTO Doc WT/DS2/9 (1996) 17.

the latter.[63] The Convention could thus operate as a reference either for interpreting the commitments undertaken by States, for example by justifying a restrictive interpretation thereof so as to ensure that WTO obligations do not undermine the Convention, or for deciding whether the challenged measures could be considered as covered by an exception to free trade commitments. The latter may, *a priori*, seem narrow. Only the GATT mentions the cultural issue via Article XX(f), which allows the restriction of free trade for the 'protection of national treasures of artistic, historic or archaeological value': Article XX(f), however, applies only to goods and would thus call for an unusually extensive interpretation in order to cover culture at large. Two other options remain, which are common to the exception provisions of GATT and GATS: that is the exceptions which allow trade restrictions in order to protect public morals,[64] but here again a particularly extensive interpretation would be required, and that of restrictive measures necessary to secure compliance with laws or regulations which are not inconsistent with GATT or GATS provisions.[65] The latter might be interesting concerning measures in application of the Convention, since the WTO Appellate Body has concluded that 'the terms "laws or regulations" cover rules that form part of the domestic legal system of a WTO Member, including rules deriving from international agreements that have been incorporated into the domestic legal system of a WTO Member or have direct effect according to that WTO Member's legal system'.[66] Nevertheless, one would at least need to prove the 'necessity'[67] of such measures, if it were admitted that the Convention was not, in itself, inconsistent with WTO law, which raises the issue of the Convention's binding character in itself[68] as well as that of its effective implementation.

---

63 *United States – Import prohibition of certain shrimp and shrimp products*, WTO Doc WT/DS58/AB/R AB-1998-4 (1998) §129. Cf the report of the Panel in *European Communities – Measures affecting the approval and marketing of biotech products*, WTO Doc WT/DS291-DS292-DS293/R (2006) [7.66–7.75], on which see L Gradoni and H Ruiz Fabri, 'L'affaire des OGM devant le juge de l'OMC : science et précaution sans principes' [2007] *Diritto del commercio internazionale* 641.

64 Article XX(a) GATT and Article XIV(a) GATS.

65 Article XX(d) GATT and Article XIV(c) GATS.

66 *Mexico – Tax measures on soft drinks and other beverages*, WTO Doc WT/DS308/AB/R (2006) [79]; see also [69–71]. See P Monnier and H Ruiz Fabri, 'Chronique du règlement des différends de l'OMC' (2005) 134 *Journal du Droit International* 1211.

67 H Ruiz Fabri, 'La nécessité devant le juge de l'OMC' in SFDI (ed.) *Le droit international et la nécessité* (Pedone, Paris, 2007) 189.

68 That is, it might be difficult to argue that trade restrictions are necessary in order to implement the Convention, given the weak obligations imposed by the Convention.

Since the receptivity of the WTO Panellist or Appellate Body member is closely linked to the fact that the acknowledged exterior treaties express long-shared concerns, the outcome will probably largely depend on the powers supporting the Convention. The prior case law does not evidence such a receptivity concerning cultural issues. Thus, in the *Canada – Periodicals* case,[69] the WTO Panel did not acknowledge the Canadian argument according to which US magazines and Canadian magazines were not, for cultural reasons, like products. The Panel did, however, specify, 'in order to avoid any misunderstandings', that 'the ability of any Member to take measures to protect its cultural identity was not at issue in the present case'.[70] This case in fact helped trigger the process of preparing the Convention.

In the meantime, the *Asbestos* case[71] provides evidence of the yielding and adaptable character of the 'like product' principle,[72] which is used to assess the existence or not of prohibited discrimination. In *Asbestos*, the EC was permitted to distinguish between products made from asbestos, and those that were not: public health considerations meant that the products were not 'like'. One could plead the lack of likeness of cultural goods and services, due precisely to their cultural dimension and its impact, for example, on the consumers' tastes and habits, and the Convention could operate as a ground for the argument through the statement of the specificity of cultural goods and services. However, cultural diversity would need to be acknowledged as of the 'same dignity'[73] as public health in the *Asbestos* case in order for this argument to be successful.

---

[69] See *Canada – Certain measures concerning periodicals*, WTO Doc WT/DS31/R (14 March 1997) (Panel Report) ('*Canada – Periodicals*'). The case came before the WTO concerning split-run periodicals, whose editorial content, which was largely produced in the US, could be electronically transmitted in order to produce the Canadian version, which contributed to reducing the production costs. Furthermore, this case would reveal the possible cumulative application of rules relating to goods and those relating to services. C Carmody, 'When "Cultural Identity was Not at Issue": Thinking about *Canada – Certain Measures concerning Periodicals*' (1999) 30 *Law and Policy in International Business* 231, G Gagné, 'Libéralisation et exception culturelle – le différend canado-américain sur les périodiques' (1999) 30 *Études internationals*, no 3; M-P Lanfranchi, 'Canada – Certaines mesures concernant les périodiques', in B Stern and H Ruiz Fabri (eds) *La jurisprudence de l'OMC – 1996–1997* (Nijhoff, Leiden, 2004) 125; A Scow, 'The Sports Illustrated Canada Controversy: Canada 'Strikes Out' in Its Bid to Protect Its Periodical Industry from U.S. Split-Run Periodicals' (1998) 7 *Minnesota Journal of Global Trade* 245.

[70] *Canada – Periodicals* [5.45].

[71] *European Communities – Measures Affecting Asbestos and Products Containing Asbestos*, WTO Doc WT/DS135/AB/R, AB-2000-11 (2001).

[72] See also *Japan – Taxes on alcoholic beverages*, WTO Doc WT/DS8/AB/R, WT/DS10/AB/R, WT/DS11/AB/R, AB-1996-2 (1996).

[73] M Hahn, above n 3, 551.

The same trigger can influence the negotiation of several pending issues, especially in the field of services,[74] and justify, in the meantime, that the opposition with regard to liberalisation commitments is upheld and exemptions are extended. Although very few States have so far undertaken commitments or declared to be inclined to do so, since most of them have again rejected any demand of liberalisation in the audiovisual sector in March 2006, such support appears all the more essential as controversies have already arisen. Exemptions, for example, while they operate as shields for several WTO Members, are vulnerable to discussion. Furthermore, pleading GATS Article XIX(1), several States[75] have already reminded Members that 'audiovisual services . . . are an integral part of the services negotiation'; have expressed 'great concern over efforts by some key participants in the negotiations to create an a priori exclusion for such an important sector', although 'above all, trade in audiovisual services results in cultural exchange, the best way to promote cultural diversity'; and have stated that this process was 'inconsistent' with the Negotiating Guidelines for the services negotiations of the Doha Development Agenda and 'with the full and open dialogue' on which the WTO is based. However, Article XIX also specifies that 'the process of liberalisation shall take place with due respect for national policy objectives and the level of development of individual Members, both overall and in individual sectors'. Clearly, this does not mean that WTO Members need to make offers and requirements simultaneously in all sectors. The objectives of national policy that the liberalisation process has to take into account can thus be objectives of cultural policy. From this perspective, it is not merely a matter of bluntly refusing any liberalisation commitment. Yet, since it is well known that it is almost impossible to call into question a commitment undertaken at the WTO, if only because it is far too expensive and out of the reach of most States, it seems essential to, first and foremost, clarify a number of issues that would

---

74 With regard to this, one can think of transversal issues such as the regime of subsidies or of safeguard measures in cases of urgency, of issues such as the distinction between audiovisual services and telecommunications which technological evolution has contributed to blur, of issues such as the treatment of e-commerce and the exact classification of the various services (since there is not, with regard to services, a unique and harmonised classification). Each State is free to not use the classification proposed within the WTO, which can lead to extensive discussions concerning the scope of application and the range of its commitments. See the long discussions held before the WTO Appellate Body in order to determine whether the sub-sector 10.D 'Other recreational services (except sporting)' covered online gambling services. *United States – Measures affecting the cross-border supply of gambling and betting services*, WTO Doc WT/DS285.AB/R (2005).

75 Communication from the United States, Hong Kong (China), Japan, Mexico and Taiwan, presented to the WTO Council for Trade in Services on 30 June 2005, WTO Doc TN/S/W/49.

help those States inclined to such commitments to undertake them knowingly and to adequately modulate them so that they are consistent with their objectives of cultural policy. This clearly pinpoints the fact that the relationship between the Convention and the ongoing negotiations in other normative spaces depends on a balance of powers in which the effective implementation of the Convention can weigh significantly.

Effective Implementation

If the Convention is to matter, it is not sufficient for it to enter into force, which is already achieved. It needs to be effectively implemented, a requirement that raises technical but also political issues.

Although it has been adopted by a very wide majority, the Convention can only be binding on those States who have ratified it. The negotiators had decided upon a requirement of 30 ratifications, which seems like quite a low benchmark, but was a deliberate choice in order to allow an entry into force as promptly as possible. The benchmark was thus reached as early as the end of 2006, so that the entry into force, planned to occur three months after the deposit of the 30th instrument of ratification, occurred on 18 March 2007. Everyone was aware, though, that this was not yet enough. The impact of the Convention depends on the level of adherence it receives. Obviously it cannot legally bind trade negotiations, but it can operate to politically mark the limit between what is negotiable and what is not, by constituting a rallying point for States. However, in order to carry out such a function, it needs a support not only quantitatively wide but also qualitatively representative.

Although the Council of Europe urged its Members, as early as February 2006, to ratify the Convention 'at the earliest opportunity' while the Francophonie did the same, as well as the African Union and various organisations from the Lusophone and Hispanophone space, one could observe, however, that UNESCO did not hurry to ensure the usual after-sales service for its conventions, even though the necessary means had been set up. The US might possibly have recovered at this stage the influence it lost during the negotiation. In any event, one can logically assume that it has undertaken every possible effort in order to limit the effects of a convention it regards as disastrous. Two complementary means of action were and are at its disposal. According to several statements made by officials of the US Department of State, one means consisted of trying to prevent States from ratifying the Convention.[76] It is difficult to assess whether it has succeeded in this respect, since the ratification is a stage individually completed by each State and thus

---

[76] Statement by Kristin Silverberg, quoted in *Le Monde* (Paris), 24 October 2005.

is a highly decentralised process, depending on internal procedures and on each government's schedule, and since, counting the ongoing or accomplished procedures, the number of accessions or ratifications had already reached 100 by the end of September 2009. The other means of action consisted of intensifying the policy of negotiating bilateral treaties, in which the balance of power obviously enables the US to be granted concessions that are elsewhere out of reach. While the Convention has clearly contributed to making States realise the effects of their liberalisation commitments, it cannot prevent them from undertaking such commitments when they feel their interests would be served thereby. However, the paradox is that this policy of bilateral treaties, which other States and the European Communities have begun to imitate, starts to raise problematic issues with regard to the WTO itself, whereas it does not entirely compromise the efficiency of the Convention, whose 'strengthening' can, on the contrary, help to negotiate provisions specific to cultural goods and services, such as those existing in several bilateral treaties.[77] However, the number of ratifications is not the only factor accounting for the Convention's influence. This depends as well on an effective application.

It is not only the number of parties to the Convention but also how they have decided to enact its provisions that will determine its true scope. Were an early sign of sufficient political will to support effective implementation to be lacking, the Convention could well have exhausted its effects in the negotiating process. While the Parties can obviously call on the Convention and refer to it from the moment of its entry into force, especially concerning their municipal measures and policies, the seriousness and coherence of their intentions regarding the Convention has to be demonstrated by the adoption of provisions essential to a complete implementation.

A complete implementation requires, in the first instance, Parties to set up the institutional infrastructure of the Convention, in order to ensure its multilateral running.[78] This has been initiated during the first meeting of the Parties in June 2007 and the first meeting of the Intergovernmental Committee in December 2007 provided the Parties with the first guidelines, especially

[77] See, for instance, the bilateral treaties between the US and Morocco, and the US and Singapore: see *Morocco – United States Free Trade Agreement*, 15 June 2004, Morocco – United States, http://www.ustr.gov/Trade_Agreements/Bilateral/Morocco_FTA/FInal_Text/Section_Index.html at 10 November 2008; *Singapore – United States Free Trade Agreement*, 15 January 2003, Singapore – United States, http://www.ustr.gov/Trade_Agreements/Bilateral/Singapore_FTA/Final_Texts/Section_Index.html at 10 November 2008.

[78] See I Bernier and H Ruiz Fabri, *La mise en œuvre et le suivi de la Convention de l'UNESCO sur la protection et la promotion de la diversité des expressions culturelles* (2005) http://www.diversite-culturelle.qc.ca/fileadmin/documents/pdf/UNESCO-anglais.pdf at 8 July 2008.

regarding the functioning of the International Fund for Cultural Diversity and the financial resources to be allocated. Other meetings are expected to take place during the next months and only their outcomes will allow an evaluation of whether the challenge of an effective multilateral running will be met, toward and maybe against the bureaucratic tendency of UNESCO. Several mechanisms such as the consultation mechanisms are particularly important to get up and running, in so far as it would demonstrate a proactive approach to the Convention, which is intended to enhance its international credibility. Nevertheless, not surprisingly, States seem reluctant to proceed quickly on this path.

But the principal factor of credibility will most likely arise from the way in which States actually implement the Convention. As pointed out above, most of the commitments in the Convention do not dictate a precise result and can at best be considered as behavioural obligations, on which one can hardly base a claim, at least from a legal standpoint, unless in terms of lack of diligence. Yet, this raises serious difficulties in terms of proof, since it belongs to States to decide in the first place under what conditions actions should take place on their territory and at the international level in order to fulfil their commitments. Thus, quite obviously, it is more incentives rather than legal constraint that will account for the Convention's implementation, whether those incentives will arise from 'civil society', which has, here again, a role to play, or from multilateral surveillance. Alongside actions undertaken at the national level, especially towards transparency and openness, the development of international cooperation appears to be the test of the Convention's credibility. In fact, the Convention remains under suspicion not only of being merely an instrument in favour of those who had already set up interventionist cultural policies and who want to protect their tools, but also of not being able to avert the threat that these States might take advantage of this circumstance. This criticism is recurrent, based on the argument that a cultural dimension can be discovered in almost anything that is man-made, from Japanese cars to French foie gras. Yet, does the incrimination of the threat of misuse truly express a criticism, since this is inherent in any permissive text and since almost none of the actors has an interest in preventing free trade, nor tries to do so? On the contrary, one should rather wonder whether trade with only one provider is actually free trade, or whether there now exists a kind of international division of cultural work, for example between 'global' movies and 'national' movies.[79]

---

[79] B J K Richardson, 'Hollywood's Vision of a Clear, Predictable Trade Framework Consistent with Cultural Diversity' in C Beat Graber et al. (eds), *Free Trade versus Cultural Diversity* (Schulthess, Zürich, 2004) 111.

The political, legal, as well as symbolic battle to which the elaboration of the Convention gave rise has not produced real victims. Undeniably, the Convention has already performed a highly significant pedagogical function by alerting States to the risks and consequences of their commitments, especially in the area of trade liberalisation. If the Convention is most certainly not the legal monster stigmatised by the US, neither is it an absolute shield against the decrease of cultural diversity through globalisation and an untempered trade liberalisation, especially considering that it never addresses the essential issue of the harm caused by cultural industries ever more concentrated, operating according to an oligopolistic logic and perfectly assessing and applying the rules of a market economy.

9. Viet Nam, human rights and trade: implications of Viet Nam's accession to the WTO

David Kinley, Hai Nguyen and Odette Murray

1. INTRODUCTION[1]

Viet Nam has taken enormous strides over the past decade. It has re-engaged with the international community; its economy is well and truly emerging; its cities are vibrant; and its people are generally much better fed, healthier and more prosperous. International trade has increased significantly since the US lifted its trade embargo in the mid-1990s, and is now set to be further increased and liberalised following Viet Nam's accession to the WTO in January 2007. But not everyone in the country has benefited, and not to the same degree. The rural poor (of which there are still millions), women and children working in the burgeoning industrial sectors, and ethnic minority groups are all faring less well. The connection between trade, economic development and human rights is nowhere more clearly demonstrated than in the plight of these groups. To varying extents, their fundamental human rights such as the rights to food, work, education, housing, adequate standards of living, non-discrimination, and cultural and religious freedoms are as yet inadequately protected, largely because the economic and political circumstances of these groups are less favourably affected by Viet Nam's transformation from a centrally planned economy into a 'market economy with a socialist orientation'.[2] This chapter analyses the interrelations of these various factors from the perspective of their impact on the protection and promotion of human rights in Viet Nam in the

[1] This is an abridged and updated version of the following publication: David Kinley and Hai Nguyen, 'Viet Nam, Human Rights and Trade: Implications of Viet Nam's Accession to the WTO' (Occasional Paper No 39, Friedrich Ebert Stiftung, 2008) http://library.fes.de/pdf-files/iez/global/05359.pdf at 10 November 2008.

[2] This goal was initially set by the Tenth Congress of the Viet Nam Communist Party and has been pursued since then: see Dinh Van An, 'Building Institutions for a Market Economy with Socialist Orientation in Vietnam' (2006) 1 *Vietnam Economic Management Review* 10.

post-WTO accession era. In the chapter we stress that trade liberalisation under the WTO is a means to an end, not an end in itself, and as such we outline legal, business and political strategies that are essential, in our view, for ensuring that trade is exploited for the benefit of the comprehensive realisation of all human rights, not the other way around.

2. VIET NAM IN A GLOBAL CONTEXT

A. The Vietnamese Economic Tiger

On 11 January 2007, Viet Nam became the 150th member of the WTO. The process of accession had formally begun 11 years earlier in 1995 and had entailed no fewer than 14 rounds of multilateral and over 40 rounds of bilateral negotiations. The economic changes undergone by the country in the final three years of this period, when negotiations were at their most intense, have been described as being 'quite remarkable, involving not only hard external negotiations, but equally, if not more difficult internal consensus building around which areas to liberalise or protect, and to what extent',[3] where 'one side wonders whether they should join the world economy, and the other side wonders how they should join the world economy'.[4]

Viet Nam's economic achievements over the past decade or so are indeed impressive: GDP has grown at an annual average rate of 7.8 per cent for the past six years (2001–2006), which translates into 6.7 per cent in per capita terms;[5] the economy has more than doubled in net worth (in real terms, measured by GDP) between 1995 and 2005; both aggregate exports and imports are expanding at over 20 per cent per annum; domestic consumption is also raging at about 20 per cent year on year increases; foreign direct investment (FDI), which has been growing steadily, exploded in 2006, increasing 50 per cent on the year before (in apparent anticipation of WTO accession);[6] and

---

3 World Bank, *Taking Stock: An Update on Viet Nam's Economic Developments* (World Bank, Washington DC, 2006) 14.

4 This was in fact said about the equally difficult process of concluding the US/Viet Nam Bilateral Trade Agreement in 2000; see J Pearson, 'The US/Viet Nam Bilateral Trade Agreement: Another Step in the Right Direction' (2002) 10 *University of Miami Business Law Review* 431, 444.

5 World Bank, *Taking Stock: An Update on Viet Nam's Economic Developments* (World Bank, Washington DC, 2007) 1. See also, Ministry of Foreign Affairs of Viet Nam, *White Paper on Human Rights* (Ministry of Foreign Affairs of Viet Nam, Hanoi, 2005) 25–7, http://www.vietnamembassy-usa.org/news/story.php?d=20050826150541 at 10 November 2008.

6 World Bank, above n 5, 4.

the country's trade and current account balances both registered surpluses in 2006 after four years of deficits. In perhaps the most poignant indication of how far *Doi Moi*[7] has brought the economy of the Socialist Republic of Viet Nam, the newly established Hanoi and Ho Chi Minh Stock Exchanges have recorded enormous increases over the past year (albeit from very modest bases) – the stock price index increasing 144 per cent in 2006, and then by another 40 per cent up to 15 May 2007.[8] The Government has itself been venturing into the international capital market to raise funds by issuing sovereign bonds to finance the expanding activities of its state-owned enterprises which do not themselves have any independent creditworthiness.[9]

At the level of individuals and households, all this has led to a sharp increase in Viet Nam's per capita GDP between 1995 (US$289) and 2002 (US$439), and a more than doubling of 'purchasing power parity' (PPP) from $1,236 per annum in 1995 to $2,745 in 2004.[10] Over the eleven-year period from 1993 to 2004, some twenty-four million people were lifted out of poverty, with the poverty rate dropping from 58.1 per cent in 1993 to only 19.5 per cent in 2004.[11] A poverty rate of 16 per cent was recorded in the most recent household survey in 2006.[12]

It is of course the relative changes in all of these statistics that are impressive. On account of rapid economic growth, Viet Nam is now no longer officially classified as a 'Least Developed Country', but still it sits only marginally above the threshold, and a substantial percentage of its people remain poor.[13] Thus, for example, while the minimum monthly wage for government employees has increased by no less than 214 per cent between

---

[7] 'Doi Moi' (renovation) is the process of economic opening of Viet Nam which started in 1986. As a result, more private enterprises were permitted by the Communist Party, and collectivisation of industrial and agricultural operations was essentially abandoned. This economic reformation from central planning to a market economy was further reflected in Viet Nam's membership of ASEAN and its Bilateral Trade Agreement with the USA.

[8] World Bank, above n 5, 15.

[9] See WTO, *Viet Nam Trade Profile* (2007), http://stat.wto.org/CountryProfile/WSDBCountryPFView.aspx?Language=E&Country=VN at 10 November 2008.

[10] United Nations Development Programme, *Human Development Report 2006* (UNDP, New York, 2006) http://hdr.undp.org/hdr2006/statistics/countries/data_sheets/cty_ds_VNM.html at 10 November 2008.

[11] Vietnamese Academy of Social Sciences, *Viet Nam Poverty Update Report 2006: Poverty and Poverty Reduction in Viet Nam 1993–2004* (VASS, Hanoi, 2006) 11.

[12] World Bank et al., 'Viet Nam Development Report 2008: Social Protection' (Joint Donor Report to the Vietnam Consultative Group Meeting, Hanoi, 6–7 December 2007) 3.

[13] See below n 43.

2003 and 2006, it is still only US$28.[14] The incidence of poverty presents a fundamental systemic challenge to the better protection of human rights in Viet Nam, to be added to the structural challenge that single-party governance poses for human rights, especially for civil and political liberties.

B. Viet Nam and Global Integration

Alongside the expansion and integration of Viet Nam's economy into the global economy, a parallel process of globalisation has been pursued in respect of Viet Nam's formal relations with the international community. From the dark days of the country's relative international isolation during much of the 1980s, it began in the early 1990s to open its doors to international engagement with, first, the resumption of normal relations with the IMF and the World Bank in 1992, to be followed, in relatively quick succession over the next six years, by membership of ASEAN, AFTA, APEC and ASEM.[15] Bilateral relations – diplomatic and trade – were also expanded over this period with a number of Western states, including, most significantly, formal re-engagement with the US. This latter process began with the lifting of the US trade embargo against Viet Nam in 1994 and the re-establishment of diplomatic relations between the two countries a year later, and reached something of an apotheosis in January 2007 when, shortly before Viet Nam's accession to the WTO, the Bush Administration signed into law Permanent Normal Trade Relations (PNTR) with Viet Nam.

C. Economic and Social Challenges

Human rights concerns in Viet Nam are inextricably linked to the country's fortunes in dealing with not only the economic and diplomatic, but also the social, political and legal challenges associated with economic growth and global integration. Thus, the foremost challenge of how, within the WTO's insistent framework of trade liberalisation, to consolidate the economic gains already made by securing long-term sustainable economic growth is key to how human rights will be protected and promoted in Viet Nam in the coming years. This is because both economic consolidation and sustainability will be, to some significant degree, dependent upon improving the breadth and depth

---

14 See World Bank, above n 3, 8–9.

15 Respectively: the Association of South East Asian States; Asia Free Trade Agreement; Asia-Pacific Economic Cooperation; and the Asia Europe Meeting. For discussion, see: United Nations' Economic and Social Commission for Asia and Pacific, *The Doha Development Agenda: Perspectives from the ESCAP Region* (UNESCAP, Bangkok, 2003) 306.

of distribution of wealth gains, and minimising the debilitating shock effects suffered by certain economic sectors and social groups. For, while economic development can certainly provide the means by which human rights can be better protected and more fully realised, so too it can distort, deny or even destroy human rights protections already existing, or the potential for them to be so protected.

Free trade protagonists are not always aware of such consequences, and even when they are, they either do not appreciate their impact, or they remove them from their frame of reference by characterising them as ignorable externalities. This explains, for example, how one of the WTO's earlier Annual Reports could declare, without apparent irony, that '[e]mpirical evidence tends to show that trade liberalization may entail non-trivial adjustment costs for certain groups'.[16] 'Adjustment costs' are especially prevalent and often grave in the agrarian sectors of developing countries such as Viet Nam, where the sudden exposure of many small farmers to the market forces of larger farmers and agri-businesses can be devastating. As John Hilary points out, 'the relationship between market changes and household level poverty has been well demonstrated in agricultural communities'.[17]

The basic causes are two-fold: (i) the undermining of local markets (by way of the combined effects of their relative uncompetitiveness and the drive to export) robs local households of their primary sources of income, and (ii) the practical failure of the theory of comparative advantage which assumes that increases in the incidence of poverty will only be temporary because substitute jobs or income sources will replace those recently lost, whereas 'in reality there may be no prospect of substitute opportunities for those groups . . . even in the long term'.[18] Much, in fact, depends on the governance capacities of states whose economics are being driven by fast-growing export markets. Thus, for example, as Chantal Thomas has pointed out, a number of sub-Saharan countries with very high export earnings relative to GDP, nevertheless languish at the bottom of the UNDP's Human Development Index on account of the fact that they typically suffer from entrenched intra-state inequality, political instability, rampant corruption, poor to non-existent infrastructure, minimal regional integration and an over-reliance on agricultural exports which are subject to high volatility and fierce competition.[19]

16 World Trade Organization, *Annual Report 1998* (WTO, Geneva, 1998) 47.

17 J Hilary, 'Trade Liberalization, Poverty and the WTO: Assessing the Realities' in H Katrek and R Strange (eds) *The WTO and Developing Countries* (Palgrave Macmillan, Basingstoke, 2004) 38, 41.

18 Ibid 42.

19 C Thomas, 'Poverty Reduction, Trade, and Rights' (2003) 18 *American University International Law Review* 1399, 1407.

3. HUMAN RIGHTS IN VIETNAM

At the level of international commitments, Viet Nam is a party to six of the nine core United Nations human rights treaties, though it does not recognise the competence of any of the committees, established under those treaties or their optional protocols, to receive individual communications. Viet Nam has also ratified five of the International Labour Organisation's eight fundamental human rights conventions within the last 11 years.[20]

At the domestic level, Viet Nam has taken considerable steps – at least in formal legal terms – to provide for the human rights embodied in its international commitments. This is reflected in the official position of the Communist Party in Viet Nam's 1992 Constitution and in the various Codes and other domestic laws enacted during the *Doi Moi* period.

In line with Viet Nam's conscious international integration, the Communist Party of Viet Nam first expressed its official viewpoint on human rights in the instruments of the IXth Congress in 2001, 'to take care of the people, to protect rights and legitimate interests of everyone, and to respect and implement international treaties on human rights that Viet Nam has ratified or acceded to.'[21] At the recent Xth Congress in 2006, the Political Report of the Party Central Committee expressly recognised the obligation of the state to institutionalise and implement citizen's rights and human rights effectively. [22]

Further, Viet Nam's 2005 White Paper on Human Rights – which, despite its propagandist overtones, is itself a significant feature of the country's willingness to engage with the international community on the subject – proclaims that 'it is Vietnam's ultimate goal to build a strong country with wealthy people in an equal, democratic and civilized society for the benefit of the people.'[23]

---

20 For details on Viet Nam's ratification of UN instruments, see the UNHCHR Treaty Body Database: http://www.unhchr.ch/tbs/doc.nsf/Statusfrset at 10 November 2008. For details regarding Viet Nam's ratification of the fundamental ILO conventions, see the ILOLEX database: http://www.ilo.org/ilolex/english/docs/declworld.htm at 10 November 2008.

21 Political Report of the Communist Party in the IX Congress in 2001, available in Vietnamese at the Communist Party website: http://www.dangcongsan.vn/tiengviet/tulieuvankien/vankiendang/details.asp?topic=191&subtopic=8&leader_topic=226&id=BT25110530192 at 10 November 2008.

22 Political Report of the Communist Party in the X Congress in 2006, available in Vietnamese at the Communist Party website: http://www.dangcongsan.vn/tiengviet/tulieuvankien/vankiendang/details.asp?topic=191&subtopic=8&leader_topic=699&id=BT1960657802 at 10 November 2008.

23 *White Paper on Human Rights*, above n 5, 4.

The 1992 Constitution recognises a broad range of human rights, including equality before the law, the right to vote, the right to work, the right to education and health care, gender equality, freedom of movement, freedom of religion, freedom of speech and the press, and the presumption of innocence.

These fundamental guarantees have provided the basis for the enactment of a number of key laws and ordinances in the field of human rights.[24] Since 1986, Viet Nam has promulgated over 40 codes and laws, over 120 ordinances, approximately 850 Government documents and more than 3,000 regulatory documents issued by Ministries and agencies.[25] Most human rights are recognised in these various laws, from fair trial rights in the 2003 Criminal Procedure Code, to the rights of women in the Law on Gender Equality, adopted on 29 November 2006.[26]

Considerable effort has been invested in providing the legal framework through which human rights concerns across the board – civil and political, as well as economic and social rights – might be addressed. The acid test, however, for these rights guarantees, is how well they are respected and enforced in practice.

A. Viet Nam's Human Rights Record

As with all countries, assessing the level of protection of human rights in Viet Nam depends upon who you ask and which rights you are talking about. Thus, in the eyes of the Government of Viet Nam, economic, social and cultural rights are undoubtedly its immediate, priority concerns as they are seen to be associated with economic development. As such, therefore, the Government proclaims in its White Paper on Human Rights, that among its greatest achievements 'in the protection of human rights [has been its] great success in poverty reduction, human development and life quality improvement'.[27]

There can be no doubt that poverty alleviation is a foundation to any serious attempts to protect and promote human rights – civil and political, as well as economic and social. However, it is not itself a guarantor of such protection, especially if its impact is uneven, as for example is the case in Viet Nam where urban communities have generally fared much better than rural ones.[28]

---

24 See generally, ibid 6.

25 Ibid 5.

26 For a fuller account of recent enactments of the Vietnamese Government in the area of human rights, see Kinley and Nguyen, above n 1, 9–11.

27 *White Paper on Human Rights*, above n 5, 25–6.

28 For example, the urban poverty rate in 2004 was 3.6 per cent, compared to a poverty rate of 25 per cent in rural areas: Vietnamese Academy of Social Sciences, above n 11, 18.

Further government action is necessary if the rights to housing, health, education, and an adequate standard of living are to be attained, let alone rights to a fair trial, privacy, expression, association, movement and political thought secured.

For example,[29] areas of significant human rights challenge still persist in respect of the death penalty (which still applies to 29 offences[30]); the right of association (which, despite being constitutionally enshrined, is yet to have formal legal protection,[31] and is, in practice, heavily curtailed[32]); the right of fair trial (which, despite legislative reform, is still undermined by the limited capacity of the judiciary and legal profession,[33] and threats to judicial independence[34]); rights of women (who earn less than their male counterparts and are concentrated in the informal economy,[35] limiting their access to social security and health care,[36] notwithstanding legislative reforms enshrining gender equality); freedom of the press (which continues to be heavily curtailed[37]); and freedom of religion (which is of particular concern

---

29 For a more comprehensive account of Viet Nam's human rights record, its achievements to date and the challenges it faces for the future, see Kinley and Nguyen, above n 1, 13–17.

30 Concluding Observations of the Human Rights Committee, 2002, UN Doc. CCPR/CO/75/VNM at para 7. For criticism, see for example, Amnesty International, *Death Penalty News, May 2006* (2006) http://web.amnesty.org/library/Index/ENGACT530022006?open&of=ENG-VNM at 10 November 2008.

31 Irene Norlund, *Filling the Gap: The Emerging Civil Society in Viet Nam* (UNDP, Hanoi, 2009) 9.

32 Concluding Observations of the Human Rights Committee, above n 30 [20].

33 Inter-Agency Steering Committee/Ministry of Justice, *Comprehensive Needs Assessment for the Development of Viet Nam's Legal System to the Year 2010* (Ministry of Justice, Hanoi, 2002) 16–17.

34 Concluding Observations of the Human Rights Committee, above n 30 [9–10].

35 There is a higher concentration of women in casual work or the informal economy (26 per cent of women compared to 19 per cent of men), rather than wage-earning employment (26 per cent women, and 41 per cent men): World Bank et al., 'Viet Nam Development Report 2007: Aiming High' (Joint Donor Report to the Vietnam Consultative Group Meeting, Hanoi, 14–15 December 2006) 111.

36 Committee on the Elimination of Discrimination against Women, *Concluding Observations of the Committee on the Elimination of All Forms of Discrimination Against Women 2007*, UN Doc CEDAW/C/VNM/CO/6 (2 February 2007) [22], http://www.unhchr.ch/tbs/doc.nsf/(Symbol)/CEDAW.C.VNM.CO.6.En?Opendocument at 10 November 2008.

37 See, for example, Human Rights Watch, *Vietnam: Crackdown of Dissent in the Wake of WTO and APEC* (2007) http://hrw.org/english/docs/2007/03/09/vietna15466.htm at 11 November 2008; and Amnesty International, *Socialist Republic of Vietnam. A Tightening Net: Web-based Censorship and Repression* (2006) http://www.amnesty.org/en/library/info/ASA41/008/2006 at 11 November 2008.

in respect of the repression of the traditional practices of indigenous minorities[38]).

4. VIET NAM, HUMAN RIGHTS AND THE WTO

Becoming a member of the WTO brings both human rights opportunities and challenges for Viet Nam. In terms of law and policy, this flows directly from the fact that now the government must balance its trade and human rights obligations under both international and domestic law. Thus, for example, its constitutionally protected human rights obligations must temper the State's economic policy (also enshrined in the Constitution) 'to make the people rich and the country strong' by various means including 'expanding intercourse with world markets.'[39]

There are at least three broad avenues of human rights opportunity. First, it is an opportunity for Viet Nam to integrate in to the global economy by accessing international goods and services equally and gaining reliable access to export markets. Economic development, in the view of the government, shall create conditions for the promotion of human rights, including the right to development, right to adequate standard of living and others. Secondly, the improvement of the domestic legal system and institutions as a requirement of joining the WTO shall foster a more favourable environment for Viet Nam when instituting legislative, administrative and judicial measures to improve human rights. And thirdly, the opening up of the economy will help Viet Nam to take further steps in human rights integration, especially through the greater breadth and depth of opportunities for interaction and dialogue with the international community that WTO membership will bring.

A. Which Rights Are of Concern?

Just as there are opportunities, there are also certain human rights challenges that are associated with rapid trade expansion and economic development. First, the harsh realities of international commercial competition that Viet Nam's businesses will now be exposed to by way of WTO-imposed liberalised trade rules will inevitably lead to business failures as well as successes. The learning curve may be very steep for Vietnamese businesses (big, small, or tiny), at least initially, as they lack experience of such competitive practices on

---

38 Concluding Observations of the Human Rights Committee, above n 30 [19].

39 *Constitution* (1992) art 16.

the global scale.[40] Business failures, of course, will have a direct effect on employment and the litany of rights that directly and substantially rely on employment for their achievement – adequate standard of living, housing, sustenance and health care. Secondly, the social impacts of joining the WTO can operate as a barrier to the enjoyment of, and access to, many human rights, particularly through the unequal distribution of benefits and the widening gap between rich and poor, both within Viet Nam and between Viet Nam and the rest of the world.[41] These challenges put certain sectors including agriculture, manufacturing, and private business at risk, and render certain groups of people including women, children and ethnic minorities more vulnerable.

In addition, there are concerns associated with a number of specific rights and groups of rights-holders.

(i) Right to food

The combination of state poverty reduction and hunger elimination programs, radical shifts in land policy that effected the distribution of agricultural land to rural households, and the general health of the national economy have brought significant improvements for Viet Nam in the guarantee of the right to food. Viet Nam has now moved from a country with a chronic lack of food to the second-largest exporter of rice. Though food poverty has dramatically decreased from 24.9 per cent in 1993 to 6.7 per cent in 2006,[42] there are still issues of concern which need to be addressed in the context of joining the WTO.

Considering that there are a large number of communities who survive just above the poverty line, the affordability of food is of fundamental importance. According to the World Bank, 53.4 per cent of people in the country live on less than two dollars a day, and 10.6 per cent on less than one

40 The effects of increased competition and the drive for efficiency have already been felt in the equitisation (privatisation) of State Owned Enterprises ('SOE'), which collectively shed more than 100,000 workers between 2000 and 2005. World Bank et al., 'Viet Nam Development Report 2006: Business' (Joint Donor Report to The Viet Nam Consultative Group Meeting, Hanoi, December 2005) 159. Further, in their conversations with the authors, participants at the workshop on 'Human Rights Implications of Viet Nam's Accession to the WTO', held in Hanoi in May 2007, stressed their particular concerns as to the ability of local Vietnamese businesses to compete with their more efficient foreign counterparts.

41 For example, see UNCTAD's analysis of the varied fortunes of LDCs who have embarked on extensive trade liberalisation, especially the difficulties they face in achieving inclusiveness in economic growth. UNCTAD, *Least Developed Countries Report 2004: Linking International Trade with Poverty Reduction* (UNCTAD, Geneva, 2004) Ch 5.

42 World Bank et al., above n 12, 4.

dollar a day.[43] While food poverty has fallen rapidly, it still affects 8.7 per cent of rural households and an alarming 29.2 per cent of ethnic minority households.[44]

It is in rural areas that more than 90 per cent of the poor population live and work,[45] and such areas are especially sensitive to changes in economic, social and natural circumstances. The liberalisation of agriculture and the reduction of subsidies necessitated by Viet Nam's accession to the WTO[46] will likely seriously threaten food security in the countryside, given the absence of any welfare assistance for families to fall back on should jobs be lost or markets evaporate.[47] There is, further, a particular risk in this regard for people living in the uplands and midlands, and ethnic minority families where over half are poor and many are living in chronic poverty. In 2004, there were about 3.5 million members of ethnic minorities living in poverty.[48]

(ii) Right to health and TRIPS

An essential feature of Viet Nam's socio-economic development strategy is improving the standard of, and access to, health care for its people. On recent figures only 38 per cent of households have health insurance or access to free health care.[49] The liberalisation of the health sector[50] will certainly affect the

---

43 World Bank et al., 'Viet Nam Development Report 2004: Poverty' (Joint Donor Report to The Viet Nam Consultative Group Meeting, Hanoi, December 2003) 15.

44 World Bank et al., above n 12, 4.

45 World Bank, *Taking Stock: An Update on Viet Nam's Recent Economic Developments* (World Bank, Washington DC, 2008) 5.

46 The Vietnamese government traditionally administered interest rate support, export bonuses and support to cover losses to enterprises exporting rice, pork, coffee and canned vegetables. Such measures are now prohibited by the terms of Viet Nam's accession agreement. In negotiating its accession, Viet Nam agreed that 'upon accession, Viet Nam would bind its agricultural export subsidies at zero in its Schedule of Concessions and Commitments on Goods, and not maintain or apply any export subsidies for agricultural products': WTO, *Report of the Working Party on the Accession of Viet Nam*, WTO Doc WT/ACC/VNM/48 (27 October 2006) 93 [366]. However, Viet Nam is permitted a measure of domestic support. Viet Nam is permitted to spend VND 3,961 billion (approx USD 246 million) on domestic support for agricultural products in any one year. See: WTO, *WTO Working Party on the Accession of Viet Nam, Domestic Support and Export Subsidies in the Agricultural Sector: Revision*, WTO Doc WT/ACC/SPEC/VNM/3/Rev.7 (2 August 2006) 7.

47 Hilary, above n 17, 41–2, and see further below, under the heading 'The special case of human rights in the agricultural sector'.

48 Vietnamese Academy of Social Sciences, above n 11, 27.

49 Ibid 24.

50 In its Schedule of Specific Commitments in Services, Viet Nam imposes no special limitations on market access or national treatment in the health and related

accessibility and affordability of health care services, but the question is whether it will necessarily be positive. The fear is that, at least in the short term, the opening up of a hitherto highly centralised industry will be detrimental to overall provision of health services, and especially for the rural poor. This fear is founded on Viet Nam's earlier experience of legalising private health services and introducing user charges at public hospitals. The result of this policy was that it shifted the burden of health care financing from the state to households, with health care costs, and especially hospital costs, constituting a serious burden on low-income families. It also exacerbated the gap between rich and poor regarding access to, and the quality of, health services. Those in the richest 20 per cent of the population have contact with a provincial or central hospital 4.5 times more often than those in the poorest 20 per cent. Low-income families are the largest users of Community Health Stations, where the quality of services is generally perceived to be of a poorer quality than that provided by public hospitals or private clinics.[51]

Viet Nam, like all poor countries, faces inherent difficulties in ensuring affordable access to pharmaceuticals for its people. Viet Nam's obligations under the *Agreement on Trade-Related Aspects of Intellectual Property Rights* (TRIPS) to recognise and enforce patent rights may compound this struggle. The issue is of particular importance in respect of the protection of the right to health of people living with HIV/AIDS. HIV has now spread throughout 64 cities and provinces. Currently, more than one hundred Vietnamese are infected by HIV every day. The estimated number of people living with HIV has more than doubled between 2000 and 2006, from approximately 122,000 to 280,000.[52] TRIPS may present an additional challenge to the implementation of the Millennium Development Goal on HIV prevention and also to the achievement of the Government's own target of ensuring that 70 per cent of HIV/AIDS patients are receiving treatment by the year 2010. Thus, both for intellectual property and human rights reasons, particular attention must be paid to the establishment and operation of foreign pharmaceutical companies in Viet Nam, such as those granted preferential access under the 2004 Viet

---

social services sector (hospital, medical and dental services), and permits foreign service suppliers to establish 100 per cent foreign-invested hospitals, provided that the minimum investment capital for a hospital is USD 20 million. See: WTO, *WTO Working Party on the Accession of Viet Nam, Schedule of Specific Commitments in Services and List of Article II MFN Exemptions*, WTO Doc WT/ACC/VNM/48/Add.2 (27 October 2006) 43.

51 United Nations Country Team Viet Nam, *User Fees, Financial Autonomy and Access to Social Services in Viet Nam* (Discussion Paper No 6, United Nations Country Team Viet Nam, 2005) 3–9.

52 UNAIDS Viet Nam, *Summary of the HIV Epidemic in Viet Nam* (2006) http://www.unaids.org.vn/facts/docs/key_messages_sep_2006_e.pdf at 11 November 2008.

Nam–EC Market Access Agreement. Under the terms of its WTO Accession Protocol, Viet Nam has a transitional period up to 1 January 2009 before it must grant foreign-owned companies the right to import pharmaceuticals.[53]

(iii) Rights of ethnic minorities

While economic liberalisation may bring benefits to the majority of the population, certain human rights of ethnic minorities such as the right to food, right to education, right to health, and right to adequate standard of living are under threat. Ethnic minority groups have not benefited from the advances Viet Nam has made over the past decade in combating poverty to the same degree enjoyed by the rest of the population. While the national poverty rate decreased significantly from 58 per cent in 1993 to 16 per cent in 2006, the poverty rate among ethnic minorities reduced respectively from 86 per cent to 52 per cent.[54] Minority groups in Viet Nam make up 14 per cent of the population (i.e. around 10 million people), but constitute 44 per cent of the poor and 59 per cent of the food poor.[55]

It has become a major concern that ethnic minorities are participating less and benefiting inadequately from the growth process. Their opportunity of accessing rights is also lessened accordingly. As a consequence, for example, 'the absolute difference in the poverty rate between the majority Kinh-Hoa and ethnic minorities has been increasing, from 32.5 percentage points in 1993 to 47.2 percentage points in 2004. In 2004, the poverty rate for ethnic minorities was 61 per cent, which is approximately 4.5 times the poverty rate for the Kinh and Hoa'.[56] Such figures signal systemic disadvantage and thereby grave, fundamental threats to the human rights of Viet Nam's ethnic peoples.

(iv) Labour and workplace rights

The combination of the speed of growth of Viet Nam's industrial sector[57] and the low base in the 1980s from which it has developed, has placed pressure on the government and on corporations to attend to issues of labour and workplace relations, as well as health and safety standards for employees. Viet Nam substantially revised its Labour Code in 2002 to incorporate the various ILO

---

53 WTO, *Report of the Working Party on the Accession of Viet Nam*, WTO Doc WT/ACC/VNM/48 (27 October 2006) 36, 155–7. See further below n 120, and accompanying text.

54 World Bank et al., above n 12, 4.

55 Ibid 13.

56 World Bank et al., above n 35, 26.

57 Based on the period from 2000–2004, 20 per cent of employed men and 13 per cent of employed women worked in the industrial sector: World Bank, *World Development Indicators* (2006) http://devdata.worldbank.org/wdi2006/contents/Table2_3.htm at 11 November 2008.

standards it has signed up to, although problems and gaps remain, which will be exacerbated by the demands of further commercial expansion and trade liberalisation.[58] Enforcement of many of these laws – in respect, for example, of forced and child labour, and unsafe work practices – is inadequate, and certain rights such as union membership are somewhat Pyrrhic (trade unions do exist, but they are not independent of Communist Party influence and control).[59] There is concern in particular regarding how to combat sweat-shop conditions, as evident, for example, in the relative prominence given to labour rights and working conditions in both the US/Viet Nam Bilateral Trade Agreement and the Trade and Investment Framework Agreement signed by both countries in June 2007.[60] Wildcat strikes in and around Ho Chi Minh City in 2006, involving thousands of workers protesting against poor pay and working conditions, elicited from the Government a 40 per cent increase in the minimum wage for workers in foreign-owned corporations (to US$54 per month), which was the first such rise since 1999.[61]

There are particular human rights concerns regarding women in the workforce, as highlighted in the burgeoning garment industry, and regarding 'internal migrant' workers.

(v) Rights of women working in the garment industry

Viet Nam's textile and garment industry accounted for 16 per cent of all exports in 2004,[62] and the garment industry has been expanding, and is expected to expand further, following WTO accession, now that exports of garments to the EU and the US – the garment industry's two biggest markets – will be free from all quotas.[63]

---

58 As the Government itself notes, 'labor is a decisive factor of the competitiveness of each enterprise and each economy': Ministry of Labor, Invalid and Social Affairs ('MoLISA'), *Labour and Social Issues Emerging from Viet Nam's Accession to the WTO* (Working Paper 18, MoLISA, 2004) 2.

59 The single, umbrella trade union – the Viet Nam Confederation of Labour – oversees and controls various subsidiary labour organisations.

60 Michael Marine, the outgoing US Ambassador to Viet Nam, nominated these issues as likely topics for the first working sessions to be held under the TIFA in late 2008: see Lien Huong, 'Vietnam: Scores of billion dollar US deals in the pipeline' (2007) http://www.bilaterals.org/article.php3?id_article=9337 at 11 November 2008.

61 Human Rights Watch, *World Report 2007 – Viet Nam* (2007) http://hrw.org/englishwr2k7/docs/2007/01/11/vietna14858.htm at 11 November 2008.

62 Naila Kabeer and Tran Thi Van Anh, *Globalisation, Gender and Work in the Context of Economic Transition: The Case of Viet Nam* (Policy Dialogue Paper 2006/2, UNDP Viet Nam, 2006) 3. Note that except where indicated otherwise all the statistics in this section and the following section have been drawn from this UNDP paper.

63 While export quotas to the EU were abolished on 1 January 2005 pursuant to Viet Nam's market access agreement with the EC, US quotas continued to be applied under the Viet Nam–US Bilateral Trade Agreement, and only ceased on WTO accession.

The export-oriented garment industry is labour intensive, and has been a significant source of new jobs, particularly for women, who make up approximately 78 per cent of garment workers. Statistical analysis of female garment workers shows that they are often young (20–30 years), generally single and without children. The overwhelming majority of female garment workers have migrated to the city from rural areas, where levels of poverty, unemployment and underemployment are all high. Most are leaving agricultural work in rural areas to seek out wage employment in the city. However, labour conditions in the garment industry are not always satisfactory. Garment workers face long hours sitting in the same position, carrying out repetitive tasks, often in hot, noisy and dusty factories, and because of this, most do not stay more than a couple of years in the industry. Surveys among female workers demonstrate that they generally work overtime, often an additional 10 to 15 hours per week,[64] which puts pressure on their ability to visit their home town or participate in cultural activities.

Garment workers receive lower levels of pay than other wage earners in the urban economy, and they are at particular risk of unemployment due to their low level of professional qualifications. Increased competition in the garment and footwear industries could increase this risk of unemployment. For example, many workers were at risk of losing their jobs following the announcement by the EC on 23 February 2006 that it would apply an anti-dumping duty to leather shoes from Viet Nam and China.[65] Such events demonstrate that these export-oriented industries, and the people they employ, are vulnerable to fluctuations in the international market.

(vi) Internal migrant workers' rights

As noted above in the case of female garment workers, there is increasing internal migration in Viet Nam, from rural to urban areas. High levels of unemployment and underemployment in the rural agricultural sector, and the promise of earning a wage in the city, have precipitated this trend. However, a particular difficulty faced by workers who migrate from rural to urban areas is that they lack formal rights to live in the city, under Viet Nam's household registration system. This can make it difficult to access municipal services, such that migrant workers may face higher housing, water and electricity costs, higher costs of medical treatment and education, and higher administrative costs. Temporary or unregistered migrants often face difficulties finding decent housing and live in more crowded accommodation.

---

64 Hai Ha, *Tại các khu công nghiệp:Lao động nữ luôn biến động, vì sao?* (2007) http://www.thuongtin.com.vn/?do=service&dtd=view&id=1041 at 11 November 2008.

65 Đông Hiêu, *Lao động nữ chịu nhiều thiết thòi trong kiến giày da* (2006) http://vietnamnet.vn/kinhte/vieclam/2006/03/548499/ at 11 November 2008.

Many who migrate to urban areas end up working in casual labour, and are especially vulnerable to abuse or violence, particularly sexual abuse which leads to a risk of HIV infection and other sexually transmitted diseases.[66] Most temporary migrants have no health insurance, and a fear of high medical costs often results in delays in seeking treatment.[67]

Despite these risks and disadvantages, internal migration has allowed many people from rural areas to find work, especially in the manufacturing industries. Many internal migrants send remittances back to their families, and studies show that this has played a critical role in poverty reduction in many rural areas.[68]

B. The Special Case of Human Rights in the Agricultural Sector

There is a coalition of economic, social and human rights reasons that warrant singling out the agricultural sector as a special case. Agriculture employs 60 per cent of Viet Nam's labour force,[69] and 45 per cent of the rural population live below the poverty line. Indeed, it is in rural areas that 'more than 90 per cent of the country's poor people live and work'.[70] The opening up of the sector to the forces of international trade will, at least in the short term, very likely compound this problem given the size and antiquated practices that predominate in the sector: farms are typically low yield, subsistence based and small – the average farm size being 0.7 hectares per household.[71] The World Bank predicts that, as land transactions become easier, the less productive (presumably poorer) households could be forced to sell some of their land to the more productive households, as market forces favour efficiency over egalitarianism.[72] It is envisaged that the size of rural sector employment will drop dramatically over the next five to ten years as people are 'pushed' out of the sector by competition, and 'pulled' out by the draw of alternative employment

---

66 Dang Nguyen Anh, 'Viet Nam Internal Migration: Opportunities and Challenges for Development' (Paper delivered at the Regional Conference on Migration and Development in Asia, Lanzhou, 14–16 March 2005) 10.

67 Ibid.

68 See Vietnamese Academy of Social Sciences, above n 11, 38–9.

69 Based on the period from 2000–2004, 58 per cent of employed men and 62 per cent of employed women worked in the agricultural sector: World Bank, *World Development Indicators* (2006) http://devdata.worldbank.org/wdi2006/contents/Table2_3.htm at 11 November 2008.

70 Oxfam, *Extortion at the Gate: Will Viet Nam Join the WTO on Pro-development Terms?* (Briefing Paper 67, 2004) 11.

71 Ibid.

72 World Bank et al., above n 40, 150–1.

in the industrial and manufacturing sectors.[73] The human rights implications of these swift and significant shifts in circumstances of rural communities, and especially of the poor, will, at least in the short term, be profound, bearing out many of the specific human rights problems outlined above.

Certainly, there are now very significant human rights challenges facing the agricultural sector, but there are also some important opportunities that membership of the WTO will provide. We consider both the challenges and opportunities in turn.

(i) Challenges

The competitiveness of Viet Nam's agricultural products is still low, largely due to low productivity, low quality and high cost, such as in the production of sugar, corn, soya bean, cotton, tobacco, milk and pork. Most of the processing factories are small and, as compared to their regional and global competitors, reliant on outdated technologies and equipment. It is estimated by the Ministry of Agriculture and Rural Development that about 70 per cent of all enterprises operating in rural areas have a capital level less than 10 billion VND (US$620,000). When import tax rates are reduced and non-tariff barriers are eliminated, local agriculture will have to face fiercer competition from imports. If efficiency and capacity are not increased, it is certain that enterprises will fail, jobs will be lost, and incomes and standards of living will decline.

Agricultural production also suffers from the failings of Vietnamese infrastructure, services and laws. Although the transportation system has been considerably improved, there are about 400 communes (or 6 per cent of the total) that do not have vehicle-grade roads to their city centres, and 50 per cent of all village roads are in poor condition. There is a lack of infrastructure in the agri-forest and aquatic products trade, including a lack of specialised ports; high costs of goods loading and unloading (for example, the at-the-port cost per tonne of exported rice in Viet Nam is nearly twice that of Thailand); and a failure to ensure food sanitation standards and consumer protection.[74]

The density of FDI is divided 34 per cent in the industrial sector, 59 per cent in the service sector, and 8 per cent in the agriculture, forest and fisheries sector.[75] Thus, a serious concern for the agricultural sector is that, in contrast

---

73 World Bank, *Accelerating Viet Nam's Rural Development: Growth, Equity and Diversification*, Volume I: Overview (World Bank, Washington DC, 2005) 3, 13.

74 Ministry of Agriculture and Rural Development, *Viet Nam's Agriculture: A Strategy Toward WTO*, http://epic.com.vn/resources/WTO_accession_agriculture_sector.pdf at 11 November 2008.

75 Information from National Centre for Social Economic Information and Forecast, available in Vietnamese: http://thongtindubao.gov.vn/Default.aspx?mod=News&cat=12&nid=2810 at 11 November 2008.

to manufacturing and textile industries, it has not attracted any significant FDI. According to the Ministry of Planning and Investment's 'Program to Attract FDI, 2006–2010', among the 94 target project requests for FDI for that period (collectively worth nearly US$26 billion) there was only one successful project for agriculture-animal raising and forestry and four projects for aquaculture.[76]

The predominance of small, family farmers, and the lack of agri-businesses on the scale anything like that which exists in the West, significantly contributes to this situation. It is being compounded by the marked increase in the conversion of farm lands into industrial zones. By 2005, land had been recovered from over 100,000 households for the development of more than 190 industrial zones and clusters.[77] It has been estimated that for around one-third of displaced households such land conversion causes severe economic disruption, particularly when all productive landholdings are recovered in any given area. Residence is disrupted, typically insufficient notice is given by the local authorities, and family members do not have the appropriate educational background or vocational skills to shift into new occupations.[78]

On top of these inherent weaknesses, Oxfam has noted that as a consequence of its WTO accession, Viet Nam is being forced to liberalise its agricultural sector above and beyond the commitments of original WTO members. Of particular significance is the issue of export subsidies: while original members currently maintain export subsidies for agricultural products,[79] Viet Nam agreed to eliminate all agricultural export subsidies immediately upon its accession, in response to pressure from developed country members of the Working Party.[80] Furthermore, under pressure from negotiating members, the average agricultural tariff which Viet Nam had to apply upon accession was

---

76 Bộ tài chính (Ministry of Finance), *Vì sao vốn FDI vào nông nghiệp quá ít?* (2006) http://www.mof.gov.vn/Default.aspx?tabid=612&ItemID=30907 at 11 November 2008.

77 Vietnamese Academy of Social Sciences, above n 11, 75.

78 Ibid.

79 Export subsidies, up to a bound level, are permitted under the Agreement on Agriculture. While developed country WTO members have agreed to eliminate their agricultural export subsidies, the time frame for the elimination of export subsidies is the subject of ongoing negotiation in the Doha Round. In the most recent revision of the draft modalities on agriculture, circulated by the chairperson of the agriculture negotiations, Ambassador Crawford Falconer, on 10 July 2008, the deadline for export subsidy elimination by developed country members is 2013, while developing countries have until 2016. See WTO Committee on Agriculture Special Session, *Revised Draft Modalities for Agriculture*, WTO Doc TN/AG/W/4/Rev.3 (10 July 2008) 26 [152–3] http://www.wto.org/english/tratop_e/agric_e/agchairtxt_july08_e.pdf at 11 November 2008.

80 See above n 46.

25.2 per cent, while its final bound tariff (following a phase-in period) will be 21 per cent[81] – a level that already threatens rural livelihoods and basic human rights standards, and which is more than 10 per cent lower than the average bound levels in neighbouring Thailand and the Philippines.[82]

Certain key agricultural concessions have been gained that bear directly on human rights concerns. Thus, based on the rationale of food security, Viet Nam is not obliged to allow foreign-owned enterprises to export rice until 1 January 2011, in accordance with the terms of its Accession Agreement.[83] And while compliance with GATT required Viet Nam to lift its pre-accession import ban on tobacco products, the Government has responded, apparently based on protecting the right to health, by declaring that a single state-owned enterprise – the Viet Nam National Tobacco Corporation – shall be the sole importer of cigarettes.[84]

There are, further, two key agricultural sectors that remain especially vulnerable to post-accession competition – coffee and sugar production. In both cases this is because of their importance, not only economically, but also socially, in respect of the numbers of people who directly or indirectly depend on them in order to attain even the most minimal social and economic goods, and thereby secure such fundamental human rights as the rights to food, work, housing, education and an adequate standard of living.

Viet Nam is the world's second-largest producer of coffee. As the cultivation and harvesting of coffee employs some 1.83 per cent of the whole national labour force and 2.93 per cent of the labour force in the agricultural sector,[85] the livelihoods of considerable numbers of rural households will be especially vulnerable as the market is quickly opened up to international competition. This vulnerability has already been demonstrated: while a sharp price increase for most of the 1990s helped many coffee growers escape poverty, the price drop in the late 1990s and the early 2000s pulled them back into poverty. This was a major cause of sluggish reduction in poverty in the Central Highlands between 1998 and 2002. Many of the poor in the Central Highlands do not participate in coffee production because they see it as 'too risky'.[86] As noted above, the export subsidies (including interest rate support, export bonuses,

---

81 World Bank, above n 3, 15.

82 Oxfam, *Do as I Say, Not as I Do: The unfair terms for Viet Nam's entry to the WTO* (Briefing Paper 74, 2005) 11.

83 WTO Working Party on the Accession of Viet Nam, *Notification on State Trading Enterprises: Revision*, WTO Doc WT/ACC/VNM/14/Rev.1 (6 October 2006) 36.

84 Ibid 15–18.

85 See Viet Nam Coffee and Coca Association, http://www.vicofa.org.vn/CautrucNganh.aspx?request=cautruc at 11 November 2008.

86 Vietnamese Academy of Social Sciences, above n 11, 47–8.

and financial support to cover losses in exportation) that Viet Nam traditionally provided to coffee producers had to be eliminated upon accession.[87] Viet Nam's final bound *ad valorem* tariff on 'green' (un-roasted) coffee is 15 per cent.

The sugar industry in Viet Nam is also a crucial part of the economy, not so much for its size – a modest yield of about 970 thousand tonnes – but for its importance in the lives of millions of rural farmers who cultivate sugarcane, often in the poorest and most remote areas of the country. The government reported during the accession process there are currently 'policies supporting the sugar sector aimed at improving the economic conditions and job creation in these disadvantaged regions'.[88] These measures have largely amounted to a movement away from the traditional production of sugar by way of household sugar mills, to the building of refineries that serve a whole community or region.[89] There are now 44 sugar factories located in different areas with the participation of more than one million labourers. On its own, this initiative will not off-set the advantages that other sugar-producing countries have established by way of subsidies (EU sugar farmers gain €833m of hidden support annually on nominally unsubsidised exports),[90] or by way of market access preferences (such as the EU's Sugar Protocol which, until recently, guaranteed EU purchase prices for the produce of certain African, Caribbean and Pacific (ACP) states).[91] The sugar industry – or more especially the sugar farmers – will in fact continue to be heavily supported by the Vietnamese Government through its allocation to the sugar industry of the vast bulk of domestic support[92] permitted to Viet Nam for the whole of the agriculture sector under the terms of its WTO accession.[93] Further, Viet Nam retains the

---

87 WTO Working Party on the Accession of Viet Nam, *Domestic Support and Export Subsidies in the Agricultural Sector: Revision*, WTO Doc WT/ACC/SPEC/VNM/3/Rev.7 (2 August 2006) 15–16, and further see above n 46.

88 WTO, Working Party on the Accession of Viet Nam, above n 53, 93 [369] (per representative of Viet Nam).

89 Ibid.

90 Oxfam, above n 82, 2. As such, Oxfam argues that 'Viet Nam must be allowed to maintain an adequate level of protection for sensitive products, including sugar, maize, and animal products, on which many poor farmers depend': ibid.

91 The long-standing arrangement has recently been denounced (September 2007): see *Background on the EU proposal to denounce the Sugar Protocol and market access for ACP sugar under EPAs* (2007) http://trade.ec.europa.eu/doclib/docs/2007/september/tradoc_135921.pdf at 11 November 2008.

92 In the form of administered minimum purchase prices that sugar processing plants must pay to farmers for their sugarcane; WTO Working Party on the Accession of Viet Nam, above n 87, 13.

93 Under the terms of its accession, Viet Nam is entitled to provide 'amber box' (that is, trade-distorting) domestic support measures to agricultural producers up to a value of 3.96 trillion dong (US$ 246 million).

right to apply tariff rate quotas on sugar, to help protect its domestic industry against a surge of competitive imports.[94]

(ii) Opportunities

All that said, joining the WTO will also create potential opportunities for the agricultural sector in Viet Nam to expand its export markets; though the key word here is 'potential'. As a non-WTO member, Viet Nam had to contend with significant import tariff rates imposed on its goods, as well as many other non-tariff barriers (such as importing-country subsidies for its competing companies in the same market). But, in theory at least, Viet Nam's accession to the WTO grants to it 'Most-Favoured-Nation (MFN)' status, which should thereby not only dismantle these barriers, but also, on account of its developing country status, actually provide Vietnamese agricultural products with some degree of preferential treatment in the global market. The extent to which practice might follow theory in this case is largely dependent on whether the Doha Round is true to its developing-country orientation, and whether the current state of endemic agricultural protectionism in the West (especially in the EU and the US) is addressed.[95] To be sure, there are economic and social arguments both ways on this issue, namely, that livelihoods and ways of life are at stake: in the EU and US if protectionist policies are substantially altered; and in countries like Viet Nam, if access to such markets is heavily qualified. However, there can be no doubt that the potential scale and extent of hardship faced by agricultural sectors in agrarian-based, developing economies like Viet Nam will be such that basic human rights to an adequate standard of living, housing, welfare, health care and even to food will be threatened in a way incomparable to that which might be experienced in the West.

The stabilization of the domestic socio-economic environment and the promise of further global economic integration have the potential to impact positively on foreign investments in agriculture. Even the comparatively modest total allocated FDI of US$2.86 billion[96] for projects in agriculture (numbering 558 to date) has already made significant contributions to the

---

94 The within-quota tariff rate for raw sugar is 25 per cent, increasing to much higher tariff rates for imports exceeding the quota. World Bank, above n 3, 18.

95 On which see Dani Rodrik, *The Global Governance of Trade: As if Development Really Mattered*, (UNDP, October 2001), 27–33. For a detailed analysis of the stalemate in the Doha Round negotiations between developed and developing countries, see: UNCTAD Trade and Development Board, *Developments and Issues in the Post-Doha Work Programme of Particular Concern to Developing Countries*, UN Doc TD/B/54/5 (6 August 2007).

96 Ministry of Agriculture and Rural Development, above n 74, 8.

development of Viet Nam's agriculture. Capacity has been enhanced, not only in investment capital, technologies and equipment, and markets, but also in infrastructure development. Some countries have made significant investments in Viet Nam's agriculture sector, namely Taiwan, Hong Kong, France and China.

Through foreign investment in agriculture, Viet Nam expects to participate more in scientific and technical cooperation programs which, through technology transfer, will enhance the capacity of Vietnamese agriculture with regard to improving its productivity, competitiveness and quality of its produce.

In terms of what this means for human rights, the challenge of this potential will be to minimise the likely problems such openness will cause in the short-term, while maximising the hoped for long-term benefits for the agriculture sector and those who depend on it.

A vital aspect of how the trade opportunities existing in all of the sectors discussed above can be exploited such as to advance the human rights of the Vietnamese people is what this chapter now turns to consider. This depends on whether and how well the main players, both inside and outside the country, understand the interrelationship between human rights and trade, and seek thereby to address human rights concerns through trade.

5. ADDRESSING HUMAN RIGHTS CONCERNS THROUGH TRADE

As this chapter has demonstrated thus far, there are evident interconnections between economic development, trade expansion and human rights protection. As a general principle, human rights will be promoted in the development context where the exploitation of potential economic benefits yielded by membership of the WTO is pursued in a way such that social benefits, including distribution, are maximised and not just viewed as a corollary to economic gain that will take care of itself. As argued by the celebrated economist Amartya Sen, we need to embrace a wider understanding of the notion of 'development': namely, that development means more than merely economic gain; it *must* also encompass gains in political and personal freedoms to be truly meaningful.[97] The challenge for Viet Nam will be to implement Sen's definition of 'development' as it harnesses the benefits of WTO accession, while mitigating its potential detriments.

---

97 Amartya Sen, *Development as Freedom* (Anchor Books, New York, 2001).

A. Three Strategic Issues

Of all the many factors that are likely to play key roles in the interaction between the domestic consequences of Viet Nam's expanded trade relations and the protection and promotion of human rights in the country over the next few years, we believe that there are three issues of particular, strategic importance: legal reform; business and human rights; and linking trade and human rights.

(i) Legal reform

In the years immediately prior to accession, the National Assembly embarked on an enormous program of reform of the administrative and business regulatory frameworks in Viet Nam. Across a vast range of matters – including banking, securities and investment, business establishment and competition laws, telecommunications, manufacturing, transport, infrastructure and construction, energy, power, water and resources management – many old laws were revised and new ones enacted to establish the legal foundations for WTO compliance.[98] The necessity and urgency of such a radical overhaul of the statute book had been well recognised by the Vietnamese authorities if the country was to meet the demands of WTO accession and, equally, if it was to exploit the economic and commercial potential that accession afforded it.

The Government-commissioned Inter-Agency Comprehensive Legal System Needs Report[99] of 2001 assesses the developing situation and charts a path to 2010 of further, necessary changes. It is a notably candid account of the present and anticipated shortcomings of the legal system, highlighting the unsystematic, less than comprehensive and somewhat superficial nature of the changes thus far effected. And it is in this assessment that much of the actual and potential human rights problems and opportunities associated with Viet Nam's legal system lie. They are, in fact, implicitly discernible rather than explicitly stated, for the Report is wholly oriented towards what needs to be done in order to better prepare Viet Nam for further international economic integration; it is not on its face concerned at all with the social, still less human rights, needs of the legal system. That fact, however, does not make these needs any less significant, just less recognised.

The Report notes the poor quality of the newly drafted laws (too often imprecise, open-ended and failing to implement the international standards they sought to incorporate); the constitutional inadequacies of how the organs

---

98 George Russell, 'Vietnam's WTO Membership: Impact on Business', *Asialaw* (Hong Kong), 1 February 2007, 1.

99 Inter-Agency Steering Committee, above n 33.

of government (Executive, Assembly and Judiciary) interrelate in respect of devising and delivering legislative programs; how ill-trained are judges and ill-equipped are courts; how endemic is the lack of respect for the notion of the rule of law within nearly all levels of the public service; how inadequate are the provisions for legal aid; and how poor is the level and delivery of tertiary legal education (notwithstanding that there are now 12 institutions nationwide that have trained nearly 100 000 law graduates over the past 15 years or so). In combination, these shortcomings can lead to abuses of the key human rights of fair trial and equality before the law, without which, so many other rights – especially economic and social rights to housing, health education, safe working conditions and adequate standard of living – are also infringed simply because of the inadequacies of the means of enforcement and redress. The systemic development of open, fair and robust legal institutions and processes is critical for Viet Nam, not only to attract and secure international trade and FDI, but also, at the same time, to ensure domestic compliance with its international human rights obligations.

In respect of legal reform, trade and human rights are interlinked. This is evident, for example, in the steady growth of the private legal profession in the country and the increasing instance of foreign law firms establishing offices in Hanoi and Ho Chi Minh City.[100] Much of this growth has been in response to the greater need for legal services as commercial enterprise and international trade expands. Indeed the lengthy and complex negotiations that preceded both the US-Viet Nam BTA and accession to the WTO required significant legal input and thereby provided direct impetus to the development of local legal capacity as well as the importation of foreign legal expertise. Nevertheless, the number of Vietnamese lawyers in practice remains small (approximately 4000)[101] and the number of those with any substantial understanding of international law miniscule (estimated to be around 50),[102] although that is apparently set to change soon following the recent announcement by the Ministry of Justice that it will establish a special training program in international law and legal practice for an annual cohort of hand-picked young Vietnamese lawyers.[103]

100 Most of these firms are from Australia, Europe, Hong Kong and the US: see David Gantz, 'Doi Moi, the VBTA and WTO Accession: The Role of Lawyers in Vietnam's Cautious Embrace of Globalization' (2007) 41 *International Lawyer* 873, 878.

101 Luật sư, *trọng tài chưa theo kịp . . . WTO*, available in Vietnamese at: http://www.vnn.vn/kinhte/2006/08/600917/ at 20 November 2008.

102 Ibid.

103 Russell, above n 98.

Irrespective of these changes, it cannot be said that the protection and promotion of human rights standards constitutes the core business of foreign and local law firms working in Viet Nam today. However, there can be little doubt that their growing presence is an important factor in the strengthening of the concept and practice of the rule of law in a country which, 20 years ago, had no notion of what the rule of law entailed, had no functioning private legal profession and trained fewer than 500 lawyers per year.[104] It is through such a framework constructed by the increased recognition of, and respect for, the rule of law that human rights can be both better expressed and protected.

There is, by the Government's own estimation, much yet to be done to truly reform the legal system and the legal services sector such that they meet the demands of international trade and commerce, let alone those of international human rights laws. The approaches to be taken to the building of Viet Nam's legal system and especially the education of its own lawyers need to be more integrated and more nuanced, such that the relationship between enhancing trade, economic development, poverty reduction and the protection of human rights are understood as part of a contiguous whole. There is a patent need for more concerted efforts to be made by the Vietnamese Government, and by its international advisers or aid donors, to stress the interdependency of trade and human rights in the development of all aspects of the country's legal system, from the policy and legislative programs, through the implementation of policies and laws by the bureaucracy, to the operation of the courts and the training and education of judges and lawyers.

(ii) Business and human rights

A crucial factor in the protection and promotion of human rights in Viet Nam at the broadest level is the degree to which the undoubted economic benefits yielded by the private sector can be harnessed for social ends; more specifically, but equally important, is the question of what the private sector can and should do directly to advance human rights standards. The first, broader contribution is secured largely through corporate taxation and the redistribution of wealth; the second, more particular question underpins the growing global movement towards making corporations socially (as well as economically) responsible for their actions, including in respect of human rights.

The private sector is the key driver of the country's integration into the international market economy, and its influence will only increase now that the Government itself is explicitly promoting private enterprise.[105] Some 160 000 new corporations have been established since 1999 and the trend is set to

[104] Gantz, above n 100, 873.

[105] *Instruments of the Xth Congress of the Communist Party of Viet Nam* (2006).

continue in coming years, even if the vast majority of these businesses are small and vulnerable to competition, especially from international corporations.[106] At the same time, following accession to the WTO and the current flood of FDI into the country, the state's role in commerce is shifting from main player to regulator, as state monopolies and state-owned enterprises are broken up and are increasingly exposed to domestic and international competition.[107] Increased integration into the world economy will both foster business activity and increase economic efficiency. But market forces will favour the productive over the less productive, the efficient over the inefficient, and this in turn will necessarily have social impacts. However, predicting which sectors or which regions will be hardest hit is difficult and imprecise.[108] In addressing the unforeseen consequences, the World Bank counsels the Vietnamese Government not to prop up ailing enterprises, but rather to focus on the people affected, through policies such as assistance to workers made redundant, and budget transfers from the provinces benefiting the most from economic reforms to those who are adversely hit.[109] Thus, when corporations fail, the state is equipped to deliver on its social responsibilities.

We ask now in this present section, what role the private sector must play in meeting its social responsibilities, and in preventing human rights abuses and promoting human rights protection. Corporations, both foreign and local, are presently subject to an array of domestic regulations when operating in Viet Nam, and some of these embrace human rights matters, such as labour laws and workplace health and safety. Compliance with such mandatory laws forms part of the notion of corporate social responsibility (CSR). But CSR also includes going 'beyond compliance' to encompass corporations voluntarily promoting social (and human rights) goods within the realms of their respective spheres of activity and influence, such as supporting the local communities in which they work by providing education and health services, or

---

106 Tấn Đức, *Vì sao chưa có doanh nghiệp tư nhân lớn?* (2006) http://www.fetp.edu.vn/inthenews/tbktsg190606_1.htm at 11 November 2008.

107 As noted above at n 40, the process of equitisation (privatisation) of former, often inefficient, State Owned Enterprises (SOEs) has resulted in job losses. However, uniquely in respect of SOEs, the Government operates a safety net for redundant SOE workers, providing severance pay packages. In 2002, the fund assisted just over one thousand workers at 34 SOEs; by 2005, the number of participating enterprises peaked at 1445, with 86 483 workers receiving redundancy pay. By 2007, a total of 218 818 workers had received assistance under the scheme: World Bank et al., above n 12, 40–1).

108 Despite sophisticated attempts to predict the social impacts of WTO accession on sectors such as livestock, fisheries, rice, coffee and textiles, the bulk of assessments are inconclusive. World Bank et al., above n 40, 156.

109 Ibid 150.

infrastructure needs, or protecting cultural practices. It must be stressed that the primary responsibility for the guarantee of human rights still rests on the shoulders of the state, but, given the power and influence that corporations can have on the economic and social well-being of developing countries, political, legal and commercial pressures have grown such that corporations are now increasingly expected not just to desist from breaches of human rights, but actively to assist in their observance and fulfilment.

The Government is, in fact, well aware of the phenomenon of CSR and of the need for it to be carefully promoted throughout the business community:

> For Vietnamese enterprises, good adoption of labor standards or CSR will certainly boost their competitiveness in the international markets. However, if improperly used, labor standards may turn to be a political issue or barrier to trade. Closely monitoring the adoption of labor standards at national and enterprise levels is needed to work out appropriate responses.[110]

The rather euphemistically expressed concern about improper use of labour standards refers to the possibility that competitor businesses (and states) will be very quick to condemn Vietnamese enterprises should their standards of CSR overall, and labour standards especially, be considered inadequate. The report from the Ministry of Labor, Invalid and Social Affairs (MoLISA) goes on to stress the particular problem that local corporations 'lack experience in keeping transparent records of CSR management and practice in their business.'[111]

There are already a number of CSR initiatives planned or in place in Viet Nam. Major transnational corporations (TNCs) operating in Viet Nam such as Adidas, Nike, GAP and Glaxo Smith Kline have their own codes of conduct and CSR programs; social audits using globally recognised social accountability standards such as SA8000 are undertaken by a number of international and local corporations; and the International Finance Corporation's Mekong Private Sector Development Facility promotes the ideas of social and environmentally sustainable business in its efforts to encourage and strengthen private enterprise in the region.[112] There is also a joint Vietnamese-Danish CSR advisory firm operating out of Hanoi,[113] and the Swedish Government has recently sponsored a number of CSR workshops in the country.

These initiatives are in themselves of marginal significance given the scale of human rights problems facing the country. The vast majority of companies in Viet Nam are small enterprises which have no notion of CSR, focusing on

---

110 MoLISA, above n 58, 8–9.

111 Ibid.

112 See http://www.ifc.org/mpdf at 11 November 2008.

113 CSR Vietnam Co Ltd: see http://www.csrvietnam.com/index.php?_MODULE=16&s=1 at 11 November 2008.

bare survival. And while most large TNCs are avowed proponents of CSR, they routinely exercise their considerable market power by way of restrictive business practices to eliminate such local (and international) competition. Such practices, though permissible under WTO rules,[114] tend to have an especially detrimental effect on local business development in poorer countries.[115] Certainly, it cannot yet be said that the private sector, in either developed or developing economies, has greeted the prospect of enhancing the human rights component of CSR – through such initiatives as the UN's Draft Human Rights Norms for Corporations – with enthusiasm; rather, corporate reactions have been almost universally sceptical, if not outright negative.[116]

Still, CSR is now a feature of the corporate landscape worldwide, and in Viet Nam the idea has been introduced early in the country's development of the private sector, and to some extent it is being implemented in practice. The task of promoting human rights observance through CSR in any developing country is enormously challenging, but is one that is now considered essential if human rights are to be effectively protected in new and emerging market economies. Conspicuously successful initiatives such the ILO-backed *Better Factories* program in Cambodia,[117] which through systematic monitoring has demonstrably improved working conditions in hundreds of export garment factories, provide templates for what can be further achieved in Viet Nam.

(iii) Linking trade and human rights

Viet Nam's accession to the WTO opens up new opportunities and challenges in respect of promoting human rights goals through the WTO's formalised regulation of international trade relations. Broadly speaking, these fall into two categories: (a) through legal means, by defending its own actions or challenging those of other member countries, under the WTO's Dispute Settlement Mechanism (DSM); and (b) through political means, by way of negotiations on specific allowances and concessions, as well as on broader questions of the direction and emphasis of the WTO. It is strategically important for many reasons, including human rights, whether and how Viet Nam utilises these processes, as well as how others use it in respect of Viet Nam in the years to come.

---

114 The Agreement on Trade Related Investment Measures ('TRIMs') effectively sidesteps the question of restrictive trade practices.

115 See Oliver Morrisey and Yogesh Rai, 'The GATT Agreement on Trade Related Investment Measures: Implications for Developing Countries and their Relationship with Transnational Corporations' (1995) 31 *Journal of Development Studies* 702.

116 See David Kinley and Rachel Chambers, 'The UN Human Rights Norms for Corporations: The Private Implications of Public International Law' (2006) 6 *Human Rights Law Review* 44.

117 See http://www.betterfactories.org/ at 11 November 2008.

(a) Legal means It can be fairly said that the DSM is almost a 'human rights-free zone'. Human rights simply did not feature in the 1946–47 negotiations on the GATT; they were seen as irrelevant to the question of the liberalisation of trade between states and were not, in any case, viewed as a problem for the democratic states that made up the original membership of the GATT.[118]

Although the term is absent from any WTO treaty provisions, there are various grounds under WTO treaties upon which the institution of protectionist measures by a country can be justified, and some of these may bear on human rights concerns. These include so-called exceptions clauses, such as GATT Article XX which allows measures that are necessary to protect public morals, human life or health, items of cultural heritage, and the conservation of exhaustible natural resources, as well as restriction on products of prison labour,[119] and GATT Article XXI which exempts actions necessary for the protection of essential security interests. Under TRIPS (Article 31), there is also provision for states to break patent restrictions (either by negotiated settlement or unilaterally) in circumstances of national emergency, for example to enable local manufacture of cheap generic medicines to counteract a health epidemic or emergency.[120]

In truth, however, there is not much in this list that provides substantial grounds for launching human rights-based arguments in the WTO context. This is starkly demonstrated by the somewhat remarkable fact that the 'product of prison labour' exception mentioned above has never yet been invoked. More fundamentally, Ernst-Ulrich Petersmann has pointed out that few, if any, of the 220 WTO cases decided thus far have involved any significant arguments that might be characterised as having a human rights focus.[121] There have been instances of heightened sensitivity to particular human health and environmental concerns in some cases, but overall the Dispute Panels and Appellate Body of the WTO have shown a marked disinclination to entertain human rights considerations in the cases before them.[122] Some argue that this

---

[118] Susan Aaronson and Jamie Zimmerman, 'Fair Trade?: How Oxfam Presented a Systemic Approach to Poverty, Development, Human Rights and Trade' (2006) 28 *Human Rights Quarterly* 998, 1001.

[119] These grounds are echoed in Article 2.2 of the *Agreement on Technical Barriers to Trade* as legitimate objectives for the imposition of technical (that is, product or process related) barriers to trade.

[120] Such a strategy has been successfully utilised by such countries as Brazil, India and Thailand.

[121] Ernst-Ulrich Petersmann, 'WTO Dispute Settlement, Developing Countries and Human Rights', (Paper presented at the Conference on WTO and Human Rights, Prato, 21 June 2007) 1.

[122] See Robert Howse and Makau Mutua, *Protecting Human Rights in a*

might change,[123] but whether or not this change occurs, it seems highly unlikely that the concerted push for raising human rights arguments in WTO disputes will come from developing countries such as Viet Nam.

When pursuing legal means to settle disputes or otherwise pressing for advantage under the rules of the WTO, developing countries are inherently disadvantaged as against developed states whose competitive edge regarding litigation and proto-litigation negotiations flows from their much greater familiarity with the system and their willingness and capacity to engage the best legal advice to advance their cause.[124] This is strikingly evident, for example, in the overwhelming statistics for the EC (86 per cent) and the US (99 per cent) as a party, or third party, to WTO dispute cases.[125] The Advisory Centre on WTO Law established by eight European countries and Canada in 1999 to provide discounted-rate legal services to developing countries in pursuing (or defending) WTO disputes has done something to redress this imbalance,[126] and there is evidence, as Gregory Shaffer notes, that 'many developing countries are learning to use the dispute settlement system more effectively'.[127]

Viet Nam has already felt the harsh impact of the adept and concerted use by developed countries of legal avenues to promote their interests against those of Viet Nam. The designation of Viet Nam as a non-market economy has made it especially vulnerable to US and EC anti-dumping duties, because the 'normal value' of products cannot be assessed against Viet Nam's own distorted 'market', but is rather assessed against some other (inevitably much more expensive) market in the same products.[128] Three such disputes, which were especially large and lengthy, have recently been concluded against Viet

---

Global Economy: Challenges for the World Trade Organization (2000) http://www.ichrdd.ca/english/commdoc/publications/globalization/wtoRightsGlob.html at 11 November 2008.

[123] Lorand Bartels, 'Trade and Human Rights', in Daniel Bethlehem et al. (eds) *The Oxford Handbook of International Trade Law* (Oxford University Press, 2009).

[124] Gregory Shaffer, 'The Challenges of WTO Law: Strategies for Developing Country Adaptation' (2006) 5 *World Trade Review* 177.

[125] Shaffer, ibid 186.

[126] The nine original signatories to the 1999 Agreement establishing the Advisory Centre on WTO Law were Canada, Denmark, Finland, Ireland, Italy, The Netherlands, Norway, Sweden and the United Kingdom. Switzerland acceded in 2004. The Centre became operational in 2001. See: http://www.acwl.ch/e/index_e.aspx.

[127] Shaffer, above n 124, 197.

[128] The practice of using a third-country market to determine the comparable 'domestic' price in the calculation of anti-dumping duties is permitted under Article VI of the GATT, and therefore, even as a WTO member, Viet Nam's designation as a non-market economy will persist.

Nam: one regarding catfish and another involving shrimp brought by the US,[129] and the third regarding footwear with leather uppers brought by the EC.[130] The consequent penalties levied against these industries in Viet Nam will adversely impact those who depend on these industries to make a living and thereby, necessarily, will impact on their levels of human rights fulfilment.

(b) Political means The WTO's DSM as presently configured has little capacity and still less inclination to operate as a vehicle for securing human rights objectives. Human rights concerns are hardly made any more explicit in the 'political' realm of the WTO either – that is, the realm in which competing interests are negotiated rather than litigated. But here at least, there is some latitude for developing countries to draw on a broader array of arguments to advance their positions, including those within the terms of the WTO that approximate to, or can accommodate more readily, human rights concerns. The Doha 'Development' Round, begun in 2001, was intended to deliver on the promise of the WTO's Marrakesh Agreement, the Preamble of which provides that trade relations between member states:

> should be conducted with a view to raising standards of living, ensuring full employment and a large and steadily growing volume of real income and effective demand, and expanding the production of and trade in goods and services, while allowing for the optimal use of the world's resources in accordance with the objective of sustainable development, seeking both to protect and preserve the environment and to enhance the means for doing so in a manner consistent with their respective needs and concerns at different levels of economic development.[131]

---

[129] Notice of Antidumping Duty Order: Certain Frozen Fish Fillets from the Socialist Republic of Vietnam, 68 Federal Register 47909 (12 August 2003); Notice of Amended Final Determination of Sales at Less than Fair Value and Antidumping Duty Order: Certain Frozen Warmwater Shrimp from the Socialist Republic of Vietnam, 70 Federal Register 5152 (1 February 2005). Also see: Joshua Startup, 'From Catfish to Shrimp: How Vietnam Learned to Navigate the Waters of "Free Trade" as a Non-Market Economy' (2005) 90 *Iowa Law Review* 1963.

[130] Council Regulation (EC) No 1472/2006, 5 October 2006, imposing a definitive anti-dumping duty and collecting definitely the provisional duty imposed on imports of certain footwear with uppers of leather originating in the People's Republic of China and Vietnam, OJ L 275/1 (6 October 2006). See also: UNDP, *Discretionary Rules: Anti-Dumping and Viet Nam's Non-Market Economy Status* (Policy Dialogue Paper 2006/4, UNDP, 2006) especially 20–9 for a discussion of the EC anti-dumping investigation on leather shoes.

[131] *Marrakesh Agreement establishing the World Trade Organisation*, opened for signature 15 April 1994, 1867 UNTS 3 (entered into force 1 January 1995).

The Doha Round has yet (if at all) to conclude,[132] but along the way it has encountered many problems principally focused on conflicts between the Northern and Southern states over the continued high levels of agricultural subsidies and domestic support in the former. Undeniably, the mainly developing nations of the South have gained in political strength as, individually and collectively, they have honed their negotiating, analytical, networking and lobbying skills as the Round has progressed. Throughout all this, when human rights issues such as the right to health and an adequate standard of living are raised (often by NGOs and commentators, rather than by states themselves), they have occupied more of a backstage role – at best, as important but ancillary or derivative concerns to the front stage issues of increased trade and economic development. The successful promotion of human rights concerns, such as that which prompted the adoption of the 2001 Doha Declaration on the TRIPS Agreement and Public Health[133] which essentially reiterated the pre-existing conditions under which compulsory licensing can occur, are the exceptions that prove this general rule.

In principle at least, the Doha Round provides the grounds upon which to pursue more development-oriented outcomes in trade, and thereby better realise human rights in developing countries such as Viet Nam. But for this to happen, trade has to be seen as a means to an end, not as an end itself. As Dani Rodrik argues 'trade is useful only insofar as it serves broader developmental and social goals'.[134] Developing countries, he continues, 'should not be obsessed with market access abroad, at the cost of overlooking more fundamental developmental challenges at home,'[135] and leeway should be accorded to countries who earnestly seek to address those challenges. Such an approach remains true to the ideals of the WTO as set out above, and clearly it opens up political space for countries such as Viet Nam to mount social arguments for the courses of economic action that they want to take. That said, such space can, and some argue[136] should, be limited where those arguments are themselves considered to act against democratic or human rights interests. This is

---

132 As *The Guardian* put it, 'trade negotiations are a bit like Mark Twain: their deaths are more rumour than fact': 'A club in trouble', *The Guardian* (London), 4 August 2008, 28. See further the comments by WTO Director-General Pascal Lamy to an informal meeting of the Trade Negotiations Committee: 'Day 9: Talks collapse despite progress on a list of issues' (29 July 2008) http://www.wto.org/english/news_e/news08_e/meet08_chair_29july08_e.htm at 11 November 2008.

133 *WTO Declaration on TRIPS and Public Health*, WTO Doc WT/MIN(01)/DEC/2 (20 November 2001) http://www.wto.org/english/thewto_e/minist_e/min01_e/mindecl_trips_e.htm at 11 November 2008.

134 Rodrik, above n 95, 27–33.

135 Rodrik, above n 95.

136 Rodrik, above n 95, 30.

in essence the rationale behind the Generalised System of Preferences (GSP) of the EU and US, both of which have arrangements that 'reward' developing and least developing countries with greater access to US and EU markets where the developing country is one which adheres to international labour standards and whose government is non-communist (in the case of the US GSP) or the country signs up to certain international human rights treaties (the EU's so-called 'GSP Plus'). Viet Nam however is ineligible for either of these on account of its Communist Party government (which disqualifies it from the US scheme) and not having ratified and implemented the required human rights treaties under the EU scheme.[137]

Evidently, the room to manoeuvre and seek advantage in the political realm of the WTO's universe serves richer states as well as it does poorer states, and often better. Furthermore, there is a marked tendency for all states to descend to particularised, tit-for-tat bargaining, which, as illustrated by the current state of the WTO Agriculture negotiations, can lead to horrendously complex, compromised and highly technical settlements that overall favour the strongest developed nations (in this case the US and the countries of the EU).[138] It also can, and has, led to an upsurge in the negotiation of bilateral trade agreements which inevitably favour the powerful over the weak and dilute the overall protective reach (albeit limited) of multilateral agreements such as those of the WTO.

The consequences for protection of human rights in this milieu are mixed. For on the one hand, their putative promotion through such trade conditionality as the GSPs of the US and EU may be welcomed, but on the other hand the same and other developed states may, through their relentless pursuit of trade liberalisation, be held responsible for the diminution or destruction of the livelihoods of millions of people in developing states, and the denial of human rights that flows therefrom. It is a dilemma recognised by the WTO's Director-General himself when he talks of the need for a new 'Geneva Consensus', even if he and all others who think like him have yet to devise the means to

---

[137] Though Viet Nam is covered by the so-called 'general arrangement' component of the EU's GSP scheme by virtue of being a developing country. To be eligible for GSP Plus, a developing country must have ratified and effectively implemented sixteen core human and labour rights conventions, and at least seven other conventions relating to the environment, narcotics, and governance principles, as listed in Annex III of Council Regulation No 980/2005 of 27 June 2005, OJ L169/1.

[138] See, for example, the 2007 'Falconer text', available at http://www.wto.org/english/tratop_e/agric_e/chair_texts07_e.htm at 11 November 2008. See Brett Williams, 'The Falconer Draft Text for the Doha Round WTO Negotiations on Agriculture – A "Ha'port of Tar" to Save the Vessel from Sinking or Just a Dab of Paint on an Irreparably Broken Hull?' (2007) 30 *University of New South Wales Law Journal* 368.

solve it, and even if the 'costs of adjustment' in human rights terms are to be inferred rather than explicitly stated:

> We cannot ignore the costs of adjustment, particularly for the developing countries, and the problems that can arise with the opening up of markets. These adjustments must not be relegated to the future: they must be an integral part of the opening-up agenda. We must create a new 'Geneva consensus': a new basis for the opening up of trade that takes into account the resultant cost of adjustment. Trade opening is necessary, but it is not sufficient in itself. It also implies assistance: to help the least-developed countries to build up their stocks and therefore adequate productive and logistical capacity; to increase their capacity to negotiate and to implement the commitments undertaken in the international trading system; and to deal with the imbalances created between winners and losers from trade opening – imbalances that are the more dangerous to the more fragile economies, societies or countries. Building the capacity they need to take advantage of open markets or helping developing countries to adjust is now part of our common global agenda.[139]

All states – developed and developing alike – will need to participate in this broad-ranging, political exercise if any progress along these lines is to be made. And as such, questions of what can and cannot be achieved by using trade to better protect human rights generally, and specifically in respect of Viet Nam, will have to play a significant part.

6. CONCLUSIONS

A direct and inevitable consequence of Viet Nam's tigerish economy and its increasing international presence, has been that greater attention is being paid to its non-trade as well as trade policies, actions and performances. In this chapter, we have sought to demonstrate that, in respect of human rights and trade issues, this attention poses both challenges and opportunities for the country and its people, as well as for those countries with which it trades. In the modern context of seemingly inexorable globalisation, the tripartite concerns of trade, development and human rights are intimately intertwined. This much can be inferred from the declared *raison d'être* of the WTO itself; from instances in which various combinations of their interrelations are trumpeted as being of vital importance by civil society organisations, and by some states; and from the Vietnamese Government's own *White Paper on Human Rights* as to the nature and significance of human rights to the country's fortunes, domestically and internationally (albeit somewhat guardedly).[140]

---

139 Pascal Lamy, *Humanising Globalization* (2006) http://www.wto.org/english/news_e/sppl_e/sppl16_e.htm at 11 November 2008.

140 *White Paper on Human Rights*, above n 5, 4–5, wherein the Government

In the new post-WTO accession era, all stakeholders in Viet Nam's progress towards making trade work for the betterment of the human rights of its people have roles to play – namely, the WTO itself, trading partners, the private sector (both local and foreign), civil society and expert commentators, and 'social intergovernmental organisations' such as the UN and its agencies and the ILO. But above all, the principal responsibilities and opportunities lie with the Government of Viet Nam. It is the international negotiator; the regulator of trade and commerce within its borders; the guardian of human rights in the country; and, ultimately, the agent of social, economic and (especially) political change. Managing the tensions and complementarities between these tasks will be no easy feat for the Government, but it is one which it now has no choice but to tackle.

stresses the principle of non-interference in a state's internal affairs at the same time as accepting the need for international cooperation, and its insistence on the interdependency of development and human rights.

10. The WTO and labor rights: strategies of linkage

Chantal Thomas

1. INTRODUCTION

While the Members of the World Trade Organization ('WTO') have yet to adopt affirmative labor obligations, the link between trade and labor has been pressed in much academic and policy discourse.[1] The judicial body of the WTO has been called on to identify some of the contours of appropriate linkage between such 'nontrade' issues and WTO rules in a series of closely watched disputes. The holdings of these cases have shifted since the WTO's establishment in 1995, away from a deep suspicion about the propriety of linking trade with nontrade issues, and towards a nuanced view that accepts the validity of linkage as long as it meets certain formal parameters.

Some have applauded this shift, while others have excoriated it. As the shape of WTO jurisprudence on linkage has shifted, calls for resolution through political negotiations have increased. Some perceive a 'legislative' solution to offer greater legitimacy because it would represent a more 'democratic' solution negotiated by the entire membership, rather than adjudicated by a panel of judges to resolve a dispute between particular members. Yet political negotiations are fraught with a host of separate problems. What might be called the 'decision costs' of a legislative solution are high, possibly prohibitively so.[2] A knotty problem arises for those concerned with linkage: there

---

[1] See generally Jagdish Bhagwati and Robert E Hudec (eds), *Fair Trade and Harmonization: Prerequisites for Free Trade?* (MIT Press, Cambridge, 1996); Symposium, 'Linkage as Phenomenon: An Interdisciplinary Approach' (1998) 19 *University of Pennsylvania Journal of International Economic Law* 201; Jose E Alvarez (ed.), ' Symposium: The Boundaries of the WTO' (2002) 96 *American Journal of International Law* 1; Andrew Guzman, *Global Governance and the WTO* (manuscript on file with author). This draft builds on the author's previous work: Chantal Thomas, 'Should the World Trade Organization Incorporate Labor and Environmental Standards' (2004) 61 *Washington and Lee Law Review* 347.

[2] See generally Joel P Trachtman, 'Economic Analysis of Prescriptive Jurisdiction' (2001) 42 *Virginia Journal of International Law* 1 (describing the trans-

seems to be an inverse relationship between perceived legitimacy, on the one hand, and decision costs on the other. The expense of negotiating a specific rule, the dangers of holdout and other strategic problems, and the specter of capture might all render the legislative option unfeasible; more seriously, they may threaten the very legitimacy that the legislation solution purports to provide.

This chapter considers the judicial and legislative responses to 'the linkage question': that is, to the incorporation of labor rights and standards within the WTO. First, the chapter recounts why the question has arisen in the first place: the relative weakness of enforcement mechanisms within international labor law. Second, the chapter reviews the range of WTO judicial responses to unilateral linkage efforts by member states, considered under existing 'negative' provisions of WTO law – a law of exceptions that allows but does not mandate linkage. Third, the chapter considers the obstacles confronting the legislative response of defining the relationship between trade and labour policies through multilateral negotiations to create 'positive' labour obligations within the WTO.

2. INTERNATIONAL LABOR LAW ENFORCEMENT MECHANISMS

The problem at the center of the 'trade linkage' question is the discrepancy between enforcement in the WTO regime and enforcement in other international legal regimes. This Part recounts the enforcement processes that have developed within international labor law and the challenges these processes continue to face.

Founded in 1919,[3] the International Labour Organization ('ILO') has established more than 180 binding conventions and 190 nonbinding resolutions on subjects ranging from human rights to occupational safety. Despite one of the oldest pedigrees in international law, however, the ILO's enforcement record has proved woeful.

An initial problem is that differing groups of countries have ratified different treaties, creating a patchwork of inconsistent legal obligations (although those conventions dealing with 'core' labour standards tend to have more uniform ratification). When a legal obligation does apply, moreover, the ILO's provisions for enforcement favor fact-finding and reporting over sanctions.[4]

action costs attendant to 'prescriptive jurisdiction' transactions'). See also below, Part 4A.

3 *Constitution of the International Labour Organization*, done at Versailles on 28 June 1919 ('*ILO Constitution*').

4 Members are required to make annual reports as to their compliance with ILO

Although the ILO constitution authorizes sanctions in the event of noncompliance, the language is vague: 'In the event of any Member failing to carry out within the time specified the recommendations [. . .] any other Member may take against that Member the measures of an economic character indicated [. . .] as appropriate to the case.'[5]

As was the case with the trade regime prior to the WTO,[6] even with respect to the most egregious labor practices, the ILO's enforcement capacity has been severely constrained, as in the case of allegations of forced labor practices in the country of Myanmar (known formerly as Burma).[7] The international outcry against Myanmar sparked a movement for economic sanctions. This mobilization resulted in, among other things, the adoption of procurement policies by several state and local governments in the United States that penalized companies for doing business with Myanmar. Within the ILO, noncompliance proceedings were triggered.[8] As provided under the ILO constitution, a coalition of 25 'worker's delegates' from a cross-section of developed and developing countries brought a formal complaint.[9] The resulting Commission of Inquiry found extensive violations of the Forced Labour Convention, amounting to 'a saga of untold misery and suffering, oppression and exploitation of large sections of the population inhabiting Myanmar by the Government, military and other public officers'.[10] The Commission

conventions to which they are parties. *ILO Constitution* Article 408. If a member fails to comply, the ILO can publicize that failure: *ILO Constitution* Article 410. A complaint can also be referred to a Commission of Inquiry, which can investigate and make findings and recommendations: *ILO Constitution* Articles 411–14. A member may then choose to pursue the matter further in the International Court of Justice ('ICJ'): *ILO Constitution* Articles 415–18.

5 *ILO Constitution* Article 419.

6 See John H Jackson, *The World Trading System: Law and International Economic Relations* (MIT Press, Cambridge, 2nd edn, 1995) 107–37 (comparing the historical processes for enforcement of GATT agreements with the improved WTO process implemented after the Uruguay Round).

7 See 'Report of the Commission of Inquiry Appointed under Article 26 of the Constitution of the International Labour Organization to Examine the Observance by Myanmar of the *Forced Labour Convention*' (1998) 80 *ILO Official Bulletin*, 2 July 1998 (describing allegations made by the ILO that the Myanmar Government facilitated forced labor practices for both public and private purposes) ('Report of the Commission of Inquiry').

8 See Ibid [1], [4] (documenting the series of ILO complaints and criticisms preceding the filing of a formal complaint and reporting on the action of the 267th meeting of the ILO Governing Body with respect to the filing of the formal complaint).

9 Ibid [1], FN1 (listing the 'workers' delegates': Lebanon, Ghana, Pakistan, France, United Kingdom, Sweden, Germany, Czech Republic, United States, Japan, Israel, Italy, Niger, India, United Republic of Tanzania, Canada, Ireland, Venezuela, Malaysia, Tunisia, Mexico, Zimbabwe, Cameroon, Barbados, and Poland).

10 Ibid [543].

condemned the 'impunity with which government officials, in particular the military, treat the civilian population as an unlimited pool of unpaid forced laborers and servants at their disposal'.[11] In response, the International Labour Conference ('ILC') voted in 2000 to compel Myanmarese compliance with *ILO Convention No 29*[12] on forced labor,[13] taking the unprecedented step of utilizing Article 33 of the *ILO Constitution* in the process,[14] a procedure reserved only for the most grave and persistent violation of international labor law. The 2000 measures were reiterated by the ILO Governing Body in 2005 due to continued recalcitrance from Myanmar.[15] In early 2007 the Myanmar junta concluded a Supplementary Understanding[16] with the ILO, which implemented on a trial basis the requested mechanism of addressing complaints over forced labor.[17] The gaoling of a local labor activist in September 2008 threw doubt on the government's compliance with this Understanding.[18] This painfully slow progress indicates that even the ILO's strongest weapon has not compelled a swift or appropriate response from the target State.

This relative institutional weakness, combined with the emergence of the relatively strong trade regime, generated the impetus for linkage of labor rights with international trade law. The remainder of this chapter examines strategies of linkage as they have unfolded within the 'judicial' and 'legislative' domains of the WTO.

---

11 Ibid [542].

12 *Convention concerning Forced or Compulsory Labour (ILO No 29)*, opened for signature 28 June 1930, 39 UNTS 55 (entered into force 1 May 1932). Myanmar (then Burma) ratified this instrument in 1955.

13 See generally ILO, 'International Labour Conference adopts Resolution targeting forced labour in Myanmar (Burma)' (Press Release, 14 June 2000). See also Gustavo Capdevila, 'Burma: ILO Gets Tough on Forced Labour' *Inter-Press Service* (Online/Rome), 16 November 2006, IPS, http://ipsnews.net/news.asp?idnews=35506 at 3 January 2009.

14 Article 33 reads: In the event of any Member failing to carry out within the time specified the recommendations, if any, contained in the report of the Commission of Inquiry, or in the decision of the International Court of Justice, as the case may be, the Governing Body may recommend to the Conference such action as it may deem wise and expedient to secure compliance therewith.

15 See ILO, 'Burma/Myanmar at the ILO Governing Body' (Press Release, 24 March 2005).

16 See *Supplementary Understanding* (26 February 2007) ILO, http://www.ilo.org/public/english/region/asro/yangon/docs/supplementary_understanding.pdf at 3 January 2009.

17 In particular, the instrument required that alleged victims of forced labor in Myanmar be given full freedom to submit complaints to the ILO Liaison Officer in Yangon and that no retaliatory measures could be taken against complainants: ILO, 'ILO concludes Understanding with Myanmar' (Press Release, 26 February 2007).

18 See ILO, 'ILO expresses concern over sentencing of Myanmar labour activist' (Press Release, 19 September 2008).

3. JUDICIAL RESPONSES TO UNILATERAL LINKAGE THROUGH INTERPRETATION?

The framework agreement of the WTO contains preambular language that affirms the importance of labour protections.[19] The Preamble recognizes that states' 'relations in the field of trade and economic endeavor should be conducted with a view to raising standards of living, ensuring full employment and a large and steadily growing volume of real income and effective demand'.[20] Beyond stating these general principles, however, the *Marrakesh Agreements* do not contain affirmative obligations to uphold labor standards. They do, however, create room for states on their own to take measures that restrict trade in order to implement social regulations.

A pivotal question in WTO jurisprudence is how much room exists under these provisions. WTO members have pursued a host of claims testing WTO law on some salient touchstones of the linkage debate. The WTO judiciary's responses have come under fire from both sides of the debate – charged at once with going too far to protect states' rights under nontrade law and not going far enough.[21] Some have charged the WTO Appellate Body with undue judicial activism.[22] Others argue that WTO judges can and should allow states

---

[19] *Marrakesh Agreement Establishing the WTO*, opened for signature 15 April 1994, 1867 UNTS 3 (entered into force 1 January 1995) ('*Marrakesh Agreement*').

[20] This language reproduces that of the 1947 *General Agreement on Tariffs and Trade*, opened for signature 1 January 1948, 55 UNTS 194 (entered into force 1 January 1948) Preamble ('GATT'): *Marrakesh Agreement* Preamble. A contrarian might argue that labor protections create 'rigidity' in the labor market, preventing full employment, so that the preamble could be read to justify the rejection, rather than the adoption, of labor protections. This familiar argument follows supply and demand but is also qualified by key assumptions. In the case of a wage increase, for example, one must assume that other variables remain constant, so that labor productivity does not increase to offset the increase in production cost, and the employer cannot regain the increase in production costs by increasing market prices. Note that this also assumes a competitive market, which prevents the employer from being able to raise prices, and that the employer was operating at a marginal labor product of zero. When the wage increases, employer demand for labor will decrease (by the amount required for the employer to recover a marginal labor product of zero). Consequently, although those employed will benefit from higher wages, the overall number of employees will be fewer. However, the reference to raising standards of living seems to make clear that what is sought is not simply full employment, but full employment that improves quality of life.

[21] See Susan Esserman and Robert Howse, 'The WTO on Trial' (2003) 82 *Foreign Affairs* 130, 133–4 (discussing the positions taken by 'antiglobalization advocates and doctrinaire free traders' against judicial activism).

[22] See Jagdish Bhagwati, 'Afterword: The Question of Linkage' (2002) 96 *American Journal of International Law* 126, 133–4 (stating that the WTO Appellate Body should avoid making drastic changes to international trade law).

to invoke international law to defend pro-labour trade restrictions.[23] An examination of WTO jurisprudence on some high-profile controversies reveals a range of interpretive possibilities in the conflict between trade rules and nontrade rules.

A. The General Exceptions of Article XX GATT

The most prominent set of 'non-trade' social regulation allowances is found in Article XX of the GATT.[24] Entitled 'General Exceptions', Article XX recognizes that the social regulation objectives of governments may lead them to take measures that restrict trade in a way that contravenes other GATT rules. Article XX permits such measures if they survive a designated test. The Article XX test requires that the measure in question possess two qualities: first, it is demonstrably germane to the stated social objective; and second, it does not abuse basic GATT/WTO principles of nondiscrimination. The measure cannot be 'applied in a manner which would constitute a means of arbitrary or unjustifiable discrimination between countries where the same conditions prevail, or a disguised restriction on international trade'. This condition is referred to as the 'chapeau' because of its location in an introductory paragraph that sits atop several brief subclauses.

The second objective is met by incorporating language that the measure at issue be in a defined nexus with the social objective – either 'related to' or 'necessary to'. Relevant provisions here include those allowing measures that are 'necessary to protect public morals', 'necessary to protect human, animal or plant life or health', 'relating to the products of prison labour', and 'relating to the conservation of exhaustible natural resources if such measures are made effective in conjunction with restrictions on domestic production or consumption'.

Apart from language in the preamble affirming 'full employment' and 'raising standards of living', however, WTO law contains no provisions that set out affirmative labor standards.[25] As with environmental standards, the potential

---

23 See Joost Pauwelyn, 'The Role of Public International Law: How Far Can We Go?' (2001) 95 *American Journal of International Law* 535, 566 (arguing that disputing parties should be allowed to invoke international laws found in sources outside of the WTO).

24 See Article XX GATT (outlining the exceptions that derive from member states' police powers).

25 The international trade regime initially envisioned after World War II would have explicitly incorporated labor standards. See *Havana Charter for an International Trade Organization*, done at Havana on 24 March 1948, Article 7 ('The Members recognize that unfair labour conditions, particularly in production for export, create difficulties in international trade, and, accordingly, each Member shall take whatever action may be appropriate and feasible to eliminate such conditions within its terri-

for recognition comes mainly via exemption. That is, the exemption clauses may allow a State, in some circumstances, to impose restrictions on goods on the basis that they have been produced in breach of labor standards. Article XX sets out several clauses that might be considered to include labor standards, most explicitly Article XX(e) which allows members to maintain measures that are otherwise WTO-inconsistent if they 'relat[e] to the products of prison labour'. Article XX also contains more general clauses that could be applied to uphold labor standards. Article XX(a) provides an exemption for measures that are 'necessary to protect public morals', and Article XX(b) allows for measures that are 'necessary to protect animal or plant life or health'. All of these clauses are subject to the chapeau's conditions relating to arbitrary or unjustifiable discrimination or disguised protection.

An early case, *Belgian Family Allowances*, suggested that differences in the treatment of foreign goods based on labor standards would violate the trade regime's basic principles of nondiscrimination.[26] However, *Belgian Family Allowances* did not discuss the applicability of Article XX's exceptions. Robert Howse has ventured that, in the contemporary context, the 'public morals' exception of Article XX(a) could allow for such measures within the conditions established by the Article XX chapeau:

> [T]here is an argument that the interpretation of public morals should not be frozen in time and that with the evolution of human rights as a core element in public morality in many post-war societies, the content of public morals extends to include disapprobation of labour practices that violate universal human rights.[27]

---

tory.'). That movement failed, and US proposals for inclusion of labor standards in the GATT regime that ultimately developed apparently failed to win the approval of the other contracting parties. See Adelle Blackett, 'Whither Social Clause? Human Rights, Trade Theory and Treaty Interpretation' (1999) 31 *Columbia Human Rights Law Review* 1, 8, FN14 (quoting an informal proposal put forth by the United States to achieve fair labor standards as part of GATT); see also Janelle M Diller and David A Levy, 'Notes and Comments, Child Labour, Trade and Investment: Toward the Harmonization of International Law' (1997) 91 *American Journal of International Law* 663, 685 6 (discussing the failure to gain support for labor standards because of the difficulty of defining unfair competition). The issue arose periodically in subsequent GATT negotiation rounds, especially the Tokyo Round, which was the last before the GATT transformed into the WTO. See Clyde Summers, 'The Battle in Seattle: Free Trade, Labor Rights, and Societal Values' (2001) 22 *University of Pennsylvania Journal of International Economic Law* 61, 62–3 (2001) (discussing the history of failed efforts to include labor standards in the GATT negotiations).

26 *Belgian Family Allowances*, GATT BISD, 1st Supp, GATT Doc DS/1S/59 (7 November 1952) (Report of the Panel) (finding that a Belgian measure that imposed a tax on government-procured imports from countries without a system of public allowances violated the Most-Favored-Nation Treatment rule of Article I GATT).

27 Robert Howse, "The World Trade Organization and the Protection of Workers' Rights' (1999) 3 *Journal of Small and Emerging Business Law* 131, 192.

Howse's premise finds support in Joost Pauwelyn's contention that WTO rules must be read in conjunction with the larger body of public international law.[28]

B. The SPS Agreement

Although the WTO has declined to take social regulations head on, its arena of operation has expanded to make that collision inevitable. During the Uruguay Round, members negotiated the *Agreement on Sanitary and Phytosanitary Measures* ('SPS Agreement'), which sought to create guidelines for the establishment of consumer health and safety regulations relating to imports.[29] The SPS Agreement expands upon GATT 1947 Article XX(I)(b) by providing that '[m]embers have the right to take sanitary and phytosanitary measures necessary for the protection of human, animal or plant life or health'. It further elaborates that '[m]embers shall ensure that any sanitary or phytosanitary measure is applied only to the extent necessary to protect human, animal or plant life or health, is based on scientific principles and is not maintained without sufficient scientific evidence'.

Viewed from one perspective, the SPS Agreement enables social regulation of trade; it seems to imply that if a country follows the SPS Agreement, its social regulations will be free from challenge under the GATT/WTO. Critics of the SPS Agreement, however, argue that the SPS Agreement imposes pressure on governments to reduce or weaken their social regulatory framework.[30] This difference of opinion was never as visible as during the recent WTO dispute in which Canada and the United States brought a complaint against the European Community ('EC'), challenging the EC's import ban on beef produced with artificial growth hormones.[31]

The so-called *EC – Hormones* case became a lightning rod for concerns about the proper role of international trade law in constraining the social regu-

---

28 Pauwelyn, above n 23, 560.

29 See *Marrakesh Agreement Establishing the WTO*, opened for signature 15 April 1994, 1867 UNTS 3 (entered into force 1 January 1995) Annex 1A (*Agreement on Sanitary and Phytosanitary Measures*) (recognizing the significance of sanitary and phytosanitary measures for health and trade).

30 See, for example, Lori Wallach and Michelle Sforza, *Whose Trade Organization? Corporate Globalization and the Erosion of Democracy* (Public Citizen, Washington DC, 1999) 59–61 (recognizing that because the SPS Agreement only permits measures based on 'sound science', nations may be forced to ignore their cultural values).

31 *European Communities – Measures Concerning Meat and Meat Products (Hormones)*, WTO Doc WT/DS26/AB/R, WT/DS48/AB/R, AB-2000-11 (16 January 1998) [2] (Report of the Appellate Body) ('*EC – Hormones*') (stating that the EC measures were inconsistent with the SPS Agreement).

latory arm of member states. The EC argued that the import ban was imposed strictly in the interests of EC consumers. The complainants argued that the import ban played on consumer fears to justify protectionist measures that only benefited EC producers.

In the resolution of the dispute, the conflict between WTO law, as currently interpreted, and other realms of international law came into stark relief. The EC justified its 'zero tolerance' approach to artificial growth hormone in beef by reference to the 'precautionary principle'. The precautionary principle of international environmental law holds that if little is known about the health implications of a particular product or process, governments are justified in imposing very strict regulations as a precaution.

The Appellate Body ultimately rejected the EC's interpretation of the precautionary principle. The AB was careful to emphasize that its interpretation of the SPS agreement did not bar Member states from establishing levels of protection that were more restrictive than predominant scientific opinion might warrant. The Appellate Body did find, however, that when a Member chose to establish a higher level of protection, a 'risk assessment' that was based on scientific research was required to support it; invocation of the precautionary principle without such scientific support failed to meet the risk assessment requirement.

C. Social Regulation or Disguised Protectionism? The Interpretive Dilemma and Challenges to Judicial Legitimacy

In the range of cases on social measures that have come before the WTO dispute settlement mechanism, few have survived. A careful reading of the Appellate Body opinions shows that in many cases it took issue not with the measure itself, but with the means by which that measure was implemented, calling for a process that was either less discriminatory or better supported by scientific evidence. Nevertheless, for many labour advocates, these outcomes suggested that reform was needed to strike a better balance between trade concerns and 'trade-related' social concerns. Ironically, from other quarters, the Appellate Body attracted criticism for being too generous to the concerns of social justice advocates. After the approval of the modified US measure protecting sea turtles, in *Shrimp – Turtle*[32] some trade analysts pronounced the Appellate Body captured by 'the persistent environmental lobbies of the North'.[33]

---

32 *United States – Import Prohibition of Certain Shrimp and Shrimp Products*, WTO Doc WT/DS/58/AB/R, AB-2001-4 (21 November 2001).

33 Bhagwati, above n 22, 133.

The criticism directed towards the Appellate Body indicates the dilemmas it faces in balancing the trade principles of the WTO with social concerns that are both policy objectives of WTO members and principles of international labor law. Some scholars argue that WTO law must be read in conjunction with these latter principles.[34] Others worry that such consideration strains the legitimacy of the Appellate Body as a body charged with applying WTO law.[35]

In the *EC – GSP* case,[36] the Appellate Body came as close as it ever has to addressing whether governments could impose sanctions on the basis of labor rights issues. India charged that the EU illegitimately had imposed conditions on its Generalized System of Preferences ('GSP') benefits. These conditionalities related to labor, environment, and drug trafficking issues, but India ultimately withdrew its complaint regarding the labor and environment aspects. That India withdrew these aspects suggests that it may have felt that the Appellate Body was positioned to rule squarely in favor of the EU on its right to impose labor and environmental conditionalities. Even with only the drug trafficking conditionalities in front of it, the Appellate Body held in favor of the EU's ability to impose conditionalities on its GSP benefits, although labor was not considered. The regime was found to be WTO-inconsistent not because these policies were incorporated, but rather only because the EU had not incorporated them in a transparent way that treated similar countries similarly.[37]

An underlying controversy on the boundary between legitimate social regulation and illegitimate protectionism charges the debate over the propriety of judicial resolution of the linkage issue.[38] If one believes in the benefits of trade and the difficulty of convincing governments to lower barriers, the rationale for this suspicion gains some validity. With a deep suspicion of the protectionist impulses of governments in mind, the import-restricting measures relating to tuna, shrimp, refined gasoline, and beef (all of which have been

---

34 Pauwelyn, above n 23, 560.

35 Guzman, above n 1.

36 *European Communities – Conditions for the Granting of Tariff Preferences to Developing Countries*, WTO Docs WT/DS246/R (1 December 2003) (Report of the Panel) ('*EC – GSP Panel*') WT/DS246/AB/R, AB-2004-1 (7 April 2004) (Report of the Appellate Body) ('*EC – GSP Appeal*').

37 In doing so, the Appellate Body adopted the 'substantive equality' model that had been part of the 'structuralist' agenda for reform of the New International Economic Order (see Raúl Prebisch, *The Economic Development of Latin America and Its Principal Problems* (United Nations, New York, 1950)) propounded by developing-country governments in the 1970s when the GSP was established. Ironically, although the principle of substantive equality drove the argument by developing-country governments for a GSP back then, in the *EC – GSP* case the substantive equality argument was adopted by the EU as respondent.

38 Robert E Hudec, 'Science and "Post-Discriminatory" WTO Law' (2003) 26 *Boston College International and Comparative Law Review* 185, 190.

challenged in GATT or WTO disputes) begin to look like poorly disguised concessions to domestic industries seeking to stave off outside competition to the detriment of consumers and ultimately to the detriment of aggregate global welfare.

Public choice literature reminds us that it is quite possible – and, under certain conditions, likely – for governments to cater to narrow protectionist interests at the expense of the wider population.[39] An insistently rosy view of the motives of governments, therefore, is not particularly appropriate. The concern about disguised protectionism is a valid one.

Given that this concern is valid, a true interpretive dilemma arises. The WTO decision-making bodies seem prepared to err on the side of enabling trade rather than enabling trade-restricting social measures. A view driven by only labor concerns might, in a similar fashion, blindly support all such measures without considering their impact on foreign producers, domestic consumers, and the world economy.

The proper interpretive stance becomes much harder to strike if one accepts both that disguised protectionism is a danger and should be discouraged, and that social regulations are nevertheless a central function of the state that are supported and required by international labor law. However difficult this puzzle is, it is quite clear that this problem cannot be avoided. The growing importance of WTO law, and of concerns relating to international labor standards, requires that the question be faced head-on and with a willingness to consider novel approaches.

This Part has examined the reasons within WTO law that negotiation of affirmative obligations might be necessary to preserve the integrity of international labor law. In other words, labor standards might better be incorporated through legislation rather than adjudication. Andrew Guzman, too, has suggested that trade and nontrade linkage 'be determined through a political process of negotiation rather than through the quasi-judicial dispute resolution processes of the WTO'.[40] The next Part looks at the basis for creating such obligations and some of the challenges that would accompany such an effort.

4. LINKAGE THROUGH LEGISLATION

This Part highlights issues that legislation of affirmative labor obligations would have to resolve. When the question of content is directly addressed, problems of form arise that are not evident simply by focusing on the question

---

39 See below, Part 4A.2.

40 Andrew T Guzman, 'Trade, Labor, Legitimacy' (2004) 91 *California Law Review* 885, 887.

from within WTO law. These problems reveal themselves when asking basic questions about constructing a set of positive rules. First, what obligations would such an agreement impose? Second, how would such obligations be enforced in the WTO system? Beyond such questions of form, however, there is the question of the substantive propriety of incorporating nontrade issues into the international trade regime. This Part observes concerns that could be raised with respect to each of these questions, but finds that these concerns by themselves should not bar pursuit of incorporation of labor standards into the WTO regime.

A. Theories of Legislative Decision-making as Applied to Trade-Labour Linkage

In determining the labor obligations to be incorporated, negotiating parties would confront several kinds of costs. As Joel Trachtman has observed, the negotiation of rights and obligations entails a host of costs.[41] The most immediate source of such costs would be the allocation of resources required to achieve greater specificity through negotiation and drafting. In addition, however, the negotiation and drafting of specific rules would be susceptible to strategic behavior that, whatever its potential benefits, might also impose costs. This Part elaborates on each of these basic insights.

(a) Negotiation and drafting issues

Critics have faulted these public international law rights for their failure to follow traditional form. Consideration of the classical contours of legal entitlements yields the conclusion that a right yields a corresponding obligation on another party. Take the right to work.[42] It may not be immediately clear whether this right generates specific individual claims or obligations broadly owed to collective populations.

In considering these difficulties, however, it should be noted that interna-

---

41 See Joel P Trachtman, 'Economic Analysis of Prescriptive Jurisdiction' (2001) 42 *Virginia Journal of International Law* 1, 51 (stating that rules cost more to develop than standards); see also Joel P Trachtman, 'The Domain of WTO Dispute Resolution' (1999) 40 *Harvard International Law Journal* 333, 350–6.

42 See *Universal Declaration of Human Rights*, GA Res 217A (III), UN Doc A/810, 71 (1948) Article 23 ('Everyone has the right to work, to free choice of employment, to just and favourable conditions of work and to protection against unemployment.'); *International Covenant on Economic, Social and Cultural Rights*, opened for signature 19 December 1966, 999 UNTS 3 (entered into force 3 January 1976) Article 6(1) ('The States Parties to the present Covenant recognize the right to work, which includes the right of everyone to the opportunity to gain his living by work which he freely chooses or accepts . . .').

tional trade law, particularly in its earliest and most fundamental documents, contains rules equally as broad and undefined in application as core rules of international labor law. For example, Article I GATT, viewed by many as the most important provision in the GATT/WTO regime, provides that all members must receive equal trade treatment from each other. Article III GATT provides that each member state must provide equal trade treatment to domestic and foreign producers. Through the dispute settlement system, member states have articulated and clarified the exact contours of the broad principles. As in constitutional law, the breadth of a principle may render it more, rather than less, suitable for elaboration through the settlement of disputes.

Another difficulty, at least as challenging, arises when one attempts to envision how the WTO's dispute settlement system as currently configured would enforce any core set of labor standards, assuming they could be identified. The complainant's standing to initiate a complaint in the system provides a significant problem.

At the international level, only governments may bring WTO disputes against another government. Typically, the complainant state alleges that the respondent state has, in violating one or more obligations under the GATT/WTO, caused 'nullification or impairment' of the complainant's entitlements under the GATT/WTO. GATT/WTO complaints derive from an asserted harm imposed by one government on another government's nationals, whose interests their government then represents in a claim against the harm-imposing government. The conceptions of harm require more indirect conception of the wrong resulting from the violation of a right than normally is recognized. The enforcement of these rules by the international trade regime would require substantial expansion of the concept of a right beyond its traditional boundaries.

Once again, these problems are not insurmountable, but they do require a broad understanding of the harms that result from a violation of international labor standards. A member wishing to bring a DSB claim must allege that its rights under the WTO have been violated by another member's noncompliance. Rendering international labor law enforceable under the WTO also requires a broad conception of harm. If, as is most likely, the victims of a respondent government's violation were the respondent's own nationals, they could not bring a complaint against their own government in the WTO dispute settlement system. Rather, another WTO member government would have to challenge the practice. The complainant state would have to allege that the respondent's failure to, for example, eliminate child labor nullifies and impairs its benefits under the agreement.

Again, this principle of cross-national harm is not alien to international labor law. The foundational document of the ILO declares that 'the failure of any nation to adopt humane conditions of labor is an obstacle in the way of other nations which desire to improve the conditions in their own countries'.[43] According to this principle, one WTO member could argue that another member's failure to honor child labor standards impedes its own ability to uphold child labor standards in its own territory. Indeed, this 'race to the bottom' argument animates much of the movement to set international labor standards. In the context of labor law, the argument concerns the economic impact of labor violations in one region on labor protections in another. The argument would be that a country's willingness to tolerate labor violations nullifies and impairs another country's protections by increasing the pressure on that country to tolerate similar labor abuses or risk losing investment to the violator.

Although empirical evidence may support some claims of indirect harm, it will undoubtedly not support all. It is of central importance to note that WTO law, however, does not require the strictures of empirically proved causation. Indeed, an important turning point for the interpretation of GATT/WTO standards was a Panel's conclusion that a complainant government did not have to show that the respondent government's violation of a rule resulted in an identifiable harm to the complainant government's nationals. Rather, the Panel adopted an irrebuttable presumption that any rule violation would necessarily harm the 'conditions of competition' for foreign nationals operating in the respondent government's market.[44] In this sense, the GATT/WTO regime has long departed from the traditional notion of a legal claim as requiring proof not only of the wrong, but also of the harm.

Based on the looser conception of actionability employed by the GATT/WTO, determining conceptions of harm required by international labor law will be less of a stretch. Under current GATT/WTO law, a complainant government argues that a respondent government's trade actions harm the 'competitive conditions' for the complainant government's nationals, established by trade. Under a trade-related labor agreement, the complainant government could argue that the respondent government's actions harm the 'conditions for securing labor standards' for its own nationals.

The issue of remedy poses similar problems. How would the WTO determine the appropriate remedy? How might the WTO measure the harm?

First, it is important to recall that the WTO dispute settlement system imposes a monetary penalty as a last resort only after the recalcitrant state has failed to reform its practices and policies satisfactorily within the stated time limit. Nevertheless, monetary penalties, in the form of suspension of conces-

---

[43] *ILO Constitution* Part XIII.

[44] *United States – Taxes on Petroleum and Certain Imported Substances*, GATT BISD, 34th Supp, GATT Doc DS/34S/136 (17 June 1987) (Report of the Panel) [5.1.9].

sions by the adversely affected government, can be and are imposed under the WTO system.

At first, the problem of measuring the appropriate remedy for infraction of labor standards seems alarming. Quantifying the damage seems impossibly nebulous when compared with a hypothetical involving an inappropriate tariff. Upon closer examination, however, it turns out that similar problems of quantification already exist in the system. For example, the system provides a remedy when a country fails to impose intellectual property protection. When such a remedy takes the form of a monetary amount, it is determined through an evidentiary analysis similar to many instances of calculating damage awards. Moreover, the suspension of concessions need not take the form of a monetary amount; rather, it can take the form of the suspension of other obligations.

The above discussion demonstrates that, even if proponents of the establishment of WTO agreements on labor standards overcome the arguments against them, real problems of legal form will accompany any attempt to establish these standards. To begin with, issues of coherence may provide difficult problems in identifying core rules for incorporation. Problems relating to the specific content of such standards, even if they could be identified, would also arise. Finally, problems of standing would arise with any attempt to enforce these standards under the current WTO dispute resolution system.

The discussions above have indicated that the same problems of coherence, content, and harm identification are not confined solely to international labor law. They have historically plagued international trade law as well.[45] The fact

---

45 During the Uruguay Round, many governments of developing countries argued that the incorporation of intellectual property rights would yield disproportionate benefits to developed countries and disproportionate costs to them. See generally Ruth Gana Okediji, 'Copyright and Public Welfare in Global Perspective' (1999) 7 *Indiana Journal of Global Legal Studies* 117; Evelyn Su, 'The Winners and the Losers: The Agreement on Trade-Related Aspects of Intellectual Property Rights andIts Effects on Developing Countries' (2000) 23 *Houston Journal of International Law* 169. For an historical account of TRIPS in the context of international law, as well as an account of how TRIPS stacks up on social issues, including public health pandemics of particular concern to some developing countries, see James Thuo Gathii, 'Rights, Patents, Markets and the Global AIDS Pandemic' (2002) 14 *Florida Journal of International Law* 261. For a more general discussion of transfer of technology, see Chantal Thomas, 'Transfer of Technology in the Contemporary International Order' (1999) 22 *Fordham International Law Journal* 2096, 2105–11.

Many now argue that the incorporation of labor and environmental standards is no more than another strategy by industrialized countries to tip the market's scales in their favor: Bhagwati, above n 22, 127–8, writes:

> By [the] test of mutual advantage [between developed countries and developing

that these difficulties of form have arisen in many different areas of international law demonstrates their prevalence in the challenge of constructing an international legal regime. The difference, therefore, is one of degree. Nevertheless, any attempt to establish affirmative labor obligations through the negotiation of WTO agreements would have to overcome these difficulties.

(b) Negotiating skews, capture and challenges to legislative legitimacy

The legislative incorporation of labor standards would confront numerous costs related to the identification and elaboration of relatively more specific rights and obligations than currently exist. The above discussion assumes, however, that given enough resources, an agreement that reflected the genuine aggregate preferences of member states would be possible. However, strategic dynamics might so skew negotiating tactics that this 'genuine' aggregation could be indeterminable, adding significantly to the challenge of negotiation.

An interest-aggregation, pluralist view of political decision-making, can decipher the WTO decision to include intellectual property – despite the existence of a 'competent body', the World Intellectual Property Organization ('WIPO') – but to exclude labor standards. To do so, however, pluralistic political decision-making must be qualified by public choice theory. In this view, when directly conflicting interests confront each other in a bid for political influence, the outcome is a product of the degree to which one interest can effectively crowd out the opposing view. A public choice model would suggest that to the extent that developed states support progress along nontrade lines, such support is secondary to and weaker than their support for trade goals. As such, it is questionable that labor and environmental standards would be pursued by developed states with intensity sufficient to produce the concessions necessary to gain their adoption.

A public choice perspective foregrounds awareness of state policy as the outcome of interaction between state actors and a host of interest groups, each with their own set of interests. A state's position on any given policy will be calculated to gain the maximum support from among potential sources of support. The distribution of preferences, *and* of preference intensities, among the state's constituencies will determine the state's position on a given issue.

---

countries], the *Agreement on Trade-Related Aspects of Intellectual Property Rights* ('TRIPS') does not belong to the WTO. It facilitates, even enforces with the aid of trade sanctions, what is in the main payment by the poor countries (which consume intellectual property) to the rich countries (which produce it) [. . .] We also demonstrated to the next set of northern lobbies that they could do the same. Thus, the unions now say: you did it for capital, so do it for 'nature'. And the poor countries that have no lobbies anywhere like the sumptuous ones such as the Sierra Club and the AFL-CIO now find themselves at the receiving end of a growing list of lobbying demands that the northern politicians are ready to concede.

Mancur Olson's classic study of trade protectionism,[46] which sought to answer why governments would adopt protectionist policies at the expense of public welfare, illustrates this dynamic (see Table 10.1). Olson argued that where the benefits of trade liberalization were widespread for consumers but also diffuse, and the costs of trade liberalization were limited but concentrated on producers, producers would have a greater incentive to organize in favor of a tariff than consumers would have to organize against it. A protectionist policy may well result even though the tariff's costs, in the aggregate, outweighed its benefits. One might dismiss Olson's analysis as counterfactual in light of the dramatic decreases in tariff levels over the post-World War II era. Surely the great gains in tariff reduction rehabilitate the possibility of legislation for the public benefit. An Olsonian logic would argue, however, that the reduction of tariffs only tracks the shift in the cost-benefit ratio of tariffs for producers. As technological advances enabled firms to capture lower production costs by moving manufacture offshore, tariffs ceased to become an attractive way of keeping competitors' goods *out of* the domestic market, and instead became a costly barrier to bringing one's own goods *into* the domestic market. Tariff reductions became possible, according to this logic, only when producer support for tariffs began to subside and producer opposition to tariffs began to grow.

The same dynamics that support trade liberalization, however, also raise red flags for 'non-trade' concerns. Assume, as I do, that stronger environmental, labor, human rights and competition policies *do* increase the public welfare. The benefits, although undeniable in the aggregate, are nevertheless relatively diffusely distributed. At the same time, such policies may raise production costs for many firms. Under Olson's analysis, industrial opposition to such policies will exceed public support for them under these conditions. If Olson's analysis is correct, firms who anticipate[47] significant costs from 'non-trade' policies will be organized to block such policies, see Table 10.2.

Table 10.1 Classic theory of regulatory capture

Policy proposal	Policy benefit	Policy cost	**Maximum welfare if:**	**Result**
Tariff	Concentrated (for producers)	Diffuse (for consumers)	*No* tariff	Tariff

46 Mancur Olson, *The Logic of Collective Action: Public Goods and the Theory of Groups* (Harvard University Press, Cambridge, 1965); *The Rise and Decline of Nations: Economic Growth, Stagflation and Social Rigidities* (Yale University Press, New Haven, 1982).

47 A line of response here would argue that firms exaggerate or misunderstand the costs involved in these policies.

Table 10.2 Updated theory of regulatory capture

Policy proposal	Policy benefit	Policy cost	**Maximum welfare if:**	**Result**
Environmental protection	Diffuse	Concentrated (for producers)	Environmental protection	*No* environmental protection
Labour protection	Diffuse	Concentrated (for producers)	Labour protection	*No* labour protection

If Olson *is* correct, however, why have the United States and the European Union, for example, come out in favor of labor and environmental policies in WTO negotiations? Olson would guide us towards an examination of the relative costs and benefits of such stated policies in light of domestic interest group dynamics. The European Union's relatively energetic support for environmental regulation, one can argue, stems from the higher utility of 'Green' policy for the EU public at large; and possibly also from the relatively lower costs for expression of preferences on a very broad and public scale such as in the European Parliament. With stronger support for Green politics, preference *for* environmental regulation begins to reach or even exceeds the intensity of firms' preferences *against* it. In the United States, by contrast, Green politics is much less well developed. Accordingly, US support for progress in international environmental law has ranged from weak to nonexistent. While interest groups have of course organized in favor of labor, environmental and other nontrade concerns, they remain largely outnumbered in the contest for policy influence within the WTO.

Turning from the interplay *within* states to the interplay *among* states, an extrapolated Olsonian logic would also worry that developed-country support for environmental and labor protections stems from a highly strategic understanding of negotiations under current conditions. Supporting such protections currently comes at little political cost to developed-country states because they know that opposition to labor and environmental negotiations will be so fierce among developing countries so as to forestall progress. Since the prospect of 'real' negotiations is nonexistent, there is no danger of angering industry, and at the same time the possibility exists to gain the support of labor and environmental groups.

If the foregoing is true, what would happen if formal departments for nontrade negotiations were established within the WTO? A public-choice prediction would augur a poor outcome. The impetus for such negotiations comes from the possibility of 'cross-issue transfers' – the kind of quid pro quo that drove the negotiation of TRIPS[48] and GATS[49] in exchange for agriculture and textile concessions during the Uruguay Round. But according to Olson's logic, developed states would quickly realize that they do not want to strengthen nontrade commitments badly enough to make serious concessions. Might the European Union form an exception to this, at least in the area of environmental policy? The offsetting 'bill' for the EU, the quid pro quo, would likely be increased market access. Market access issues strike at the heart of the EU, however, and may trump its support for environmental policy.

To press the public choice argument, Olson would wager that the foregoing dynamics offer not only predictive but also descriptive value. As a descriptive matter, the public choice model may better explain past and present negotiations both in the WTO and in other venues such as the United Nations – and in particular, the failure of nontrade negotiations to produce institutionally significant results in any forum. In short, the very reasons why many nontrade regimes have failed to gain authoritativeness outside the WTO would also greatly impede the progress of nontrade negotiations within the WTO. Confronted with the challenge to 'walk the talk', and given the intensity of developing-country opposition to some kinds of 'nontrade' policies, developed states might well abandon such concerns.[50]

B. The TRIPS Precedent

This Part makes the observation that the WTO's intellectual property ('IP')

---

48 *Marrakesh Agreement Establishing the WTO*, opened for signature 15 April 1994, 1867 UNTS 3 (entered into force 1 January 1995) Annex 1C (*Trade-Related Aspects of Intellectual Property Rights*) ('TRIPS').

49 *Marrakesh Agreement Establishing the WTO*, opened for signature 15 April 1994, 1867 UNTS 3 (entered into force 1 January 1995) Annex 1B (*General Agreement on Trade in Services*) ('GATS').

50 The example of TRIPS can be read as a strong counterpoint; Guzman, above n 40, relies heavily on TRIPS here (as I have elsewhere with similar objectives). International intellectual property law was weak prior to incorporation into the WTO, and strong afterwards. The transition supports the argument that the institutional context can generate important substantive consequences – the intuition that underlies all pro-linkage arguments. An Olsonian perspective would, however, raise questions about whether the institutional context was the independent variable. Under this perspective, the increased authoritativeness of international intellectual property did not *result* from the institutional shift into the WTO. Rather, *both* the institutional shift *and* the increased authoritativeness resulted from a relatively rapid and marked increase in the intensity of industry preferences for increased intellectual property protection. To follow through on the logic, without this underlying industry support, the institutional shift would not have happened, or if it did happen the negotiations would have been far less productive.

law has followed an arc similar to that recommended by advocates for WTO incorporation of labor obligations. A primary objective of the WTO's establishment in 1995 was to extend trade discipline to areas of international economic activity that had been excluded under the previous international trade regime of the GATT. The WTO retained the existing regime defined by the GATT and significantly expanded it. For example, agreements on intellectual property, such as TRIPS, and trade in services, such as GATS, resulted from this effort.

The rationale for a WTO agreement regulating trade in services is clear: services are a category of trade, just as goods are. By the time the Uruguay Round began in the 1980s, the importance of internationally provided services justified the inclusion of services in the regulatory scope of international trade law, an area previously concerned only with goods. The rationale for a WTO agreement regulating IP is quite another matter. Although countries can trade IP rights across borders in licensing and other rights transferring agreements, they need not trade such rights in order for the TRIPS Agreement to apply. The TRIPS signatories adopted the agreement because trade affects IP rights. The value of the IP right increases with the capacity of the right-holder to enforce it and decreases when the information can be accessed without going through the right-holder. The latter may occur because the producer is operating in a region where the right does not exist or is underenforced.

As with IP protection, labor standards can affect trade flows by affecting production costs for goods and services. Just as the value of an IP right will decrease if it can be evaded through trade, the value of a labor right will also decrease if evasion through trade is an option. Moreover, the rights themselves may erode, a phenomenon known as the 'race to the bottom'.

Without considering TRIPS, the trade versus nontrade distinction might appear to justify exclusion of labor standards. Considered in isolation, the institutional competence argument that the WTO should not incorporate labor issues because they are not themselves the subject of trade, even if they clearly influence and are influenced by trade, appears more persuasive. Upon consideration of TRIPS, however, this distinction finds itself on very shaky ground. TRIPS concerns itself primarily with IP rights not as a subject of trade, but as a body of standards that affect trade flows. In this respect, international IP law is indistinguishable from international labor law in its relation to trade. After considering the TRIPS Agreement, the trade versus nontrade distinctions fail to explain the exclusion of labor rights. The IP case shares other similarities with international labor law: the relevant international enforcement regime that had developed was relatively weak. In addition, GATT law harbored a 'negative' exception for IP law in Article XX, similar to those that might apply for labor standards, but the TRIPS signatories ultimately made the political decision to strengthen this early incorporation with clearer and more rigorous positive obligations.

Article XX GATT, the General Exceptions provision, contains clause (d) which allows governments to take trade-restricting measures necessary to enforce IP law.[51] If the General Exceptions measure does provide all the support necessary for governments to enforce trade-related measures that might restrict imports, presumably no need to negotiate TRIPS would have arisen. TRIPS was negotiated, however, notwithstanding both a recognition of IP protection in the GATT's General Exceptions provision and a well-developed body of existing international law outside of the GATT. The fact that negotiation occurred lends credence to the argument that some integration of affirmative obligations to labor standards is required for these standards' proper enforcement and that the current exceptions-driven regime is inadequate.

Legislating affirmative IP obligations required confronting problems of diffuseness and nonjusticiability. At first blush, these problems seem much less troublesome in international IP law. Enumerated procedures identify IP rights owed to the right-holder, for example, the right to 'prevent' others from 'making, using, offering for sale, selling, or importing'.[52] Every government who is a party to the agreement, which now includes all WTO members, owes these rights. The right generates entitlements to certain types of legal protections – the right to deploy the state's enforcement power to exclude others from using the IP to which the right attaches.

Hindsight should not obscure the fact that real difficulties of this sort arose in the drafting of TRIPS, however. Although the *Paris Convention*[53] and the *Berne Convention*[54] were paramount in international IP law, a number of other international agreements developed. The *Universal Copyright Convention*,[55] for example, was a parallel instrument to the *Berne Convention*. Moreover, contracting parties put into force several versions of the Paris and Berne conventions. As a result of these numerous agreements, states significantly disagreed as to which international IP obligations were fundamental. For

---

51 See Article XX(d) GATT (allowing for trade-restrictive measures 'necessary to secure compliance with laws or regulations which are not inconsistent with the provisions of this Agreement, including those relating to [. . .] the protection of patents, trade marks and copyrights').

52 Article 28(1)(a) TRIPS.

53 *Paris Convention for the Protection of Industrial Property*, opened for signature 20 March 1883, 828 UNTS 107, as last revised at Stockholm 14 July 1967, 828 UNTS 305 ('*Paris Convention*').

54 *Berne Convention for the Protection of Literary and Artistic Works*, opened for signature 9 September 1886, as last revised at Paris, 24 July 1971, 828 UNTS 221 ('*Berne Convention*').

55 Opened for signature 6 September 1952, 943 UNTS 178 (entered into force 10 July 1974).

example, European states tended to regard the 'moral rights' of authors against degradation of their work under the *Berne Convention* as fundamental, whereas the United States did not.

In addition to the issue of uniformity of principles, serious problems arose because the vagueness of the principles allowed for substantial variation across countries. For example, although the *Paris Convention* established the basic principle of patent protection, it allowed for much more variation among member states than the specific obligations imposed by TRIPS. Indeed, the frustration of the United States at the lack of uniformity of IP protection abroad provided a major incentive for its pursuit of IP negotiations in the trade regime. Moreover, awareness of the lack of uniformity of protections was acute in the context of the TRIPS negotiations; the primary achievement of the negotiations was to resolve these differences and arrive at a single set of 'core' substantive standards.

A final distinction departs from any appeal to structural or substantive logic, but appeals purely to pragmatic considerations. Particularly in the wake of the WTO's newfound institutional rigor, many commentators worry about the increased likelihood that the international trade regime will reach a 'breaking point'.[56] The new WTO sets much loftier ambitions for institution-building than did the old GATT. Commentators worry that, while the GATT was flexible and therefore never broke, the WTO may be overly rigid and overshoot the mark in seeking to establish a 'legalistic' regime.[57] The result might be a backlash of states that would erode the precious legitimacy that the global regime has built up over the postwar era.

The jury is still out as to whether the WTO is institutionally viable over the long run. The dispute settlement system garnered early acclaim by resolving contentious issues between powerful members with relative success. The first new agreement-making meeting in Singapore went relatively smoothly and succeeded in making anticipated gains. However, the highly visible failure of the next ministerial conference in Seattle revived the old institutional concerns. The Seattle experience demonstrated that state sovereignty still had

---

[56] See Robert E Hudec, 'The New WTO Dispute Settlement Procedure: An Overview of the First Three Years' (1999) 8 *Minnesota Journal of Global Trade* 1, 14 (anticipating that, because international legal systems depend on voluntary member government compliance, the WTO legal system cannot expect unanimous governmental compliance with its legal rulings).

[57] Ibid 12 (displaying skepticism that member countries will be receptive to greater legal discipline in the WTO system); Miquel Montañà i Mora, 'A GATT with Teeth: Law Wins over Politics in the Resolution of International Trade Disputes' (1994) 31 *Columbia Journal of Transnational Law* 103, 178 (explaining that some scholars have observed a preference for informalism in international economic law and observing that this preference explains the law's reluctance to employ rigid mechanisms).

bite; that is, if the member states desired, they could refuse to adhere to the built-in agenda, impeding the progressive development of the institution. Thus, the anticipated progress in negotiations on services, agriculture, and other areas failed to materialize.

Particularly in the wake of Seattle, one might argue that at some point institutional modesty is required: the addition of items to the negotiation agenda would be too taxing. There may be some validity to this perception. It does not justify, however, the special exclusion of labor concerns, as opposed to other issues that are placed on the agenda. For example, negotiations on competition policy would require reconciling many different and complex regulatory regimes, but WTO members continue to consider the possibility of framing an agreement on competition.[58] However, controversy and disagreement continue to run high over the matter, and formal efforts to frame an agreement have not begun.

In reviewing these political dynamics, one might notice that developing countries' interests, at least as commonly construed in this particular debate,[59] run counter to IP protection as well as to labor concerns. At the time of the Uruguay Round negotiations, many developing countries staunchly opposed the incorporation of IP rights. The argument sounded quite similar to those made in the context of labor debates. Developing countries argued that the administration of IP rights properly belonged to the United Nations organization traditionally charged with that duty, the WIPO.

General opposition to IP standards in developing countries resulted not in an absolute opposition to their incorporation, but rather in a quid pro quo approach. Having reconciled themselves to the need to establish a comprehensive trade regime, many developing countries sought to leverage their willingness to countenance IP negotiations for the purpose of including negotiations on sectors of interest to them. Textiles and agriculture were two such notable sectors. Trade groups in the United States, which had an interest in maintaining the status quo of high protectionist barriers to imports, staunchly opposed negotiations on both of these topics.

Were labor negotiations to begin, the quid pro quo approach would undoubtedly re-emerge. That is, if industrialized countries wanted better labor practices in poor countries, the industrialized countries would have to agree,

---

[58] At the conclusion of their 1996 meeting in Singapore, WTO members agreed to 'establish a working group to study issues [. . .] relating to the interaction between trade and competition policy [. . .] in order to identify any areas that may merit further consideration in the WTO framework': see *Singapore Ministerial Declaration*, WTO Doc WT/MIN(96)/DEC (18 December 1996) [20].

[59] Of course, there are many reasons to believe that poor countries, or at least significant populations therein, stand to benefit from such protections.

at least partially, to fund the process of acquiring those practices. This approach has been a staple of recent international environmental law, in which the principle of environmental protection is now wedded to the goal of development in poor countries.[60]

Developing countries' resistance to linkage will likely continue as long as proponents of the trade-labor/environment linkage fail to construct cost-sharing arrangements, as in the case of labor regulations, or construct only partial arrangements, as in the case of environmental regulations. However, it is important to note that in many cases integrating trade and labor regulations would impose no new obligations on member states. Particularly with respect to the most salient international agreements on labor, most rich and poor countries have reached agreement. The fact that poor countries have already assumed these obligations seems to neutralize any legitimate protest on their part to integrating into a regime that might provide more effective enforcement.[61] However, as Jose Alvarez has argued, state accession to international law instruments is often conditional precisely on their relatively weak enforceability and the relatively high residual state autonomy to determine compliance.[62]

C. The History of Legislative Action on Labor Rights

The establishment of the WTO in 1995 raised alarms for political actors, particularly in the global North, who became concerned that the extensively revamped and unprecedentedly rigorous institutional and enforcement struc-

---

60 See Edith Brown Weiss, 'Introductory Note', United Nations Conference on Environment and Development, 31 *ILM* 814, 814–15 (outlining areas of concern and priorities relating to sustainable development and implementing economic progress while using resources in a clean and efficient manner).

61 See Clyde Summers, 'The Battle in Seattle: Free Trade, Labor Rights, and Societal Values', (2001) 22 *University of Pennsylvania Journal of International Economic Law* 61, 67. Summers argues that:

> It is ironic that Egypt, Brazil, Indonesia and Pakistan, which were among those most vocal in opposing the [proposal to incorporate labour discussions into WTO talks in Seattle] have ratified conventions on all of these subjects, with the exception of Pakistan's failure to ratify a convention on child labour. They expressed outrage that [President] Clinton would suggest [in his proposal on labour] that they should be required to observe the conventions that they had ratified.

62 See Jose E Alvarez, 'How Not to Link: Institutional Conundrums of an Expanded Trade Regime' (2001) 7 *Widener Law Symposium Journal* 1, 1 (noting that the WTO is rare among international law regimes because it usually 'secures at least procedural (if not always substantive) compliance').

ture of the new multilateral trade regime would accelerate a 'race to the bottom' brought about by globalization and accompanying regulatory competition. Within civil society, trade unions became the most organized and concentrated locus for this broad-based concern. By 1997, both the United States and British heads of state (Tony Blair and Bill Clinton) had been elected by constituencies that incorporated this concern, and those governments among others raised the question of incorporating labor standards directly into the WTO.

The early phase of the trade–labor linkage debate was characterized by a perception that the international labor law regime needed to 'harden' in order to be able to stand up to the trade regime. This impulse bore some resemblance to an earlier and more successful initiative to incorporate intellectual property standards into the WTO, precisely out of recognition that the existing United Nations-based structure provided inadequate enforcement. As Part 4B above suggests, at least theoretically, the establishment of a 'Trade-Related Labour Rights Agreement' similar to the TRIPS Agreement that was adopted by WTO members might have been possible.

The question of whether to incorporate labor standards was 'hard-fought' at the WTO's first two member-wide general assembly meetings, called Ministerial Conferences.[63] Nevertheless, a justification for exclusion on grounds of institutional competence emerged early on. At the first-ever Ministerial Conference, in Singapore in 1996, the WTO member governments adopted a declaration that formally established that 'the [ILO] is the competent body to set and deal with [labor] standards.'[64] While the *Singapore Declaration* endorsed the work of the ILO, it also took pains to clarify that differential labor costs should be viewed as an *advantage* rather than a social problem.[65]

After the issue was raised again at the next Ministerial, in Seattle, contributing to the disintegration of talks at that meeting, the 'hard linkage' strategy, the strategy to incorporate labor standards through 'transplanting' them into the WTO, would seem to have played itself out. A final, somewhat half-hearted effort at the next Ministerial Conference, led only to a reaffirmation of the Singapore conference's initial decision on the division of labor from trade.[66]

63 World Trade Organization, *Understanding the WTO* (WTO, Geneva, 3rd edn, 2007) 75.

64 *Singapore Ministerial Declaration*, above n 58[4].

65 Ibid. ('We reject the use of labour standards for protectionist purposes, and agree that the comparative advantage of countries, particularly low-wage developing countries, must in no way be put into question.')

66 *Doha Ministerial Declaration*, WTO Doc WT/MIN(01)/DEC/1 (20 November 2001) [8] ('We reaffirm our declaration made at the Singapore Ministerial Conference regarding internationally recognized core labour standards.').

In the meantime, the ILO tried to 'harden' itself. The WTO's 1996 declaration that the ILO was the competent body for administering international labor law sparked a renewed effort by the ILO at consolidation and streamlining. One important result was the ILO *Declaration on Fundamental Principles and Rights at Work*.[67] The Declaration identifies the following four core labor standards:

(a) freedom of association and the effective recognition of the right to collective bargaining;
(b) the elimination of all forms of forced or compulsory labor;
(c) the effective abolition of child labor; and
(d) the elimination of discrimination in respect of employment and occupation.

The Declaration appears to be the ILO's explicit recognition of the institutional challenge articulated by the WTO. It also appears to recognize that a critical aspect of meeting this institutional challenge was to articulate obligations that are finite and concrete rather than expansive and diffuse.

Although the *Doha Ministerial Declaration* reaffirmed the division of labor from trade, the period from the turn of the century to the present day demonstrates, beyond this 'hard' separation of formal law, that a variety of clues to a slowly changing institutional culture has emerged. Still very limited, they nonetheless indicate a permeation of *values* within the trade organization. The first indication here is the Joint ILO-WTO Study of 2007.[68] This study directly addressed the costs of trade liberalization on employment security, and acknowledged that trade liberalization could create both winners and losers. As such, it can be seen as a shift towards a shared vocabulary.

Surveying the history of actual legislative efforts at linkage bears out the theoretical prediction that direct action on the legislative front is beset with insurmountable difficulties arising from transaction costs and capture. Consequently, it is not surprising that proponents of linkage have shifted away from the effort at direct, formal, explicit incorporation of labor rights – 'transplant' – and towards a strategy of 'osmosis' in which labor rights values are incorporated by means that are diffuse but ultimately pervasive. What the

---

[67] See *ILO Declaration on Fundamental Principles and Rights at Work*, 37 ILM 1233 (entered into force 19 June 1998) Article 2 (stating that all member states have an obligation to promote the four core labor standards).

[68] ILO and WTO Secretariats, *Trade and Employment: Challenges for Policy Research* (2007) WTO, http://www.wto.org/english/res_e/booksp_e/ilo_e.pdf at 3 January 2009.

osmosis strategy lacks in definite objectives, it makes up for in ambition, for it seeks no less than a transformation of 'consciousness'.[69]

This trend is supported more broadly by the general turn, largely initiated by scholars of international relations,[70] to the study of 'governance' rather than 'government'.[71] Three trends in particular are important: the disaggregation of regulatory practices and decisions into a series of interactions amongst both government and nongovernment actors with a wide range of interests;[72] a focus on the ways in which those interests are constructed by the identities, shaped in turn by social and cultural norms and ideals, of the actors involved;[73] and an emerging belief in the priority of international cooperation (rather than realpolitik conflict).[74] In sum, scholars have recognized the emerging importance of studying what I will call *cultures of governance*, in which mobilization for change by social movements and political actors unfolds in a macrocosmic setting of interconnected but incongruous spheres of meaning and interest.

This last, a belief in the importance of cooperation, finds its juridical counterpart in work on 'legal pluralism' that announces, with palpable anxiety,[75] the challenge posed to the international order by international legal regimes that are not integrated.[76] The puzzle of how to realize international law's 'presumption against normative conflict'[77] has perhaps yielded, in the absence

---

69 See also Chapter 2, pp. 41–2.

70 Important early exceptions amongst US international law scholars include Louis Henkin and Harold Koh. See Louis Henkin, *How Nations Behave* (Columbia University Press, New York, 1979); Harold Hongju Koh, 'Transnational Legal Process' (1996) 75 *Nebraska Law Review* 181, 183–4.

71 See, for example Joseph S Nye and John D Donahue, *Governance in a Globalizing World* (Brookings Institution Press, Washington DC, 2000).

72 Andrew Moravcsik, 'Taking Preferences Seriously: A Liberal Theory of International Politics' (1997) 51 *International Organization* 516.

73 Alexander Wendt, *Social Theory of International Politics* (Cambridge University Press, Cambridge, 1999) 92–120.

74 Robert O Keohane, *After Hegemony: Cooperation and Discord in the World Political Economy* (Princeton University Press, Princeton, 1984) 49–64.

75 G Hafner, *Risks Ensuing from Fragmentation of International Law*, UN Doc A/55/10 annex (2000).

76 Andreas Fischer-Lescano and Gunther Teubner, 'Regime-Collisions: The Vain Search for Legal Unity in the Fragmentation of Global Law' (2004) 25 *Michigan Journal of International Law* 999, 1004 ('Global legal pluralism [. . .] is not simply a result of political pluralism, but is instead the expression of deep contradictions between colliding sectors of a global society').

77 Martti Koskenniemi, *Fragmentation of International Law: Difficulties Arising from the Diversification and Expansion of International Law: Report of the Study Group of the International Law Commission*, UN Doc A/CN.4/L.682 (13 April 2006) [37]; see also Howse and Teitel, Chapter 2, footnote 3, citing same to advocate for '[r]econstructing globalisation on the basis of a human rights consciousness'.

of clear doctrinal solutions, an urgency to the project of resolving conflicts among spheres of international law by bringing colliding worldviews closer together. It is possible that this groundwork in the 'legislative' arena has in turn made decisions such as the *EC – GSP* case discussed above possible. The hypothesis here, which future research would hopefully bear out, is that a shifting institutional culture in the WTO will emerge which reaffirms formal institutional separation of trade and labor mandates but simultaneously moves towards a shared vocabulary that bridges that formal institutional gap, and creates an atmosphere of greater legitimacy for judicial interpretations that strengthen that bridge.

5. CONCLUSION

On reflection, this debate between the judicial and legislative responses to incorporation at an international level seems to parallel a tension between competing attributes of legitimacy in decision-making within domestic legal systems: expertise and independence on the one hand, versus accountability and representativeness on the other. Although the legislative response to linkage is politically more desirable, it appears to be less plausible. Judicial response may represent the best option, particularly at an early stage. Moreover, judicial response might have an 'action-forcing' effect, in which the relative benefit of codification through legislation increases over time to correct any deficiencies in the rules established by the legislature. However, potentially prohibitive decision costs might reduce overall welfare by barring collective action, resulting in the continuation of a rule that does not represent the aggregate preferences of the members and their respective constituencies.

On either side, however, the purported virtues can be seen as vices: one can regard the expertise of the judiciary as 'insider' bias, and the accountability of the legislature is susceptible to capture. Even more complexly, recently these charges of insider bias and capture have sometimes strayed outside their traditional realms: critics have charged the WTO judiciary with capture and the representatives of member states with insider bias. In the current 'Development Round' of WTO negotiations, the international debate on integrating trade and labor must determine not only the appropriate substance and form of the rule, but also the appropriate decision-making institution and process.

11. Public opinion and the interpretation of the World Trade Organisation's Agreement on Sanitary and Phytosanitary Measures

Caroline E. Foster[1]

1. INTRODUCTION

With the passage of over a decade since the adoption of the World Trade Organisation ('WTO') Agreement on Sanitary and Phytosanitary Measures ('SPS Agreement'), it is time to examine experience to date in light of the SPS Agreement's basic rationales. WTO panels and the Appellate Body have gradually established a jurisprudence that consolidates accepted interpretations of the SPS Agreement's provisions and identifies how its provisions can work together. This chapter evaluates the state of that jurisprudence and makes proposals for further developments in the interpretation of the SPS Agreement, focusing on the troubled question of the role that may permissibly be played by public opinion in decision-making under the SPS Agreement.

Concluded at the end of the Uruguay Round of trade negotiations in 1994, the SPS Agreement regulates barriers to trade that are adopted to counter sanitary and phytosanitary risks by requiring them to be based on science. To the extent of their overlap, the Agreement provides a more disciplined footing to the exceptions found in Article XX of the General Agreement on Tariffs and Trade ('GATT') which allow Contracting Parties to impose barriers to trade in order to protect human, animal and plant life and health. Under the SPS Agreement, sanitary and phytosanitary measures (defined as measures to combat pests, diseases, and additives and contaminants in food) must be grounded in science. The SPS Agreement thus offers a relatively solid bulwark against economic protectionism in this field by WTO Members. The disciplines

[1] A version of this chapter is also published as C E Foster, 'Public Opinion and the Interpretation of the World Trade Organisation's Agreement on Sanitary and Phytosanitary Measures' (2008) 11 *Journal of International Economic Law* 427.

detailed in the SPS Agreement are intended to ensure that Members' entitlement to adopt sanitary and phytosanitary measures will not be abused or used as a cloak to protect other interests, including the interests of those sectors of a Member's own economy that are in competition with imported goods. The row over the EC's ban on the import and marketing of beef from cattle treated with growth promotion hormones formed the backdrop for negotiation of the SPS Agreement, and the *EC – Hormones* case[2] exemplifies a situation characterised by alleged economic protectionism of the type the Agreement was designed to counter.

The SPS Agreement was a major achievement for agricultural exporters at the conclusion of the Uruguay Round. During the negotiations the Cairns group of agricultural exporting countries had pushed hard for the commitments it contains, and they were pleased with the outcome. The SPS Committee, established in 1995, carries out a vital role within the WTO in facilitating ongoing discussion among Members on sanitary and phytosanitary issues and trade-inhibiting developments on the ground. Meantime, WTO Panels have dealt with disputes about alleged violations of the SPS Agreement in five cases: the *EC – Hormones* case,[3] the *Australia – Salmon* case,[4] the *Japan – Agricultural Products II* case,[5] the *Japan – Apples* case,[6] and the *EC*

---

[2] Panel Report, *EC Measures Concerning Meat and Meat Products (Hormones), Complaint by Canada*, WTO Doc WT/DS48/R/CAN (1998), modified by Appellate Body Report, WTO Doc WT/DS26/AB/R, WT/DS48/AB/R, DSR 1998: II (1998) 235 ('*EC – Hormones* PR'). Panel Report, *EC Measures Concerning Meat and Meat Products (Hormones), Complaint by the United States*, WTO Doc WT/DS26/R/USA (1998), modified by Appellate Body Report, WTO Doc WT/DS26/AB/R, WT/DS48/AB/R, DSR 1998: III (1998), 699. The two panel reports are almost identical. The relevant paragraphs of the Canadian report will be referred to with respect to points made in this chapter. For the Appellate Body Report, DSR 1998: I, 135.

[3] Above n 2.

[4] Panel Report, *Australia – Measures Affecting Importation of Salmon*, WTO Doc WT/DS18/R and Corr 1 (1998), modified by Appellate Body Report, WT/DS18/AB/R, DSR 1998:VIII (1998) 3407 (*Australia-Salmon* PR); Appellate Body Report, *Australia – Measures Affecting Importation of Salmon*, WTO Doc WT/DS18/AB/R, DSR 1998:VIII (1998) 3327 ('*Australia-Salmon* ABR'); Panel Report, *Australia – Measures Affecting Importation of Salmon – Recourse to Article 21.5 of the DSU by Canada*, WTO Doc WT/DS18/RW, DSR 2000:IV (2000) 2031 ('*Australia-Salmon* CPR').

[5] Panel Report, *Japan – Measures Affecting Agricultural Products*, WTO Doc WT/DS76/R (1999), modified by Appellate Body Report, WTO Doc WT/DS76/AB/R, DSR 1999:I (1999) 315 ('*Japan-Agricultural Products II* PR'); Appellate Body Report, *Japan – Measures Affecting Agricultural Products*, WTO Doc WT/DS76/AB/R, DSR 1999:I (1999) 277 ('*Japan-Agricultural Products II* ABR').

[6] Panel Report, *Japan – Measures Affecting the Importation of Apples*, WTO Doc WT/DS245/R (2003), upheld by Appellate Body Report, WTO Doc

– *Biotech* case.[7] In all of these cases, the importing Member has been found to have failed in certain respects fully to observe its obligations under the Agreement.

The question of public opinion about sanitary and phytosanitary risks has arisen most directly in the context of dispute settlement. The most concerning of the five SPS cases referred to just above have been the *EC – Hormones*[8] and the *EC – Biotech*[9] disputes. These two cases have involved high levels of public concern about the safety of the products intended to be imported into the EC. In *EC – Hormones*, the risk in question has been food safety, so a fundamental aspect of this dispute has been how people feel about meat that might contain residues from growth promotion hormones where these residues could increase, even very minimally, the chance of cancer in the population. Food safety concerns have also arisen in *EC – Biotech*. However, in *EC – Biotech* the most significant risk in question has, arguably, been the potential danger to biodiversity that is posed as a result of genetically modified organisms. Therefore, in addition to food safety concerns, a fundamental part of this litigation has been how the importance of biodiversity is valued, for its own sake and because of the uncertainty attaching to such anthropogenic alterations to the ecosystem. In both the *EC – Hormones* and *EC – Biotech* cases, compliance with WTO rulings has been an issue. The result has been to undermine the WTO dispute settlement system.[10]

The interpretation of the SPS Agreement to date is such that it can be divided notionally into two sets of core requirements: those that focus on the need for SPS measures to have a scientific basis, and those that incorporate other requirements, such as the requirement that a Member select the least trade-restrictive measure available to ensure its chosen level of risk protection. So far, the significance of public opinion has remained outside the interpretation of the first of these sets of provisions, and there has been a strong tendency to regard those requirements as excluding non-scientific considerations. Risk assessment

---

WT/DS245/AB/R, DSR 2003:IX (2003) 4481 ('*Japan-Apples* PR'); Appellate Body Report, *Japan – Measures Affecting the Importation of Apples*, WTO Doc WT/DS245/AB/R, DSR 2003:IX (2003) 4391 ('*Japan-Apples* ABR'); Panel Report, *Japan – Measures Affecting the Importation of Apples – Recourse to Article 21.5 of the DSU by the United States*, WTO Doc WT/DS245/RW (2005) ('*Japan-Apples* CPR').

7 Panel Report, *European Communities – Measures Affecting the Approval and Marketing of Biotech Products*, WTO Doc WT/DS291/R, WT/DS292/R, WT/DS293/R, Corr 1 and Add 1, 2, 3, 4, 5, 6, 7, 8 and 9 (2006) ('*EC-Biotech* PR').

8 Above n 2.

9 Above n 7.

10 For an analysis of one suggestion on how this problem is to be addressed, see S Charnovitz 'An Analysis of Pascal Lamy's Proposal on Collective Preferences' (2005) 8 *Journal of International Economic Law* 449.

has been regarded as a purely scientific activity, and the idea of a distinction between risk assessment and risk management has prevailed, despite the expression of doubts on this score by the Appellate Body in the very first SPS case, *EC – Hormones*. The need to take account of public opinion has been regarded as an aspect of risk management and is governed by the second set of provisions in the SPS Agreement.

A striking feature of the five cases decided to date under the SPS Agreement is that decisions have for the most part been made under the first set of provisions referred to. These provisions comprise in particular Articles 2.2, 5.1 and 5.7 of the SPS Agreement, which set out the basic requirements that SPS measures be based on scientific grounds and on risk assessments. Article 2.2 of the SPS Agreement states that measures must be based on scientific principles and must not be maintained without sufficient scientific evidence. Article 2.2 cross-refers to Article 5.7, which envisages the use of SPS measures on a temporary or provisional basis where there is insufficient scientific evidence. Except where Article 5.7 applies, or where SPS measures conform to international standards (see Article 3.2), the SPS Agreement requires all SPS measures to be based on a full risk assessment, in accordance with Article 5.1 of the SPS Agreement.

The second set of provisions in the SPS Agreement includes Articles 5.5 and 5.6. Article 5.5 imposes an obligation to avoid arbitrary or unjustifiable distinction in the levels of protection that Members consider appropriate in different situations, if these distinctions result in discrimination or a disguised restriction on international trade. Article 5.6 requires Members to ensure their sanitary and phytosanitary measures are not more trade-restrictive than required to achieve their appropriate level of sanitary or phytosanitary protection. A Member's capacity to take into account the public's appreciation of a risk's magnitude has been viewed as being accommodated largely through the concept that WTO Members are entitled to set their own level of protection against a risk, as seen in Articles 5.5 and 5.6 of the Agreement, as well as Article 3.3. This concept has not played any significant part in determining the consistency of Members' measures with Articles 2.2, 5.1 and 5.7.

The type of deep-rooted difficulties seen in the *EC – Hormones* and *EC – Biotech* disputes are a result of this bifurcation in thinking under the SPS Agreement, and an implicit systemic determination to view the first set of provisions as excluding considerations relating to public opinion. Taking a position that rejects the notional distinction described above, this chapter sets out to take a fresh look at the interpretation of each of the relevant SPS provisions. Proceeding step by step through the provisions, the chapter will assess the arguments for and against greater recognition within SPS jurisprudence of the significance of public opinion in decision-making about risks to human health and the environment.

The order in which these provisions will be considered follows a natural logic in relation to the problem at hand, rather than the numerical scheme of the SPS Agreement. First the chapter will address the central requirement under Article 2.2 of the Agreement that SPS measures be based on sufficient scientific evidence, with particular attention to the meaning of 'sufficient'. Second, the important concept of a Member's chosen level of protection is considered, and suggestions are made for giving a higher profile to Article 5.6. Third, a considerable portion of the chapter is devoted to exploring arguments that public opinion may potentially be of significance within the requirement in Article 5.1 that SPS measures be based on a risk assessment. Fourth, the application of the non-discrimination provision in Article 5.5 is considered. The subsequent sections of the chapter then address proposals to recognize the place of public opinion within Article 5.1 and to give greater prominence to Article 5.6, taking into account some of the practical problems that arise and proposing solutions. Support for the proposals made is drawn from broader public international law, in the form of international human rights law and, in the chapter's concluding section, international environmental law.

The central argument in the chapter is that, in a context of scientific uncertainty, a WTO Member should be able to defend sanitary or phytosanitary measures on the basis that its population simply does not want to run a given risk. Even though SPS measures are rarely adopted with entirely pure motives, it remains essential that the SPS Agreement is interpreted in a way that will accommodate an instance where public concern about an uncertain risk is legitimately a primary factor.

This new approach would be consistent with basic democratic principles, as well as being beneficial for the WTO system. At its present stage of development, the approach taken to the Agreement's interpretation is a halfway house, in which the likelihood that WTO Members may have mixed motives for the adoption of SPS measures generates an ongoing determination within the WTO system to interpret the SPS Agreement in a way that will not permit such measures to stand. The possibility that these mixed motives include genuine motives goes unacknowledged and is never tested. As a direct result, problems in implementing dispute settlement determinations persist. In this chapter, the view is taken that it is time to move beyond this halfway house. There will be a price to pay. In a case of mixed motives, a genuine motive will have to be acknowledged and permitted to prevail in determinations of a measure's legality. The most difficult aspect of this argument is a concern that increased scope for economic protectionism may result. The chapter acknowledges this, but remains steadfast in the view that there is a need to develop an increasingly sophisticated approach to SPS law that can better accommodate the dimension of public opinion.

At the outset it needs to be emphasized that the chapter is not proposing an abandonment of scientific standards under the SPS Agreement. Science will always have a central role to play in rules to assess the legality of sanitary and phytosanitary measures. The question is how best to combine scientific risk assessment and non-scientific aspects of decision-making about risk within a multilateralised international system.[11] If this can be achieved, it will help ensure consistency between international economic law and broader public international law. In particular, there will be more scope for a better accommodation of the right to political participation of Members' populations as reflected in international human rights treaties and international environmental law.

2. THE PROVISIONS OF THE SPS AGREEMENT

A. 'Sufficient' Scientific Evidence and Article 2.2

Article 2.2 is the central provision of the SPS Agreement. This provision embodies the Agreement's primary obligation, a requirement that Members ensure their SPS measures are based on scientific principles and are not maintained without *sufficient* scientific evidence, except as provided for under Article 5.7, and to ensure they are applied only to the extent necessary. How does public opinion fit into Article 2.2? In particular, are the views of a Member's population considered pertinent for determining the 'sufficiency' of the scientific evidence supporting an SPS measure under Article 2.2? Jurisprudence on this point to date is limited. It is commonly understood that in *EC – Hormones* the Appellate Body effectively acknowledged that it is to be expected that the 'sufficiency' of the scientific evidence supporting a measure will be assessed in the light of the seriousness of the risk in question:

> [A] Panel charged with determining, for instance, whether 'sufficient scientific evidence' exists to warrant the maintenance by a member of a particular SPS measure may, of course, and should bear in mind that responsible, representative governments commonly act from perspectives of prudence and caution where risk of irreversible, e.g. life-terminating, damage to human health is concerned.[12]

However, the Appellate Body referred here only to recognising the adoption of a precautionary stance by governments. While governments may be respond-

---

[11] For related discussion, see J Peel, Risk 'Regulation under the WTO SPS Agreement: Science as an International Normative Yardstick? (Jean Monnet Working Paper 02/04, NYU School of Law, New York, 2004).

[12] *EC-Hormones* ABR 124; *Japan-Apples* CPR 8.105; *EC-Biotech* PR 786.

ing, at least in part, to the concerns of their populations, the genuine fears of the individuals concerned are recognised only indirectly. In any event, most WTO Members would probably take the view that the concepts of irreversible or life-threatening damage arguably reflect essentially only objective measurements of the magnitude of the risk concerned. Whether there is scope to incorporate greater recognition of Members' populations' subjective perspectives on risks within the concept of 'sufficiency' of scientific evidence remains an unanswered question.

A complementary point may be made in relation to Article 5.7 of the SPS Agreement, which permits the adoption of SPS measures on a provisional basis where relevant scientific evidence is *insufficient*. The reference here to 'insufficiency' has been found to refer to insufficiency specifically for the purposes of conducting a risk assessment.[13] Article 5.7 obviously operates in such a way as to allow for precautionary responses to risks. What we are interested in here is the degree to which public appreciation of risks may be relevant in the interpretation and application of Article 5.7. In this respect it can be suggested that determinations of whether the scientific evidence in a case is 'insufficient' for a risk assessment should take into account the seriousness of the risk in question. For example, where a risk is understood to be particularly serious and to threaten highly valued interests, and yet relatively little information about the risk is available, then these factors must surely contribute to a determination of whether it should be possible to rely on Article 5.7. However, it might be noted that the Panel in *EC – Biotech* did not respond positively to the EC's arguments that 'insufficiency', like 'sufficiency', was a 'relational' concept in the sense that the insufficiency of scientific evidence was to be assessed with reference to matters of concern to a legislator.[14]

B. A Member's Chosen Level of Protection: Articles 3.3 and 5.6

The concept that a Member's chosen level of protection against a risk must be respected is an important part of SPS jurisprudence. The same concept has received strong recognition also in cases under the environmental and health exceptions in the GATT, even though it has no direct roots in the text of the GATT.[15] Article 3.3, and particularly Article 5.6, are the provisions of the SPS Agreement that expressly acknowledge the importance of a Member's chosen level of protection. Article 3.3 has a relatively self-contained impact. The effect of Article 3.3 is simply that Members may choose to disregard international

13 *Japan-Apples* ABR 179.

14 *EC-Biotech* PR 7.3226, 7.3234, 7.3238, and also 7.3052f.

15 *Korea – Various Measures on Beef* ABR 54, 176; *US-Gambling* ABR 308.

sanitary and phytosanitary standards in favour of standards based on their desire for higher levels of protection than are provided in the international standards.[16] Article 5.6 is of more interest here. As noted above, Article 5.6 provides that Members are to ensure their sanitary and phytosanitary measures 'are not more trade-restrictive than required to achieve their appropriate level of sanitary or phytosanitary protection'. A footnote to the provision explains that a measure may be considered more trade-restrictive than required if another less trade-restrictive measure is available that will allow the Member to achieve the same level of protection. A Member may choose to set its level of protection at zero tolerance of any risk of harm, provided that the risk to which its measures is directed is an ascertainable risk.[17]

In both *EC – Hormones* and *EC – Biotech* the panels charged with assessing the parties' cases opted not to consider Article 5.6. In the *EC – Hormones* case, the reason given was judicial economy. In *EC – Biotech*, Article 5.6 was not considered to be potentially applicable to the EC's moratorium on GMOs or to the EC's product specific measures, because neither was found by the Panel to involve a substantive SPS measure, but rather they were both found to involve solely procedural delay.[18] In relation to the potential application of Article 5.6 to individual EC Member States' safeguard measures, the Panel exercised judicial economy.[19]

Yet Article 5.6 is a strength of the SPS Agreement, because it carves out protected scope for national level decision-making that may be based on public opinion about risks. The provision in Article 5.6 is already taking an increasing profile at the stage of compliance proceedings, as findings under Article 5.6 may cast light on alternative measures that could be implemented by a party to bring it into compliance with the Agreement.[20]

To the extent that consideration of consistency with Article 5.6 can be brought forward from the compliance stage to the stage of original panel proceedings, Article 5.6 may be a provision of the future for SPS jurisprudence. From a Panel's point of view, a potentially rather awkward aspect of assessing the implementation of this provision is that in some cases this is likely to require a close engagement in the science in order to determine the availability of alternative measures that could be applied by a Member. Provided that Panels are able to come to terms with both the science of a case and the appropriate procedural approach to adopt, the remaining issue will be whether available alternative measures would actually achieve a Member's

16 See generally *EC-Hormones* ABR.

17 *EC-Hormones* ABR 186.

18 *EC-Biotech* 7.1398–7.1407 and 7.1715–7.1729.

19 *EC-Biotech* PR 7.3377.

20 *Japan-Apples* CPR; *Australia-Salmon* CPR.

level of protection. Determination of this point may be difficult for panels, especially in cases where a Member has not clearly articulated its level of protection. The point is likely to be a highly politicized one, and the difficulties would be heightened in cases other than the more routine quarantine disputes like *Japan – Apples* and A*ustralia – Salmon.*

The potential to apply Article 5.6 in an increasingly significant way is bolstered through reference to related aspects of the developing jurisprudence under the exceptions found in Article XX of the GATT and Article XIV of the General Agreement on Trade in Services (GATS). For example, under Article XX(b) of GATT (which permits Members in certain circumstances to adopt trade restrictions to protect human, animal plant life or health) the Article XX necessity test has been recognised as including a test of whether there are any reasonably available less trade-restrictive alternative measures.[21] An emphasis is, in practice, increasingly placed on this approach to necessity despite the formal adoption by the Appellate Body of a 'weighing and balancing' test for assessing necessity under Article XX.[22] However, the relationship between the two tests remains unclear, as the 'weighing and balancing' test and the 'alternative measures' test have been woven together in all of the relevant cases decided to date under both the GATT and the GATS.[23] This apparent development may be the forerunner of the development of an increased role for Article 5.6 of the SPS Agreement.

C. Risk Assessment and Public Opinion: Article 5.1

Arguably the most significant procedural discipline in the SPS Agreement is found in the requirement in Article 5.1 that all trade-inhibiting measures to protect human, animal and plant life and health from pests, diseases and food

---

[21] See, inter alia, GATT Panel Report, *United States Section 337 of the Tariff Act of 1930*, GATT Doc L/6439BISD 36S/345 (1989) [5.26]; Appellate Body Report, *Korea – Measures Affecting Imports of Fresh, Chilled and Frozen Beef*, WTO Doc WT/DS161/AB/R, WT/DS169/AB/R, DSR 2001:I (2001) 5, [159ff] ('*Korea – Various Measures on Beef*'); Appellate Body Report, *European Communities – Measures Affecting Asbestos and Asbestos-Containing Products*, WTO Doc WT/DS135/AB/R, DSR 2001:VII (2001) 3243 ('*EC-Asbestos* ABR') [170ff].

[22] *Korea – Various Measures on Beef* ABR 162, citing the Report of the Panel at 675, and 164; Appellate Body Report, *Dominican Republic – Measures Affecting the Importation and Internal Sale of Cigarettes*, WTO Doc WT/DS302/AB/R (2005) 70 ('*Dominican Republic-Cigarettes*').

[23] *EC-Asbestos* ABR 172; Appellate Body Report, *United States – Measures Affecting the Cross-Border Supply of Gambling and Betting Services*, WTO Doc WT/DS285/AB/R (2005) 306–7; *Dominican Republic-Cigarettes* ABR 66–70; *Brazil – Measures Affecting Imports of Retreaded Tyres*, WTO Doc WT/DS332/R (2007) PR 7.737, 7.843.

additives and contaminants (as defined in Annex A(1) of the SPS Agreement) must be based on a risk assessment. Article 5.1 gives practical effect to Article 2.2. To date there has been considerable emphasis on compliance with Article 5.1 of the SPS Agreement. Here, some hard questions must be asked. For example, are SPS measures potentially to be regarded as 'based on' a risk assessment in accordance with Article 5.1 in all cases where the scientific uncertainty in relation to a risk exceeds the purely theoretical?[24] Behind such questions lies the broader, vital issue of the role to be played by public opinion in determining whether a Member is in compliance with Article 5.1.

In order to address this issue, it is helpful to come back to basics, and consider how 'risk' is best understood. Institutional strategies for estimating risks were, historically, employed earliest in sectors seeking to capitalise on the subjugation of risks to organised management to the fullest extent possible, such as gambling, insurance and investment.[25] Subsequently, engineers[26] and economists[27] developed specialised approaches to understanding risk. The classic formula for risk assessment in these disciplines requires the likelihood of a risk to be multiplied by the gravity of the harm that would be caused, to produce an overall indicator of a given risk: 'However and wherever it is discussed, it seems that there is a consensus that the essence of risk consists of the probability of an adverse event and the magnitude of its consequences.'[28]

Risk is thus generally understood to involve two components: likelihood and magnitude, that is to say, probability and severity. This understanding of risk can be developed further, as follows. The likelihood of a risk can be assessed technically. The magnitude of a risk has two aspects: the 'subjective aspect' of determining the magnitude of a risk may be counterposed with the 'objective aspect' of determining the magnitude of a risk. The 'objective' aspect of magnitude can, like likelihood, be assessed technically. The 'subjective aspect' of determining the magnitude of a risk consists in the value judgement that is made, by those who are subject to the risk, about the scale or magnitude of the consequences that will follow if the risk eventuates. For example, the subjective magnitude of risks associated with artificial interference in ecosystems depends on the value that is attached to biodiversity, both

---

24 A threshold established by the Appellate Body in *EC-Hormones* ABR [186].

25 P L Bernstein, *Against the Gods: The Remarkable Story of Risk* (John Wiley, New York, 1996).

26 C Starr, 'Social Benefit versus Technological Risk' (1969) 165 *Science* 1232.

27 K J Arrow, *Essays in the Theory of Risk-Bearing* (Markham Publishing, Chicago, 1971).

28 S Rayner and R Cantor, 'How Fair is Safe Enough? The Cultural Approach to Societal Technology Choice' in R E Löfstedt and L Frewer (eds) *The Earthscan Reader in Risk and Modern Society* (Earthscan, London, 1998) 91, 91 citing the seminal work of Starr, above n 26.

for its own sake and in light of the unknown potential practical consequences for human beings. The overall assessment of a particular risk must hinge on a combination of its estimated likelihood with both objective and subjective determinations of its magnitude.

The approach to risk adopted by the International Law Commission (the ILC) might usefully be referred to at this point. The ILC has defined 'risk' by applying the concepts of likelihood and magnitude: '[r]isk of causing significant transboundary harm includes risks taking the form of a high probability of causing significant transboundary harm and a low probability of causing disastrous transboundary harm'.[29] The ILC has also commented on the role played by value determinations within assessments of the significance of a risk: '[t]he term "significant", while determined by factual and objective criteria, also involves a value determination which depends on the circumstances of a particular case and the period in which such determination is made [. . .]'.[30] A similar point may be made in relation to the provisions of the Cartagena Protocol on Biosafety to the Convention on Biological Diversity.[31] The Protocol provides that risk assessments are to entail evaluation of the possible adverse effect of living modified organisms on the conservation and sustainable use of biodiversity, including specifically both an evaluation of the likelihood of such effects being realised and an evaluation of the consequences, combining to create an estimation of the overall risk.[32]

The definition of risk assessment for the purposes of the SPS Agreement is found in Annex A, para 4 of the SPS Agreement:

> Risk assessment – The evaluation of the likelihood of entry, establishment or spread of a pest or disease within the territory of an importing Member according to the sanitary or phytosanitary measures which might be applied, and of the associated potential biological and economic consequences; or the evaluation of the potential for adverse affects on human or animal health arising from the presence of additives, contaminants, toxins, or disease-causing organisms in food, beverages or feedstuffs.

This definition has two limbs. The first limb relates to pests and diseases. The second limb relates to additives, contaminants, toxins, and disease-causing organisms in food, beverages and feedstuffs. The Panel in the *Australia –*

---

[29] *Articles on Prevention of Harm from Transboundary Activities 2001* Art 2(a). Report of the International Law Commission on the work of its Fifty-third session, Official Records of the General Assembly, Fifty-sixth session, Supplement No 10 (A/56/10) Ch V http://www.un.org/law/ilc/texts/prevention/preventionfra.htm at 8 July 2008.

[30] Above n 29, commentary on Article 2 [7].

[31] 39 ILM (2000) 1027.

[32] Ibid; see Article 15, Annex III 8d and 8e.

Salmon case, and subsequently the Appellate Body, have parsed the first limb of the definition in such a way that it requires three steps:

a) Identifying the disease and its potential consequences;
b) Evaluating the likelihood of entry, etc. as well as the potential biological and economic consequences; and
c) Evaluating the likelihood of entry, etc. according to the SPS measures that might be applied.[33]

The most curious aspect of this analysis is that there remains an ambiguity about the extent to which the first limb of the definition of risk assessment entails an appreciation of the magnitude of a risk at all, let alone the subjective dimensions of such an appreciation. In both *Australia – Salmon*,[34] and *Japan – Apples*,[35] respective panels focused essentially on the question of whether Members' risk assessments had appropriately assessed the likelihood of entry, establishment or spread of a pest or disease within the territory of an importing Member, and the Appellate Body did not demur. The same was largely true in *EC – Biotech*,[36] in relation to both the first and second limbs of the definition of risk assessment.

The second limb of the Annex A definition of risk assessment was applied in *EC – Hormones* and in *EC – Biotech*. The Appellate Body essentially endorsed the application by the Panel in that case of a two-step process involving firstly the identification of the adverse effects in question and secondly an evaluation of the potential or probability of the occurrence of the events.[37] One concern articulated by the Appellate Body was that 'probability' was not a good synonym for 'potential' because 'probability' implied a quantitative assessment of likelihood.[38] The Appellate Body's emphasis was on likelihood only. No reference was made to the question of a risk's magnitude. The same was true of the Panel's approach in *EC – Biotech*. The studies referred to by

---

33 *Australia-Salmon* PR 8.71, ABR 120–1; *Japan-Apples* ABR 196; *EC-Biotech* PR 7.3040.

34 *Australia-Salmon* PR 8.55 and 8.80; ABR 121–31; CPR 7.44–7.47. However, in the context of its reasoning under Article 5.5 the Appellate Body appeared to adopt the opposite point of view: 'We recognize that the definition of a risk assessment requires a risk assessment to evaluate the consequences of the "entry, establishment and spread of a disease"': *Australia-Salmon* ABR 149.

35 *Japan-Apples* PR 8.234–8.280, ABR 198–206.

36 See in general *EC-Biotech* PR 7.3027 and, as an example of the application of the approach emphasizing likelihood, PR 7.3045–7.3046.

37 *EC-Hormones* PR 8.101, 8.113.

38 *EC-Hormones* ABR 184.

Member States in support of their safeguard measures were found not to constitute risk assessments because they did not evaluate likelihood.[39]

Questions of magnitude, whether objective or subjective, have effectively slipped out of the picture altogether in the jurisprudence that has developed under the SPS Agreement. However, guidance for undertaking risk assessments found in the applicable standards of the Food and Agriculture Organisation ('FAO'),[40] the Codex Alimentarius,[41] and the Office International des Epizooties ('OIE'),[42] which WTO Members are obligated to take into account, reflects the need to address both the likelihood and the magnitude or 'consequences' of risks. Indeed, the SPS Committee itself has recognized that '[r]isk in the context of the SPS Agreement refers to the likelihood that an adverse event (pest or disease) will occur *and* the magnitude of the associated consequences on plant or animal life or health of the adverse event.'[43] Further, reference may be made to Article 5.3 of the SPS Agreement, which provides that Members are to take into account certain economic factors in assessing risks to animal or plant life or health. The listed factors are: the potential damage in terms of loss of production or sales in the event of the entry, establishment, or spread of a pest or disease; the costs of control or eradication in the territory of the importing Member; and the relative cost-effectiveness of alternative approaches to limiting risks. These factors clearly go to the magnitude of risk.

Thus, the institutional framework surrounding the SPS Agreement does clearly recognize that magnitude is an essential component of risk, even though this is not reflected in dispute settlement reports. However, the common understanding, as reflected in Article 5.3, is that determining the magnitude of a risk involves essentially only what might be called the 'objective' assessment of magnitude. The components of risk assessment are often understood to include determination of the nature and severity of adverse

---

[39] *EC-Biotech* PR 7.3047ff.

[40] See for example the *FAO Pest Risk Analysis for Quarantine Pests including Analysis of Environmental Risks and Living Modified Organisms 2004 International Standards for Phytosanitary Measures* (ISPM No 11).

[41] See for example the *Guideline for the Conduct of Food Safety Assessment of Foods Produced Using Recombinant-DNA Micro-organisms*, CAC/GL 46-2003; *Guideline for the Conduct of Food Safety Assessment of Foods Derived from Recombinant-DNA Plants*, CAC/GL 45-2003; *Principles for the Risk Analysis of Foods Derived From Modern Biotechnology*, CAC/GL 44-2003. See also the various documents referred to by the Panel in *EC-Hormones* PR 8.106.

[42] See for example the OIE, *World Organisation for Animal Health, Aquatic Animal Health Code 2004, Guidelines for Risk Assessment* Art 1.4.2.1.

[43] *Guidelines to Further the Practical Implementation of Article 5.5* G/SPS/15 (2000) [A4], [B2] (emphasis original).

effects as part of 'hazard characterisation', which, alongside a technical evaluation of likelihood, then feeds into the risk assessment's overall final 'risk characterisation'. These determinations are usually limited to scientific delineation of the magnitude of risks.[44] The question that remains is whether risk assessments should incorporate public opinion about the magnitude of a risk, which we might call the 'subjective' assessment of magnitude.

This is difficult territory, indeed. Many will claim that there is no role for public opinion within the concept of risk assessment, which must remain a purely scientific process in order to guarantee the transparency on which the SPS Agreement relies so strongly. On the other hand, accepting that both the likelihood and magnitude of a risk are central elements in an assessment of a risk, a strong argument can be made that risk assessment can never be a value-free process. While it may be possible to estimate the likelihood of a risk in technical terms, the question of a risk's magnitude will always hinge partly on value judgements by the society that is to be subjected to the risk. In many cases, the value judgements of the individuals conducting a risk assessment may tacitly have been injected into the risk assessment in lieu of the societal view, and the judgements of these individuals may be mistakenly taken as a substitute for societal views in reading and employing the final conclusions of the risk assessment. Where the societal view and the view of authors of a risk assessment do not sufficiently coincide, it is not possible to say that a full and complete risk assessment has actually been conducted.[45]

The argument for considering giving greater recognition to the subjective dimension of the magnitude of risk is also bolstered by the advice of the Appellate Body in *EC – Hormones* that, when addressing the factors to be taken into account in carrying out a risk assessment in accordance with Article 5.2 of the SPS Agreement, there is nothing to indicate that the list of factors specified in the SPS Agreement was intended to be a closed list.[46] Also of

---

[44] See, for example, the *Communication from the Commission on the Precautionary Principle* COM(2000) 1.

[45] Such a view is consistent with perspectives reflected in one of the amicus curiae briefs submitted in the *EC–Biotech* case: D Winickoff et al., 'Adjudicating the GM Food Wars: Science, Risk, and Democracy in World Trade Law' (2005) 30 *Yale Journal of International Law* 81. See also C Foster, 'Social Science Experts and Amicus Curiae Briefs in International Courts and Tribunals: The WTO Biotech Case' [2005] *Netherlands International Law Review* 433.

[46] As the Appellate Body said, '[i]t is essential to bear in mind the risk that is to be evaluated in a risk assessment under Article 5.1 is not only risk ascertainable in a science laboratory operating under strictly controlled conditions, but also risk in human societies as they actually exist, in other words, the actual potential for adverse effects on human health in the real world where people live and work and die': *EC-Hormones* ABR 187.

direct relevance are the Appellate Body's remarks to the effect that the reference to risk assessment in Article 5 of the SPS Agreement should not be read down by drawing a strict dividing line between the two processes of assessing risk (risk assessment) and managing risks (risk management).[47] In light of the Appellate Body's comments, and the absence of attention to the issue in the cases to date, it is strongly arguable that the question of the role of public opinion within risk assessment can be regarded as an open one at present.

There is also another, distinct, argument in favour of moving beyond a restrictive approach to risk assessment which excludes the question of public opinion. A lack of emphasis on the subjective aspect of the magnitude of risks within WTO jurisprudence means there is little transparency in relation to this dimension of Panels' decision-making. Panels, inevitably, form a subjective view of their own on the magnitude of the risk at issue in a dispute. Their evaluation of the legal aspects of the dispute will be influenced, tacitly, by that view of the magnitude of the risk. For example, in *EC – Hormones* the Panel's appreciation of the magnitude of the risks of cancer associated with consumption of beef from cattle treated with growth promotion hormones may well have differed from the EC's appreciation of the same risk. In the recent *EC – Biotech* case, the Panel seems possibly to have held the view that the magnitude of the risks associated with biotech products was not great, a view seemingly not shared by Austria, France, Germany, Italy, Greece and Luxembourg. At the same time, it has to be said that the Panel's views on the magnitude of the risks in question are not readily apparent from the Panel's report. The need to make findings that might have depended more closely on any evaluation of the magnitude of the risks was avoided, as the Panel chose to focus on the EC's compliance with the procedural aspects of the SPS agreement. This is an intriguing outcome in a case in which transcripts of the Panel's consultation with independent experts indicate good grounds for concern about the risks associated with biotech products. One explanation is, of course, that the Panel did appreciate the concerns identified in consultation with its independent experts, but in the circumstances of the case felt unable to deal differently with the issues raised.[48]

There are thus a number of arguments in favour of recognising public opinion as an inherent aspect of risk assessment. At the same time, taking such a step would raise a variety of practical problems which will be considered below. First, however, it is important to complete the survey of relevant provisions of the SPS Agrement by contemplating the interpretation of Article 5.5.

---

47 *EC-Hormones* ABR [86].

48 In adopting its final conclusions the Panel stated that it was not making any findings on the safety of biotech products, although noting that there were some documented risks: *EC-Biotech* PR 8.5.

D. Non-discrimination and Article 5.5

Article 5.5 of the SPS Agreement needs to be interpreted carefully in light of the arguments developed above. Article 5.5 requires Members to aim for consistency in the application of the concept of appropriate level of protection, and, as noted above, imposes an obligation to avoid arbitrary or unjustifiable distinction in the levels of protection that Members consider appropriate in different situations, if these distinctions result in discrimination or a disguised restriction on international trade.[49] Carrying forward the reasoning set out earlier in relation to Article 5.1, it would follow that a distinction based on a genuine fear may not be an arbitrary or unjustifiable distinction and that the result may be a genuine, rather than a disguised, restriction on international trade. Indeed, the supposedly similar situations in question may in some cases not even be comparable.

Given the potential value of Article 5.5 in combating protectionism, panels will have to continue to give careful consideration to its application in practice. Some guidance may be taken from the comments of the Appellate Body in past cases. The Appellate Body has noted that there is no legal obligation of consistency of appropriate levels of protection; this is merely a goal. Nor does the goal posit absolute or perfect consistency.[50] The Appellate Body has also emphasised that different situations subjected to comparison must, to begin with, be comparable, that is they must have sufficient common elements.[51] There may therefore be scope to argue that differences in a Member's population's appreciation of the magnitude of risks will in some cases render risks incomparable. In *EC – Hormones* the Appellate Body overruled the Panel's finding that the EC had adopted an arbitrary and unjustifiable distinction between the levels of protection applied in relation to hormones used for growth promotion (whether synthetic or natural) and hormones occurring endogenously in meat and other foods. The point made by the Appellate Body was that the comparison between these situations became an absurdity in light of the 'comprehensive and massive governmental intervention in nature and in the lives of ordinary people' that would be required to ensure consistent levels of protection.[52] That populations are likely to have a different appreciation of the risks from added hormones compared with the risk from endogenous hormones may also have been a factor in the mind of the Appellate Body. The same could conceivably be said in relation to the distinction drawn by the compliance Panel in *Australia – Salmon* between fish diseases already present

49 *Australia-Salmon* ABR 213, CPR 7.91.
50 *EC-Hormones* ABR 213.
51 *EC-Hormones* ABR 217.
52 *EC-Hormones* ABR 221.

in Australia and fish diseases that might be introduced by imports.[53] Populations are likely to have a different appreciation of the risks from introduced diseases compared with diseases that are already present in a country. In addition, the text of Article 5.5 itself recognises that people's attitudes to risk vary, including because of such factors as whether exposure to a risk is voluntary.[54]

Setting aside the question of the comparability of different situations under Article 5.5, the question remains of whether a distinction based on a genuine fear may nevertheless be arbitrary or unjustifiable, and may result in discrimination or a disguised restriction on international trade. It would seem that such a distinction could, depending on the circumstances, be considered unjustifiable, and could potentially result in discrimination, but a finding that there is a disguised restriction on international trade is unlikely to follow where the distinction is made on the basis of the genuine fears of a Member's population. In *EC – Hormones*, the EC successfully defended itself at the appellate stage against claims that it had acted inconsistently with Article 5.5. The Appellate Body agreed with the Panel that the EC had maintained an unjustifiable distinction in the level of protection implemented in relation to anti-microbial agents used in pigs compared with growth promotion hormones used in cattle.[55] However, the Appellate Body overrode the Panel's finding that this had resulted in discrimination or a disguised restriction on international trade. The Appellate Body was not prepared to accept the inference drawn by the Panel that the ban on beef raised using growth promotion hormones was not intended to protect the population against cancer but rather to protect domestic beef products.[56] The Panel's finding was erroneous as a matter of law.[57] The Appellate Body's comment is worth noting, because of its relevance to the discussion in the next section of this chapter:

> The documentation that preceded or accompanied the enactment of the prohibition of the use of hormones for growth promotion and that formed part of the record of the Panel makes clear the depth and extent of the anxieties experienced within the European Communities concerning the results of the general scientific studies (showing the carcinogenicity of hormones), the dangers of abuse (highlighted by scandals relating to black-marketing and the smuggling of prohibited veterinary

---

53 *Australia-Salmon* CPR 7.93.

54 Article 5.5 notes 'the exceptional character of human health risks to which people voluntarily expose themselves', as noted by the Appellate Body in *EC-Hormones* ABR 118. See also the SPS Committee's *Guidelines to Further the Practical Implementation of Article 5.5* G/SPS/15 (2000) [A8].

55 *EC-Hormones* ABR 235.

56 *EC-Hormones* ABR 245.

57 *EC-Hormones* ABR 246.

> drugs in the European Communities) of hormones and other substances used for growth promotion and the intense concern of consumers within the European Communities over the quality and drug-free character of the meat available in its internal market.

There continues, in addition, to be an important role for science to play under Article 5.5. As in the case of Article 5.6, Panels may need to engage quite closely with the science of a dispute. For example, in *EC – Hormones*, the Appellate Body referred to several respects in which the Panel had relied on the views of the independent scientific experts that had been appointed to assist the Panel.[58]

3. APPLYING THE PROPOSED NEW APPROACH: PROBLEMS AND SOLUTIONS

If the subjective element of assessing the magnitude of risks was to be reintegrated into risk assessment under the SPS Agreement, what would be the outcome from a practical point of view? In addition to scientific analyses of the likelihood of a risk and objectively assessable dimensions of its magnitude, it could be envisaged that in certain cases the views expressed by the Member's population would be taken directly into account by a WTO Panel dealing with a dispute over a Member's compliance with the requirement in Article 5.1 to base its measures on a risk assessment, and potentially also in relation to a Member's compliance with the requirements of Article 2.2. The authenticity of those views could be established through a documented account of appropriate processes of public deliberation within that WTO Member's domestic jurisdiction.[59]

Two main types of problems arise in connection with this proposal. The first type of problem arises because of the scope that would be introduced for doubts about such questions as whether the views expressed by the public in a particular case were genuinely held, particularly where those views were not consistent with what was thought to be a rational appreciation of the risk

---

[58] *EC-Hormones* ABR 226, 231, 232, 233. See also *Australia-Salmon* CPR 7.92, 7.96.

[59] Joanne Scott and Ellen Voss advocate the demonstration of the authenticity of public opinion in J Scott and E Voss, 'The Juridification of Uncertainty: Observations on the Ambivalence of the Precautionary Principle within the EU and the WTO' in C Joerges and R Dehousse (eds) *Good Governance in Europe's Integrated Market* (Oxford University Press, Oxford, 2002) 253, 286. By way of precedent, the Appellate Body's analysis of the EC's compliance with Article 5.5 in the SPS Agreement in *EC-Hormones* may be considered. See below.

involved. The response to be made on this point is that subjective perspectives on the magnitude of a risk must obviously continue to be combined with objective assessments of magnitude. A potential way forward in dealing with this problem, in the form of an indicative proportionality test, will be discussed further below.

The second type of problem arises at a practical level. How feasible is it to expect WTO panels to assess the robustness of public consultation processes, and to interpret the information arising from them? What are the resource implications, for example the costs of employing qualified experts to help panels on this issue?[60] Further, how realistic is it to expect WTO Members to conduct the types of public consultation processes that are envisaged? To the extent that this is more practicable for developed than developing countries, would a system that expected such processes to be carried out unduly favour more developed countries in defending their risk-response measures? On the other hand, it can be noted that seeking the views and evidence of interested parties, including consumer organizations, is already a required element of the specified process for the adoption of anti-dumping measures and subsidies under the Anti-Dumping Agreement,[61] and of the Agreement on Subsidies and Countervailing Measures,[62] respectively. Further thought should be given to whether the practical difficulties associated with consulting the public constitute a good reason to hold back from pursuing such a development if it is otherwise sound in principle.

Nevertheless, the need remains to consider such problems as whether the views expressed by the public in a particular case are genuinely held, and even whether these views reflect the best choice or decision for the individuals who are consulted. The complex relationships between human emotion and human cognition may produce preferences for decisions that are, in a sense, biased.[63] Additionally, the way in which risks are handled through the media is likely to result in their amplification. While the politicisation of selected issues is a feature that is difficult to eliminate from democratic systems, the protection of human life and health in particular is an area in which this tendency may be

---

[60] See Foster, above n 45.

[61] *Agreement on Implementation of Article VI of the General Agreement on Tariffs and Trade* Art 6.

[62] *Agreement on Subsidies and Countervailing Measures* Art 12.

[63] C R Sunstein, *Laws of Fear: Beyond the Precautionary Principle* (Cambridge University Press, Cambridge, 2005). Cognitive psychologists have established that the lay-person's perception of risks will privilege unduly factors such as, for example, the potential for a catastrophic outcome, and the possibility that individuals and their close family members may be affected. See D M Kahan et al., 'Fear of Democracy: A Cultural Evaluation of Sunstein on Risk' (2006) 119 *Harvard Law Review* 1071 and C R Sunstein. 'Misfearing: A Reply' (2006) 119 *Harvard Law Review* 1110.

accentuated. These problems are, of course, also a part of everyday life and debate in the domestic democratic polity. Prominent among the remedies that have been promoted in relation to this problem is the provision of better information to the public. Further, the value of deliberation should not be underestimated. When an iterative approach is adopted that invites individuals to discuss and rethink their positions in the light of increased information flow, better outcomes should be achieved. The difference in the international setting is that a party that is affected economically by another party's trade barriers may be able to do relatively little to influence the debate within the importing party. The provision to importing parties' populations of full and accurate information from all perspectives is to be emphasised, and there may be ways to reflect the responsibility of importing Members in this regard.

This last point might be addressed under the umbrella of a broader structural remedy that could readily find a home within SPS jurisprudence: an indicative proportionality test might be applied under Article 5.1 in assessing whether a measure was based on a risk assessment. Where a Member's response to a risk did not appear disproportionate in the light of objective indicators of a risk's likelihood and magnitude, no further enquiry into the evaluation of the magnitude of the risk would be necessary. On the other hand, a finding by a Panel that it considered a trade restrictive measure to be a disproportionate response to a risk could be used as an indicator that close attention should be paid in assessing the genuineness of a Member's estimates of magnitude, and a trigger for undertaking further examination into the extent of the Member's government's consultation with its own populus. In the course of that examination, a Panel would look, inter alia, for indications that the population had been given the most accurate information available on the objective aspects of the magnitude of the risk in question.

It should be emphasised that what is proposed would be an indicative proportionality test only, not a definitive test. In this chapter the view is taken both that disproportionate measures could possibly be a result of a population's genuinely held views and that in order to become more functionable the SPS Agreement has to be interpreted in such a way as to accommodate this possibility. There is therefore no suggestion here that a Panel's view of the proportionality of risk-response measures should be determinative of their legality. It should remain the primary task of a WTO Panel only to examine whether an SPS measure bears an appropriate connection back to the Member's assessment of the risk, taking into account that the Member had consulted its population.

The proposal made in this chapter contrasts in this respect with the remarks of the Panel in *Japan – Apples*, where the Panel relied on a concept of disproportionality to support a finding that Japan's quarantine measures did not bear a rational relationship with relevant science under Article 2.2 of the

Agreement.[64] It may be noted that the Appellate Body did not adopt the Panel's approach in that case.[65] It may also be noted that the absence of a proportionality test in WTO jurisprudence contrasts with the requirement in Section 3 S1 of the International Standard for Phytosanitary Measures No. 11, on pest risk analysis for quarantine pests, that measures be in proportion to a risk, as referred to by the Panel's independent experts in the *EC – Biotech* case.[66] However, there was little direct indication that the panel in the *EC – Biotech* case was inclined towards application of a proportionality test.[67]

4. PRACTICAL APPLICATION OF PROPOSALS

How would the proposals that have been set out in this chapter work in practice? The situation seen in the *EC – Hormones* case might be considered. It will be recalled that the Panel and, ultimately the Appellate Body, found against the EC in that case because the EC's prohibition on the importation and marketing of beef from cattle treated with growth promotion hormones was not 'based on' a risk assessment as required by Article 5.1 of the SPS Agreement.[68] It was held that, even assuming that the studies carried out within the EC constituted a risk assessment, they did not rationally support the EC ban. If risk assessment were to be regarded, as suggested in this chapter, as incorporating the subjective appreciation of a risk's magnitude alongside an estimation of likelihood and an assessment of the objective aspect of magnitude, it would be considerably more likely in such a case for a Member's response to be found to be 'based on' a risk assessment. However, in the *EC – Hormones* case, the EC would quite possibly have failed to pass an indicative proportionality test, because the EC's measure was not greatly proportionate to the risk in question as seen from a scientific perspective.

Accordingly, it would have been necessary for the Panel to address the question of the part played within the EC's 'risk assessment' by estimations of the magnitude of the risk, particularly objective estimations of magnitude and with particular attention to the way in which the views of populations of Member States on this issue had been garnered. A close examination of the internal consultation processes carried out with those populations would have

64 See *Japan-Apples* PR 8.181, 8.198.
65 *Japan-Apples* ABR 163, 147.
66 For the Panel's written consultation with experts, see *EC-Biotech* [1049].
67 Although see *EC-Biotech* PR 7.3064.
68 *EC-Hormones* ABR 208.

been required. Although as a matter of principle the burden of proof would have remained with the complainants, much of the necessary information would in fact need to have been furnished by the responding party. The complainants would have had to establish that the EC's public consultation processes were unsound. The claim that the EC was out of compliance with Articles 2.2 and 5.1 would have failed if the complainants could not establish an unrebutted prima facie case that the EC's measure was ungrounded either in science or in a genuine fear of the population.

The next hurdle in such a case would be to apply Article 5.6, in order to determine whether alternative measures would have sufficed, such as labelling and monitoring. Here the science supporting the measure would possibly have come under further close scrutiny, although continued reference to the views of the population would still have formed part of the equation, as embodied in the chosen level of protection.

For those who will ask whether the subjective appreciation of a risk could prove to be the determining factor in relation to the Article 5.1 test in certain types of case, the answer is therefore 'yes'. However, this subjective appreciation has to be clear on the evidence, and evaluation of that evidence should not necessarily be regarded as a straightforward matter. Further, the role of science in establishing the legality of SPS measures must not be disregarded: Article 2.2 of the Agreement continues to require that measures be based on scientific principles and not maintained without sufficient scientific evidence, and Article 5.1 continues to require a risk assessment that incorporates a large volume of scientific input and sound scientific analysis.

5. CONSISTENCY WITH INTERNATIONAL HUMAN RIGHTS LAW

Further support for the proposals made above is to be found in international human rights law. A number of human rights provisions dealing with the right to health refer to the right of political participation in decisions relating to health, including at the international level. The corollary of this right to political participation is surely that States should be able to have confidence that international legal provisions will be interpreted in such a way as to recognise and accept a situation where their populations genuinely reject a product or technology because of its attendant risks.

The relevant human rights provisions may readily be outlined. Article 25 of the *International Covenant on Civil and Political Rights* ('ICCPR') deals with the right to participate in public affairs, voting rights and the right of equal access to public service. Article 25(a) states that every individual is to have the right and the opportunity to 'take part' in the conduct of public affairs, directly or through freely chosen representatives.[69] As noted by the United Nations High Commissioner for Human Rights in 2005, this participatory right includes 'the exertion of influence on decision-making through public debate and dialogue'.[70] Further, the Human Rights Committee, the monitoring body established under the ICCPR, has advanced an interpretation of political participation in the 'take part' clause that extends to the international level.[71] General Comment 25 says that the conduct of public affairs is a broad concept relating to the exercise of political power, and covers all aspects of public administration, as well as the formulation and implementation of policy at *international*, national, regional and local levels.[72] Article 21 of the Universal Declaration of Human Rights 1948 refers to the individual's 'right to take part in the government of his country, directly or through freely chosen representatives'.[73] The argument might be made that the government of one's country today has inescapable international dimensions.

There has been relative silence on the question of how the 'take part' clause in the ICCPR is to be viewed, with the *travaux* casting little light on this issue.[74] However, it has been argued insightfully that the right to political participation may be seen as a 'programmatic right' in the same way as many of the economic and social rights recognized in the International Covenant on

---

69 This may be referred to as the 'take part' clause, while the provision in paragraph (b) of Article 25, which embodies the right to vote in genuine periodic elections, can be called the 'elections' clause. H J Steiner, 'Political Participation as a Human Right' (1988) 1 *Harvard Human Rights Year Book* 77. See the parallel provision in Article 23 of the *American Convention on Human Rights 1969*: 9 ILM (1970) 673. See also Chapter 12, p. 313.

70 Analytical study of the High Commissioner for Human Rights on the Fundamental Principle of Participation and its Application in the Context of Globalization, Report of the High Commissioner, UN Doc E/CN.4/2005/41 (23 December 2004) [14], citing General Comment 25: The Right to Participate in Public Affairs, Voting Rights and the Right of Equal Access to Public Service (Article 25), UN Doc CPR/C/21/Rev.1/Add.7 ('General Comment 25').

71 General Comment 25, above n 70.

72 Paragraph 5 of the General Comment states:

> The conduct of public affairs, referred to in paragraph (a), is a broad concept which relates to the exercise of political power, in particular the exercise of legislative, executive and administrative powers. It covers all aspects of public administration, and the formulation and implementation of policy at *international*, national, regional and local levels. (Emphasis added.)

73 UN Doc A/810. See also *African Charter on Human and Peoples' Rights 1981*: 9 ILM (1981) 58, Art 13.

74 Steiner, above n 69, 94; G H Fox, 'The Right to Political Participation in International Law' (1992) 17 *Yale Journal of International Law* 539, 555.

Economic, Social and Cultural Rights.[75] On this view, the obligations associated with the right to political participation would expand as ideas evolve as to what is necessary to secure a way of life that is consistent with human dignity.[76] The content of the right must accordingly be open to 'experimental reformulation' as new needs emerge.[77] On this basis it can be argued that the right to political participation is to be interpreted in the light of the contemporary constitutional debate inspired by international economic integration.

Reference should also be made to the right to the highest attainable standard of health, as found in Article 12 of the *International Covenant on Economic, Social and Cultural Rights*.[78] In 2000 the UN Committee on Economic, Social and Cultural Rights issued General Comment No 14 on the right to health.[79] The right to health was interpreted as an inclusive right that embraced not only the provision of timely and appropriate health care, but also obligations relating to the underlying determinants of health, such as access to safe drinking water, an adequate supply of food and housing, access to health-related information, and healthy occupational and environmental conditions.[80] The Committee noted that an important aspect of the right to health 'is the participation of the population in all health-related decision-making at the community, national and *international* levels'.[81]

From this brief survey of the most significant authorities, the consistency between the proposals in this chapter and international human rights law is clear.

6. CONCLUSION

The SPS Agreement has dual aims. On the one hand, the SPS Agreement is a highly valuable instrument for combating unfounded sanitary and phytosani-

---

75 Steiner, above n 69, 130.

76 Ibid 132.

77 Ibid: 'One cannot identify broadly shared and stable views of its import, or even crystallized disputes about appropriate forms of institutionalization or about the types of governmental duties that it imposes.'

78 See also the *International Convention on the Elimination of All forms of Racial Discrimination 1965* Art 5(e)(iv); *Convention on the Elimination of All forms of Discrimination against Women 1979* Art 11(1)(f), 12; *Convention on the Rights of the Child 1989* Art 24.

79 *Substantive Issues Arising in the Implementation of the International Covenant on Economic Social and Cultural Rights*, General Comment No 14 (2000) The Right to the Highest Attainable Standard of Health E/C. 12/2000/4 (11 August 2000).

80 Ibid [11].

81 Ibid (emphasis added).

tary measures. On the other hand, it is the Agreement's intention to allow for the bona fide protection of human, animal and plant life and health. A scientific foundation for SPS measures is required in all cases, but science is often incomplete and uncertain. The crucial question at this juncture in the Agreement's ongoing interpretation, particularly in disputes involving greater rather than lesser scientific uncertainty, is the extent to which public opinion is relevant in determining whether measures are consistent with the SPS Agreement.

As discussed in this chapter, interpretations of risk assessment requirements in the SPS Agreement have followed a distinctive but artificial course, in that they have implicitly viewed the SPS Agreement as having removed from the risk assessment process the subjective dimension of the estimation of a risk's magnitude. The concept of a Member's chosen 'level of protection' is referred to instead. The primary driving factor behind the employment of this concept to date has largely been the intention to make it easier to combat economic protectionism by ensuring that States' internal views on risks to human health and the environment are regarded as irrelevant in determining the WTO-consistency of a measure.

On the one hand the concept of a chosen 'level of protection' is helpful, as it offers a way to insulate value-based domestic appreciations of the magnitude of risks from substantive review at the international level. On the other hand, in practice the results of the associated bifurcation between science and public opinion have started to prove troubling, as shown by the ongoing dispute over compliance with the *EC – Hormones* and *EC – Biotech* rulings.

The need to increase both the legitimacy and the functionability of the multilateral trade regime demands greater recognition of public opinion. Processes for engaging the public in discussion of particular risks are becoming increasingly important internationally. Greater emphasis must be placed in WTO jurisprudence on the acceptability, the importance, and even the necessity of encouraging the formation and expression of the public's diverse responses to risks. Contemporary thinking on the inherent nature of societies' response to risk increasingly emphasises the importance of public deliberation on risks to human health and the environment.[82] It is not coincidental that commentary on the precautionary principle increasingly speaks of the importance of public participation, or that international treaties in the environmental field are incorporating provisions expressly requiring public consultation in

[82] See, inter alia, E Fisher and R Harding, 'The Precautionary Principle: Towards a Deliberative, Transdisciplinary Problem-Solving Process' in R Harding and E Fisher (eds) *Perspectives on the Precautionary Principle* (The Federation Press, Annandale, 1999) 290.

decision-making processes.[83] Indeed, the 'canonical' texts of the US National Research Council have been cited in support of the need for ensuring there is broad-based public participation in both risk assessment and risk management.[84] Increasingly, processes are being developed domestically to accommodate input from the citizenry in relation to new forms of risk and the associated need for value-based judgements to which decisions about these risks give rise. In the Netherlands, techniques of 'constructive technology assessment' (CTA) have been developed,[85] while in the United Kingdom work is being done on 'deliberative mapping' (DM) methods.[86]

The importance of an approach that accommodates public opinion was recognised in Principle 10 of the *Rio Declaration on Environment and Development* of 1992, which observed that 'Environmental issues are best handled with the participation of all concerned citizens, *at the relevant level* [. . .]'.[87] With the negotiation of the *Aarhus Convention on Access to Information, Public Participation in Decision-Making and Access to Justice in Environmental Matters* in 1998, the principles involved have undergone further development.[88] The objective of the Aarhus Convention is to ensure the protection of the right of every person of present and future generations to live in an environment adequate to his or her health and well-being, including through guaranteeing the rights of access to information, *public participation in decision-making*, and access to justice in environmental matters.[89] Parties

---

[83] See for example the *Espoo Convention on Environmental Impact Assessment in a Transboundary Context 1991*, 30 ILM (1971) 802, Art 2(2); *ILC Articles on Prevention of Harm from Transboundary Activities*, above n 39, Art 13. See also J Ebbesson, 'The Notion of Public Participation in International Environmental Law' (1997) 8 *Yearbook of International Environmental Law* 51.

[84] See Winickoff et al., n 45, at 17–19 and 25, citing the National Research Council, *Understanding Risk: Informing Decisions in a Democratic Society* (National Academy Press, Washington DC, 1996) ix; National Research Council, *Building Consensus through Risk Assessment and Management of the Department of Energy's Environmental Remediation Program* (National Academy Press, Washington DC, 1994) 26; National Research Council, *Science and Judgment in Risk Assessment* (National Academy Press, Washington DC, 1994) 267.

[85] P Harremoës et al., *The Precautionary Principle in the 20th Century: Late Lessons from Early Warnings* (Earthscan, London, 2002) 211.

[86] A Stirling, 'Risk, Uncertainty, and Precaution: Some Instrumental Implications from the Social Sciences' in F Berkhout et al. (eds) *Negotiating Environmental Change: New Perspectives from Social Science* (Edward Elgar, Cheltenham, UK and Northampton, MA, 2003) 33.

[87] Emphasis added.

[88] *Aarhus Convention on Access to Information, Public Participation in Decision-Making and Access to Justice in Environmental Matters 1998*, 38 ILM (1999) 517.

[89] Article 1 (emphasis added).

are to promote application of the Convention's principles in international environmental decision-making processes.[90] The public is to be informed about proposed activities that may have a 'significant effect' on the environment (which could potentially include trade-related decisions),[91] and to be allowed to make submissions on them, in writing or at a public hearing.[92] Parties to the Aarhus Convention are to ensure that due account is taken of the outcome of such public participation.[93] Within this overall approach, provision of full and accurate information to the public and the need for reasoned deliberation must be emphasised.[94]

Ongoing research and experimentation is taking place in a number of countries on how to structure processes of informing and consulting the public about new technologies and new risks to human health and the environment and how to generate public participation and deliberation in order to produce clear and meaningful outcomes. For example, in relation to the risks and opportunities of genetic technology in particular, reference might be made to the experience in the United Kingdom and in New Zealand respectively. In the United Kingdom, public concerns about GM crops led to the establishment of the Agriculture and Environment Biotechnology Commission, in 2000, which was given a formal responsibility for advising the Government on strategic issues at the interface of public values and scientific knowledge. In New Zealand, reference may be made to the public enquiry into genetic modification that produced the Report of the Royal Commission on Genetic Modification 2001, and the subsequent establishment of the Bioethics Council, Toi te Taiao, with the aim of enhancing New Zealand's understanding of the cultural, ethical and spiritual aspects of biotechnology, and ensuring that the use of biotechnology has regard for New Zealanders' values.[95]

For international trade law to benefit in the long run, developments in domestic practice, and in both international human rights law and international environmental law should be taken fully into account when considering the ongoing interpretation of the SPS Agreement.

---

[90] Article 3(7).

[91] Article 6(2)(e).

[92] Article 6(7).

[93] Article 6(8).

[94] There has already been an emphasis provision of full and accurate information for some decades. See, for example, A M Weinberg, 'Science and Trans-Science' (1972) 10 *Minerva* 209, 222; as well as J D Fraiberg and M J Trebilcock, 'Risk Regulation: Technocratic and Democratic Tools for Regulatory Reform' (1998) 43 *McGill Law Journal* 835, 883.

[95] For more information on the Bioethics Council, see http://www.bioethics.org.nz/ at 2 July 2008.

12. Democratic deficit, participation and the WTO

Sarah Joseph

This chapter will analyse arguments that the World Trade Organization ('WTO') suffers from a 'democratic deficit', which casts doubt on the legitimacy and desirability of its rules and policies. First, this chapter outlines the two strands of this accusation of 'democratic deficit'. That is:

1. That the WTO unduly undermines the regulatory capacity of States, and
2. That democratic deficiencies exist within WTO internal processes, such as negotiations and dispute settlements.

Secondly, I examine the relevance to this issue of international human rights law, particularly the right of political participation in Article 25 of the *International Covenant on Civil and Political Rights 1966* ('ICCPR').[1] Thirdly, many of the alleged democratic deficits of and within the WTO afflict other international regimes. In this regard, a comparison between the WTO regime and the international human rights regime is undertaken in order to identify whether democratic deficiencies within the WTO are of greater concern than the general democratic deficiencies that exist at the international level of governance. Fourthly, potential limits to the WTO's mandate, which might strike a more appropriate balance between national regulatory powers and international rules in light of democratic deficiencies in WTO internal processes, are discussed. The fifth section concludes this chapter.

1. THE TWO COMPONENTS TO THE WTO/DEMOCRATIC DEFICIT ARGUMENT

There are generally two strands to the 'democratic deficit' arguments. First,

[1] *International Covenant on Civil and Political Rights*, opened for signature 16 December 1966, 999 UNTS 14668 (entered into force 23 March 1976).

there are arguments regarding the substance of WTO rules, the WTO's 'output'.[2] A general contention of critics is that WTO rules unduly restrict the regulatory capacities of States, which is particularly problematic if WTO rules undermine the ability of States to enact laws that reflect the democratic will of their people.[3] For example, in the *Beef Hormone* case, the Panel and the Appellate Body in the WTO decided that the ban on the import of hormone-treated meat by the European Communities ('EC') was a breach of the Agreement on the Application of Sanitary and Phytosanitary Measures ('SPS').[4] The lifting of the ban would apparently be against the wishes of the majority of European peoples and consumers, who fear that such hormones could be unsafe for human health. Hence, the EC chose to maintain the ban and suffer consequent trade sanctions in accordance with WTO rules.[5] A similar issue could arise in the future regarding the EC's restrictions on imports of genetically modified organisms ('GMOs').[6]

The second and intrinsically related component to the 'democratic deficit' arguments concerns WTO internal processes,[7] that is its 'input'. If the WTO's

---

2 I have respectfully borrowed the terminology of 'output' and 'input' (below) from Robert O Keohane and Joseph S Nye Jr, 'The Club Model of Multilateral Cooperation and Problems of Democratic Legitimacy' (Working Paper No 4, John F Kennedy School of Government), http://www.ksg.harvard.edu/visions/publication/keohane_nye.pdf at 21 July 2008.

3 Jeffrey L Dunoff, 'The Death of the Trade Regime' (1999) 10 *European Journal of International Law* 733, 758.

4 *European Communities – Measures Affecting Meat and Meat Products*, WTO Doc WT/DS26/AB/R, WT/DS48/AB/R, AB-1997-4 (13 February 1998) (Appellate Body Report) ('*EC – Hormones*').

5 See Grace Skogstad, 'International Institutions and Food Safety Regulation: Values in Conflict', in I Holland and J Flemings (eds) *Government Reformed: Values and New Political Institutions* (Ashgate, Dartmouth, 2003) 121. Indeed, the EC is now challenging the continued trade sanctions on the basis of new scientific evidence of the effect of hormones in beef. While the Panel Report was circulated on 31 March 2008, the EC has requested that the Appellate Body review certain issues of law contained therein; see http://www.wto.org/english/tratop_e/dispu_e/cases_e/ds320_e.htm at 21 June 2008.

6 *European Communities – Measures Affecting the Approval and Marketing of Biotech Products*, WTO Doc WT/DS291/R, WT/DS292/R, WT/DS293/R (29 September 2006) (Panel Report) ('*EC – Biotech*') concerned a challenge to a de facto moratorium on the approval of GMOs by the EC, as well as bans on GMOs issued by certain individual EC States. The relevant moratorium and bans were found to breach the SPS on the basis that risk assessments on GMOs had not been carried out, or had been unduly delayed. Thus, the substantive issue of whether imports of GMO foods can be restricted or banned is not addressed.

7 Thomas Cottier, 'Preparing for Structural Reform of the WTO' (2007) 10 *Journal of International Economic Law* 497, 499.

input legitimacy is lacking, that circumstance casts doubt on the legitimacy of the substantive rules generated by those processes.[8]

There is commonly little democratic input into a State's decision to join the WTO, even though that decision generates binding WTO obligations which can have a profound impact on people's livelihoods. For example, ratification is often a function of the executive government, rather than the more representative legislative arm of a national government.

In any case, people are rarely well informed of the process of negotiating agreements, standards, or accession deals, which are historically negotiated by trade technocrats in secret. Negotiating teams have generally represented a very narrow range of interests, and are not necessarily skilled at appreciating the non-trade impacts (for example, in the fields of human rights, environment, and health) of trade deals. Indeed, Nobel laureate Joseph Stiglitz has suggested that trade negotiations are too important to be left to trade ministries.[9] This trade bias is exacerbated by the fact that non-governmental bodies involved in negotiations will normally represent business interests rather than other elements of civil society.[10]

Given the undoubted trade ethos of the major players in WTO negotiations and the effective exclusion of non-trade interests, such as human rights, environmental and other civil society groups, it is arguable that the WTO lacks the credentials to legitimately make decisions that impact significantly on non-trade areas.[11] A related argument is that the priority given to trade values within the WTO undermines the ability of States to respect international obligations in the non-trade arena. For example, it has been argued that the *Beef Hormone* decision, if implemented, would undermine the duty of the States in the European Union ('EU') to respect the right to an adequate standard of health care (here, in the context of food safety).[12]

---

[8] Kal Raustiala, 'Rethinking the Sovereignty Debate in International Economic Law' (2003) 6 *Journal of International Economic Law* 841, 862; Daniel C Esty, 'The World Trade Organization's Legitimacy Crisis', (2002) 1 *World Trade Review* 7, 15–16.

[9] Joseph Stiglitz, 'Social Justice and Global Trade' (2006) 169 *Far Eastern Economic Review* 18, 22.

[10] Ilan Kapoor, 'Deliberative Democracy and the WTO' (2004) 11 *Review of International Political Economy* 522, 530.

[11] This a point commonly made by David M Driesen, 'What is Free Trade? The Real Issue Lurking behind the Trade and Environment Debate' (2001) 41 *Virginia Journal of International Law* 279, 324. See also Esty, above n 8, 13.

[12] Caroline Dommen, 'Raising Human Rights Concerns in the World Trade Organization: Actors, Processes and Possible Strategies', (2002) 24 *Human Rights Quarterly* 1, 17–19. The cogency of such an argument is beyond the scope of this chapter.

There have been improvements in this regard in WTO practices. WTO rules are now more widely known, and the WTO website is an excellent resource which improves transparency. Some negotiating positions are now published in advance, which allows some time for national public consultation, and non-business NGOs have been part of some negotiating teams in some discussions. Furthermore, one must also note that NGOs themselves lack democratic credentials, as stressed in an influential report on WTO reform.[13] Nevertheless, as Charnovitz has argued, NGO input is important to improve the ultimate outcome of WTO negotiations: NGO participation ensures that alternative ideas and values are injected into the WTO policy-making and legislative process.[14]

Just as there is a bias within the WTO against non-trade interests, there is a bias in WTO processes against developing States in favour of industrialised States. WTO members are driven by domestic political agendas to attempt to carve a bargain that is most favourable to themselves, rather than a fair bargain.[15] Of course, a fair deal might still eventuate by default, as negotiators are forced to compromise if everyone has the same win/lose attitude, but only if negotiating teams possess equal power. However, the strongest Members within the WTO, such as the US and the EC, have clearly been able to exercise greater influence over agendas and outcomes of WTO negotiations (and those within its predecessor negotiating forum, the General Agreement on Tariffs and Trade ('GATT')) than weaker countries, especially small developing countries. Given the real imbalances between negotiating teams, it is not surprising that current WTO rules favour the rich and economically powerful States over the poor and comparatively powerless States.[16] Such has been recently conceded by Pascal Lamy, the Director-General of the WTO.[17]

---

13 Consultative Board of the Director-General of the WTO, *The Future of the WTO* (WTO, Geneva, 2004) 45 ('Sutherland Report').

14 Steve Charnovitz, 'The WTO and Cosmopolitics' (2004) 7 *Journal of International Economic Law* 675, 680.

15 Gregory Schaffer has previously commented on 'mercantilist rivalries' in dispute resolution, which, it is argued, are likely to be reflected in negotiating strategies: Gregory C Shaffer, *Defending Interests: Public Private Partnerships in WTO Litigation* (Brookings Institution Press, Washington DC, 2003), 137.

16 See generally, Sarah Joseph, 'Trade to Live and Live to Trade', in M Baderin and R McCorquodale (eds) *Economic, Social and Cultural Rights in Action* (Oxford University Press, Oxford, 2006) 391; Oxfam, *Rigged Rules and Double Standards: Trade, Globalisation and the Fight Against Poverty* (Oxfam, London, 2002); Amrita Narlikar, *The World Trade Organization: A Very Short Introduction* (Oxford University Press, Oxford, 2005).

17 Pascal Lamy, 'It's Time for a new "Geneva Consensus" on making trade work for development' (Address delivered at New York University, New York, 30 October 2006), www.wto.org/english/news_e/sppl_e/sppl45_e.htm at 21 July 2008.

There are a number of disadvantages for poorer States in WTO negotiations. Even though WTO treaties are adopted by consensus, Cottier has suggested that the WTO 'in fact operates under a system of de facto preponderance, reflecting political clout and market size'.[18] Negotiators and other relevant personnel from developing States may lack the technical expertise to effectively represent their nations' interests.[19] For example, huge discrepancies may arise in the size of negotiating delegations. In the Hong Kong Ministerial meeting in 2005, the US had 356 delegates while Burundi had three. Given the intense ongoing nature of WTO negotiations one can surmise that the US personnel were far better informed (and slept!) than those from Burundi.[20] The least developed WTO members are unable to maintain WTO missions in Geneva, so they cannot participate in the numerous interim meetings at WTO headquarters.[21]

Disturbingly, Narlikar states that some developing States did not comprehend the extent of their WTO commitments adopted after the Uruguay Round in 1995, noting that a number believed that the *Agreement on Trade Related Aspects of Intellectual Property* ('TRIPS') was 'limited to counterfeit goods'.[22] In fact, TRIPS imposes far-reaching obligations regarding the protection of all intellectual property rights.

The negotiating culture of the GATT/WTO served to exclude numerous Members from important aspects of deal-brokering. Policies and treaties were negotiated in notorious 'Green Room' meetings, to which only certain Members were invited, and in which discussions were secret. Green Room decisions were then presented to other Members as faits accomplis. Of course, this process generated not only substantively unfair outcomes (unsurprisingly favouring the Green Room participants) but also generated feelings of marginalisation and resentment amongst those excluded.[23]

Under-participation by developing States at various stages in WTO negotiating processes means that the ensuing substantive outcomes of the Uruguay

---

18 Cottier, above n 7, 502.

19 See generally, United Nation High Commissioner for Human Rights ('UNHCHR'), 'Analytical Study of the High Commissioner for Human Rights on the fundamental principle of participation and its application in the context of globalization', UN Doc E/CN.4/2005/41 (23 December 2004) 13.

20 See Oxfam, *What Happened in Hong Kong?* (Briefing Paper 85, Oxfam, 2005) 5, http://www.oxfam.org/en/files/bp85_hongkong/download at 31 January 2006.

21 Kapoor, above n 10, 529.

22 Narlikar, above n 16, 82. See *Marrakesh Agreement Establishing the World Trade Organization*, opened for signature 15 April 1994, 1867 UNTS 3 (entered into force 1 January 1995), annex 1C (*Agreement on Trade Related Aspects of Intellectual Property*).

23 Ibid 18.

Round, such as the adoption of TRIPS, are less likely to be in their interests.[24] Arguments regarding iniquities in the WTO agreement of 1995 are beyond the scope of this chapter, but are noted above (regarding TRIPS) and in my previous writings.[25]

There have been improvements in WTO processes, designed to facilitate greater Member participation. The Green Room has been significantly reformed, with more invitees and a more transparent process. The focus in these smaller group discussions is on consensus building rather than on decision-making, so Members not involved in the particular discussions are not presented with 'take it or leave it' propositions.[26] The WTO is attempting to provide greater technical support to improve the capacity of developing countries through, for example, the *Integrated Framework for Trade-Related Technical Assistance to Least Developed Countries*.[27] Furthermore, in the current Doha round of WTO negotiations, developing States have formed stronger coalitions to counterbalance the traditional power of the US and the EC.[28] The negotiating clout of big developing States with huge markets such as India, Brazil, and China cannot be doubted. One may note, however, that the increasing balancing of power within WTO negotiations has helped to stall the current negotiations, so the 1995 rules (unfair according to this author) prevail.

Finally, there are criticisms regarding the accountability and transparency of the WTO's dispute settlement bodies ('DSBs'), the Panel and the Appellate Body. The WTO's dispute settlement system ('DSS') is unusually powerful within the international system: States tend to implement their decisions,[29] or else they expose themselves to economic sanctions.[30] Developed states again have the advantage when it comes to the enforcement of decisions. Retaliatory trade sanctions imposed by a rich industrialised nation on a poor nation will

---

24 UNHCHR, above n 19 [33], [34]. TRIPS has generated a flow of wealth from developing to developed States, as most intellectual property rights are held by companies in industrialised countries: see United Nations Development Programme ('UNDP'), *Human Development Report 2005: International Cooperation at a Crossroads: Aid, Trade and Security in an Unequal World* (2005) 135, http://hdr.undp.org/reports/view_reports.cfm?type=1 at 31 January 2005.

25 See generally Joseph, above n 16.

26 Narlikar, above n 16, 146

27 WTO Doc WT/MIN (96)/14 (7 January 1997).

28 See Narlikar, above n 16, 112–13.

29 Sharyn O'Halloran, 'US Implementation of WTO Decisions' (Address delivered at WTO at Ten: Dispute Settlement and Developing Countries, Columbia University, 6 April 2006).

30 The EC response to *EC – Hormones* was an example of non-compliance; claimant States in that litigation are consequently imposing countervailing sanctions on the EC.

generally have a greater impact than the reciprocal situation. Furthermore, mounting a WTO challenge is an expensive business which requires considerable technical skills.[31]

There are concerns about the decision-making processes within the DSS. Hearings are closed to the public unless all parties consent. Decisions at first instance are made by trade experts, who may not be particularly conversant with non-trade issues, such as human rights, which can again lead to an undue dominance of trade values over potentially competing values. Whilst the Panels *may* take other areas of international law into account in interpreting WTO rules,[32] they do not have to do so outside the field of customary international law.[33] In making decisions under the WTO, WTO rules will prevail over any inconsistent alternative rules of international law,[34] except in the case of *jus cogens* norms.[35] For example, in *Beef Hormone*, the Appellate Body found that the 'precautionary principle' derived from environmental law could not override the terms of the SPS, regardless of whether that principle was a customary norm.[36]

The DSBs are disproportionately powerful within the WTO.[37] Their decisions can only be overruled by consensus, which is improbable given that a vindicated Member is unlikely to vote against its own victory. The 'law-making' role of the WTO's 'judiciary' is presently more consequential than was possibly ever envisaged, as the legislative process is presently stalled

31 Shaffer above n 15, 161–2.

32 *United States – Import Prohibition of Certain Shrimp and Shrimp Products*, WTO Doc WT/DS58/AB/RW, AB-2001–4 (21 November 2001) [126]–[134] (Report of the Appellate Body).

33 In *EC – Biotech* [7.68], the panel found that it was only required to take another treaty into account in interpreting WTO provisions if all WTO members were party to that treaty. As WTO membership has been extended to several non-States (Hong Kong, EC, Chinese Taipei), there are no treaties to which all WTO members are party.

34 *Korea – Measures Affecting Government Procurement*, WTO Doc WT/DS163/R (19 June 2000) [7.96] (Panel Report).

35 *Vienna Convention on the Law of Treaties*, opened for signature 23 May 1969, 1195 UNTS 311 (entered into force 27 January 1980) Article 53. See also Martti Koskenniemi, 'Fragmentation of International Law: Difficulties Arising from the Diversification and Expansion of International Law' [2006] 2 *Yearbook of the International Law Commission* UN Docs A/CN.4/L/682 and A/CN.4/L/682/corr 1, [365]–[373].

36 *EC – Hormones* [120]–[125]. See Dommen, above n 12, 19. The Appellate Body found that the status of the norm as custom was unclear.

37 See Jeffery Atik, 'Democratizing the WTO' (2000–2001) 33 *George Washington International Law Review* 451, 455.

during the Doha round.[38] States may increasingly seek to further their trade interests via favourable interpretation in the DSBs, rather than seek to achieve outcomes through negotiation and compromise.

Even though the dispute settlement process is only open to States, private commercial interests have been effectively represented in that dispute settlement process.[39] For example, some cases are colloquially known by the names of the private interests behind the litigation, rather than by the States who 'fought' the case: the 'Kodak/Fuji' case is a classic example.[40] In contrast, NGOs have participated on only an indirect basis by submitting amicus briefs. The panels can accept unsolicited briefs, but they do not have to.[41] It is not clear whether such briefs have been significant in the making of any decisions.[42] The unique level of participation by commercial bodies in WTO dispute settlement processes again prioritises a trade focus to the possible detriment of non-trade interests.

A final comment on the DSS is to note that Panel decisions and, to a lesser extent, Appellate Body decisions, are extremely long and technical. The *EC – Biotech* decision was over one thousand pages long, certainly a huge disincentive for anyone wishing to read it and analyse its implications. Though this concern might sound petty, the arcane nature of the decisions poses an unnecessary artificial barrier to involvement by 'outsiders'. Members of the panels and the Appellate Body must learn not to summarise every point and every duplicative argument by multiple claimants, and to deliver decisions that are more easily readable.[43]

WTO procedures and processes are currently biased in favour of commercial trade interests and developed States. This systemic bias is likely to gener-

---

38 Joost Pauwelyn, 'The Sutherland Report: A Missed Opportunity for Genuine Debate on Trade, Globalization and Reforming the WTO' (2005) 8 *Journal of International Economic Law* 329, 336. See also Keohane and Nye, above n 2, 24.

39 See generally, Shaffer, above n 15.

40 See Jeffrey L Dunoff; 'The Misguided Debate over NGO Participation at the WTO' (1998) 1 *Journal of International Economic Law* 433, 441–8. The official name of the case is *Japan – Measures Affecting Consumer Photographic Film and Paper*, WTO Doc WT/DS44/R (31 March 1998) (Panel Report).

41 *United States – Import Prohibition of Certain Shrimp and Shrimp Products*, WTO Doc WT/DS58/AB/R (12 October 1998) [110] (Report of the Appellate Body) ('*Shrimp Turtle* Case').

42 Nathalie Bernasconi-Osterwalder, 'Democratizing international dispute settlement: the case of trade and investment disputes' (Paper presented at the 6th International Conference of New or Restored Democracies, Doha, 29 October–1 November 2006) 3–4. See also Pauwelyn, above n 38, 346.

43 See generally John A Rogosta, 'Unmasking the WTO-Access to the DSB System: Can the WTO DSB Live up to the Moniker "World Trade Court"?' (1999–2000) 31 *Law and Policy in International Business* 739, 765–7.

ate outcomes that favour such interests, and therefore act to the detriment of other interests, such as those of developing States or non-trade (for example, human rights, environmental) interests, if the respective sets of interests should conflict.

It must be noted that developing States are generally against the greater involvement of NGOs in the WTO negotiation or interpretation process.[44] They fear that NGO involvement could exacerbate the dominance of industrialised States within the WTO, as Northern NGOs are 'louder' and more experienced advocates than their Southern counterparts. Such concerns assume some sort of dissonance between the goals of Northern and Southern NGOs.[45] However, strong NGOs do exist in the South, for example in India and Brazil, and there are vibrant North/South NGO partnerships.[46] Furthermore, the existence of conflict between Northern and Southern NGOs over trade issues has been exaggerated. For example, there is evidence that trade unions from both North and South favour explicit linkage of labour and trade in the WTO, contrary to common assertions that Southern trade unions fear protectionist abuse of such clause to the detriment of their members.[47] There has also been some convergence in the positions of some Northern NGOs and the negotiating positions of developing States during the Doha round.[48] For example, numerous Northern NGOs supported developing States in their attack on the effect of TRIPS on access to medicines, which helped produce the *Doha Declaration on TRIPS and Public Health* in 2001.[49] Indeed, some NGOs, such as Oxfam and the Catholic Agency for Overseas Development ('CAFOD'), have advised developing States on their negotiating positions in the Doha round.[50] Finally, the continued exclusion of NGOs (whether from North or South) will continue to skew WTO outputs in favour of trade and commercial interests, and away from social justice and other non-trade interests.[51] A

---

44 Keohane and Nye, above n 2, 8.

45 See, for example, Jagdish Bhagwati, 'Afterword: the Question of Linkage' (2002) 96 *American Journal of International Law* 126; Kathleen Newland, 'Workers of the World, Now What?' (1999) 114 *Foreign Policy* 52, 56–7.

46 See also Keohane and Nye, above n 2, 19.

47 See, generally, Gerard Griffin et al., 'Trade Unions and the Social Clause: A North South Union Divide?' (Working Paper No 81, National Key Centre in Industrial Relations, Monash University, 2002), http://www.buseco.monash.edu.au/mgt/research/working-papers/nkcir-working-papers/nkcir-workingpaper-81.pdf at 4 November 2007.

48 See, generally, Oxfam, *Rigged Rules and Double Standards*, above n 16.

49 Robert Wai, 'Countering, Branding and Dealing: Using Economic and Social Rights in and Around the International Trade Regime' (2003) 14 *European Journal of International Law* 35, 72, 79.

50 Sutherland Report, above n 13, 44.

51 Autocratic governments such as those in China and Burma, which arise more

continued trade bias within the WTO, while its output continues to impact on non-trade areas, is no more legitimate than a continued bias in favour of developed States.[52]

2. THE RELEVANCE OF INTERNATIONAL HUMAN RIGHTS LAW

What human rights are engaged by the issue of democratic deficit in an international organisation such as the WTO? First, one may note that it is problematic to identify breaches of human rights by the WTO per se. For example, it is a non-State actor that has not ratified any human rights treaties. The human rights obligations of the WTO itself are beyond the scope of this chapter. Suffice to note that if certain practices within the WTO prejudice the enjoyment of human rights, then human rights violations by the individual State members may be found, and/or the ability of a State to abide by its human rights obligations will be undermined.[53]

The surrender of autonomous regulatory power by the State over important issues, such as food safety and intellectual property protection, could breach the right of peoples to self-determination, protected under Article 1 of ICCPR, the *International Covenant on Economic Social and Cultural Rights* ('ICESCR'),[54] and under customary international law. Article 1(1) of each Covenant guarantees the right of peoples to 'freely pursue their economic, social and cultural development'. Furthermore, all States parties to both Covenants have duties under common article 1(3) to respect and promote the right of self-determination of others, so they should avoid actions, such as enforcement of WTO rights, if such action might prejudice enjoyment of the right.

in the developing world rather than the North, are hostile to the overt promotion of social justice interests by non-governmental groups, whether at the national or international levels. In such circumstances, those governments are not necessarily representing the interests of their people, as opposed to their own interests. That is, their 'democratic' credentials are highly suspect.

52 See also Sara Dillon, 'A Farewell to "Linkage": International Trade Law and Global Sustainability Indicators' (2002) 51 *Rutgers Law Review* 87, 130–5; Robert Howse, 'From Politics to Technocracy – and Back Again: the Fate of the Multilateral Trading Regime' (2002) 96 *American Journal of International Law* 94, 115.

53 See Statement of the UN Committee on Economic Social and Cultural Rights to the Third Ministerial Conference of the World Trade Organization, UN Doc E/C.12/1999/9 (26 November 1999) [7].

54 *International Covenant on Economic, Social and Cultural Rights*, opened for signature 16 December 1966, 999 UNTS 3 (entered into force 3 January 1976).

The transfer of national regulatory power upwards to an international regime per se cannot constitute a breach of Article 1, lest nearly all international regimes prejudice that right. The question of breach must therefore depend on the degree of the removal of regulatory power. It is difficult to characterise the WTO regime as constituting a greater interference with State power than other regimes in terms of subject matter. It is not, for example, 'broader' in substantive terms than human rights or environmental treaties. As noted below in Part 3, however, the intensity of the interference by the WTO in those areas in which it impacts is probably stronger than most other international regimes, and its enforcement mechanisms are certainly stronger. Therefore, it is possible that WTO obligations can be characterised as somehow breaching the right of self-determination. Nevertheless, it seems unlikely; no such breach was, for example, identified in a comprehensive report on globalisation and participation by the United Nations High Commissioner for Human Rights in 2004.[55]

Article 25 of the ICCPR delineates an individual right to participate in political processes. Democratic rights are not only about elections and the free choice of government by the majority; they entail individual rights to have an opportunity to take part in the political process. Majority preferences do not always have to be satisfied, but the routine flouting by a State of majority preferences would signal inadequate protection of this right. The right has been interpreted broadly by the Human Rights Committee ('HRC'), the monitoring body established under the ICCPR, to encompass rights to participate in 'all aspects of public administration, and the formulation of policy at the *international*, national, regional and local levels'.[56]

Participatory rights are also recognised in Articles 7, 8 and 14(2) of the *Convention on the Elimination of All Forms of Discrimination against Women* ('CEDAW'),[57] as well as Article 5 of the *International Convention on the Elimination of All Forms of Racial Discrimination* ('ICERD').[58] In General Recommendation 23, the CEDAW Committee has elaborated the requirements of CEDAW with regard to participation of women in international bodies and decision-making:

---

55 See generally UNHCHR, above n 19.

56 UNHRCR, *General Comment 25*, UN Doc CCPR/C/21/Rev.1/Add.7 (12 July 1996) [5] (emphasis added). See also UNHCHR, above n 19 [8].

57 *Convention on the Elimination of All Forms of Discrimination against Women*, opened for signature 18 December 1979, 1249 UNTS 13 (entered into force 3 September 1981).

58 *International Convention on the Elimination of All Forms of Racial Discrimination*, opened for signature 21 December 1965, 660 UNTS 195 (entered into force 4 January 1965). See also UNHCHR, above n 19 [7].

> The globalization of the contemporary world makes the inclusion of women and their participation in international organizations, on equal terms with men, increasingly important. The integration of a gender perspective and women's human rights into the agenda of all international bodies is a government imperative. Many crucial decisions on global issues, such as . . . economic restructuring . . . are taken with limited participation of women.[59]

Therefore, women should be given equal opportunities to 'represent their governments at the international level and to participate in the work of international organizations', such as the WTO.[60]

Finally, the *Declaration on the Right to Development* describes the right to development as:

> [a]n inalienable human right by virtue of which all peoples are entitled *to participate in*, contribute to, and enjoy economic, social, cultural and political development, in which all human rights and fundamental freedoms can be fully realized.[61]

It is often argued that WTO rules and policies, which largely promote freer trade, are compatible with the right to development, specifically the economic aspects thereof.[62] It is arguable, however, that the participatory aspects of the right have been neglected by States when acting through the WTO, which might prejudice the enjoyment of such rights.

The United Nations High Commissioner for Human Rights has conceded that the exact parameters of participatory rights at the global level are unclear.[63] What is clear is that participatory rights are not confined within national borders, so the inherently limited participation within WTO processes, whether they be negotiation, treaty-making, or dispute resolution, risks classification as a breach of human rights by its Member States, especially given the significant outcomes of those processes.[64]

---

59 CEDAW, *General Comment* 23, UN Doc A/52/38/Rev.1 (31 January 1997) [39].

60 UNHCHR, above n 19 [35].

61 *Declaration on the Right to Development*, GA Res 41/128, UN GAOR, 41st sess, 97th plen mtg, UN Doc A/RES/41/128 (4 December 1986) Article 1 (emphasis added).

62 Robert Howse, 'Mainstreaming the right to development in international trade law and policy at the World Trade Organization', UN Doc E/CN.4/Sub.2/2004/17 (9 June 2004) [50].

63 UNHCHR, above n 19 [18].

64 UNHCHR, above n 19 [18]. On the other hand, it may be noted that Article 25 rights are explicitly conferred on 'citizens', which may undermine its potential impact at the international level, as there is no notion of a global 'citizen', unless it simply refers to the citizens of State members of international organisations. See also Susan Marks, *The Riddle of All Constitutions* (Oxford University Press, Oxford, 1999) Ch 4, 109–20.

That said, rights of participation are not absolute. Article 25 ICCPR anticipates 'reasonable' restrictions. Most relevantly, the right of *direct* participation in public affairs is possibly limited to the rights outlined in Article 25(b) (right to vote and stand for elections) and 25(c) (equal access to a State's public service).[65] This issue arose in *Mikmaq Tribal Society v Canada*,[66] which concerned a complaint by an indigenous tribe regarding Canada's failure to invite it to a constitutional conference on indigenous rights to which other indigenous tribes had been invited. The HRC stated at [5.4]:

> Surely, it cannot be the meaning of article 25(a) . . . that every citizen may determine either to take part directly in the conduct of public affairs or to leave it to freely chosen representatives. It is for the legal and constitutional system of the State party to provide for the modalities of such participation.

At [5.5], the HRC added:

> [A]rticle 25(a) of the Covenant cannot be understood as meaning that any directly affected group, large or small, has the unconditional right to choose the modalities of participation in the conduct of public affairs.

In *Beydon v France*,[67] the complainants were members of an NGO, the DIH, an organisation which campaigned for the creation of the International Criminal Court ('ICC'), and for France's full participation in and cooperation with that Court. It did not approve of France's decision, upon its ratification of the Statute of the International Criminal Court,[68] to make a declaration which limited ICC jurisdiction over war crimes. The complainants alleged a violation of Article 25 entailed in the French government's failure to take into account 'the widespread public opposition expressed both directly and through their elected representatives to the French declaration under Article 124'.[69] The HRC found the complaint inadmissible, and noted at [4.5]:

> The Committee has . . . noted the [complainants'] claim under article 25 (a), that they were deprived, by the State party, of their right and opportunity to take part in the conduct of public affairs *relating to the negotiations, and subsequent adhesion*

---

65 Sarah Joseph et al., *The International Covenant on Civil and Political Rights: Cases, Materials and Commentary* (2nd edn, Oxford University Press, Oxford, 2004) 657.

66 UN Doc CCPR/C/43/D/205/1986 (3 December 1991).

67 UN Doc CCPR/C/85/D/1400/2005 (28 November 2005) ('*Beydon*').

68 *Rome Statute of the International Criminal Court*, opened for signature 12 September 2003, 2187 UNTS 90 (entered into force 31 December 2003) ('*Rome Statute*').

69 *Beydon* [3.1].

> *of France to the ICC Statute* with a declaration . . ., the Committee recalls that citizens also take part in the conduct of public affairs by exerting influence through public debate and dialogue with their representatives or through their capacity to organize themselves. In the present case, the [complainants] have participated in the public debate in France on the issue of its adhesion to the ICC and on the issue of [A]rticle 124 declaration; they acted through elected representatives and through their association's actions. In the circumstances, the Committee considers that the [complainants] have failed to substantiate . . . that their right to take part in the conduct of public affairs has been violated (emphasis added).

Thus, the limited participation of the complainants in France's decisions regarding negotiation and ratification of the *Rome Statute* did not breach Article 25.[70]

From *Beydon* we can extrapolate that citizens, at least those in democratic States, are indirectly participating in the process through the agency of government representatives. WTO power is legitimised as the organisation is merely exercising the authority delegated to it under treaties negotiated by and assented to by those representatives.

Even if Article 25 rights are not breached, related rights, such as minority rights in Article 27 ICCPR, and the right of non-discrimination in Article 26 ICCPR, may be threatened. Regarding Article 27, the HRC has clearly stated that minority groups have rights of direct participation (for example, consultation with governments) in decisions that impact their interests.[71] Furthermore, exclusion of certain groups from WTO processes, either at the national or international level, raises concerns regarding discrimination in conjunction with the right of political participation. The HRC stated in General Comment 25 on Article 25 at [6]: 'Where a mode of direct participation by citizens is established, no distinctions should be made between citizens as regards their participation on the grounds mentioned in article 2, paragraph 1,[72] and no unreasonable restrictions should be imposed.'

The historical narrowness of interests represented by WTO negotiators, the greater input into WTO processes by business compared to other civic groups, the general lack of input by historically marginalised groups such as the poor, women[73] and indigenous peoples,[74] all raise legitimate queries regarding the

---

70 See also *Brun v France*, UN Doc CCPR/C/88/D/1453/2006 (23 November 2006).

71 See UNHCHR, *General Comment 23*, UN Doc CCPR/C/21/Rev.1/Add.5 (8 April 1994) [7]; see also Joseph et al., above n 65, 778, 781–2.

72 The prohibited grounds of discrimination enumerated in Article 2(1) ICCPR are: race, colour, sex, language, religion, political or other opinion, national or social origin, property, birth or other status.

73 See Dillon, above n 52, 146–8, commenting on the general absence of women in the international trade field. See also Shelley Wright, 'Women and the Global

adequacy of the level of participation in WTO negotiations and decision-making. As noted by Esty:

> [T]o limit their participation in global politics to electing national representatives who will designate trade ministry officials to represent the nation in a narrowly confined intergovernmental dialogue produces a terribly thin reed of popular sovereignty on which to build the legitimacy of the WTO.[75]

The exercise of greater rights of participation by constituencies not traditionally involved in WTO processes at the national and international levels would serve a normative function in helping to ensure against breaches arising from participation deficit, such as breaches of Article 25 ICCPR and non-discrimination obligations. They would also serve an instrumental function in helping to ensure that the substantive outcomes of negotiations conform with other human rights. For example, the consideration by WTO panels of *amicus curiae* briefs from a variety of groups would help to ensure that they are aware of a range of non-trade interests that may be impacted by their decision. As noted, the lobbying by civil society at national and international levels, along with the negotiation stances of governments from developing States, led to the adoption by the WTO of the *Doha Declaration on TRIPS and Public Health* in 2001. This Declaration, along with subsequent decisions and a TRIPS amendment, has arguably alleviated some detrimental effects of WTO rules on the right to enjoy adequate standards of health care in Article 12 ICESCR.[76]

3. DEMOCRATIC DEFICIT AND INTERNATIONAL REGIMES: WHY SINGLE OUT THE WTO?

WTO membership removes certain policy choices from Member States under international law, as is the case with most international law regimes. Furthermore, other international regimes also allocate power and decision-making upwards to international bodies, which are more remote from people than their own national bodies. Therefore, it is arguable that most international legal regimes impact negatively on the participatory rights of national populations. The United Nations itself has noted the paradox that the substance of politics has become internationalised (for example, in the areas of trade,

Economic Order: a Feminist Perspective' (1995) 10 *American University International Law Review* 861.

74 UNHCHR above n 19, 9.

75 Esty, above n 8, 15.

76 See UNHCHR, above n 19, 15.

human rights, environment), while political processes and institutions have remained largely national.[77]

Is the democratic deficit within the WTO somehow a 'worse' threat to democratic rights than democratic deficit in other international bodies? Is the allocation of particular power to the WTO as an international institution more or less appropriate than comparable allocations of power to other international bodies? I will make some observations on this issue by comparing the WTO with international human rights regimes.

Indeed, international human rights regimes have also been portrayed at times as threats to the legitimate regulatory power of States, and the democratic choices of a State's people. For example, there has been outrage in the UK regarding certain decisions of the European Court of Human Rights, such as those which have found British counterterrorism measures to breach international human rights standards.[78] In Australia, the conservative Liberal Party, in opposition and in government, has commonly impugned findings of violation against Australia by the HRC and other human rights bodies, on the basis that the decisions lack legitimacy in challenging decisions reached by Australian democratic processes.[79]

The purpose of international human rights law is in many ways counter-majoritarian. Though all people have human rights, they are probably most important for certain vulnerable minorities. In democracies, majorities are generally able to take care of themselves.[80] Minorities, however, are in greater need of the support of international human rights regimes to guard against the arbitrary exercise of power by majorities. Majority rule per se is unlikely to cater for the human rights of unpopular minorities such as suspected or actual criminals and terrorists, or vulnerable minorities whose interests simply do not coincide with those of the majority. The notion of individual human rights would be considerably undermined if their extent was ultimately determined

---

77 Report of the Panel of Eminent Persons on United-Nations Civil Society Relations, *We the Peoples: Civil Society, the United Nations and Global Governance*, UN Doc A/58/817 (11 June 2004) 8, [7]–[10].

78 See Kieran McEvoy, 'Law, Struggle, and Political Transformation in Northern Ireland' (2000) 27 *Journal of Law and Society* 542, 557; Sarah Joseph, 'Denouement of the Deaths on the Rock: the Right to Life of Terrorists' (1996) 14 *Netherlands Quarterly of Human Rights* 5, 6, 22.

79 See generally David Kinley and Penny Martin, 'International Human Rights Law at Home: Addressing the Politics of Denial' (2002) 26 *Melbourne University Law Review* 466.

80 Of course, human rights are precarious for majorities in non-democracies, governed by dictatorships, such as Burma, or minority rule, such as apartheid South Africa. International human rights law of course also seeks to curb the arbitrary exercises of power of non-democratic governments.

merely by the exercise of majority choices. Indeed, another limit to the right of political participation is that majorities cannot compel government policies that breach other human rights. Of course, many States incorporate constitutional protections for minorities which apparently constrain the government from implementing policies that reflect oppressive majority preferences. In such cases, international obligations and supervision act as a backstop to guard against the manipulation of municipal constitutional norms against minorities, and/or decision-making that unduly reflects majority preferences. Therefore, the removal of regulatory power from States under international human rights law may be justified despite its counter-majoritarian consequences.

In any case, the extent of the interference by international human rights law with State regulatory power is quite weak. The findings of the human rights bodies at the global level are not legally binding, though they do have persuasive value. Numerous States have impugned the findings of these bodies on the basis of their non-legal status.[81] Indeed, Donoho claims that enforcement under the global human rights treaties has been delegated 'almost exclusively'[82] to the municipal systems of States, due to institutional incapacities at the global level. An even greater role for national supervision and enforcement mechanisms is envisaged in some of the newest human rights treaties such as the *Optional Protocol to the Convention against Torture and other Inhuman, Cruel or Degrading Treatment or Punishment*[83] and the *Convention on the Rights of Persons with Disabilities*.[84]

The negotiation of global human rights treaties is an open process, with significant NGO participation in bodies such as the Human Rights Council and its predecessor, the Commission on Human Rights. Though commercial NGOs have not been so involved, they could be involved so long as they are accredited by the United Nations. Despite arguments that human rights are imbued by 'Western' concepts, developing States have played a significant

[81] See, for example, Australia's response to the adverse finding of the HRC in *A v Australia*, UN Doc CCPR/C/59/D/560/1993 (30 April 1997): Darryl Williams MP, Attorney General, 'Australian Government responds to the United Nations Human Rights Committee' (Press Release, 17 December 1997).

[82] Douglas Lee Donoho, 'Relativism versus Universalism in Human Rights: the Search for Meaningful Standards' (1991) 27 *Stanford Journal of International Law* 345, 372–3.

[83] Optional Protocol to the Convention against Torture and other Inhuman, Cruel or Degrading Treatment or Punishment, UN Doc A/RES/57/199 (18 December 2002).

[84] *Convention on the Rights of Persons with Disabilities*, UN Doc A/RES/61/106 (24 January 2007) ('CRPD'). The CRPD was opened for signature on 30 March 2007 and came into force with the deposit of the 20th ratification thereof on 8 May 2008.

role in drafting human rights treaties.[85] In any case, no State has to ratify a human rights treaty even if it agrees on the texts thereof, and it can normally enter reservations thereto.

States have considerable discretionary room for manoeuvre with respect to the implementation and enforcement of most internationally recognised human rights. Economic social and cultural rights are inherently flexible, with a State's obligations under the ICESCR being constrained by a State's 'maximum available resources', and by the progressive nature of most aspects of those rights. Most civil and political rights are constrained by concepts such as proportionality and reasonableness.[86] For example, the right to freedom of expression in Article 19 ICCPR may be limited by measures that are 'provided by law and are necessary' to protect national security, public order, public health, public morals, and/or the rights of others. Minority rights in article 27 ICCPR have been limited in order to accommodate reasonable economic development programmes.[87]

Civil society has significant input into human rights monitoring processes, such as reporting processes before the treaty bodies and Universal Periodic Review before the Human Rights Council. Individuals can access grievance procedures under some human rights treaties.[88] Hearings in regional courts are public, but deliberations over individual complaints at the global level are not. All final decisions are easily accessible, for example via the internet.

A human rights complaint will often have already been litigated at the national level, giving an opportunity for interested parties to submit *amicus* briefs, if allowed, to national courts. Material from those national decisions is made available to the international body. There is considerable deference to national authorities in international human rights decision-making, with the utilisation of doctrines such as the margin of appreciation,[89] the need for

---

85 See, for example, Susan Waltz, 'Universalizing Human Rights: the Role of Small States in the Construction of the Universal Declaration of Human Rights' (2001) 23 *Human Rights Quarterly* 44.

86 There are, exceptionally, some absolute rights, which may never be qualified in any circumstance, such as rights to freedom from torture and freedom from slavery.

87 See Joseph et al., above n 65, 772–9.

88 For example, individuals may submit petitions against a State for alleged violations of their rights under the ICCPR if the relevant State has ratified the First Optional Protocol to the ICCPR: *Optional Protocol to the International Covenant on Civil and Political Rights*, opened for signature 16 December 1966, 999 UNTS 302 (entered into force 23 March 1976) Article 1.

89 The 'margin of appreciation' is a doctrine used by the European Court of Human Rights in interpreting the European Convention on Human Rights. It is akin to a 'benefit of the doubt' given to the State party in implementing certain human rights. If a certain measure is deemed to fall within a State's margin of appreciation, no violation is found.

complainants to exhaust domestic remedies before seeking international remedies, and the fact that the international bodies will normally defer to local findings of fact and evidence.[90]

It is concluded that it is appropriate to delegate certain decision-making powers 'upwards' to international human rights bodies. A balance is maintained between national decision-making powers and the competence of international bodies. Furthermore, the outputs of human rights bodies are justified by the extent of the inputs. In fact, a common criticism of human rights is that the powers of international bodies are too weak, rather than too strong. Such criticisms often concern the weakness of human rights enforcement, which is discussed below.

Let us compare that short overview of human rights systems with the WTO. Trade law does not have the same counter-majoritarian purpose as human rights law.[91] One argument in favour of an international trade organisation is to prevent capture of the State by protectionist producer interests that seek to undermine the utilitarian benefits of a liberalised economy for all.[92] Protectionist producer interests are often concentrated and politically mobilised, and are therefore able to manipulate the domestic political process.[93] The WTO helps States to reinforce rational majority interests by protecting consumers (a disparate group who often lack a coherent political voice), who benefit from access to cheaper goods, and, according to the theory of comparative advantage, the interests of the importing State as a whole as its industries are forced to become more competitive and efficient.[94]

The WTO also helps protect the legitimate interests of overseas traders from State B who might otherwise be at the mercy of populist decision-making by State A. The WTO enhances the participatory rights of those traders, who are particularly vulnerable to being abused as political pawns as they are excluded from State A's political community.[95] Under international human rights law, only citizens have rights of political participation in a particular State. However, modern global economic interdependence indicates that the right may be permissibly limited in order to prevent undue harm to the interests of non-citizens, such as foreign exporters whose livelihoods depend on access to State A's markets.

However, there are fears that the WTO itself has been captured by special interests. Keohane and Nye have noted that the domestic power of protectionist interests in the developed world shrunk with each round of GATT talks,

---

90 See, for example, Joseph et al., above n 65, 22–3.
91 Dunoff, above n 3, 758.
92 Raustiala, above n 8, 854–5, 864–7.
93 Narlikar, above n 16, 5; Esty, above n 8, 11.
94 Narlikar, above n 16, 5; Raustiala, above n 8, 864.
95 Raustiala, above n 8, 873–4.

with a corresponding increase in the influence and power of their exporter opponents.[96] It is arguable that the WTO now serves to reinforce the power of multinational corporations, who are the major engines and direct beneficiaries of world trade.[97] It does not enhance participatory rights if the WTO is effectively promoting the interests of the already powerful.[98]

The WTO does not defer to national regimes in the way that international human rights institutions do, by use of such doctrines as exhaustion of domestic remedies or the margin of appreciation. Furthermore, WTO norms are less flexible than most human rights norms. Most human rights norms can be limited in proportionate or reasonable circumstances to achieve a number of broad objectives, including protection of 'the rights of others'. In contrast, WTO exceptions, such as those listed in Article XX of the GATT, seem to cover a narrower range of objectives, though the scope of Article XX(a), allowing trade restrictions on the basis of 'public morals', remains largely unexplored.[99] The Panels and the Appellate Body have been stricter in interpreting and applying limitations to WTO norms than have human rights bodies in interpreting and applying limitations to human rights norms. An exception must overcome two hurdles before it will be acceptable under WTO law: it must satisfy a strict test of 'necessity' in achieving the desired objective,[100] and it must satisfy a second strict test imposed under the chapeau of Article XX: the measure must not constitute 'arbitrary' or 'unjustifiable' discrimination. The single hurdle human rights test of 'proportionality' is a less onerous hurdle for the application of exceptions or qualifications than the double-barrelled test applied by the DSBs.[101]

---

96 Keohane and Nye, above n 2, 6.

97 Atik, above n 37, 459; Esty, above n 8, 11. It is true that the interests of multinational corporations and those of consumers can coincide. For example, the entry of such corporations into a market can give consumers access to cheaper goods. However, their interests are not identical. For example, the two sets of interests diverge over measures designed to ensure product quality, and arguably over intellectual property laws (as the latter restrict competition and drive prices up).

98 See also Pauwelyn, above n 38, 331

99 In *United States – Measures Affecting the Cross Border Supply of Betting and Gambling Services*, WTO Doc WT/DS285/AB/R (7 April 2005) [296]–[299] (Report of the Appellate Body), the Appellate Body upheld the Panel's definition of public morals as 'standards of right and wrong conduct maintained by or on behalf of a community or nation'.

100 The 'necessity' test does not apply to all exceptions in Article XX but it does apply to those most relevant to human rights, Article XX(a) (public morals) and XX(b) (protection of human, animal or plant life or health).

101 See United Nations High Commissioner for Human Rights, *Human Rights and World Trade Agreements: Using General Exception Clauses to Protect Human Rights* (Office of the High Commissioner for Human Rights, New York and Geneva,

The process of negotiating WTO treaties and human rights treaties is not comparable. WTO negotiations are conducted in secret. They are characterised by trade-offs of interests: one WTO member might for example trade off its domestic sugar interests in order to gain advantages for its domestic cotton interests. WTO members do not wish the 'selling out' of a domestic industry to be visible.[102] In contrast, human rights treaties are negotiated in open meetings, and often with NGO participation.[103] There is no comparable 'give and take': a State does not for example trade children's rights for the rights of political prisoners. Finally, less is at stake when negotiating a human rights treaty. A State can vote to adopt a treaty yet never ratify it, or, in most cases, may ratify it with reservations. In the WTO, negotiations yield 'all or nothing' propositions. States negotiate treaties and then must sign up to the 'single undertaking', that is the package deal, without reservation.[104]

Almost all WTO complaints concern systemic issues in a State's economy, so many people's interests might be involved in the resolution of those complaints. This circumstance heightens the need for public participation in the dispute resolution process. In contrast, some human rights complaints concern scenarios in which no one beyond the protagonists is concerned.

Finally, the WTO is a stronger regime than most international human rights regimes in terms of enforcement. Breach of WTO obligations can expose a State to economic countermeasures, effectively trade sanctions, from an aggrieved State. In contrast, if a State is found in violation of a UN human rights treaty and fails to take remedial action, it will rarely suffer consequences beyond condemnation and shame, if that. Such consequences simply do not compare to the effects of 'punishment' within the WTO system.

It must be noted that the decisions of regional human rights courts are binding. Europe, through the mechanisms developed under the European Convention on Human Rights, has easily the most developed regional system. Execution of judgments is supervised by the Committee of Ministers within the Council of Europe, which can exert heavy political pressure in the case of non-compliance. In general, the Committee has been able to secure execution

---

2005) 15, http://www.fao.org/righttofood/kc/downloads/vl/docs/AH311.pdf at 18 October 2007.

102 See Sutherland Report, above n 13, 45; Keohane and Nye, above n 2, 19.

103 See Robert McCorquodale, 'An Inclusive International Legal System' (2004) 17 *Leiden Journal of International Law* 477, 493–4.

104 Narlikar, above n 16, 31–2. There are two plurilateral deals, which only bind States that voluntarily ratify them, concerning civil aircraft and government procurement; two further deals have now expired. There are also some flexibilities in the main WTO deals, such as the ability of States to choose which services they will liberalise under the General Agreement on Trade in Services ('GATS'). Reservations are explicitly allowed to a few WTO treaties, but this author is unaware of any.

of judgments through 'constructive and cooperative dialogue' with States.[105] In this regard, one may note that the European human rights system stands alongside a very strong regional free trade system, the EU, which also incorporates some coordination and harmonisation on economic and social rights.[106] Thus, human rights agendas have not been marginalised during the process of European economic integration. By comparison, the WTO is not counterbalanced by a comparably strong global human rights body, or indeed any global social justice body. The coordinated progress of free trade and human rights commitments in Europe contrasts starkly with the uncoordinated progress at the global level.[107]

Democratic deficit is a criticism that can probably be levelled at all international bodies, as there is little popular input into their processes compared to national political processes. However, democratic deficit in the context of the WTO deservedly generates a greater level of concern than democratic deficit in many other contexts, due to a number of characteristics of that system that are highlighted in the above comparison between the WTO and international human rights regimes.

4. POSSIBLE REFORM OF THE WTO'S MANDATE: WHERE SHOULD THE LINE BE DRAWN?

This writer accepts that an international trade regime with a supervisory organisation such as the WTO is generally a good idea. It helps, for example, to save the traders from State B from the destructive acts of State A, and to save State A from populist nationalist protectionism, which is self-defeating and hurts its economy. Despite the participation advantages of the big economic powers, at least the WTO imposes some sort of rule of law on those States. It also provides a forum for the peaceful resolution of trade disputes, a benefit for global peace and security.[108]

---

105 See Council of Europe, 'Human Rights and Legal Affairs: Frequently Asked Questions', http://www.coe.int/t/e/human_rights/execution/01_Introduction/02_FAQ.asp (14 August 2008).

106 In respect of the latter, see Bob Hepple, *Labour Laws and Global Trade* (Hart, Oxford, 2005), Ch 8–9. See also Dillon, above n 52, 123 (FN140).

107 See, for example, World Commission on the Social Dimension of Globalisation, *A Fair Globalization: Promoting Opportunities for All* (ILO, Geneva, 2004).

108 Joel R Paul, 'Do International Trade Institutions Contribute to Economic Growth and Development?' (2003) 44 *Virginia Journal of International Law* 285, 338–9.

However, that does not mean that the WTO's mandate to override national decision-making power is correctly drawn. In light of the problems regarding its input legitimacy, should its power or output be restricted? This section raises some suggestions regarding possible redrawing of the scope of the substantive power of the WTO. These suggestions are raised for discussion, rather than as recommendations.

A. Deferential Doctrines

Should the WTO dispute settlement bodies make greater use of deferential doctrines like the margin of appreciation? For example, Winickoff et al. argue that States should be given significant leeway under the SPS agreement, perhaps akin to a margin of appreciation, when they are applying standards in areas where there is low certainty regarding potential risks, and low consensus on those risks (such as in the case of GMOs).[109] The interpretation of limitations could also be loosened: for example the interpretation of 'necessity' in Article XX could converge more with the interpretation of 'reasonable' in the context of human rights limitations. Only the most unreasonable trade restrictions would be clearly disallowed, whereas 'borderline' restrictions would generally be acceptable. More decision-making power would be restored to national levels. Of course, more trade restrictions would inevitably be allowed under such a system.

B. Return to the Scope of the GATT

Should the WTO return to its humbler GATT roots, and only target discriminatory protectionism, rather than branching out into the realm of minimum standards as in the TRIPS and SPS agreements?[110] Regarding TRIPS, the justification for its inclusion is that it promotes research and development and helps to promote technology transfer. Nevertheless, it is difficult to justify the extraordinary protections offered to one set of individual (often corporate) rights, intellectual property rights, compared to other rights, such as human rights, in the current international system.[111] TRIPS has of course been

---

[109] David Winickoff et al., 'Adjudicating the GM Food Wars: Science, Risk, and Democracy in World Trade Law' (2005) 81 *Yale Journal of International Law* 81, 86, 107–8.

[110] See Driesen, above n 11, 327–9, Esty, above n 8, 17. See also Deborah Z Cass, *The Constitutionalization of the World Trade Organization* (Oxford University Press, New York, 2005) 213–16; Dillon, above n 52, 115; Howse, above n 52, 112.

[111] See, for example, Paul, above n 108, 329. See also Tom G Palmer, 'Are Patents and Copyrights Morally Justified? The Philosophy of Property Rights and Ideal

severely criticised for its alleged undermining of several human rights, through for example its impact on the price of essential drugs, undermining the right to an adequate standard of healthcare. TRIPS is an odd inclusion in the WTO agreements, given that its implementation mandates the restriction of trade rather than trade liberalisation.[112]

The SPS agreement prohibits discriminatory application of sanitary and phytosanitary standards in its preamble, and in Articles 2(3) and 5(5). It also requires States to adhere to certain minimum procedural standards (as opposed to the minimum substantive standards in TRIPS) under Articles 3(3), 5(1) and 5(2) of the SPS in determining whether a potential risk justifies the application of a sanitary or phytosanitary standard.[113] The *Agreement on Technical Barriers to Trade* ('TBT') also imposes minimum procedural standards.[114] These Agreements therefore demand that sanitary, phytosanitary, and technical standards be 'rational' rather than merely non-discriminatory. 'Rationality' in the context of the SPS is equated with 'scientific justification'. 'Using science to enforce harmonization is a more ambitious goal than using it to combat protectionism', and it raises greater problems 'in terms of cultural autonomy and democratic legitimacy'.[115] Scientific assessments are not value-free or culturally uniform.[116] Therefore, perhaps States should enjoy 'regulatory self-determination' and be able to demand high precautionary standards, so long as they are applied in a non-discriminatory fashion.[117]

Ultimately, as Robert Hudec noted, removal of 'minimum standards' such as those in the SPS (or the TBT) and a retreat to non-discrimination involves a value judgement that the danger of excessive protectionism is not as bad as the danger of inadequate or inappropriate minimum standards in the relevant areas.[118] From the point of view of economic efficiency, the former value

Objects' (1990) 13 *Harvard Journal of Law and Public Policy* 911, 914; Peter Drahos, 'The Rights to Food and Health and Intellectual Property in the Era of "Biogopolies" in S Bottomley and D Kinley (eds) *Commercial Law and Human Rights* (Ashgate, Dartmouth, Aldershot) 215, 227.

112 See generally, Jagdish Bhagwati, 'Symposium: The Boundaries of the WTO – Afterward: The Question of Linkage' (2002) 96 *American Journal of International Law* 126, 128.

113 See, for example, Driesen, above n 11, 293–4.

114 *Marrakesh Agreement Establishing the World Trade Organization*, opened for signature 15 April 1994, 1867 UNTS 3 (entered into force 1 January 1995), annex 1A (*Agreement on Technical Barriers to Trade*) Article 2.2.

115 Winickoff et al., above n 109, 91, 92.

116 Winickoff et al. trace the differing social science and regulatory experiences of the EC and the US in the context of 'testing' GMOs: Ibid 93–6.

117 Ibid, 108.

118 Robert Hudec, '"Circumventing" Democracy: the Political Morality of Trade Negotiations' (1993) 25 *NYU Journal of International Law and Politics* 311, 321.

outweighs the latter. However, from the point of view of non-trade lobbies and possibly consumers, that equation is probably reversed.

It must be noted, however, that the dividing line between discriminatory protectionist provisions and non-discriminatory provisions is often unclear.[119] It is difficult to distinguish between protectionism and 'sanctionable science with trade-distorting effects'.[120] As unusually high standards will require foreign producers to set up separate production lines to continue exports to the relevant State, discrimination in effect (indirect discrimination) might almost always arise.[121] In the *Shrimp* disputes, the impugned US trade measure was a ban on shrimp harvested without a turtle excluder device ('TED'). The measure was aimed at both US and foreign fishing fleets. Nevertheless, the measure was found to be discriminatory, contrary to the chapeau of Article XX of GATT, as the regulation did not take into account the 'different conditions' that might arise in foreign States, so the effect of the measure was discriminatory.[122] Nothing in the decision however identifies why it was difficult for other States to install TEDs.[123] Driesen persuasively argues that the decision indicates that the discrimination was somehow entailed in the US's failure to discriminate *in favour of* the foreign fleets by exempting them from the TED requirement.[124] In that case, any neutral measure that somehow obstructs international trade, even if applied equally to domestic trade, might be construed as discriminatory.[125]

---

119 See discussion in Driesen, above n 11, 330–7.

120 Winickoff et al., above n 109, 109.

121 Hudec, above n 118, 318.

122 *Shrimp Turtle* Case [164].

123 Driesen, above n 11, 333.

124 Driesen concedes that the Appellate Body's separate argument regarding the differential treatment of some trading partners as opposed to others, in that the US had negotiated turtle protection with some partners and not others, was a plausible basis for finding discrimination: Ibid.

125 More recently, the Appellate body appeared to significantly narrow the test of discrimination in *Dominican Republic – Measures Affecting the Importation and Internal Sale of Cigarettes*, WTO Doc WT/DS302/AB/R (25 April 2005) [96] (Report of the Appellate Body): '[T]he existence of a detrimental effect on a given imported product resulting from a measure does not necessarily imply that this measure accords less favourable treatment to imports *if the detrimental effect is explained by factors or circumstances unrelated to the foreign origin of the product* . . .' (emphasis added)

This test arguably goes so far as to apply only to *de jure* rather than *de facto* discrimination. And yet it is well understood in many instances that *de facto* discrimination, such as indirect discrimination arising from facially neutral rules, should also be prohibited. Bartels has suggested that the *Dominican Republic* test applies if a measure always, or almost always, detrimentally affects foreign goods, rather than only sometimes affects them. See Lorand Bartels, 'Trade and Human Rights' in D Bethlehem et al. (eds) *Oxford Handbook of International Trade* (Oxford University Press, Oxford, 2008, forthcoming) 17.

C. The WTO and 'Inward Measures'

Perhaps greater deference should be given when the WTO deals with so-called 'inward measures', those designed to protect national populations, compared to outward measures, those aimed at protecting other people or somehow changing behaviour overseas. The latter will often concern the production processes in another state. For example, the trade restrictions in *EC – Hormone* were aimed at keeping hormone-treated beef out of Europe, rather than convincing overseas producers not to use hormones. Less deference would arise in cases like the *Tuna Dolphin* disputes,[126] GATT cases where the US attempted to influence fishing practices abroad by restricting the import of tuna that had not been caught in a 'dolphin-friendly' manner: the ban was aimed at saving dolphins. States should have more discretion regarding the imposition of inward measures, as they have considerable international obligations to protect their own people and comparatively fewer extraterritorial obligations to people in other States. For example, international human rights law demands that States guarantee the human rights of their own people. States do have some extraterritorial obligations not to harm the human rights of people in other States. That said, States do not have clear obligations to coerce other States into protecting the human rights of their people (as opposed to obligations to cooperate with other States to promote human rights). Outward measures are more likely to constitute illegitimate interferences into the sovereign domains of other States, so there is more justification for international supervision in that regard.[127]

On the other hand, it might on occasion be difficult to distinguish between inward and outward measures: the purpose of a law is not always clear. For example, the *Tuna Dolphin* ban could be reconceptualised as an inward measure, designed to protect the sensitivities of US consumers, who did not wish to be complicit via their purchases in the slaughter of dolphins. It was perhaps arguable that the measure protected the 'public morals' of US consumers. Furthermore, an 'inward' purpose does not preclude an 'outward'

---

[126] *United States – Restrictions on Imports of Tuna*, GATT Doc DS21/R (3 September 1991) (Report of the Panel). *Tuna Dolphin* was a case brought by Mexico and others against the US under Articles XI, XIII and III GATT. The panel report was circulated in 1991, but never adopted. Consequently, it does not have the status of a legal interpretation of GATT law: http://www.wto.org/english/tratop_e/envir_e/edis04_e.htm at 24 July 2008.

[127] UNHCHR, above n 101, 16–17. One may note that it does appear acceptable for a State to 'regulate' external matters under Article XX GATT according to *United States – Import Prohibition of Certain Shrimp and Shrimp Products*, WTO Doc WT/DS58/AB/RW, AB-2001-4 (21 November 2001) [107], [137] – [138] (Report of the Appellate Body). See also Howse, above n 52, 111.

effect.[128] For example, the EU bans on the import of GMOs are probably designed to safeguard the health of European consumers, and to comply with the general wishes of European consumers. However, the effect probably has been to put farmers in other States off using GMOs, for fear of jeopardising their European markets.[129]

D. Respecting Consumer Choice

Given that free trade is partly designed to enhance consumer choice, perhaps consumer choices should be respected, at least with regard to their perceptions of their own welfare.[130] For example, if Europeans do not want hormone-treated meat to be imported into Europe, why force it on them? Why insist that consumer choice be 'rational', or, as required under the SPS, based on science?[131] As consumers are effectively the people of a State in a commercial guise, the respecting of consumer choices arguably equates with respecting the democratic choices of a State. Indeed, consumer choice has been relevant in some aspects under WTO law. In determining whether products made from white asbestos and the same products made without asbestos were 'like products' for the purposes of Article III of GATT, the Appellate Body in *EC – Asbestos* took consumer tastes, such as a general aversion to asbestos, into account in deciding that the products were not like.[132]

Problematically, such a proposal assumes that consumer choice can actually be established. Furthermore, consumer choice might be manipulated for protectionist ends. For example, regarding the GMO issue, it has been argued that European consumers are being brainwashed by a barrage of GMO-propaganda from protectionist farmers, who cannot compete in the GM arena, in an unholy alliance with loud politically influential NGOs.[133]

---

128 See, for example, Driesen, above n 11, 311.

129 See, for example, Lawrence A Kogan, 'Trade protectionism: Ducking the truth about Europe's GMO policy', *International Herald Tribune* (New York), 27 November 2004.

130 Such a restriction would not permit consumers to insist on choices that result in outward measures, such as consumer preferences against goods made by children. Of course, similar arguments to those canvassed directly above would arise regarding potential 'moral injuries' to consumers.

131 See also Driesen, above n 11, 319.

132 *European Communities – Measures Affecting Asbestos and Asbestos-Containing Products*, WTO Doc WT/DS135/AB/R (00-1157) AB-2000-11 (5 April 2001) [130], [139] (Report of the Appellate Body). As the products were not 'like', the EU was permitted to treat them differently without breaching WTO non-discrimination provisions.

133 See Kogan, above n 129.

The forced import of goods under WTO rules does not force a consumer to actually consume those goods. The GMO example, however, demonstrates that consumer choice is not necessarily easy to exercise. Concerns have been raised, regarding GMOs, of uncontrolled cross-contamination, meaning that it might become impossible to guarantee that a certain type of food is in fact GM-free. Unsuspecting consumers may not be aware of GMOs in meals that are not home-cooked, or in meals that their children consume outside the home.

In this regard, it is submitted that labelling should be allowed to ensure that consumers have genuine freedom of choice regarding the characteristics of the goods they are consuming. Indeed, labels regarding production processes such as child labour ('outward' issues) should also be allowed. Ultimately, such labelling would ensure the provision of relevant information to consumers (in accordance with the right to freedom of information guaranteed in, for example, Article 19 ICCPR), and would allow consumers to make their choices accordingly. Full disclosure would allow market forces to actually 'decide' if it is acceptable for goods to have certain characteristics (for example, to contain GM ingredients) or be manufactured by an undesirable process (which, for example, hurts labourers or the environment). That said, the compatibility of labelling systems with WTO law, thus far untested within the DSS, cannot be presumed.[134] Furthermore, labelling requirements should reasonably reflect consumer concerns: spurious labelling requirements could impose an intolerable burden on exporters, particularly from developing States which might lack certain technical capacities.

E. Deferring to Expert Opinion

Perhaps WTO bodies should regularly defer to other experts when an issue concerns serious non-trade issues, such as the Office of the High Commissioner for Human Rights if human rights issues should arise, or the International Labor Organization ('ILO') in respect of labour issues.[135] The extent of its mandate could be maintained, but other international expert bodies could be integrated into WTO processes regarding issues that clearly straddle the trade and non-trade divide. In extreme cases, the resolution of

---

[134] In *EC – Biotech*, the Panel alluded to the possibility that EC regulations on the labelling of GMOs breached the SPS agreement at [7.392]. See, for example, Carlos Lopez-Hurtado, 'Social Labelling and the WTO' (2002) 5 *Journal of International Economic Law* 719; Nick Covelli and Viktor Hohots, 'The Health Regulation of Biotech Foods under the WTO Agreements' (2003) 6 *Journal of International Economic Law* 773.

[135] See Esty, above n 8, 17–18.

relevant disputes could effectively be ceded to that other body. For example, persistent and egregious labour rights abuses in Burma have resulted in the exceptional authorisation of trade (and other) sanctions by the ILO under article 33 of the *ILO Constitution* in 2000.[136] The US has accordingly imposed sanctions on Burma in 2003. So far, the US has not been criticised by or within the WTO for these measures. The WTO has stayed 'out of the way', perhaps an appropriate example of 'forbearance' regarding an issue that is a serious human rights issue and only incidentally a trade issue.[137]

The above suggestions for WTO reform are raised to prompt debate. All suggestions have some merit, but all are potentially problematic. A combination of some of the above suggestions may be the best way forward.

An alternative or complementary strategy is to reform the WTO's internal processes. Enormous challenges, however, are entailed in reforming internal processes to render them more inclusive. For example, richer States will always have greater economic power than poorer States and will always be tempted to abuse their superior bargaining positions (though the identity of richer States may change). Furthermore, it may be impossible to accommodate all of the various agendas of trade and non-trade NGOs, not to mention the agendas of the various States, within the WTO negotiating framework.[138] The stalling of the Doha round indicates that the reformed negotiation processes, such as the more open Green Room and the increased clout of certain developing States, have reduced the possibility of consensus agreement.

Nevertheless, given that the stakeholders in the WTO process extend far beyond the traditional GATT/WTO trade negotiators, continued exclusion of non-trade interests from, and continued negotiation disadvantage for poorer States within, WTO internal processes, are not justifiable. It may also be impossible to proceed with WTO negotiations without a significantly improved democratic pedigree.[139] An increase in input legitimacy is needed in order to justify the WTO's output legitimacy. Paradoxically, it may be inevitable that more inclusive 'input' will reduce the strength of the WTO's output.[140] The stakes of the WTO's output, in terms for example of a single

[136] Constitution of the International Labour Organization (1919).

[137] See Rob Howse et al., 'The World Trade Organization and Labour Rights: Man Bites Dog' in V A Leary and D Warner (eds) *Social Issues, Globalisation and International Institutions* (Martinus Nijhoff, Leiden, 2006) 173–4, 189, 194–8, 223 and 229–31. See also Dunoff, above n 3, 757ff.

[138] UNHCHR, above n 19 [45]; Sutherland Report, above n 13, 44–5; Keohane and Nye, above n 2, 8; Howse, above n 52, 112.

[139] Howse makes some comment on the potential veto power of 'outsiders' generated by their ability to expose 'fault lines' in proposed deals, which must become public at some stage prior to ratification: Howse, above n 52, 116.

[140] See Pauwelyn, above n 38, 337–46.

undertaking and strong legal enforcement of obligations, may have to be lowered, allowing, for example, for more plurilateral agreements or 'exit options' for States.[141] An easing of the 'legal' side of the WTO to accommodate its political side may be necessary.[142] This may sound like a weak option, especially given that the strong judicialisation of trade law has often been regarded as the jewel in the WTO's crown. On the other hand, a better democratic pedigree is likely to make the eventual agreements more legitimate and effective.[143]

A final option is to introduce greater balance into the system of global governance, to offset the effect of the WTO's output.[144] That is, the output of international institutions in non-trade areas, such as human rights, labour, development, poverty alleviation, and the environment could be significantly strengthened in terms of enforcement. This strategy involves 'equalising up' rather than bringing the WTO 'back to the pack'. It would 'even out' the systemic advantages conferred within the trade regime to developed States and trade interests, as alternative interests would be strengthened within those other forums. For example, developing States as well as certain non-trade interests would benefit hugely from the provision of enforcement mechanisms, which are currently absent, for the Millennium Development Goals. At the moment, such a strategy is perhaps utopian, given the lack of political will to strengthen these other areas of global governance. Such balance, however, could evolve over time, as has for example occurred within the free trade area of Europe.

5. CONCLUDING REMARKS

Democratic deficit probably characterises most international organisations, including the WTO. However, the unusual power of the WTO, as well as particular characteristics of its internal processes (such as the high level of secrecy within negotiations, and the notion of a single compulsory undertaking), generate more acute anxieties about its democratic deficit.

Current WTO output probably exceeds its current input legitimacy, which justifies a dilution of its powers. Indeed, increased input would likely lead to a dilution of WTO outputs. Such dilution could take the form of decreased

---

141 Ibid 340, 343.

142 See also Joost Pauwelyn, 'The Transformation of World Trade' (2005–2006) 104 *Michigan Law Review* 1.

143 See also Keohane and Nye, above n 2, 27; Raustiala, above n 8, 862. See also Cass, above n 110, 221–3.

144 See generally Dillon, above n 52, Part V.

legalisation, a retreat from the imposition of minimum standards, or greater deference to national decision-making or national consumer preferences. Deceleration in the global free trade project will be viewed by many as an unfortunate compromise, a 'second-best' option. That said, it may be the only option that is currently politically feasible. An alternative strategy would be to boost the strength of non-economic areas of international governance in order to provide for a greater balance of interests and agendas at the international level. Such an option does not seem politically achievable in the short term, but should be a long-term goal of the international community.

13. Energy security, economic development and climate change: carbon markets and the WTO

Graciela Chichilnisky

1. INTRODUCTION

At a time when China and India are flexing their geopolitical muscles and the developing countries rapidly increase energy use, the world faces the environmental consequences of a long and successful period of Western industrialization. Two centuries of industrialization based on fossil fuels emitted large amounts of carbon dioxide into the atmosphere and created a serious risk of climate change. For many the results are unfolding in front of our eyes. Entire towns in Alaska are sinking in the melting permafrost and warming seas[1] and Florida is the next most vulnerable US site.[2] It is widely accepted that catastrophic change could happen, and the possibility by itself calls for action. Yet the thirst for fossil fuels continues unabated across the world. China is building a new coal plant every two weeks, and the US consumer uses more energy than ever, facing the highest oil prices since the OPEC embargoes in the 1970s and 1980s.[3] An understandable desire for energy independence creates a powerful incentive to use abundant coal resources in China as well as in the US, so as to meet the rapidly growing need for energy.[4]

---

1 W Yardley, 'Engulfed by Climate Change, Town Seeks Lifeline' *New York Times*, 27 May 2007, 1. The permanently frozen subsoil, known as permafrost, upon which the town of Newtok and many other Native Alaskan villages rest is melting, yielding to warming air temperatures and a warming ocean. Erosion has already made Newtok an island, the village is now below sea level and sinking, and studies say that the entire town will be washed away in a decade. The US Army Corps of Engineers has estimated that to move Newtok could cost at least $130 million, which comes to almost $413,000 for each of its 315 residents.

2 See generally, OECD, 'Ranking of the World's Cities most exposed to Coastal Flooding Today and in the Future', http://www.oecd.org/dataoecd/16/10/39721444.pdf (23 October 2008).

3 G Chichilnisky and G Heal, *Oil and the International Economy* (Clarendon Press, Oxford, 1989).

4 P Eisenberger and G Chichilnisky, *Reducing the Risk of Climate Change*

Developing nations play a key role in the global warming problem: they are expected to be the largest emitters in 20 to 30 years' time, when they complete their process of industrialization. While their emissions represent less than 40 per cent of total emissions currently, developing nations will suffer the worst risks from climate change – floods, desertification, drops in agricultural production, lack of water and sea level rise – which could sink the Maldives Islands and Bangladesh beneath the seas. Yet there is no concerted strategy on the part of the G77 or any other regional bodies from Latin America, Asia or Africa, to address this issue in the context of the climate negotiations. Nor is there any consideration of global warming strategies for developing nations within the framework of the WTO. Indeed, the WTO has not considered global environmental markets (such as the carbon market) as part of its portfolio. This chapter argues that environmental markets are among the most important markets of the twenty-first century, including markets for water and biodiversity, and that they ought to become a key part of the WTO negotiations and statutes.

The importance of environmental markets is apparent in the carbon market of the Kyoto Protocol that I helped to create and which became international law in 2005. This market trades the right to emit carbon dioxide from the burning of fossil fuels. In reality fossil fuels tie together into a Gordian knot three key global issues: energy security, economic development and climate change.[5] In the fossil fuel age developing nations face a cruel choice: economic development and energy independence clash against a stable climate. We cannot have them all. The attendant geopolitical conflicts take several forms. Fossils generate about 87 per cent of energy used in the world today. Since they are unevenly distributed on the earth's crust, they have led to wars and conflicts and violations of human rights, prompting understandable calls for energy security and independence.

At the same time economic development still depends on the use of energy, and in today's economy, this means fossil fuels. In the longer term, the only way out is to disentangle the use of energy from carbon emissions, making available clean, abundant renewable energy sources. But this is not feasible in the short term because of the sheer scale of the fossil infrastructure that must be replaced: about $40 trillion today, and with current trends about $400 trillion by the end of the century.[6]

---

while Producing Renewable Energy (Columbia University, New York, 2007) ref 4. The US coal industry presented recently an ambitious plan to secure enormous subsidies for coal production in the name of energy independence.

5 G Chichilnisky, *Beyond the Global Divide* (2010, forthcoming).

6 Data from the International Energy Agency, IEA.

In June 2009, the UN General Assembly placed global warming within the scope of the UN Security Council, and it is now considered a security and human rights issue. Energy security and independence raise issues regarding the right to self-determination, and the rights of peoples to livelihoods and adequate standards of living. Global warming threatens numerous rights, such as the rights to food, water, housing, and adequate standards of health and the right to life.

There is no connection at present between the new global carbon market and the WTO. The carbon market is not part of the WTO portfolio, even though it will probably be the most important world market this century. The WTO should be involved in the global climate negotiations as the very existence of the carbon market depends on the Kyoto Protocol whose provisions end at present in 2012. At the end of the chapter we examine the possible role of the WTO in helping bridge the gap between the rich and the developing nations through international trade in rights to emit, and the dynamics of how the carbon market can help implement a transition from a fossil economy into a renewable energy economy.

2. SHORT-TERM GOALS AND LONG-RUN OBJECTIVES

A transition away from fossils sources seems inevitable in the long run, because they are limited in supply. Alternative sources of energy are a necessary condition for sustainable development in the long run, and the rapidly growing world demand for energy[7] will require a variety of alternative sources. Supplies are not the problem. Solar, on its own, can easily meet a tenfold increase using only 1 per cent of the energy that hits the planet's surface, and within known technologies.[8] In the long run, the solution is transition to renewable sources of energy.

The long run solution, however, is not appropriate for the short run. A transition to alternative energy sources is expected to take a long time, since 87 per cent of the energy used in the planet today is obtained from fossil fuels such as oil and coal. Change will take time and require a massive new and expensive infrastructure. Yet as long as we continue to use fossil fuels and emit carbon we increase the concentration of greenhouse gases, and the risk of catastrophic climate change.[9] Stabilizing the level of emissions is certainly helpful, but

---

[7] World demand for energy is projected to be, by the end of this century, five to ten times larger than today's energy use (IEA data).

[8] IEA data.

[9] Scientists agree that we need to consider the possibility of a 'tipping point', namely a level of heating that triggers catastrophic climate change, which is typical of

stabilizing at the current level of 24 billion tons of carbon dioxide will continue to build up carbon dioxide in the atmosphere and increase risk. For this reason the IPCC asserts that we need to decrease emissions of carbon dioxide by about 60 to 80 per cent within the next fifteen or twenty years.[10] Clearly long-run policies do not suffice to deal with the immediate problem we face. Immediate action is required to manage the risk of climate change.

The short-run problem is acute. Making the transition away from fossil fuels in a short period of time could increase the risk of social disruption, which could be catastrophic in its own right, since most human life is dependent on energy. Both rich and poor nations could be seriously affected by a drastic decrease in the use of fossil fuels. Rapidly growing nations such as China and India are heavily dependent on coal, and so are the US and Russia. It does not seem feasible to drastically decrease the use of fossil fuels in the short term, which is why there is an increasing call to capture the carbon emitted by fossil fuels plants and store it safely, at least as part of a short-run solution.

Managing risks in the short and in the long run – are quite different problems and require different solutions. For the long run a transition is needed to a non-fossil fuel economy, one that can accommodate the rapidly growing needs of 80 per cent of the world's population, who are starting their path to industrialization and a tenfold increase in energy use within this century. For the short run, we need instead a continuation of fossil fuel energy use and a simultaneous *decrease* in the carbon content of the planet's atmosphere. This is a major challenge.

Short-term goals must be compatible with long-term objectives, to avoid the trap of defeating long-run aims by focusing solely on short-run targets.

The technology strategy should accommodate both the short- and long-term goals, and the transition of the short term into the long term. This is a tall order because such a technology must simultaneously facilitate the transition to alternative sources providing for massive increases in supplies for the long run, while in the short run it allows the continued use of fossil fuels *and* decreases the carbon content in the planet's atmosphere.

---

physical systems that have complex feedback effects. The earth's climate is believed to be one of them. In general, one views the risks as having 'heavy tails' so that the possibility of rare events turns out to be much larger than expected.

10 As we reach 500 carbon parts per million, the average global temperature is expected to increase by 3° C, which means three times this amount in the polar caps triggering sea-level rise.

3. A BRIEF WORD ON PROPERTY RIGHTS

Critics of globalization suggest that property rights are somehow antithetical to human rights, Article 17 of the Universal Declaration of Human Rights states that '(1) everyone has the right to own property alone as well as in association with others; (2) no-one shall be arbitrarily deprived of his property'. In addition, there are many instances where efficient allocation of property rights is a necessary precondition to, although not a guarantor of, the effective attainment of human rights. For example, while it might appear to be morally and politically desirable to speak of the common heritage of mankind in relation to such resources as air and sea, it has long been understood that communal ownership or at least open access, will tend to lead to over-exploitation and a disincentive to efficient use.

The latter argument was encapsulated in a paper by Harold Demsetz in relation to property rights,[11] which in turn was a central element in Garrett Hardin's seminal paper on the 'tragedy of the commons'.[12] Demsetz noted that where land is communally owned, a person seeking to maximize the value of their communal rights would tend to over-hunt and over-work the land because some of the costs of doing so are borne by others. Hardin used the example of an open pasture available to a large number of cattle herders. Because the costs of over-grazing of the open access land are borne by all, the cost for each herder is far outweighed by the individual benefit they obtain by adding an extra cow to their personal herd. If they simply pursue their own personal net benefit they are each likely to continue to increase the size of the herd, thus leading to serious over-grazing of the land.

Conversely, where a single person owns the land, that person will seek to maximize its present value by selecting among alternative future streams of benefits and costs, that which maximizes present value. Sustainable uses will generally be more valuable in terms of protecting and enhancing the property's value. Property rights thus provide incentives for the use of efficient resource allocation.

Similarly, where aspects of the environment such as air and water are available for unconstrained use by all, there is a greater incentive for individuals to engage in activities harmful to the environment because once again the costs of that harm do not fall solely or even predominantly on them. Pollution by manufacturers is an obvious example.

Economists describe the harm to those not involved in these transactions as a *negative externality*. Economic theory proposes that absent any serious

---

[11] Harold Demsetz, 'Toward a Theory of Property Rights' (1967) 57 *American Economic Review* 347.

[12] Garrett Hardin, 'The Tragedy of the Commons' (1968) 162 *Science* 1244.

market failure, the market is the best means by which to allocate scarce resources. Markets operate by using a price mechanism as the key means to achieve an equilibrium between supply and demand of various activities in the face of scarcity. The more consumers want something, the more they will be prepared to pay. The higher this demand, the more that suppliers will enter the market to meet that demand. Yet if the parties to a transaction are not required to cover the cost of such negative externalities, they will not build it into the price and the market mechanism inappropriately under-prices the activity and hence allows for an incentive towards such harmful behaviour.

The negative externality is an example of market failure. In the face of any form of market failure, it is appropriate for government to intervene and redress or prevent the problem. One regulatory response in relation to the above examples is for the government to impose a tax on the transaction at a level that builds in enough additional cost to counter the negative costs that the transaction will occasion. An alternative regulatory approach is to prohibit certain forms of negative externalities or make the parties liable to third parties for the damage. A third alternative noted above is to provide for property rights in a broader range of things so that there is a disincentive for the owner to engage in the harmful activity in the first place. Then one can allow the trading of these rights for added flexibility. This is the carbon market of the Kyoto Protocol. In each case, whether one solution is to be preferred or whether the particular response chosen will achieve its aims will depend on the way it is defined and applied. There is also commonly overlap between the differing regulatory responses and governments might use a combination of each.

Where a property rights solution is adopted or contemplated, this should remind us that property is a social institution supported by a particular State's legal regime. A government allocates property rights as one of a range of means to regulate its society's control over resources, understanding the notion of resources in the broader sense to include land, sea, air, commodities, artistic and commercial works and inventions. Because property is in part a legal construct, where appropriate a regulator is able to create a number of discrete legal property rights that relate to the one physical asset. More fundamentally, property and property law rights can be looked at as a means of regulating the relationships between people as they relate to various things.[13] Nevertheless, the insight from economics is that in many cases, the mere absence of property rights can be expected to lead to undesirable outcomes. Regulators should thus consider how a property rights solution might benefit certain policy goals. This is why the carbon market is so important and why the WTO should help regulate it.

---

13 Felix Cohen, 'Dialogue on Private Property' (1954) 9 *Rutgers Law Review* 357.

4. PROPERTY RIGHTS IN RESOURCES AND THE GLOBAL ENVIRONMENT

In reality, international markets led to global environmental problems such as global warming, and should be part of their resolution. The core of the problem is that in developing nations natural resources such as fossil fuels and forests are owned as common property, while industrial nations own these as private property.[14] This historical difference creates a pattern of north–south trade where developing nations over-extract resources for the export market without real comparative advantage and without true gains from trade.

Resource trade handicaps the economic progress of developing nations.[15] It leads to the over-extraction and under pricing of resources in global markets, and the attendant global over-use of fossil fuels. Distorted market prices undermine energy security in industrial nations, and cause over-consumption of fossils and global warming risks. Economic development requires energy, but since 87 per cent of the world's energy derives from fossil fuels, its use conflicts with the need to avert global warming, creating a cruel choice.

The Kyoto Protocol created a *carbon market* to resolve the dilemma and correct unduly low resource prices – overcoming missing property rights for fossil fuels such as oil, coal and gas, in developing nations by introducing global property rights on the use of the atmosphere of the planet to emit carbon as a by-product of burning fossil fuels. The Kyoto Protocol defined such global property rights on emissions – by providing limits that each OECD nation accepted on their own carbon emissions, making sure that the global total of emissions always remained below the 1995 level. Once property rights are created this means the rights to emit carbon up to a certain limit – the carbon market give nations a flexibility of emitting over or under their limits on a given year, while always remaining within the global total. This way the Protocol ensures that total carbon emissions in the world will be reduced as needed, with the market providing a degree of flexibility, but always remaining within the global total. The carbon market is the main and most distinguishing feature of the 1997 Kyoto Protocol of the United Nations, which became international law in 1995. There is no other international agreement that is based on a global assignation of property rights and a market mechanism to trade these rights, as

14 See, for example, G Chichilnisky, 'North South Trade and the Dynamics of Renewable Resources' (1993) 4 *Change and Economic Dynamics* 219; G Chichilnisky, 'North–South Trade and the Global Environment' (1994) 84 *American Economic Review* 851.

15 G Chichilniskry and G Heal, *The Evolving International Economy* (Cambridge University Press, Cambridge, 1986, 2006).

the Protocol is. As proposed by Chichilnisky,[16] in the Kyoto Protocol's carbon market, rich nations agreed to limits on their rights to use the planet's atmosphere to emit carbon dioxide, and the Protocol allowed these rights to be traded, in order to correct for the lack of private property on fossil fuels in developing nations. Through the Kyoto Protocol the world's emissions, in total, always remain below an acceptable total that reduces emissions below today's levels. Its carbon market uses a market mechanism to penalize over emitting and reward reduced emissions.

5. THE CARBON MARKET AND ITS IMPACT ON THE ABATEMENT OF GLOBAL EMISSIONS

The key economic incentive to make the transition away from fossil fuels to renewable energy is provided by the creation of a so-called 'price signal' for carbon. A 'price signal' is a mechanism that creates costs on emitting carbon and rewards under-emitting. These are imposed by the recent international agreements that resulted in the creation of the carbon market.[17] Simply put, a negative incentive to emit is created by charging an emitter a price to emit each ton of carbon, which is determined by supply and demand in the newly created carbon market.

The carbon market was born from the commitments of governments to reduce total carbon emissions. The commitments emerged from the 1992 UN Framework Convention on Climate Change, its 1997 Kyoto Protocol signed by 160 nations, and from Europe's carbon constraints for electricity generators and industry under the European Union Emissions Trading Scheme ('EU ETS') and from the ratification of the Kyoto Protocol into international law in 2005. At present the Protocol itself is in a period of flux, since the governmental obligations to restrict emissions it provides expire in 2012. New follow-up rules are being negotiated at present. At Bali, Indonesia, in December 2007, the US for the first time indicated its willingness to accept binding limits on its emissions as part of the so-called Bali Roadmap, a process that will culminate in Copenhagen COP XV on December 2009, and has as an objective to extending and modifying as appropriate the Kyoto Protocol's provisions – including its carbon market – after 2012.

---

16 See G Chichilnisky, 'Development and Global Finance: The Case for an International Bank for Environmental Settlements' (Discussion Paper No 10, UNESCO and UNDP, 1996); G Chichilnisky, 'An Axiomatic Approach to Choice under Uncertainty with Catastrophic Risks' (2000) 22 *Energy and Resource Economics* 221.

17 See K Capoor and P Ambrosi, *State and Trends in the Carbon Market, 2007* (World Bank, Washington DC, 2007).

Why is the Protocol's assignation of 'property rights on emissions' to the various OECD nations so crucial in this context? Before any carbon market can exist and operate, there has to be a firm agreement among the nations to ceilings on emissions – or more precisely as in this case to *reduce* total world emissions, and who has the right to emit what. Therefore, a strict numerical limit on overall emissions must be agreed by the traders – otherwise, there is no carbon market. This feature makes the market approach more attractive than taxes when overall limits on emissions are urgently needed, as they are now. Taxes do not ensure caps on emissions of any sort, while market quotas do.[18] The emissions limits and carbon market of the Kyoto Protocol have unique characteristics that distinguish this market mechanism from other markets, which are discussed below. The mechanism of the Kyoto Protocol provides preferential treatment for poor nations, in a manner that increases the market's efficiency, although it is expected that as they reach the same level of development as others, the poor nations will face similar caps on their own emissions. No other market has the characteristic of joining efficiency with preferential treatment for poor nations. This characteristic derives from the fact that the carbon dioxide concentration in the planet's atmosphere is a 'privately produced public good'.[19] This means that carbon emissions are privately produced. But at the level of consumption carbon dioxide distributes evenly and stably throughout the entire planet's atmosphere – so that it has the characteristic of a 'non-rival' public good, instead of a private good. Indeed, the carbon concentration in the planet's atmosphere is a global public good.[20]

What do carbon traders trade? The traders either buy rights to emit above their caps, or sell rights to emit by emitting below their cap. The Kyoto Protocol and its carbon market ensure a total global ceiling on emissions that trade does not change. Therefore this market approach secures a total ceiling for the global emissions of those who participate. At present neither the US

---

18 See G Chichilnisky and G Heal, 'Markets for Tradeable CO_2 Emission Quotas: Principles and Practice' (Working Paper No 153, OECD Paris, 1999).

19 See G Chichilnisky and G Heal (1995), 'Who should Abate: an International Perspective', *Economic Letters*, G Chichilnisky and G Heal, *OECD Markets for Tradable Emission Permits: Theory and Policy*, OECD Economic Division Report No. 52, Paris, France, see www.chichilnisky.com; Chichilnisky, above n. 16; G Chichilnisky and G Heal, *Environmental Markets: Equity and Efficiency* (Columbia University Press, New York, 2000). The unique characteristics of the carbon markets in this regard make them counter-intuitive to what might be considered the 'ordinary' logic of the free market.

20 See G Chichilnisky (1992), 'The Abatement of Carbon Emissions in Industrial and Developing Nations', in G Chichilnisky (2010) (ed.), *The Economics of Climate Change*, Edward Elgar, UK, forthcoming; and G Chichilnisky and G Heal (1995), 'Who should Abate: an International Perspective', *Economic Letters*, cf. www.chichilnisky.com

(which emits about 25 per cent of total global emissions) nor the developing nations (who emit 40 per cent in total) have committed to such 'caps', even though they are both signatories of the 1997 Protocol. As a result, the Kyoto Protocol actually governs less than 40 per cent of global carbon emissions. These considerations exemplify the important role that the WTO can bring to the global climate negotiations, perhaps prompting the nations of the world to trade freely in the carbon market so as to increase the market's reach beyond 40 per cent of emissions and regulate the market for efficient outcomes.

Despite the continued resistance from the US, the carbon market has been quite active trading \$60 billion annually[21] and has already shown great promise in reducing carbon emissions. It is worth noticing that a similar market was established in the US for SO_2 and it is widely known as successful in controlling SO_2 emissions within the US after the Clean Air Act became law, although the SO_2 market differs from the carbon market in that it treats all traders equally. All signals indicate that soon the US may adopt a 'cap and trade approach' for carbon emissions – either participating in the global carbon market of the Kyoto Protocol or by creating a separate carbon market within the US territory, and several proposals have been advanced to date.[22] In June 2009 the US House of Representatives passed an Energy Bill which provides for emission limits and cap and trade legislation. Currently the US still does not abide by the Kyoto Protocol rules that it signed in 1997.

The following provides basic statistics and summarizes how the carbon market operates, who are the buyers and sellers, what they trade, and what has been achieved up to 2008 in terms of reductions in emissions. Two years after becoming international law, in 2007, the carbon market grew in value to an estimated US\$60 billion, three times greater than in the previous year.[23] In 2006 the market was dominated by the sale and resale of European Union Allowances ('EUAs') under the EU ETS. Project-based activities primarily through the Clean Development Mechanism ('CDM') of the Kyoto Protocol, and Joint Implementation (JI) projects also grew sharply to a value of about \$23 billion in transactions up to 2007. The voluntary market for reductions by corporations and individuals is much smaller, but it also grew by an estimated US\$100 million in 2006. Both the Chicago Climate Exchange ('CCX') and the New South Wales Market ('NSW') saw record volumes and values traded in 2006. These statistics indicate that the carbon market is functioning, how it trades, and what has been achieved so far.

---

21 World Bank Report, *Status and Trade of the Carbon Market*, 2006 and 2007.

22 See Capoor and Ambrosi, above n 17.

23 Further statistics on the carbon market can be found in Capoor and Ambrosi, above n 17.

Who are the buyers in the carbon markets? The main compliance buyers in the carbon market are:

1. European private buyers interested in EU ET;
2. Government buyers interested in Kyoto compliance;
3. Japanese companies with voluntary commitments under the Keidanren Voluntary Action Plan;
4. US multinationals operating in Japan and Europe and preparing in advance for the regional Greenhouse Gas Initiative (RGGI) in the Northeast US States or the California Assembly Bill 32 establishing a state-wide cap on emissions;
5. Power retailers and large consumers regulated by the NSW market in Australia; and
6. North American companies with voluntary but legally binding compliance objectives in the CCX.

Who dominates the carbon markets? In 2006 European buyers dominated the primary CDM and JI markets with 86 per cent of market share (versus 50 per cent in 2005), while Japanese purchases were only 7 per cent of the primary market. The UK led the market with about 50 per cent of project-based volumes, followed by Italy with 10 per cent. Private sector buyers, predominantly banks and carbon funds, continued to buy large numbers of CDM assets, while public sector buyers continued to dominate JI purchases.

To evaluate the performance of the carbon market we now discuss the impact of its creation. The EU ETS (Phase I) demonstrated that a *carbon price signal* in Europe succeeded in stimulating emissions abatements both within Europe and especially in developing countries. Following the release of verified 2005 emissions data, it became clear that the 2005–6 emissions cap was not set at an appropriate level relative to actual emissions in that period, as prices dropped rapidly during 2006.[24] In the second part of 2006, the market shifted its attention to Phase II based on expectations that those caps would be much more stringent, ensuring higher and more stable prices. In the following section we explain this phenomenon from a theoretical viewpoint.

From the physical view point, it is important to keep track of the carbon reductions that the carbon market has achieved. In contrast with the highly volatile 2006 EUA market, project-based assets showed great price stability,

---

[24] In 2006 the EU Commission stated that Phase I was only a 'learning phase' and promised to assess the second period (Phase II) plans in a manner that 'ensures the correct and consistent application of the criteria and sufficient scarcity of allowances of EU ETS': see www.epped.eu/climatechange/docs/COM(2006)725final.doc at 10 November 2008.

while transacted volumes also grew steadily, and developing countries supplied nearly 450 $MtCO_2$ of primary CDM credits for a total market value of $5 billion. Average prices for Certified Emissions Reductions ('CER') from developing countries were up marginally in 2006 at US$10.90, with the vast majority of transactions in the range US$8 to 14. China continued to have a dominant market-share of the CDM with 61 per cent and set a relatively stable price floor for global supply of CERs. In 2007 it grew to $60 billion/annual trade with over $23 billion in CDM projects under the Kyoto Protocol's Clean Development Mechanism.

In sum, since 2002 a cumulative 920 $MtCO_2$, the equivalent to 20 per cent of EU emissions in 2004, have been transacted through primary CDM transactions for a value of over US$23 billion.

6. HOW THE MARKET SETS CARBON PRICES, AND WHAT DETERMINES PRICE STABILITY

The previous section showed how, starting from a unique theoretical construct in the 1997 Kyoto Protocol, a functioning market was achieved, a carbon market that traded over $60 billion annually and has succeeded in reducing carbon emission from the EU while transferring about, to date, $23 billion in clean technology projects to developing nations for CDM carbon reduction.

Despite the success of the market strategy, the stability of the carbon market discussed in the previous section remains a source of concern for private industry, which seeks firm targets to plan for costs and opportunities in the years ahead. Non-experts are understandably confused about how prices are set in the carbon market, and believe that they are set by free floating supply and demand forces of the traders. In reality, prices do fluctuate in the short term with supply and demand forces, but it is possible to identify market 'fundamentals' that determine carbon prices, and these have nothing to do with short-term supply and demand forces on the part of the traders. For example, the drop in prices during 2006 was due to too lenient (or high) emission caps, as was recognized in a statement by the European Union Commission. This section will explain how carbon markets function to determine carbon prices, and how these prices fluctuate over time. We show that in an economy dominated by fossil fuels, there are two 'fundamentals' that determine prices in the carbon market:

1. Emission caps, which are a measure of scarcity and the extent of demand for 'permits to emit' and imposed by the EUTS; and
2. The efficiency of existing technology in transforming fossil fuels into goods and services, which is equivalent to the cost of abatement.

To explain how the carbon market 'fundamentals' work, we provide a brief overview of the theory underlying the global carbon market. The body of theory underlying the carbon market was developed by the author when she proposed the creation of the Kyoto Protocol 'cap and trade' system to the international community in 1995 and 1996 designed and crafted by the author, while it was presented in various meetings of the OECD, the World Bank and the United Nations Framework Convention of Climate Change, and in the actual writing of the Protocol in Kyoto, December 1997.[25]

The background is as follows. In today's economy, fossil fuel energy is used to produce most goods and services. We know that about 87 per cent of all the energy used in the world today comes from fossil sources, so to simplify the exposition assume that all energy comes from fossils. Due to the physical characteristics of fossil fuels, using more fossil fuels emits more carbon dioxide. The more energy is used, the more carbon one emits and the less carbon abatement is obtained. Lower concentrations of CO_2 are associated with a more stable climate regime, while higher concentrations of CO_2 increase average temperatures that cause turbulent weather, sea level rise and the risks of catastrophic climate change. The 'good' in question can also be described as the 'abatement' of carbon dioxide, namely a decrease in carbon emissions measured from today's baseline. The abatement of carbon can be considered a good because it can improve our welfare.

Abatement is actually a 'public good' due to the physical characteristics of carbon dioxide, which diffuses uniformly and stably throughout the planet's atmosphere. Private goods are those where we have a choice about consumption that is independent from each other – for example we can choose to consume a certain amount of bananas, bread and cars independent of other people. That the quality of the atmosphere is a 'public good' is neither an economic nor a political statement – it is a physical reality. I can theoretically consume one banana while you choose to consume two or none. But it is physically impossible for me to face 430 ppm (parts per million) of carbon in the atmosphere, while you face 280 ppm. The entire atmosphere has a single carbon concentration, which is the same across all nations. This is a physical fact and an important feature for the global climate negotiations. This means that all nations in the world face the same concentration of CO_2, the problem of global warming in that sense unifying the nations of the world.

---

[25] Some of the results discussed below have been published in G Chichilnisky, above n 14 (1993); Chichilnisky, above n 16 (1996); Chichilnisky and Heal, above n 18; Chichilnisky and Heal, above n 19. They show that although carbon markets operate in some ways that are similar to standard markets, in other ways they are quite distinct and behave differently.

In the fossil fuel economy, the more energy we use the less carbon abatement we produce. This translates into a cruel trade-off that identifies our environmental dilemma: the choice between more goods and a better climate. This is why in the fossil fuel economy, industrialization and consumerism are viewed as the 'culprits' for climate change. Indeed, in the fossil economy the more goods we produce, the lower is our atmospheric quality.

Below we illustrate geometrically how the carbon market works. Figure 13.1 below illustrates a world economy with two nations. Each of them is represented by a frame: the left frame corresponds to Nation 1 and the right frame to Nation 2. The horizontal axis represents consumption levels of goods and services, and the vertical axis represents levels of abatement, the public good. The transformation frontier that is illustrated for each nation with a curved line in Figure 13.1 indicates the trade-off between the public good and the private good – between more carbon abatement (the public good) and more private goods and services produced. The curve indicates that the more private goods we produce the more carbon we emit. This is therefore the same trade-off that was mentioned above (that is, society faces a cruel trade-off between more goods and services versus a more stable climate). Each nation has a different curve because each nation may use a different production technology, which uses energy to make private goods, which is represented in Figure 13.1 by the convex transformation curve. Therefore each nation in Figure 13.1 may have a different transformation or trade-off curve, because each may have a different production technology, each nation transforms energy into private goods potentially differently. For example, Nation 2 has more efficient technologies, so it is able to produce more goods with the same amount of abatement. Both nations, however, use fossil fuels; therefore in both nations the more fossil fuel energy the nation uses, the more goods and services it produces and the more carbon it emits – and the less abatement it produces. For this reason in each of the two frames in Figure 13.1, the convex curve slopes downward, even though they may be different curves – illustrating in both nations the negative connection between goods and services (private goods) produced and abatement (public goods) produced that is typical of the fossil fuel economy. In sum: the more goods are produced, the more energy is used and the more carbon is emitted in the fossil economy.

We now introduce property rights and trading in the carbon market. For example, rich nations that are parties to the Kyoto Protocol's carbon market have assumed an abatement obligation, known as a 'commitment' or a 'cap', to limit or reduce their carbon emissions. Each nation has a different cap.[26] Recall

---

[26] See G Chichilnisky and G Heal (2000), *Environmental Markets Equity and Efficiency*, Colombia University Press, and the Kyoto Protocol that appears therein, see www.chichilnisky.com

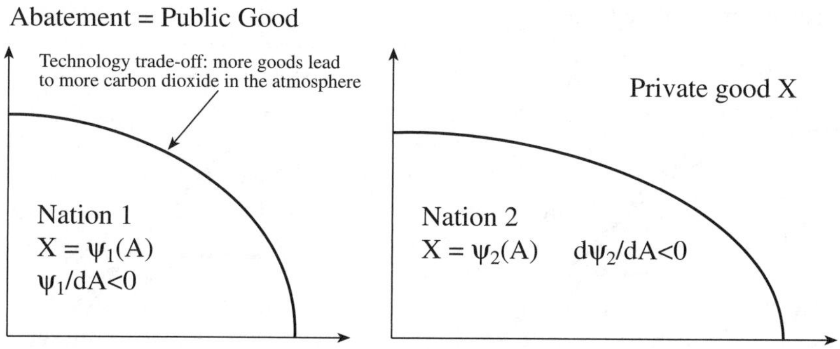

Figure 13.1 *Two nations in the fossil fuel economy. Each faces a technological trade-off: producing more goods and using more energy, or emitting less carbon*

that the vertical line in these figures represents the amount of the public good (abatement of carbon). Then one can interpret the height of this vertical line as the quantity of abatement that the nation has committed to do, and therefore the height is called its 'commitment' or 'cap'. The levels A1 and A2 in Figure 13.2 below denote the 'emission caps' in Nations 1 and 2 respectively.

The total amount of abatement in the world is of course the sum of what is abated by both nations, namely A1 + A2. The total carbon abated is the same for both nations because of the physical properties of CO_2. Therefore there is a common horizontal dotted line in Figure 13.2 that is valid for both nations, denoting the total decrease in emissions in the world economy, or 'world abatement'.

Using Figure 13.2, we can now illustrate the working of a 'cap and trade' system and how prices are set by the market 'fundamentals'. The 'cap and trade' system represented here could be either a trading system in the world economy, or within one country, and in the latter case the traders may be states, provinces, cities, or utilities depending on how the system is structured. However, in the latter case, the total amount abated will be determined not just by the particular country's 'caps', but also by the emission caps in the rest of the world. This is because, as already mentioned all nations produce CO_2, the overall level of carbon dioxide in the planet's atmosphere is the same for all people on the planet. The overall level of carbon in the planet's atmosphere is in fact the sum of the emissions originating from every nation in the world. This property is what ties together the welfare of every nation in the global warming dilemma, and what makes possible the sharing of the same goal by developing nations and industrial nations in limiting emissions. Put simply, carbon emissions in India cause the rise in the level of the sea in America, and vice versa.

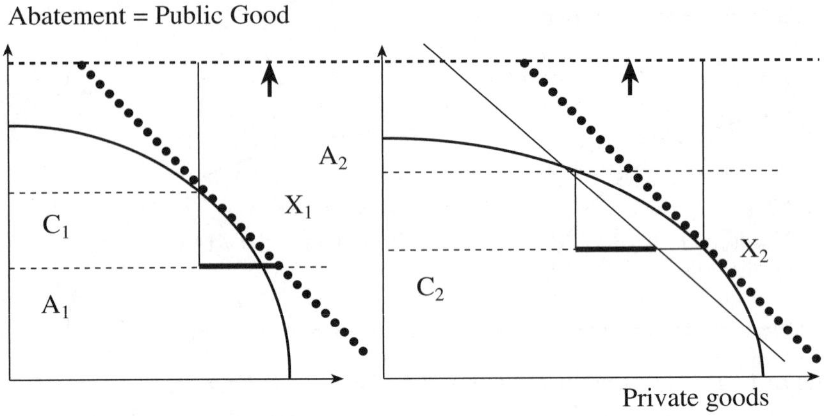

Figure 13.2 *The carbon price is represented by a sloped line with black spheres. It is the same for both nations, due to competitive markets. The slope of this line indicates the 'exchange rate' between carbon and goods. This price depends solely on technology and on the chosen 'caps'. The solid horizontal segment in nation 2 represents the value that nation 2 pays for importing 'permits' to emit from nation 1, paid in the goods it exports to nation 2 in exchange for those permits.*

Each nation optimizes welfare in terms of its consumption of private good X (measured in the horizontal axis) and environmental quality A (the public good measured in the vertical axis) within their technology possibilities (given by the curved line that is the 'transformation technology' that transforms goods into emissions) and subject to a constraint in its national income. What is this constraint? Each nation will consume a certain amount of goods X and environmental quality A that maximize its welfare, given that it produces X using A, and that it trades X and its rights to emit with the other nation. Market equilibrium means a price for permits, production and consumption levels for which supply equals demand so that both markets clear, for goods and for permits, and each nation maximizes its welfare within its income. Market clearing means that the total amount abated equals the sum of what is abated by both nations, and that the amount of goods consumed equals what is produced.

In Figure 13.2 above the small upward arrows indicate the market solution once trading takes place. Each nation produces goods and abatement so as to maximize its welfare within its income, where national income is measured taking into account the value of goods (and services) and of carbon permits. The price of permits in Figure 13.2 is given by the slope of the line with black spheres. Market equilibrium occurs when supply equals demand in all markets.

Since we have introduced a carbon market in this second figure, here supply includes not just supply of goods (and services) but also supply of 'permits' to emit, which are traded across nations in the carbon market. Optimality conditions require that each nation produces at the tangency point between the price line and the transformation frontier, so that Nation 1 produces at X_1 and Nation 2 produces at X_2 – where the points X_1 and X_2 are as indicated in Figure 13.2. Nation 1 in Figure 13.1 abates *more* at its production level X_1 than what is required (the requirement is point A_1, while Nation 1 produces at X_1, and the height of point X_1 that indicates its abatement level, namely C_1, is higher than A_1). Nation 2, instead, abates less than what it is required to abate (the requirement is at point A_2, which is higher than C_2, which is the height of point X_2). Therefore one nation will buy and the other will sell permits to emit. In fact Nation 1 will be a net seller of carbon permits, while Nation 2 will be a net buyer of permits, as shown in Figure 13.2. The two nations produce goods, and there is international trade of carbon permits among them as well as of goods. Nation 1 ends up using the extra income from the export of permits to import more goods, and its final consumption in market equilibrium is at the point indicated with an arrow. This nation exports permits, and imports goods with the income obtained, so it ends up consuming more goods than it produces. The opposite happens with Nation 2, which must buy permits from Nation 1, and has to export goods to Nation 1 in order to pay for its permits. Nation 2 ends up consuming fewer goods than it produces at market equilibrium, at the point indicated with an arrow. Supply for permits must equal demand for permits, and this occurs when the amount of permits that Nation 1 sells is the same as the amount of permits that Nation 2 wants to buy. The carbon market price adjusts until supply equals demand both in the goods market and the market for permits. In a competitive market this price depends on two important parameters that we call the market 'fundamentals':

1. The technological transformation between more goods and more abatement; and
2. The level of 'abatement' or 'caps' that are externally provided by governments.

The lower the caps, the higher the obligation to abate and therefore the higher the price of carbon. This is how the market operates. Observe that this is exactly as was indicated by the EU Commission in 2006, when it discovered that carbon prices were dropping because the caps on carbon emissions were set too high, so the caps were adjusted accordingly.[27] By setting the caps, the

---

27 World Bank Report, Status and Trends of the Carbon Market, 2006, 7 and 8, op. cit.

governments determine the demand of permits and influence the price of carbon up and down.

Additionally it is important to appreciate that the production technology, or 'transformation frontier', plays a key role. A fundamental result in the theory of competitive markets ensures that the price that equates supply and demand for goods should be equal to the rate of technological transformation between those goods – namely the slope of the transformation curve in Figures 13.1 and 13.2. However, it is worth pointing out that these fundamental results hold only in well-behaved competitive markets. These are markets where all traders share the same information, and no trader dominates the market as in monopolistic situations. Under these conditions, the technology that transforms energy into goods and abatement plays a key role in determining the price of carbon, as do the overall market 'caps' that are determined by governments.

7. CONCLUSIONS: THE CARBON MARKET AND THE WTO

The developing nations play a key role in the resolution of the global warming problem, since they are expected to be the largest emitters in 20 to 30 years' time. Today they share a small part of the global emissions, about 40 per cent or less, but nevertheless in the short run they will bear most of the burden of the climate change risks. Yet there is no concerted strategy on the part of the G77 or any other regional bodies from Latin America, Asia or Africa, to address the global warming issue. Nor is the WTO involved in any effort to organize this important market.

The WTO can play a key role in the continuation and expansion of the carbon market into the future, as well as in the creation of other global environmental markets that can play an important role this century. Specifically the WTO can participate in the global climate negotiations, working to ensure the continuation of the limitations on emissions that are the foundations of the carbon market, and going beyond the current 2012 deadline within the Kyoto Protocol.

This proposal would require that the WTO initiates a separate effort or division to participate in the efforts of the United Nations Framework Convention for Climate Change, participating in the annual meetings of the UN Convention of the Parties ('COP') and developing specific research projects and publications to explain the connection between the objectives of the WTO and the objectives of the Climate Convention of the United Nations. It is critical that the WTO creates an expert academic body that can take a clear and logical position on the important issue of exports of natural resources from poor nations: how they affect the global environment, particularly on the issue of global warming and exports of fossil fuels; how they affect violence and regional conflict; and how they can create or worsen poverty and violations of human rights. This issue was studied extensively by the author[28] and more recently a well-established negative empirical connection between opening to trade and income inequality at the global level was shown also by Robert Barro.[29] The issue of trade with ill-defined property rights on resources should be central to this exercise, as well as the development of a new policy within the WTO about the real connection between Trade and the Environment. This must show how international trade *can* be consistent with sustainable development once *global property rights* are introduced on the key global environmental assets (such as global rights to use the planet's atmosphere to emit carbon, or use of water) as in the Kyoto Protocol and its carbon markets (or the equivalent for other environmental assets).

Additionally, the WTO can participate with other international organizations, such as the World Bank and the IMF, ensuring competitive behaviour in the carbon market to avoid the loss of efficiency that may occur otherwise. This is a standard role of ensuring market efficiency and fair trading that the WTO plays in standard markets, understanding however that in the context of environmental markets there is a positive association between efficiency and preferential treatment of poor nations in the assignment of property rights on the use of the global public good,[30] a connection that does not exist in the conventional markets that the WTO usually deals with, which are markets trading private goods.

Another option for the WTO is to provide an avenue for creating Pilot Projects, Working Groups and bringing developing nations' representatives to discuss concerns and potential interests in the carbon market and the CDM mechanism of the Kyoto Protocol, from the point of view of world trade. 'Capacity building' on the part of the WTO would help developing nations

---

28 G Chichilnisky, 'Terms of Trade and Domestic Distribution: Export Led Growth in Abundant Labour' (1981) 8 *Journal of Development Economics* 163; G Chichilnisky (1992), 'North South Trade and the Global Environment', *American Economic Review*; and G Chichilnisky (2010), 'Beyond the Global Divide', in press, www. chichilnisky.com.

29 R J Barro, 'Inequality and Growth: A Revision' (2007) 324 *Boletin Informativo Techint* 9.

30 See G Chichilnisky et al., 'Equity and Efficiency in Environmental Markets: Global Trade in Carbon Dioxide Emissions' in G Chichilnisky and G Heal (eds) *Environmental Markets: Equity and Efficiency* (Columbia University Press, New York, 2000) 46; G Chichilnisky and G Heal 'Who should Abate Carbon Emissions: An International Perspective', *Economic Letters*; and 'Markets for Tradable Emissions Permits: Theory and Policy', OECD Report No. 52, Economics Division of the OECD, Paris, France, above n 19.

take better advantage of the financial mechanism and facilities that are currently provided by the CDM of the Kyoto Protocol. The WTO can offer such capacity building in the area of market mechanisms and how to best use these for sustainable development.

The WTO could also provide a forum for working out cooperative solutions for the energy issues and the global warming issues that arise from the working of the carbon market – such as stability of market prices.

The WTO can help create and regulate derivative markets of the Kyoto Protocol Carbon Market – such as future markets, which are known to help stabilize market prices in the energy field, for example oil prices.

Finally, the WTO could provide an avenue for improving stability and liquidity in the carbon market through options and forward markets, as well as asset-backed securities that can be floated in global capital markets with the support of other Bretton Woods institutions.

The carbon market is only the tip of the iceberg. As the twenty-first century advances, new environmental issues will surely emerge – in some cases, they have already emerged – connected with the availability of water, the conservation of biodiversity, and even the global airwaves.[31] The entire world could benefit from a well-organized WTO participation in such markets, since by some measures environmental markets could be the most important global markets in the rest of our century.

---

31 See Chichilnisky, above n 16 (1996).

14. From *realpolitik* of international trade to the Geneva Consensus

Shervin Majlessi[1]

1. INTRODUCTION

This chapter comprises a commentary on presentations delivered during the Monash/Sydney Universities' Conference on *The World Trade Organisation and Human Rights: Interdisciplinary Perspectives* upon which the chapters in this collection are based. In the spirit of the interdisciplinary presentations during the conference this comment focuses on developments in the area of GATT/WTO law, from *realpolitik* of international trade to an institutionalist one, and its connection with human rights law. The commentary is in part a variation of the fragmentation narrative presented in Andrew Lang's chapter,[2] according to which the evolution of theory and practice of the discipline of GATT/WTO law, at least until very recently, happened outside what should have been its natural course (that is, in the context of an international economic law or international trade law,[3] which in turn would be a branch of international law).

I propose, therefore, that a different approach is needed to address the conflict between trade and human rights. It is submitted that Pascal Lamy's proposed Geneva Consensus creates some space for that different approach based on a different theory of international economic *relations*.[4]

---

1 The views expressed herein are those of the author, and cannot be attributed to the United Nations.

2 See Chapter 7.

3 Already the different names of this field of law demonstrate some of the confusion in study of the subject which goes beyond mere questions of semantics. We sometimes refer to international economic law and sometimes to international trade law when talking about WTO issues and very often use them interchangeably. Professor Bardhan and Professor Chichilnisky focus on an economic perspective of trade issues to demonstrate that economics is not the science of commerce that explains choices, but rather that economics is the science of allocation of scarce resources. The result of this distinction is that international trade or economic law should have very different meanings. See, respectively, Chapters 4 and 13.

4 The interpretative approach which is presented by Howse and Teitel in their

2. INTERNATIONAL ECONOMIC *LAW* OR INTERNATIONAL ECONOMIC *RELATIONS*

Whether we consider WTO law to be part of international trade or economic law, as Petersmann has pointed out in his chapter, we can distinguish between a more economic-centered North American and a more legal European approach to this field.[5]

Surprisingly until very recently there was not a single textbook entitled 'International Economic *Law*' in North America. The leading American scholar in this field is John H Jackson, to such a degree that he is believed to have 'pioneered [the] new academic discipline'[6] of international trade law with his book, *World Trade and the Law of GATT* in 1969.[7] For more than forty years now, Professor Jackson has been researching, teaching and publishing in the field of international trade law and the law of the GATT/WTO.[8] Because of Jackson's influence on scholarly works and teaching in the field of international economic law, and in order to trace the differences between the North American and European approaches, it is interesting to examine the formation of what I have labelled 'Jackson's Paradigm'. I believe that Jackson's Paradigm has been instrumental in shaping the methodology of study of WTO law as a discipline of international economic law.

Jackson's first book[9] had a limited ambition. It was intended to be a treatise on the law of the GATT and to present a pragmatic analysis for govern-

---

chapter is indeed very constructive in addressing the current conflict between human rights and trade obligations (see Chapter 2). However, in order to address the linkage between trade and human rights in a more comprehensive manner it is proposed that future developments in WTO law should be based on a different theory of international economic *relations*.

5 See Chapter 3. We are not addressing a developing country approach in this context because such an approach – if it exists – does not appear to have had an impact on the methodology of study in this field of law.

6 M Bronckers and R Quick (eds) *New Directions in International Economic Law: Essays in Honour of John H Jackson* (Kluwer, The Hague, 2000) ix ('*Essays in Honour of Jackson*').

7 *World Trade and the Law of GATT* (Bobbs-Merrill, 1969) ('*The Law of GATT*').

8 See the 12-page bibliography of Jackson's principal publications as of January 2000 in *Essays in Honour of Jackson*, above n 6, 571–82. After years of teaching at Michigan Law School, Jackson joined Georgetown University's Law Center, Washington DC, in 1998, where he is also heading the Institute of International Economic Law: See http://www.law.georgetown.edu/iiel at 16 November 2008. In the same year he started the *Journal of International Economic Law* published by Oxford University Press and has been its editor-in-chief since. See *Journal of International Economic Law* online: http://www.jiel.oupjournals.org at 16 November 2008.

9 *The Law of GATT*, above n 7.

ment or GATT officials, private attorneys and legal scholars.[10] As evidenced by its title and content that book was not intended as, and had no claim to being, a treatise on international economic law or even international trade law. It was this 'pragmatic analysis' that laid the cornerstone for later works by Jackson and other scholars working in this field. In fact, it opened the door to the unexplored and unfamiliar field of GATT law, which was exotic and technical to international lawyers.[11]

What distinguishes Jackson's early work from the contemporary works of his European counterparts is a focus on GATT issues, an ambiguous position on the role of GATT law in the broader picture of international law, and a distinct policy-oriented approach. He refers to the position of law in the GATT system of that time in the following terms:

> One of the more puzzling questions facing a legal scholar is the question of what role 'law' plays in international affairs. The question in the context of GATT is perhaps slightly more perplexing than the same question in the context of international relations generally. One of the reasons that makes the GATT an interesting object of scrutiny with respect to this question is that it was intended to contain precisely formulated legal rules, some times termed 'contractual', which were to be directly applied without further elaboration.[12]

After comparing GATT with other international economic organizations he observed that 'GATT [. . .] has no legal staff. Its legal framework is sketchy and inadequate'.[13]

In his major book on world trade[14] in a section entitled 'International Law and International Economic Relations: An Introduction', Jackson dedicated merely a page to 'international economic law'.[15] He takes note of differing ideas about the meaning of the term and first presents the broad view that 'cast a very wide net, and embrace[d] almost any aspect of international law that relate[d] to any sort of economic matter'.[16] From his treatment of the subject, however, it appears that he favors a more restrained definition that 'would embrace trade, investment, and services when they [were] involved in transactions that cross national borders, and those subjects that involve[d] the establishment on national territory of economic activity of persons or firms

---

10 Ibid ix.

11 D McRae, 'The Contribution of International Trade Law to the Development of International Law' (1996) 260 *Recueil des Cours* 99, 113–15.

12 *The Law of GATT*, above n 7, 12.

13 Ibid 13.

14 John H Jackson, *The World Trading System: Law and Policy of International Economic Relations* (MIT Press, Cambridge, 1997).

15 Ibid 25.

16 Ibid.

originating from outside that territory'.[17] In this meaning, international economic law does not seem any different from international trade law.[18] Jackson's definition almost coincides with the definition presented by European scholars; it is only narrower in scope. But as will be discussed below, the real difference between North American and European views is in their approach to the subject-matter and not in their definitions.[19]

3. INTERNATIONAL ECONOMIC RELATIONS APPROACH

It is telling that Jackson is hesitant to use the term *international economic law*[20] and is inclined to use *international economic relations* – as evidenced in the title of his book.[21] This use of international economic relations instead of international economic law brings to mind the distinction between international law ('IL') and international relations theory ('IR'). From the viewpoint of the IR scholar, international lawyers have 'a highly formalistic and exclusively technical international legal positivist approach to international relations'[22] and are not concerned 'about the international society in which that law operates, about the nations and the relations between nations which that law orders, about the national interests and policies which that law furthers'.[23] From the perspective of international law scholars, the field of international

17 Ibid.

18 Jackson himself continues by stating that '[i]n any event, clearly the subject of international trade whether in goods or in services (or both), is at the core of international economic law': ibid.

19 In his more recent writings, however, Jackson has adopted a broader approach which reflects the broader questions of international law: see John H Jackson, *Sovereignty, the WTO and Changing Fundamentals of International Law* (Cambridge University Press, Cambridge, 2006) 46.

20 Ironically, Jackson is the author of the 'Economic Law, International' entry in the *Encyclopedia of Public International Law*. In his article he favorably quotes Carreau et al.'s definition of international economic law, but his treatment of the subject is no different than his book: R Bernhardt (ed.) *Encyclopedia of Public International Law*, (Amsterdam, North-Holland Pub Co, 1985) vol 8, 150.

21 It is interesting to note that since there is no 'international economic law' subject heading in the Library of Congress cataloguing system, all of the books on this subject are classified under the 'international economic relations' subject heading.

22 F Boyle, *World Politics and International Law* (1958) 59, cited in K W Abbott, 'Modern International Relations Theory: A Prospectus for International Lawyers' (1989) 14 *Yale Journal of International Law* 335, 336.

23 Louis Henkin, *How Nations Behave: Law and Foreign Policy* (New York, Columbia University Press, 2nd edn, 1979) ix.

relations is so dominated by a realist and neo-realist paradigm that they see 'little point in a dialogue with adherents of this view'.[24] It is only during the past two or three decades that major interdisciplinary works in these two fields have emerged.[25]

Similar to that IR/IL distinction, use of the term *law of international economic relations* ('IER') underlines the economic realities of the world trading system where – as evidenced by the chapter of Ken Shadlen – factors

---

[24] Abbott, above n 22, 338.

[25] As A M Slaughter points out, '[t]he discipline of international relations was born after World War I in a haze of aspirations for the future of world government': A M Slaughter, 'International Law and International Relations Theory: A Dual Agenda' (1993) 87 *American Journal of International Law* 205, 207. After World War II, however, the high aspirations for a world government and international rule of law gave way to Political Realism, according to which the law on an international level was a law of politics and politics was 'a struggle for power': H J Morgenthau, *Politics Among Nations: The Struggle for Power and Peace* (Alfred A Knopf, New York, 4th edn, 1967). Abbott observes that, 'Realism, the dominant IR theory for over two thousand years, has had little to say to students of international law': above n 22, 337. From this traditional perspective law and politics were seen as two different domains, often uninformed by the developments of one another. Until not very long ago, that estrangement of law and politics on the international level continued. Even though theoretical works on international law existed, they could not be considered as interdisciplinary works on international law and international relations. See, for example, M McDougal, *Studies in World Public Order* (New Haven, Yale University Press, 1960), or C de Visscher, *Théories et Réalités en Droit International Public*, (Pedone, Paris, 4th edn, 1970). In 1968, in his preface to the first edition of his interdisciplinary work, *How Nations Behave*, Henkin noted how scholarly works on international relations were empty of any reference to international law, and vice versa. Henkin, above n 23, ix. But as other schools of international relations (institutionalism, constructivism, liberalism, neoliberalism and so forth) developed, more common ground between international law and international relations theory was found. In 1989, Abbott noted how regime theory could be useful for international lawyers: above n 22. Things are different nowadays. More and more – especially North-American – authors attempt interdisciplinary approaches to international legal issues. For a bibliography of interdisciplinary scholarship involving IR and IL see A M Slaughter et al., 'International Law and International Relations Theory: A New Generation of Interdisciplinary Scholarship' (1998) 92 *American Journal of International Law* 367, 393–7. For a brief overview of IR theories see P J Katzenstein et al., '*International Organization* and the Study of World Politics' (1998) 52 *International Organization* 645 and J Brunnée and S J Toope, 'International Law and Constructivism: Elements of an Interactional Theory of International Law' (2000) 39 *Columbia Journal of Transnational Law* 19; see also the special issue of *International Organization* on legalization (vol 54) which includes articles on Legalization and World Politics, Legalization and Dispute Resolution, Law and Economic Integration and Legalization in Three Issue Areas, and also a critique of that volume in M Finnemore and S J Toope, 'Alternatives to "Legalization": Richer Views of Law and Politics' (2001) 55 *International Organisation* 734.

which count are economic, negotiating power or notion of risk, as opposed to an abstract legal environment of an international economic law ('IEL') built by lawyers.[26]

This understanding is reinforced by Professor McRae's approach in his lectures at the Hague Academy of International Law[27] as well as by Professor Lowenfeld's approach in *International Economic Law*.[28] McRae, unlike Jackson, does not refer expressly to the law of international economic relations, but his conclusions are also more of an *economic relations*, rather than *economic law*, type. In all three cases the authors use illustrative examples to present Ricardo's theory of comparative advantage as 'a powerful intellectual underpinning' of the liberal trade ideal.[29] This starting point marks the divergence of their approach from formalistic public international law.[30] This would have been similar to adopting one of several IR theories (structuralist, institutionalist or constructivist), as presented in Shadlen's paper, as the underlying theory and starting point of public international law. As a result of this dominant approach, until very recently the question of the relationship of WTO law and international law remained greatly unresolved.

4. INADEQUACY OF THE TWO APPROACHES

In my view neither the formalist legal European approach, nor the economics-centered North American analysis provides an adequate general theoretical framework for regulating international trade relations of states. On the one hand, a formalistic international law approach to international trade issues will

---

[26] See Chapter 5.

[27] McRae acknowledges the influence of Jackson's works on his own writings in D M McRae, 'GATT Article XX and the WTO Appellate Body' in *Essays in Honour of Jackson*, above n 6, 218, 218.

[28] Lowenfeld, *International Economic Law* (Oxford University Press, New York 2002). Lowenfeld's is the only North American treatise entitled *International Economic Law*.

[29] Jackson, above n 14, 15; see also McRae, above n 11, 139–42. According to Lowenfeld, the 'doctrine of comparative advantage has informed, if not quite dominated, the GATT since its creation in the early post-war years, and has sustained that fragile enterprise for half a century, exclaimed by establishment of the World Trade Organization in 1994'. After presenting the theory he goes on to address its shortcomings from a policy-making perspective: above n 28, 3, 7 (footnote omitted).

[30] Professor Deardorff, a professor of International Economics at the University of Michigan, tells us how for many years, at the very beginning of Professor Jackson's trade law class, he gave two lectures about the theory of comparative advantage: A V Deardorff, 'The Economics of Government Market Intervention and Its International Dimension' in *Essays in Honour of Jackson*, above n 6, 70, 70.

be misleading, or at least incomplete, as it will not recognize the driving force behind trade liberalization. It is not informed by economic theories of international economic relations and it largely ignores the most important issues in this field.[31] On the other hand, the North American approach fails to take into account a wide range of more elaborate economic theories – for example, the model presented in Prof. Chichilnisky's chapter in this book[32] – while taking a purely economic paradigm too far. Extending Ricardo's theory from domestic markets to the international scene is problematic, because domestically even in the purest models of capitalism the government plays a balancing role between public interest and individual rights.[33] In fact, Article XX GATT (which refers to policies that may justify exceptions to the principles of free trade) and inclusion of the concept of sustainable development in the preamble of the *Agreement Establishing the World Trade Organization*[34] indicate that concerns of the international trade regime have to go beyond the concept of comparative advantage and call for a more comprehensive approach to the regulation of trade.[35]

Indeed in the past few years there has been a gradual shift away from the *realpolitik* of international trade to a more encompassing view of international economic law.[36] In the same vein it is important to note that according to the

---

[31] Some works of this stream of literature ignore the most important issues in this field. For instance, to my great surprise, the latest 'revised edition' of Seidl-Hohenverldern's *International Economic Law*, includes references to the WTO on only 3 of its 250 pages and dedicates two lines to the dispute settlement system of that organization: I Seidl-Hohenverldern, *International Economic Law* (Kluwer, The Hague 3rd rev edn, 1999).

[32] See Chapter 13.

[33] It has to be noted that in recent years, as world trade issues have attracted more attention among international lawyers, some interesting attempts have been made to discern different perspectives in the field of international economic law. The focus on two approaches in this commentary should not lead to ignoring these other perspectives. On the contrary, studying the range of different perspectives reinforces our conclusions regarding the limited scope of the two mainstream perspectives highlighted in this commentary: see, for example, A H Qureshi (ed.) *Perspectives in International Economic Law* (Kluwer Law International, The Hague, 2002), which brings together a range of perspectives including legal, institutional, developing country, regional, human rights, feminist, ideological, goal-oriented, subject-based perspectives.

[34] *Marrakesh Agreement Establishing the World Trade Organization*, opened for signature 15 April 1994, 1867 UNTS 3 (entered into force 1 January 1995).

[35] G Marceau, 'A Call for Coherence in International Law: Praises for the Prohibition against "Clinical Isolation" in WTO Dispute Settlement' (1999) 33 *Journal of World Trade* 87, 87–8.

[36] Jackson's recent book is an example of this shift. See Jackson, above n 19. Pauwelyn also convincingly argued for the relevance of international law in international trade: Joost Pauwelyn, *Conflict of Norms in Public International Law* (Cambridge University Press, Cambridge, 2003).

current Director-General of the WTO, Pascal Lamy, 'by definition sustainable development calls for the consideration of fundamental values other than those of market opening to include, for instance, the protection of the environment, human rights and other social values'.[37] The question, however, is how can the international trade regime take other concerns and values into account.

5. GENEVA CONSENSUS

In response to that broad question Lamy has proposed the 'Geneva Consensus': 'a belief that trade opening does work for development, on the condition that the imbalances it creates, both domestically and internationally, are properly addressed'.[38] Lamy's call for a Geneva Consensus is accompanied by a call for a global governance system, to enhance and promote the interdependence of our world, comprising three elements: '*common values*, *actors with sufficient legitimacy*, and *mechanisms of governance* that are truly effective and can arbitrate values and interests in a legitimate way'.[39]

The elements to which Lamy refers bring to mind first and foremost the constructivist theory of international relations ('values' and 'actors') and then an institutionalist one ('mechanisms of governance'), as explained in Shadlen's chapter.[40] I would argue that the international human rights system can contribute to the elaboration of all three elements of the Geneva Consensus.[41]

A. Human Rights as Common Values

Lamy calls for 'common values' which 'may allow us to define the common goods or benefits that we would like to promote and defend collectively on a global scale' and which 'goes further than the UN Charter of Rights which is 60 years old'.[42]

---

37 Pascal Lamy, 'Towards Global Governance?' (Speech delivered at the Institut d'Etudes Politiques de Paris, Paris, 21 October 2005) http://www.wto.org/english/news_e/sppl_e/sppl12_e.htm at 16 November 2008 (emphasis added).

38 Pascal Lamy, *Message to Garnet Network of Excellence* (2006) Garnet, http://www.garnet-eu.org/index.php?id=197 at 16 November 2008.

39 Pascal Lamy, 'Humanising Globalization' (Speech delivered in Santiago de Chile, 30 January 2006) http://www.wto.org/english/news_e/sppl_e/sppl16_e.htm at 16 November 2008 (emphasis added).

40 See Chapter 5.

41 See L Arbour and S Majlessi, 'Placing Human Rights in the Geneva Consensus' in G Sampson (ed.) *The WTO and Global Governance: Future Directions* (United Nations University, Tokyo, 2008).

42 Lamy, above n 39.

The *Universal Declaration on Human Rights*[43] ('UDHR'), which was adopted parallel to the *Havana Charter for an International Trade Organisation*, encompasses values common to different cultural, philosophical and religious traditions,[44] and has been complemented with several other human rights instruments which, in the field of economic, social and cultural rights, impose obligations on their member states to respect, protect and fulfil these rights.[45] During the World Conference on Human Rights in Vienna, Member States of the United Nations recognized that human rights are 'the first responsibility of Governments'.[46] WTO members should therefore respect their concurrent obligations to promote and protect human rights when negotiating and implementing international rules on trade liberalization.

B. Principle of Participation and its Application in the Context of Globalization

The second element of a system of global governance according to Lamy is 'actors who have sufficient legitimacy to get public opinion interested in the debate'.[47] But it could equally be suggested, as pointed out in chapters by Sarah Joseph and Caroline Foster,[48] that, based on the principle of participation, the broader public should be involved in the WTO. Political rights and the right to participate in the conduct of public affairs as outlined in the UDHR and the *International Covenant on Civil and Political Rights*[49] ('ICCPR') are expressions of the principle of participation.[50]

---

43 GA Res 217A (III), UN Doc A/810, 71 (1948).

44 See Chapter 6.

45 All members of the WTO have ratified at least one human rights instrument, 126 have ratified the *International Covenant on Economic, Social and Cultural Rights*, opened for signature 16 December 1966, 999 UNTS 3 (entered into force 3 January 1976) ('ICESCR'), and 149 have ratified the *Convention on the Rights of the Child*, opened for signature 20 November 1989, 1577 UNTS 3 (entered into force 2 September 1990). An additional four WTO members have signed but not ratified the ICESCR (Belize, Pakistan, South Africa and the United States).

46 *Vienna Declaration and Programme of Action of the World Conference on Human Rights*, UN Doc A/CONF.157/23 (25 June 1993) Part I [1].

47 Lamy, above n 39.

48 See Chapters 11 and 12.

49 Opened for signature 16 December 1966, 999 UNTS 171 (entered into force 23 March 1976).

50 Art 21 UDHR; Art 25 ICCPR. Furthermore, the principle of participation can be found in the context of combating discrimination against women in the *Convention on the Elimination of All Forms of Discrimination against Women*, opened for signature 18 December 1979, 1249 UNTS 13 (entered into force 3 September 1981) ('CEDAW') and, in the area of racial discrimination, in the *International Convention*

According to the High Commissioner for Human Rights, the question of participation in the context of globalization can be examined at three levels: participation of individuals nationally; participation of States, as the primary human rights duty bearers and subjects of international law, at the global level and, direct participation of individuals and groups at the international level in global institutions. The latter is also important because increasingly decisions affecting people locally are being taken globally.[51]

C. Mechanisms of Governance and What Role for Trade and Human Rights Mechanisms in Arbitrating the Values?

Finally, Lamy turns his attention to a mechanism to 'arbitrate values and interests in a legitimate way', as the third element of a system of global governance.[52] The trade liberalization process may in certain circumstances lead to the adoption of retrogressive measures that can roll back the progress towards realization of certain human rights which require time, resources and planning. It is, therefore, important for the WTO mechanisms to ensure that the process of progressive trade liberalization is not at odds with progressive realization of socio-economic rights.[53] As Lamy has acknowledged

---

on the Elimination of All Forms of Racial Discrimination, opened for signature 7 March 1966, 660 UNTS 195 (entered into force 4 January 1969) ('ICERD'), which prohibits racial discrimination in connection with participation in political and public life: Art 7 and 14 CEDAW; Art 5 ICERD. The Human Rights Committee has interpreted the right to take part in the conduct of public affairs broadly, noting that the conduct of public affairs covers 'all aspects of public administration, and the formulation and implementation of policy at the international, national, regional and local levels': Human Rights Committee, *General Comment No 25: The right to participate in public affairs, voting rights and the right of equal access to public service*, UN Doc CCPR/C/21Rev.1/Add.7 (12 July 1996) [5]; see also Committee on the Elimination of Discrimination against Women, *General Recommendation No 23: Article 7 (Political and Public Life) and Article 8 (International Level)* (1997) [35], http://www.bayefsky.com/general/cedaw_genrecom_23.php at 16 November 2008.

51 For more details see United Nations High Commissioner for Human Rights, *Analytical study of the High Commissioner for Human Rights on the fundamental principle of participation and its application in the context of globalization: Report of the High Commissioner for Human Rights submitted in accordance with Commission for Human Rights resolution 2004/24*, UN Doc E/CN.4/2005/41 (23 December 2004).

52 Lamy, above n 38.

53 The Appellate Body of the WTO has already taken note of non-WTO legal norms in different WTO disputes; for example, in interpreting 'exhaustible natural resources' or in recognizing that certain species were endangered in the *Shrimp/Turtle* case: *United States – Import Prohibition of Certain Shrimp and Shrimp Products*, WTO Doc WT/DS58/AB/R (12 October 1998) (Report of the Appellate Body) ('*Shrimp/Turtle*')

the WTO is a sophisticated system for rules making and for ensuring their enforcement. But this does not mean that the WTO is hegemonic and does not take into account other international norms and other international organisations. On the contrary, the WTO is not more important than other international organisations and WTO norms do not necessarily supersede or trump other international norms.[54]

The specific role of WTO bodies and mechanisms, including the *Trade Policy Review Mechanism*[55] ('TPRM') and the Dispute Settlement System, and the human rights mechanisms, including treaty bodies,[56] the special procedures[57] and the new process of Universal Periodic Reviews of the Human Rights Council, in ensuring coherence and arbitrating the conflicts between trade rules and human rights obligations, has to be further studied and explored. In the interim, as demonstrated in Kinley, Nguyen and Murray's chapter, methodologies for human rights impact assessment of trade policies need to be developed in order to provide empirical evidence on the linkage between trade and human rights.[58]

6. CONCLUSION

Solutions to problems related to conflicts between trade and human rights obligations cannot be found solely by recourse to conflict of – international – laws techniques. Lasting solutions in this area have to be based on an interdisciplinary understanding of issues as was the ambition of this workshop. The goal of this commentary was to highlight changes in the study of international trade law that have made an interdisciplinary approach more relevant.

The discipline of international trade law has gone through a long transformation since the GATT days: from a 'mélange of law and non-law, institutions and non-institutions' to 'diplomat's jurisprudence' (to use the words of Robert

54 Pascal Lamy, 'The WTO in the Archipelago of Global Governance' (Speech delivered at the Institute of International Studies, UC Berkeley, 14 March 2006) http://www.wto.org/english/news_e/sppl_e/sppl20_ e.htm at 16 November 2008.

55 *Marrakesh Agreement Establishing the World Trade Organization*, opened for signature 15 April 1994, 1867 UNTS 3 (entered into force 1 January 1995) annex 3 (*Trade Policy Review Mechanism*).

56 Examples include the Human Rights Committee, the Committee on Economic, Social and Cultural Rights, and the Committee on the Elimination of All Forms of Discrimination Against Women.

57 Examples include the Special Rapporteur on the right to food, the Special Rapporteur on the right of everyone to the enjoyment of the highest attainable standard of physical and mental health, and the Special Representative of the Secretary-General on human rights and transnational corporations and other business enterprises.

58 See Chapter 9.

Hudec)[59] and then with the advent of the WTO it came closer to a 'Wilsonian Institutional Liberalism' (as Anne-Marie Slaughter calls it),[60] which replaced the old realism. It is now time to move a step further in recognizing the relevance of the broader context of international law. While the primary role of ensuring policy coherence within different international bodies rests with Member States of the United Nations and WTO, the Geneva Consensus advocated by the current Director General of the WTO presents an opportunity to address the question of coherence at the multilateral level.

59 Robert Hudec, *The GATT Legal System and World Trade Diplomacy* (Butterworth Legal Publishers, Salem, 2nd ed, 1990) 30.

60 A M Slaughter, 'Liberal International Relations Theory and International Economic Law' (1995) 10 *American Journal of International Law and Policy* 717.

Index